10.00

THE LOEB CLASSICAL LIBRARY

FOUNDED BY JAMES LOEB, LL.D.

EDITED BY

E. H. WARMINGTON, M.A., F.R.HIST.SOC.

FORMER EDITORS

† T. E. PAGE, C.H., LITT.D. † E. CAPPS, PH.D., LL.D.

† W. H. D. ROUSE, LITT.D. L. A. POST, L.H.D.

CICERO

XXII

LETTERS TO ATTICUS

BOOKS I-VI

7

CICERO.
BUST IN THE CAPITOLINE MUSEUM, ROME.

CICERO

IN TWENTY EIGHT VOLUMES

XXII

LETTERS TO ATTICUS

BOOKS I–VI

WITH AN ENGLISH TRANSLATION BY

E. O. WINSTEDT, M.A.

OF MAGDALEN COLLEGE, OXFORD

LONDON

WILLIAM HEINEMANN LTD

CAMBRIDGE, MASSACHUSETTS

HARVARD UNIVERSITY PRESS

MCMLXX

American
SBN 674 99008-0

British
SBN 434 99007-8

First printed 1912
Reprinted 1919, 1920, 1927, 1939, 1944,
1956, 1962, 1970

Printed in Great Britain

CONTENTS

LIST OF CICERO'S WORKS

SHOWING THEIR DIVISION INTO VOLUMES IN THIS SERIES

A. Rhetorical Treatises

Five volumes

B. Orations

Ten volumes

LIST OF CICERO'S WORKS

LIST OF CICERO'S WORKS

LIST OF CICERO'S WORKS

INTRODUCTION

THE letters contained in this volume cover a large and important period in Cicero's life and in the history of Rome. They begin when he was thirty-eight years of age; and at first they are not very numerous. There are only two of that year (68 B.C.), six of the following year, one of the year 66, when he held the praetorship, and two of 65. Then there is a gap in his correspondence. No letters at all survive from the period of his consulship and the Catilinarian conspiracy; and the letters to Atticus do not begin again until two years after that event. Thereafter they are sufficiently frequent to justify Cornelius Nepos' criticism, that reading them, one has little need of an elaborate history of the period. There are full—almost too full—details, considering the frequent complaints and repetitions, during the year of his banishment (58–57 B.C.), and the correspondence continues unbroken to the year 54. Then after a lapse of two years or more, which Atticus presumably spent in Rome, it begins again in 51, when Cicero was sent to Cilicia as pro-consul, much against his will; and the volume ends with a hint of the trouble that was brewing between Caesar and Pompey, as Cicero was returning to Rome towards the end of the next year.

The letters have been translated in the traditionary order in which they are usually printed. That order, however, is not strictly chronological; and, for the convenience of those who would read them in their historical order, a table arranging them so far as

possible in order of date has been drawn up at the end of the volume.

For the basis of the text the Teubner edition has been used; but it has been revised by comparison with more recent works and papers on the subject. Textual notes have only been given in a few cases where the reading is especially corrupt or uncertain; and other notes, too, have been confined to cases where they seemed absolutely indispensable. For such notes and in the translation itself, I must acknowledge my indebtedness to predecessors, especially to Tyrrell's indispensable edition and Shuckburgh's excellent translation.

There remain two small points to which I may perhaps call attention here in case they should puzzle the general reader. The first is that, when he finds the dates in this volume disagreeing with the rules and tables generally given in Latin grammars and taught in schools, he must please to remember that those rules apply only to the Julian Calendar, which was introduced in 45 B.C., and that these letters were written before that date. Before the alterations introduced by Caesar, March, May, July and October had thirty-one days each, February twenty-eight, and the other months twenty-nine. Compared with the Julian Calendar this shows a difference of two days in all dates which fall between the Ides and the end of the months January, August, and December, and of one day in similar dates in April, June, September, and November.

The second point, which requires explanation, is the presence of some numerals in the margin of the text of letters 16 to 19 of Book IV. As Mommsen pointed out, the archetype from which the existent

INTRODUCTION

MSS. were copied must have had some of the leaves containing these letters transposed. These were copied in our MSS. in the wrong order, and were so printed in earlier editions. In the text Mommsen's order, with some recent modifications introduced by Holzapfel, has been adopted; and the figures in the margin denote the place of the transposed passages in the older editions, the Roman figures denoting the letter from which each particular passage has been shifted and the Arabic numerals the section of that letter.

The following signs have been used in the apparatus criticus :—

$M =$ the *Codex Mediceus* 49, 18, written in the year A.D. 1389, and now preserved in the Laurentian Library at Florence. M^1 denotes the reading of the first hand, and M^2 that of a reviser.

$\Delta =$ the reading of M when supported by that of the *Codex Urbinas* 322, a MS. of the 15th century, preserved in the Vatican Library.

$E = $ *Codex Ambrosianus* E, 14, a MS. probably of the 14th century, in the Ambrosian Library at Milan.

$N = $ the *Codex ex abbatia Florentina* n. 49 in the Laurentian Library, written in the 14th or 15th century.

$P = $ No. 8536 of the Latin MSS. in the Bibliothèque Nationale at Paris, a MS. of the 15th century.

$R = $ No. 8538 of the same collection, written in the year 1419. These four MSS. *E, N, P, R*, with some others form a separate class; and

$\Sigma = $ the reading of all the MSS. of this class, or of a preponderant number of them.

INTRODUCTION

C = the marginal readings in Cratander's edition of 1528, drawn from a MS. which is now lost.

Z = the readings of the lost *Codex Tornaesianus*, Z^b denoting the reading as preserved by Bosius, and Z^l that testified to by Lambinus.

I = the reading of the *editio Jensoniana* published at Venice in 1470.

Rom. = the edition published at Rome in 1470.

CICERO'S LETTERS
TO ATTICUS
BOOK I

M. TULLI CICERONIS
EPISTULARUM AD ATTICUM
LIBER PRIMUS

I

CICERO ATTICO SAL.

Scr. Romae
m. Quint. a
689

Petitionis nostrae, quam tibi summae curae esse scio, huius modi ratio est, quod adhuc coniectura provideri possit. Prensat unus P. Galba. Sine fuco ac fallaciis more maiorum negatur. Ut opinio est hominum, non aliena rationi nostrae fuit illius haec praepropera prensatio. Nam illi ita negant vulgo, ut mihi se debere dicant. Ita quiddam spero nobis profici, cum hoc percrebrescit, plurimos nostros amicos inveniri. Nos autem initium prensandi facere cogitaramus eo ipso tempore, quo tuum puerum cum his litteris proficisci Cincius dicebat, in campo comitiis tribuniciis a. d. xvi Kalend. Sextiles. Competitores, qui certi esse videantur, Galba et Antonius et Q. Cornificius. Puto te in hoc aut risisse aut ingemuisse. Ut frontem ferias, sunt, qui etiam Caesonium putent. Aquilium non arbitrabamur, qui denegavit et iuravit morbum et illud suum regnum iudiciale opposuit. Catilina, si iudicatum erit meridie non lucere, certus erit competitor. De Aufidio et Palicano non puto te exspectare dum scribam. De iis, qui nunc petunt, Caesar certus putatur. Thermus cum Silano conten-

CICERO'S LETTERS
TO ATTICUS
BOOK I

I

CICERO TO ATTICUS, GREETING.

With regard to my candidature, in which I know you take the greatest interest, things stand as follows, so far as one can guess at present. P. Galba is the only canvasser who is hard at work; and he meets with a plain and simple, old-fashioned, No. As people think, this unseemly haste of his in canvassing is by no means a bad thing for my interests: for most refusals imply a pledge of support to me. So I have hope that I may derive some advantage from it, when the news gets abroad that my supporters are in the majority. I had thought of beginning to canvass in the Campus Martius at the election of tribunes on the 17th of July, the very time that, Cincius tells me, your man will be starting with this letter. It seems certain that Galba, Antonius, and Q. Cornificius will be standing with me. I can imagine your smile or sigh at the news. To make you tear your hair, there are some who think Caesonius will be a candidate too. I don't suppose Aquilius will. He has said not, pleading his illness and his supremacy in the law courts in excuse. Catiline will be sure to be standing, if the verdict is, No sun at midday. Of course you will know all about Aufidius and Palicanus, without waiting for letters from me. Of those who are standing, Caesar is thought to be a certainty: the real fight is expected

dere existimatur; qui sic inopes et ab amicis et existimatione sunt, ut mihi videatur non esse ἀδύνατον
Curium obducere. Sed hoc praeter me nemini videtur. Nostris rationibus maxime conducere videtur
Thermum fieri cum Caesare. Nemo est enim ex iis,
qui nunc petunt, qui, si in nostrum annum reciderit,
firmior candidatus fore videatur, propterea quod
curator est viae Flaminiae, quae tum erit absoluta
sane facile. Eum libenter nunc Caesari consuli ac-
cuderim.[1] Petitorum haec est adhuc informata cogitatio. Nos in omni munere candidatorio fungendo
summam adhibebimus diligentiam, et fortasse, quoniam videtur in suffragiis multum posse Gallia, cum
Romae a iudiciis forum refrixerit, excurremus mense
Septembri legati ad Pisonem, ut Ianuario revertamur.
Cum perspexero voluntates nobilium, scribam ad te.
Cetera spero prolixa esse his dumtaxat urbanis competitoribus. Illam manum tu mihi cura ut praestes,
quoniam propius abes, Pompei, nostri amici. Nega
me ei iratum fore, si ad mea comitia non venerit.
Atque haec huius modi sunt.

Sed est, quod abs te mihi ignosci pervelim. Caecilius, avunculus tuus, a P. Vario cum magna pecunia
fraudaretur, agere coepit cum eius fratre A. Caninio
Satyro de iis rebus, quas eum dolo malo mancipio
accepisse de Vario diceret. Una agebant ceteri creditores, in quibus erat L. Lucullus et P. Scipio et, is
quem putabant magistrum fore, si bona venirent, L.

---

[1] que cum (tum *Z*) erit—libenter nunc ceteri (nuntitere
M marg.: nunciteri *Z*) consuli (concili *Z*), acciderim (acci-
derunt *Z*) *MZ*[1]: *the reading in the text is that of Boot.*

to lie between Thermus and Silanus. But they are so unpopular and so unknown, that it seems to me to be on the cards to smuggle in Curius. Nobody else thinks so, however. It would probably suit our book best for Thermus to get in with Caesar: for, of the present batch of candidates, he would be the most formidable rival if he were put off to my year, as he is commissioner for the repairing of the Flaminian road. That will easily be finished by then: so I should like to lump him together with Caesar now. Such is the present rough guess of the chances of the candidates. I shall take the greatest care to fulfil all a candidate's duties: and, as Gaul's vote counts high, I shall probably get a free pass and take a run up to visit Piso, as soon as things have quieted down in the law courts here, returning in January. When I have discovered the views of the upper ten, I will let you know. The rest I hope will be plain sailing, with my civilian rivals at any rate. For our friend Pompey's followers you must be responsible, as you are quite close to them. Tell him I shall not take it unkindly if he does not come to my election. So much for that.

But there is a thing for which I have to crave your pardon. Your uncle, Caecilius, was cheated out of a large sum of money by P. Varius, and has taken an action against his brother, A. Caninius Satyrus, about some property which he says was fraudulently made over to him by Varius. The other creditors have made common cause with him: and among them are L. Lucullus and P. Scipio and the man who was expected to act for them at the sale, if the goods were put up for auction, L. Pontius.

Pontius. Verum hoc ridiculum est de magistro. Nunc cognosce rem. Rogavit me Caecilius, ut adessem contra Satyrum. Dies fere nullus est, quin hic Satyrus domum meam ventitet; observat L. Domitium maxime, me habet proximum; fuit et mihi et Quinto fratri magno usui in nostri petitionibus. Sane sum perturbatus cum ipsius Satyri familiaritate tum Domiti, in quo uno maxime ambitio nostra nititur. Demonstravi haec Caecilio simul et illud ostendi, si ipse unus cum illo uno contenderet, me ei satis facturum fuisse; nunc in causa universorum creditorum, hominum praesertim amplissimorum, qui sine eo, quem Caecilius suo nomine perhiberet, facile causam communem sustinerent, aequum esse eum et officio meo consulere et tempori. Durius accipere hoc mihi visus est, quam vellem, et quam homines belli solent, et postea prorsus ab instituta nostra paucorum dierum consuetudine longe refugit.

Abs te peto, ut mihi hoc ignoscas et me existimes humanitate esse prohibitum, ne contra amici summam existimationem miserrimo eius tempore venirem, cum is omnia sua studia et officia in me contulisset. Quodsi voles in me esse durior, ambitionem putabis mihi obstitisse. Ego autem arbitror, etiamsi id sit, mihi ignoscendum esse,

ἐπεὶ οὐχ ἱερήιον οὐδὲ βοείην.

Vides enim, in quo cursu simus et quam omnes gratias non modo retinendas, verum etiam acquirendas

6

But it is absurd to talk of acting for them at present. Now for the point. Caecilius asked me to take a brief against Satyrus. Now there is hardly a day but Satyrus pays me a visit. He is most attentive to L. Domitius and after him to me, and he was of great assistance to me and to my brother Quintus when we were canvassing. I am really embarrassed on account of the friendliness of Satyrus himself and of Domitius, who is the mainstay of my hopes. I pointed this out to Caecilius, assuring him at the same time that, if he stood alone against Satyrus, I would have done my best for him : but, as things were, when the creditors had combined and were such influential persons that they would easily win their case without any special advocate whom Caecilius might retain on his own account, it was only fair for him to consider my obligations and my circumstances. He seemed to take it more ungraciously than I could have wished or than a gentleman should : and afterwards he withdrew entirely from the intimacy which had grown up between us in the last few days.

Please try to forgive me and to believe that delicacy prevented me from appearing against a friend whose very good name was at stake, in the hour of his misfortune, when the friendly attentions he had paid to me had been unfailing. If you cannot take so kind a view, pray consider that my candidature stood in the way. I think even so I may be forgiven : for there is not " a trifle, some eightpenny matter," [1] at Iliad xxii, 159 stake. You know the game I am playing, and how important it is for me to keep in with everyone and

---

[1] Lit. " Since it was not for a victim for sacrifice nor for an oxhide shield [they strove]."

putemus. Spero tibi me causam probasse, cupio quidem certe.

Hermathena tua valde me delectat et posita ita
belle est, ut totum gymnasium eius ἀνάθημα [1] esse
videatur. Multum te amamus.

II

CICERO ATTICO SAL.

Scr. Romae
paulo post
ep. 1 a. 689

L. Iulio Caesare, C. Marcio Figulo consulibus filiolo
me auctum scito salva Terentia. Abs te tam diu nihil
litterarum! Ego de meis ad te rationibus scripsi
antea diligenter. Hoc tempore Catilinam, competi-
torem nostrum, defendere cogitamus. Iudices habemus, quos volumus, summa accusatoris voluntate.
Spero, si absolutus erit, coniunctiorem illum nobis
fore in ratione petitionis; sin aliter acciderit, humaniter feremus.

Tuo adventu nobis opus est maturo; nam prorsus
summa hominum est opinio tuos familiares nobiles
homines adversarios honori nostro fore. Ad eorum
voluntatem mihi conciliandam maximo te mihi usui
fore video. Quare Ianuario mense, ut constituisti,
cura ut Romae sis.

III

CICERO ATTICO SAL.

Scr. Romae
ex. a. 687

Aviam tuam scito desiderio tui mortuam esse,
et simul quod verita sit, ne Latinae in officio non
manerent et in montem Albanum hostias non ad-

---

[1] eius ἀνάθημα *Schütz*: eiut αναθμα *M*: eliu onaohma *C*.

8

even to make new friends. I hope I have justified
myself to you. I am really anxious to do so.

I am highly delighted with your Hermathena,
and have found such a good position for it, that the
whole class-room seems but an offering at its feet.[1]
Many thanks for it.

II

CICERO TO ATTICUS, GREETING.

I beg to inform you that on the very day that *Rome,*
L. Julius Caesar and C. Marcius Figulus were elected *shortly after*
to the consulship I was blessed with a baby boy; *letter 1,* B.C.
and Terentia is doing well. It is ages since I had a *65*
letter from you! I have written before and told you
all my affairs. At the present minute I am thinking
about defending my fellow candidate Catiline. We
can have any jury we like with the greatest goodwill
of the prosecutor. I hope, if Catiline is acquitted,
it will make us better friends in our canvassing: but,
if it does not, I shall take it quietly.

I badly want you back soon: for there is a wide-
spread opinion that some friends of yours among the
upper ten are opposed to my election, and I can see
that you will be of the greatest assistance to me in
winning their goodwill. So be sure you come back
to town in January, as you proposed.

III

CICERO TO ATTICUS, GREETING.

I beg to inform you that your grandmother has *Rome,*
died of grief at your absence and of fear that the *towards the*
Latin tribes would revolt and not bring the beasts *end of* B.C.

_____
[1] ἀνάθημα is generally used of an offering at a shrine, and Cicero *67*
seems to speak here of the Hermathena as the goddess to whom
the whole room was dedicated. But the reading is uncertain.

ducerent. Eius rei consolationem ad te L. Saufeium missurum esse arbitror. Nos hic te ad mensem Ianuarium exspectamus ex quodam rumore an ex litteris tuis ad alios missis; nam ad me de eo nihil scripsisti. Signa quae nobis curasti, ea sunt ad Caietam exposita. Nos ea non vidimus; neque enim exeundi Roma potestas nobis fuit. Misimus, qui pro vectura solveret. Te multum amamus, quod ea abs te diligenter parvoque curata sunt.

Quod ad me saepe scripsisti de nostro amico placando, feci et expertus sum omnia, sed mirandum in modum est animo abalienato. Quibus de suspicionibus etsi audisse te arbitror, tamen ex me, cum veneris, cognosces. Sallustium praesentem restituere in eius veterem gratiam non potui. Hoc ad te scripsi, quod is me accusare de te solebat. In se expertus est illum esse minus exorabilem, meum studium nec sibi nec tibi defuisse. Tulliolam C. Pisoni L. f. Frugi despondimus.

IV

CICERO ATTICO SAL.

Scr. Romae in. a. 688

Crebras exspectationes nobis tui commoves. Nuper quidem, cum iam te adventare arbitraremur, repente abs te in mensem Quintilem reiecti sumus. Nunc vero sentio, quod commodo tuo facere poteris, venias

to the Alban hill for sacrifice.[1] No doubt Saufeius will send you a letter of condolence. I am expecting you back by January—from mere hearsay, or was it perhaps from letters you have sent to others? You have not said anything about it to me. The statues you have obtained for me have been landed at Caieta. I have not seen them yet, as I have not had a chance of getting away from town; but I have sent a man to pay for the carriage. Many thanks for the trouble you've taken in getting them—so cheaply too.

You keep writing to me to make your peace with our friend. I have tried every means I know: but it is surprising how estranged he is from you. I expect you have heard what he thinks about you: anyhow I'll let you know when you come. I have not been able to restore the old terms of intimacy between him and Sallustius, though the latter was on the spot. I mention it because Sallustius used to grumble at me about you. Now he has found out that our friend is not so easy to appease, and that I have done my best for both of you. Our little Tullia is engaged to C. Piso Frugi, son of Lucius.

IV

CICERO TO ATTICUS, GREETING.

You keep on raising our hopes of seeing you: and just the other day, when we thought you were nearly here, we find ourselves suddenly put off till July. Now I really do think you ought to keep your pro-

Rome, at the beginning of B.C. 66

---

[1] The point is not very clear. My translation follows Mr. Strachan Davidson's interpretation that the old lady was thinking of the Social War, which took place twenty years earlier. Others understand *feriae* with *Latinae* and take it to refer merely to possible delays of the festival.

ad id tempus, quod scribis; obieris Quinti fratris
comitia, nos longo intervallo viseris, Acutilianam
controversiam transegeris. Hoc me etiam Peducaeus
ut ad te scriberem admonuit. Putamus enim utile
esse te aliquando eam rem transigere. Mea inter-
cessio parata et est et fuit. Nos hic incredibili ac
singulari populi voluntate de C. Macro transegimus.
Cui cum aequi fuissemus, tamen multo maiorem
fructum ex populi existimatione illo damnato cepimus
quam ex ipsius, si absolutus esset, gratia cepissemus.

Quod ad me de Hermathena scribis, per mihi
gratum est. Est ornamentum Academiae proprium
meae, quod et Hermes commune omnium et Minerva
singulare est insigne eius gymnasii. Quare velim, ut
scribis, ceteris quoque rebus quam plurimis eum
locum ornes. Quae mihi antea signa misisti, ea nondum vidi; in Formiano sunt, quo ego nunc proficisci
cogitabam. Illa omnia in Tusculanum deportabo.
Caietam, si quando abundare coepero, ornabo.
Libros tuos conserva et noli desperare eos me meos
facere posse. Quod si adsequor, supero Crassum
divitiis atque omnium vicos et prata contemno.

V

CICERO ATTICO SAL.

*Scr. Romae
paulo ante
IV K. Dec.
686*

Quantum dolorem acceperim et quanto fructu sim
privatus et forensi et domestico Luci fratris nostri
morte, in primis pro nostra consuetudine tu existimare potes. Nam mihi omnia, quae iucunda ex

mise and come if you can possibly manage it. You will be in time for my brother Quintus' election; you will see me after all this long while; and you will settle the bother with Acutilius. The latter point Peducaeus, too, suggested that I should mention to you: we think it would be much better for you to get the thing settled at last. I am and have long been ready to use my influence for you. You would never believe how pleased everyone is with my conduct of Macer's case. I might certainly have shown more partiality to him: but the popularity I have gained from his condemnation is far more important to me than his gratitude at an acquittal would have been.

I am delighted at your news about the Hermathena. It is a most suitable ornament for my Academy, since no class-room is complete without a Hermes, and Minerva has a special appropriateness in mine. So please do as you suggest and send as many ornaments as possible for the place. The statues you sent before I have not seen yet. They are in my house at Formiae, where I am just thinking of going. I'll have them all brought to my place at Tusculum, and if that ever gets too full I'll begin decorating Caieta. Keep your books and don't despair of my making them mine some day. If I ever do, I shall be the richest of millionaires and shan't envy any man his manors and meadows.

V

CICERO TO ATTICUS, GREETING.

You, who know me so well, can guess better than anyone the grief I have felt at the death of my cousin Lucius and the loss it means to me both in my public and in my private life. He has always *Rome, shortly before Nov. 27, B.C. 68*

humanitate alterius et moribus homini accidere possunt, ex illo accidebant. Quare non dubito, quin
tibi quoque id molestum sit, cum et meo dolore
moveare et ipse omni virtute officioque ornatissimum
tuique et sua sponte et meo sermone amantem
adfinem amicumque amiseris.

Quod ad me scribis de sorore tua, testis erit tibi
ipsa, quantae mihi curae fuerit, ut Quinti fratris
animus in eam esset is, qui esse deberet. Quem cum
esse offensiorem arbitrarer, eas litteras ad eum misi
quibus et placarem ut fratrem et monerem ut
minorem et obiurgarem ut errantem. Itaque ex iis,
quae postea saepe ab eo ad me scripta sunt, confido
ita esse omnia, ut et oporteat et velimus.

De litterarum missione sine causa abs te accusor.
Numquam enim a Pomponia nostra certior sum factus
esse, cui dare litteras possem, porro autem neque
mihi accidit, ut haberem, qui in Epirum proficisceretur, nequedum te Athenis esse audiebamus. De
Acutiliano autem negotio quod mihi mandaras, ut
primum a tuo digressu Romam veni, confeceram;
sed accidit, ut et contentione nihil opus esset, et ut
ego, qui in te satis consilii statuerim esse, mallem
Peducaeum tibi consilium per litteras quam me dare.
Etenim, cum multos dies aures meas Acutilio dedissem, cuius sermonis genus tibi notum esse arbitror,
non mihi grave duxi scribere ad te de illius queri-
moniis, cum eas audire, quod erat subodiosum, leve
putassem. Sed abs te ipso, qui me accusas, unas mihi
scito litteras redditas esse, cum et otii ad scribendum
plus et facultatem dandi maiorem habueris.

Quod scribis, etiamsi cuius animus in te esset

been kindness itself to me, and has rendered me every service a friend could. I am sure you, too, will feel it, partly out of sympathy with me, and partly because you will miss a dear and valued friend and relative, who was attached to you of his own accord and at my prompting.

You mention your sister. She herself will tell you the pains I have taken to make my brother Quintus behave as he should to her. When I thought he was a little annoyed I wrote to him trying to smooth matters down with him as a brother, to give him good advice as my junior, and to remonstrate with him as in error. Judging by all the letters I have had from him since, I trust things are as they should be and as we wish them to be.

You have no reason to complain of lack of letters from me, as Pomponia has never let me know when there was a messenger to give them to. Besides it has so happened that I have not had anyone starting for Epirus and have not yet heard of your arrival at Athens. Acutilius' business I settled according to your directions, as soon as ever I got to Rome after your departure: but, as it happened, there was no hurry, and, knowing I could trust your good judgement, I preferred Peducaeus to advise you by letter rather than myself. It was not the bother of writing you an account of his grievances that I shirked. I spent several days listening to him, and you know his way of talking; and I did not mind, though it was a bit of a bore. Though you grumble at me, I've only had one letter from you, let me tell you, and you have had more time to write and a better chance of sending letters than I've had.

You say, " if so and so is a little annoyed with

offensior, a me recolligi oportere, teneo, quid dicas,
neque id neglexi, sed est miro quodam modo adfectus.   Ego autem, quae dicenda fuerunt de te, non
praeterii; quid autem contendendum esset, ex tua
putabam voluntate me statuere oportere.   Quam si
ad me perscripseris, intelleges me neque diligen-
tiorem esse voluisse, quam tu esses, neque neglegen-
tiorem fore, quam tu velis.

De Tadiana re mecum Tadius locutus est te ita
scripsisse, nihil esse iam, quod laboraretur, quoniam
hereditas usu capta esset.   Id mirabamur te ignorare,
de tutela legitima, in qua dicitur esse puella, nihil usu
capi posse.   Epiroticam emptionem gaudeo tibi
placere.   Quae tibi mandavi, et quae tu intelleges
convenire nostro Tusculano, velim, ut scribis, cures,
quod sine molestia tua facere poteris.   Nam nos ex
omnibus molestiis et laboribus uno illo in loco con-
quiescimus.   Quintum fratrem cotidie exspectamus.
Terentia magnos articulorum dolores habet.   Et te et
sororem tuam et matrem maxime diligit salutemque
tibi plurimam ascribit et Tulliola, deliciae nostrae.
Cura, ut valeas et nos ames et tibi persuadeas te
a me fraterne amari.

VI

CICERO ATTICO SAL.

*Scr. Romae
paulo post
IV K. Dec.
a. 686*

Non committam posthac, ut me accusare de epistularum neglegentia possis; tu modo videto, in
tanto otio ut par in hoc mihi sis.   Domum Rabiria-
nam Neapoli, quam tu iam dimensam et exaedifica-

you," I ought to patch things up. I know what you mean, and I have done my best: but he is in a very odd mood. I have said all I could for you. I think I ought to follow your wishes as to what special arguments I should use. If you will write and tell me your wishes you will find that I did not wish to be more energetic than you were, nor will I be less energetic than you wish.

In that matter about Tadius' property, he tells me you have written him that there is no necessity for him to trouble any more about it: the property is his by right of possession. I wonder you forgot, that in the case of legal wards—and that is what the girl is said to be—right of possession does not count. I am glad you like your new purchase in Epirus. Please carry out my commissions, and, as you suggest, buy anything else you think suitable for my Tusculan villa, if it is no trouble to you. It is the only place I find restful after a hard day's work. I am expecting my brother Quintus every day. Terentia has a bad attack of rheumatism. She sends her love and best wishes to you and your sister and mother: and so does my little darling Tullia. Take care of yourself, and don't forget me. Your devoted friend.

VI

CICERO TO ATTICUS, GREETING.

I will take care that you shall not have any reason *Rome,* to complain of my slackness in writing to you in the *shortly after* future. See to it yourself that you keep up with *Nov. 27,* me. You have plenty of spare time. M. Fontius B.C. *68* has bought Rabirius' house at Naples, which you had in your mind's eyes ready mapped out and finished,

tam animo habebas, M. Fontius emit HS cccɔɔ x̄x̄x̄. Id te scire volui, si quid forte ea res ad cogitationes tuas pertineret. Quintus frater, ut mihi videtur, quo volumus animo, est in Pomponiam, et cum ea nunc in Arpinatibus praediis erat, et secum habebat hominem χρηστομαθῆ, D. Turranium. Pater nobis decessit a. d. IV Kal. Dec.

Haec habebam fere, quae te scire vellem. Tu velim, si qua ornamenta γυμνασιώδη reperire poteris, quae loci sint eius, quem tu non ignoras, ne praetermittas. Nos Tusculano ita delectamur, ut nobismet ipsis tum denique, cum illo venimus, placeamus. Quid agas omnibus de rebus, et quid acturus sis, fac nos quam diligentissime certiores.

VII

CICERO ATTICO SAL.

*Scr. Romae
ante Id.
Febr. 687*

Apud matrem recte est, eaque nobis curae est. L. Cincio HS x̄x̄cd constitui me curaturum Idibus Febr. Tu velim ea, quae nobis emisse et parasse scribis, des operam ut quam primum habeamus, et velim cogites, id quod mihi pollicitus es, quem ad modum bibliothecam nobis conficere possis. Omnem spem delectationis nostrae, quam, cum in otium venerimus, habere volumus, in tua humanitate positam habemus.

for about £1,150.[1] I mention it in case you still hanker after it. My brother is getting on as well as we can wish, I think, with Pomponia. He is living with her at his estate at Arpinum now, and has with him a *littérateur*, D. Turranius. My poor father died on the 27th of November.

That is about all my budget of news. If you can come across any articles of *vertu* fit for my Gymnasium, please don't let them slip. You know the place and what suits it. I am so pleased with my house at Tusculum that I am never really happy except when I am there. Send me a full account of your doings and of what you are thinking of doing.

VII

CICERO TO ATTICUS, GREETING.

Things are all right at your mother's : and I have got my eye on her. I have arranged to deposit £180 [2] with L. Cincius on February the 13th. Please hurry up with the things you say you have bought and got ready for me. I want them as soon as possible. And keep your promise to consider how you can secure the library for me. All my hopes of enjoying myself, when I retire, rest on your kindness.

Rome before Feb. 13, B.C. 67

---

[1] 130,000 sesterces.   [2] 20,400 sesterces.

MARCUS TULLIUS CICERO

VIII

CICERO ATTICO SAL.

Scr. Romae
post Id.
Febr. a. 687

Apud te est, ut volumus. Mater tua et soror a me Quintoque fratre diligitur. Cum Acutilio sum locutus. Is sibi negat a suo procuratore quicquam scriptum esse et miratur istam controversiam fuisse, quod ille recusarit satis dare amplius abs te non peti. Quod te de Tadiano negotio decidisse scribis, id ego Tadio et gratum esse intellexi et magno opere iucundum. Ille noster amicus, vir mehercule optimus et mihi amicissimus, sane tibi iratus est. Hoc si quanti tu aestimes sciam, tum, quid mihi elaborandum sit, scire possim.

L. Cincio HS cciↄↄ cciↄↄ cccc pro signis Megaricis, ut tu ad me scripseras, curavi. Hermae tui Pentelici cum capitibus aeneis, de quibus ad me scripsisti, iam nunc me admodum delectant. Quare velim et eos et signa et cetera, quae tibi eius loci et nostri studii et tuae elegantiae esse videbuntur, quam plurima quam primumque mittas, et maxime quae tibi gymnasii xystique videbuntur esse. Nam in eo genere sic studio efferimur, ut abs te adiuvandi, ab aliis prope reprehendendi simus. Si Lentuli navis non erit, quo tibi placebit, imponito. Tulliola deliciolae nostrae, tuum munusculum flagitat et me ut sponsorem appellat; mi autem abiurare certius est quam dependere.

20

VIII

CICERO TO ATTICUS, GREETING.

All's well—as well as could be desired—at home. *Rome,*
Quintus and I are looking after your mother and *after Feb.*
sister. I have spoken to Acutilius. He says his *13,* B.C. *67*
broker has not advised him, and is much surprised
there should have been such a fuss because he refused
to guarantee that there should be no further claims
on you. The settlement that you have arranged
about Tadius' affairs is, I am sure, very good news for
him, and he is pleased about it. That friend of
mine, who is really quite a good soul and very amiable
to me, is exceedingly annoyed with you. When I
know how deeply you take it to heart, I may be able
to lay my plans accordingly.

I have raised the £180 [1] for L. Cincius for the
statues of Megaric marble, as you advised me. Those
figures of Hermes in Pentelic marble with bronze
heads, about which you wrote, I have already fallen
in love with: so please send them and anything else
that you think suits the place, and my enthusiasm
for such things, and your own taste—the more the
merrier, and the sooner the better—especially those
you intend for the Gymnasium and the colonnade.
For my appreciation for art treasures is so great that
I am afraid most people will laugh at me, though I
expect encouragement from you. If none of Lentulus' boats are coming, put them on any ship you like.
My little darling, Tullia, keeps asking for your
promised present and duns me as though I were
answerable for you. But I am going to deny my
obligation rather than pay up.

[1] 20,400 sesterces.

MARCUS TULLIUS CICERO

IX

Scr. Romae post ep. 8 a. 687

Nimium raro nobis abs te litterae adferuntur, cum et multo tu facilius reperias, qui Romam proficiscantur, quam ego, qui Athenas, et certius tibi sit me esse Romae quam mihi te Athenis. Itaque propter hanc dubitationem meam brevior haec ipsa epistula est, quod, cum incertus essem, ubi esses, nolebam illum nostrum familiarem sermonem in alienas manus devenire.

Signa Megarica et Hermas, de quibus ad me scripsisti, vehementer exspecto. Quicquid eiusdem generis habebis, dignum Academia tibi quod videbitur, ne dubitaris mittere et arcae nostrae confidito. Genus hoc est voluptatis meae; quae γυμνασιώδη maxime sunt, ea quaero. Lentulus naves suas pollicetur. Peto abs te, ut haec diligenter cures. Thyillus te rogat et ego eius rogatu Εὐμολπιδῶν πάτρια.

X

CICERO ATTICO SAL.

Scr. in Tusculano ante Quintil. a. 687

Cum essem in Tusculano (erit hoc tibi pro illo tuo: " Cum essem in Ceramico ") verum tamen cum ibi essem, Roma puer a sorore tua missus epistulam mihi abs te adlatam dedit nuntiavitque eo ipso die post meridiem iturum eum, qui ad te proficisceretur. Eo factum est, ut epistulae tuae rescriberem aliquid, brevitate temporis tam pauca cogerer scribere.

IX

CICERO TO ATTICUS, GREETING.

Your letters are much too few and far between, *Rome,*
considering that it is much easier for you to find B.C. *67*
someone coming to Rome than for me to find anyone going to Athens. Besides, you can be surer
that I am at Rome than I can be that you are in
Athens. The shortness of this letter is due to my
doubts as to your whereabouts. Not knowing for
certain where you are, I don't want private correspondence to fall into a stranger's hands.

I am awaiting impatiently the statues of Megaric
marble and those of Hermes, which you mentioned
in your letter. Don't hesitate to send anything else
of the same kind that you have, if it is fit for my
Academy. My purse is long enough. This is my
little weakness; and what I want especially are those
that are fit for a Gymnasium. Lentulus promises his
ships. Please bestir yourself about it. Thyillus asks
you, or rather has got me to ask you, for some books
on the ritual of the Eumolpidae.

X

CICERO TO ATTICUS, GREETING.

When I was in my house at Tusculum—that's tit *Tusculum,*
for tat against your "When I was in Ceramicus"— *before July,*
but when I really was there, your sister sent a man B.C. *67*
from Rome with a letter from you, and told me that
someone was going to start for Greece that very
afternoon. So for lack of time I must make a very
short answer to your letter.

MARCUS TULLIUS CICERO

Primum tibi de nostro amico placando aut etiam plane restituendo polliceor. Quod ego etsi mea sponte ante faciebam, eo nunc tamen et agam studiosius et contendam ab illo vehementius, quod tantum ex epistula voluntatem eius rei tuam perspicere videor. Hoc te intellegere volo, pergraviter illum esse offensum; sed, quia nullam video gravem subesse causam, magno opere confido illum fore in officio et in nostra potestate.

Signa nostra et Hermeraclas, ut scribis, cum commodissime poteris, velim imponas, et si quod aliud οἰκεῖον eius loci, quem non ignoras, reperies, et maxime quae tibi palaestrae gymnasiique videbuntur esse. Etenim ibi sedens haec ad te scribebam, ut me locus ipse admoneret. Praeterea typos tibi mando, quos in tectorio atrioli possim includere, et putealia sigillata duo. Bibliothecam tuam cave cuiquam despondeas, quamvis acrem amatorem inveneris; nam ego omnes meas vindemiolas eo reservo, ut illud subsidium senectuti parem.

De fratre confido ita esse, ut semper volui et elaboravi. Multa signa sunt eius rei, non minimum, quod soror praegnans est. De comitiis meis et tibi me permisisse memini, et ego iam pridem hoc communibus amicis, qui te exspectant, praedico, te non modo non arcessi a me, sed prohiberi, quod intellegam multo magis interesse tua te agere, quod agendum est hoc tempore, quam mea te adesse comitiis. Proinde eo animo te velim esse, quasi mei negotii

First I promise to patch up the quarrel between you and our friend, even if I cannot quite make peace. I should have done it before of my own accord: but now that I see from your note that you have set your heart on it, I will give my mind to it and try harder than ever to win him over. I would have you to know that he is very seriously annoyed with you: but, as I cannot see any serious ground for his annoyance, I hope I shall find him pliable and amenable to my influence.

Please do as you say about the statues and the Hermeraclae: and have them shipped as soon as you can conveniently, and any other things you come across that are suitable for the place—you know what it is like—especially for the Palaestra and Gymnasium. That's where I am sitting and writing now, so my thoughts naturally run on it. I give you a commission, too, for bas-reliefs for insertion in the stucco walls of the hall, and for two well-covers in carved relief. Be sure you don't promise your library to anyone, however ardent a suitor you may find for it. I am saving up all my little gleanings to buy it as a prop for my old age.

My brother's affairs are, I trust, as I have always wished them to be and striven to make them. Everything points that way, and not the least that your sister is enceinte. As for my election, I have not forgotten that I gave you leave to stop away: and I have already warned our common friends, who expect you to come, that I have not only forborne to ask you to do so, but even forbidden it, knowing that present business is of much more importance to you than your presence at my election would be to me. I should like you to feel exactly as though it were my business

causa in ista loca missus esses; me autem eum et
offendes erga te et audies, quasi mihi, si quae parta
erunt, non modo te praesente, sed per te parta sint.
Tulliola tibi diem dat, sponsorem me appellat.

XI

CICERO ATTICO SAL.

Scr. Romae
Quint. aut
Sext. a. 687

Et mea sponte faciebam antea et post duabus epistulis tuis perdiligenter in eandem rationem scriptis
magno opere sum commotus. Eo accedebat hortator
adsiduus Sallustius, ut agerem quam diligentissime
cum Lucceio de vestra vetere gratia reconcilianda.
Sed, cum omnia fecissem, non modo eam voluntatem
eius, quae fuerat erga te, recuperare non potui, verum
ne causam quidem elicere immutatae voluntatis.
Tametsi iactat ille quidem illud suum arbitrium, et
ea, quae iam tum, cum aderas, offendere eius animum
intellegebam, tamen habet quiddam profecto, quod
magis in animo eius insederit, quod neque epistulae
tuae neque nostra adlegatio tam potest facile delere,
quam tu praesens non modo oratione, sed tuo vultu
illo familiari tolles, si modo tanti putaris, id quod,
si me audies et si humanitati tuae constare voles,
certe putabis. Ac, ne illud mirere, cur, cum ego
antea significarim tibi per litteras me sperare illum
in nostra potestate fore, nunc idem videar diffidere,
incredibile est, quanto mihi videatur illius voluntas
obstinatior et in hac iracundia offirmatior. Sed haec

which had taken you away. And you will find and hear from others that my feelings towards you are just as they would be if my success, supposing I have any, were gained not only with you here, but by your aid.

My little Tullia is for having the law of you, and is dunning me as your representative.

XI

CICERO TO ATTICUS, GREETING.

I had been working for you of my own free will, *Rome, July* and my energies were redoubled by the receipt of *or Aug.,* two letters from you insisting on the same point. B.C., *67* Besides, Sallustius was continually pressing me to do my best to replace you on your old friendly footing with Lucceius. But when I had done the uttermost, I failed not only to win back his old affection for you, but even to extract from him the reason for his change of feelings towards you. Though he is continually harping on that arbitration case of his, and the other things which I noticed provoked him when you were here, there is something else, I am sure, which is rankling in his mind. And this your presence, a talk with him, and still more the sight of your familiar face, would do more to remove than either your letters or my services as intermediary, if you think it worth while to come. And, if you will listen to me and are disposed to act with your usual courtesy, you will certainly think it worth while. You would never believe how self-willed and stiff-necked he seems to be on the point: so don't be astonished that I now appear to doubt my ability to manage him, though in former letters I hinted that I thought he would be under my thumb. But that will all be

aut sanabuntur, cum veneris, aut ei molesta erunt, in utro culpa erit.

Quod in epistula tua scriptum erat me iam arbitrari designatum esse, scito nihil tam exercitum esse nunc Romae quam candidatos omnibus iniquitatibus, nec, quando futura sint comitia, sciri. Verum haec audies de Philadelpho.

Tu velim, quae Academiae nostrae parasti, quam primum mittas. Mire quam illius loci non modo usus, sed etiam cogitatio delectat. Libros vero tuos cave cuiquam tradas; nobis eos, quem ad modum scribis, conserva. Summum me eorum studium tenet sicut odium iam ceterarum rerum; quas tu incredibile est quam brevi tempore quanto deteriores offensurus sis, quam reliquisti.

XII

CICERO ATTICO SAL.

Scr. Romae K. Ian. a. 693

Teucris illa lentum sane negotium, neque Cornelius ad Terentiam postea rediit. Opinor, ad Considium, Axium, Selicium confugiendum est; nam a Caecilio propinqui minore centesimis nummum movere non possunt. Sed ut ad prima illa redeam, nihil ego illa impudentius, astutius, lentius vidi. " Libertum mitto, Tito mandavi." Σκήψεις atque ἀναβολαί; sed nescio an ταὐτόματον ἡμῶν. Nam mihi Pompeiani prodromi nuntiant aperte Pompeium acturum Antonio succedi

put right when you come, or he will smart for it who deserves it.

You say in your note that my election is thought certain; but let me tell you that candidates are plagued to death nowadays with all sorts of unfairness, and even the date of the election is not fixed. But you will hear about that from Philadelphus.

Please send what you have purchased for my Academy as soon as possible. It is astonishing how the mere thought of the place raises my spirits even when I am not in it. Be sure you don't get rid of your books. Keep them for me as you promise. My enthusiasm for them increases with my disgust at everything else. You would never believe how changed for the worse you will find everything has been in the short time you have been away.

XII

CICERO TO ATTICUS, GREETING.

Teucris [1] is an unconscionably slow coach and Cornelius has never come back to Terentia : so I suppose I shall have to turn to Considius, Axius, or Selicius. Even his relatives can't screw a penny out of Caecilius at less than 12 per cent. But to return to the point ; Teucris' behaviour is the most shameless mixture of cunning and laziness I have ever seen. " I'm sending a freedman," says she, or " I've given Titus a commission." All excuses and delays ! But perhaps " *dieu dispose* " ; [2] for Pompey's advance party bring news that he is going to move for

Rome, Jan. 1, B.C. 61

---

[1] Probably a pseudonym for some agent of Gaius Antonius, though some suggest that it stands for Antonius himself.

[2] Menander, ταὐτόματον ἡμῶν καλλίω βουλεύεται.

29

oportere, eodemque tempore aget praetor ad populum. Res eius modi est, ut ego nec per bonorum nec
per popularem existimationem honeste possim hominem defendere, nec mihi libeat, quod vel maximum
est. Etenim accidit hoc, quod totum cuius modi sit,
mando tibi, ut perspicias. Libertum ego habeo sane
nequam hominem, Hilarum dico, ratiocinatorem et
clientem tuum. De eo mihi Valerius interpres nuntiat, Thyillusque se audisse scribit haec, esse hominem
cum Antonio; Antonium porro in cogendis pecuniis
dictitare partem mihi quaeri et a me custodem com-
munis quaestus libertum esse missum. Non sum me-
diocriter commotus neque tamen credidi, sed certe
aliquid sermonis fuit. Totum investiga, cognosce,
perspice et nebulonem illum, si quo pacto potes, ex
istis locis amove. Huius sermonis Valerius auctorem
Cn. Plancium nominabat. Mando tibi plane totum,
ut videas cuius modi sit.

Pompeium nobis amicissimum constat esse. Divortium Muciae vehementer probatur. P. Clodium,
Appi f., credo te audisse cum veste muliebri deprehen-
sum domi C. Caesaris, cum pro populo fieret, eumque
per manus servulae servatum et eductum; rem esse
insigni infamia. Quod te moleste ferre certo scio.

Quod praeterea ad te scribam, non habeo, et mehercule eram in scribendo conturbatior. Nam puer
festivus anagnostes noster Sositheus decesserat, meque plus quam servi mors debere videbatur, commo-

Antony's retirement, and a praetor will bring the motion forward. In my circumstances I couldn't honourably champion him. I should lose the respect of both parties if I did: and what's more, I wouldn't, if I could, in view of certain things that have happened, to which I should like to call your attention. There's a freedman of mine, an utter scoundrel—Hilarus I mean—an accountant and a client of yours. Valerius the interpreter sends me news of him, and Thyillus says he has heard, too, that the fellow is with Antony, and that Antony, when he is making requisitions, always asserts that part is levied on my authority, and that I have sent a freedman to look after my share. I am considerably annoyed, though I hardly believe the story: but there has been a good deal of talk. Look into the matter thoroughly and try to get to the bottom of it, and, if you possibly can, get that rascal shifted. Valerius mentioned Cn. Plancius as his authority for the statement. I leave the whole matter entirely in your hands to investigate.

I am assured that Pompey is on the best of terms with me. Mucia's divorce meets with everyone's approval. I expect you have heard that P. Clodius, son of Appius, was discovered in woman's clothes in C. Caesar's house, where the sacrifice was going on: but a servant girl managed to smuggle him out. It has created a public scandal: and I am sure you will be sorry to hear of it.

I don't think I have any other news for you: and I'm sorry to say I've been rather upset while writing. My reader Sositheus, a charming fellow, has died; and I am more upset about it than anyone would suppose I should be about a slave's death. Please

verat. Tu velim saepe ad nos scribas. Si rem
nullam habebis, quod in buccam venerit, scribito.
Kal. Ianuariis M. Messalla, M. Pisone coss.

XIII

CICERO ATTICO SAL.

Scr. Romae
VI K. Febr.
a. 693

Accepi tuas tres iam epistulas, unam a M. Cornelio,
quam Tribus Tabernis, ut opinor, ei dedisti, alteram,
quam mihi Canusinus tuus hospes reddidit, tertiam,
quam, ut scribis, ancora soluta [1] de phaselo dedisti;
quae fuerunt omnes,[2] ut rhetorum pueri loquuntur,
cum humanitatis sparsae sale tum insignes amoris
notis. Quibus epistulis sum equidem abs te lacessitus
ad rescribendum; sed idcirco sum tardior, quod non
invenio fidelem tabellarium. Quotus enim quisque
est, qui epistulam paulo graviorem ferre possit, nisi
eam pellectione relevarit? Accedit eo, quod mihi non
est notum ut quisque in Epirum proficiscitur. Ego
enim te arbitror caesis apud Amaltheam tuam victi-
mis, statim esse ad Sicyonem oppugnandum profectum, neque tamen id ipsum certum habeo, quando ad
Antonium proficiscare, aut quid in Epiro temporis
ponas. Ita neque Achaicis hominibus neque Epiro-
ticis paulo liberiores litteras committere audeo.

Sunt autem post discessum a me tuum res dignae
litteris nostris, sed non committendae eius modi periculo, ut aut interire aut aperiri aut intercipi possint.
Primum igitur scito primum me non esse rogatum
sententiam praepositumque esse nobis pacificatorem

---

[1] ancora sublata *Lambinus*: ora soluta *Peerlkamp*. *But
Schmalz* (*Antibarbarus*, ii. 588, 7th ed.) *points out the reading
of the MSS. is defensible as a contamination of* ancora sublata
and nave soluta.

[2] ut rhetorum pueri *Madvig*: rethorum pure *MSS.*

write frequently. If you have no news, write the first thing that comes into your head.

January 1, in the consulship of M. Messalla and M. Piso.

XIII

CICERO TO ATTICUS, GREETING.

I have had your three letters: one from M. Cor- *Rome, Jan.* nelius, to whom you gave it, I think at the Three *25,* B.C. *61* Taverns; another brought by your host at Canusium; and a third, which you say you posted from the boat just as you got under way. All three of them were, as a pupil in the rhetorical schools would say, at once sprinkled with the salt of refinement and stamped with the brand of affection. They certainly provoke an answer: but I have been rather slow about sending one, for lack of a safe messenger. There are very few who can carry a letter of weight without lightening it by a perusal. Besides, I don't hear of every traveller to Epirus. For I suppose when you have offered sacrifice at your villa Amalthea you will start at once to lay siege to Sicyon. I'm not certain either how or when you are going to join Antony or how long you will stay in Epirus. So I dare not trust at all outspoken letters to people going either to Achaia or to Epirus.

Plenty of things worth writing about have happened since your departure, but I dared not commit them to the risk of the letters being either lost or opened or intercepted. First, then, let me tell you I was not asked my opinion first in the House, but had to play second fiddle to the " peace-maker " of the

33

Allobrogum, idque admurmurante senatu neque me invito esse factum. Sum enim et ab observando homine perverso liber et ad dignitatem in re publica retinendam contra illius voluntatem solutus, et ille secundus in dicendo locus habet auctoritatem paene principis et voluntatem non nimis devinctam beneficio consulis. Tertius est Catulus, quartus, si etiam hoc quaeris, Hortensius. Consul autem ipse parvo animo et pravo tamen cavillator genere illo moroso, quod etiam sine dicacitate ridetur, facie magis quam facetiis ridiculus, nihil agens cum re publica, seiunctus ab optimatibus, a quo nihil speres boni rei publicae, quia non vult, nihil speres mali, quia non audet. Eius autem collega et in me perhonorificus et partium studiosus ac defensor bonarum. Qui nunc leviter inter se dissident. Sed vereor, ne hoc, quod infectum est, serpat longius. Credo enim te audisse, cum apud Caesarem pro populo fieret, venisse eo muliebri vestitu virum, idque sacrificium cum virgines instaurrassent, mentionem a Q. Cornificio in senatu factam (is fuit princeps, ne tu forte aliquem nostrum putes); postea rem ex senatus consulto ad virgines atque ad pontifices relatam idque ab iis nefas esse decretum; diende ex senatus consulto consules rogationem promulgasse; uxori Caesarem nuntium remisisse. In hac causa Piso amicitia P. Clodi ductus

34

Allobroges.[1] Nor did I mind much, though the
senate murmured disapproval. It has freed me from
the necessity of bowing to a crotchety individual, and
sets me at liberty to preserve my political dignity in
spite of him. The second place carries nearly as much
weight with it as the first, and one's actions are not
so much bound by obligation to the consul. The
third place fell to Catulus : the fourth, if you want to
go as far, to Hortensius. The consul is petty-minded
and perverse, a quibbler who used that bitter kind of
sarcasm which raises a laugh even when there is no
wit in the words, on the strength of his expression
rather than his expressions. He is no politician at
all, he stands aloof from the conservatives : and one
cannot expect him to render any good services to the
State, because he does not wish to do so, nor any
bad, because he does not dare. But his colleague is
most polite to me, a keen politician and a bulwark of
the conservative party. There is a slight difference
of opinion between them at present : but I am afraid
that the contagion may spread. No doubt you have
heard that, when the sacrifice was taking place in
Caesar's house, a man in woman's clothes got in ; and
that after the Vestal Virgins had performed the sacrifice afresh, the matter was mentioned in the House
by Cornificius. Note that he was the prime mover
and none of us. Then a resolution was passed, the
matter was referred to the Virgins and the priests,
and they pronounced it a sacrilege. So the consuls
were directed by the House to bring in a bill about
it. Caesar has divorced his wife. Piso's friendship

[1] C. Calpurnius Piso, consul in 67 B.C. and governor of
Gallia Narbonensis in 66–65 B.C. He had temporarily pacified the Allobroges, but they were already in revolt again.

operam dat, ut ea rogatio, quam ipse fert et fert ex senatus consulto et de religione, antiquetur. Messalla vehementer adhuc agit severe. Boni viri precibus Clodi removentur a causa, operae comparantur, nosmet ipsi, qui Lycurgei a principio fuissemus, cotidie demitigamur, instat et urget Cato. Quid multa? Vereor, ne haec neglecta a bonis, defensa ab improbis magnorum rei publicae malorum causa sit. Tuus autem ille amicus (scin, quem dicam?), de quo tu ad me scripsisti, posteaquam non auderet reprehendere, laudare coepisse, nos, ut ostendit, admodum diligit, amplectitur, amat, aperte laudat, occulte, sed ita, ut perspicuum sit, invidet. Nihil come, nihil simplex, nihil ἐν τοῖς πολιτικοῖς illustre, nihil honestum, nihil forte, nihil liberum. Sed haec ad te scribam alias subtilius; nam neque adhuc mihi satis nota sunt, et huic terrae filio nescio cui committere epistulam tantis de rebus non audeo.

Provincias praetores nondum sortiti sunt. Res eodem est loci, quo reliquisti. Τοποθεσίαν, quam postulas, Miseni et Puteolorum, includam orationi meae. "A. d. III Non. Decembr." mendose fuisse animadverteram. Quae laudas ex orationibus, mihi crede, valde mihi placebant, sed non audebam antea dicere; nunc vero, quod a te probata sunt, multo mi ἀττικώτερα videntur. In illam orationem Metellinam

for Clodius is making him do his best to have the bill
shelved, though he is the person who has to bring it
forward under the House's orders—and a bill for
sacrilege too! Messalla at present takes a strict
view of the case. The conservatives are dropping
out of it under persuasion from Clodius. Gangs of
rowdies are being formed. I, who at first was a
perfect Lycurgus, am daily cooling down. Cato,
however, is pressing the case with energy. But
enough. I am afraid that what with the lack of
interest shown in the case by the conservatives, and
its championship by the socialists, it may cause a lot
of mischief to the State. Your friend [1]—you know
whom I mean, the man who, you say, began to praise
me as soon as he feared to blame me—is now parading
his affection for me openly and ostentatiously; but
in his heart of hearts he is envious, and he does not
disguise it very well. He is totally lacking in
courtesy, candour, and brilliancy in his politics, as well
as in sense of honour, resolution, and generosity.
But I'll write more fully about that another time.
I've not got hold of the facts properly yet, and I
dare not trust an important letter to a man in the
street like this messenger.

The praetors have not drawn their provinces yet:
and things are just as they were when you left. I
will insert a description of Misenum and Puteoli in
my speech as you suggest. I had already spotted
the mistake in the date, Dec. 3. The passages in
my speeches which took your fancy were, do you
know, just those that I was proud of, but didn't like
to say so before: and after Atticus' approval they
look much more Attic in my eyes. I have added a

[1] Pompey.

addidi quaedam. Liber tibi mittetur, quoniam te amor nostri φιλορήτορα reddidit.

Novi tibi quidnam scribam? quid? etiam. Messalla consul Autronianam domum emit HS $\overline{\text{cxxxiiii}}$. " Quid id ad me? " inquies. Tantum, quod ea emptione et nos bene emisse iudicati sumus, et homines intellegere coeperunt licere amicorum facultatibus in emendo ad dignitatem aliquam pervenire. Teucris illa lentum negotium est, sed tamen est in spe. Tu ista confice. A nobis liberiorem epistulam exspecta. vi Kal. Febr. M. Messalla, M. Pisone coss.

XIV

CICERO ATTICO SAL.

Scr. Romae Id. Febr. a. 693

Vereor, ne putidum sit scribere ad te, quam sim occupatus, sed tamen ita distinebar, ut huic vix tantulae epistulae tempus habuerim atque id ereptum e summis occupationibus. Prima contio Pompei qualis fuisset, scripsi ad te antea, non iucunda miseris, inanis improbis, beatis non grata, bonis non gravis; itaque frigebat. Tum Pisonis consulis impulsu levissimus tribunus pl. Fufius in contionem producit

38

little to my reply to Metellus. I'll send the book
to you, since your affection for me has given you a
taste for rhetoric.

Is there any news to tell you? Let me see—yes.
The consul Messalla has bought Autronius' house for
£1,200.[1] What business is that of mine, you will ask.
Only that it proves that my house was a good invest-
ment, and is beginning to open people's eyes to the
fact that it is quite legitimate to make use of a
friend's pocket to buy a place that gives one a social
position. That Teucris is a slow coach; but it is not
hopeless yet. Mind you get your part finished. I'll
write less guardedly soon.

Jan. 25, in the consulship of M. Messalla and M.
Piso.

XIV

CICERO TO ATTICUS, GREETING.

I'm afraid you'll be heartily sick of my pleas of *Rome, Feb.*
business, but I'm so driven from pillar to post that I *13, B.C. 61*
can hardly find time for these few lines, and even that
I have to snatch from important business. I have
already written and told you what Pompey's first
public speech was like. The poor did not relish it,
the socialists thought it pointless, the rich were not
pleased with it, and the conservatives were dissatisfied: so it fell flat. Then at the instance of the
consul Piso, an untrustworthy tribune, Fufius, must

---

[1] There seems to be some mistake about the numeral, as
£1,200 (134,000 sesterces) is too little for a house which
could be compared with Cicero's, which cost £30,000. If it
is supposed to stand for |c̅x̅x̅x̅i̅v̅| (i.e. 13,400,000 sesterces)
it would be too large. Tyrrell suggests reading |x̅x̅x̅i̅v̅|
(i.e. 3,400,000 sesterces), about £30,000.

Pompeium. Res agebatur in circo Flaminio, et erat
in eo ipso loco illo die nundinarum πανήγυρις. Quaesivit ex eo, placeretne ei iudices a praetore legi, quo
consilio idem praetor uteretur. Id autem erat de
Clodiana religione ab senatu constitutum. Tum Pompeius μάλ' ἀριστοκρατικῶς locutus est senatusque
auctoritatem sibi omnibus in rebus maximam videri
semperque visam esse respondit et id multis verbis.
Postea Messalla consul in senatu de Pompeio quaesivit, quid de religione et de promulgata rogatione
sentiret. Locutus ita est in senatu, ut omnia illius
ordinis consulta γενικῶς laudaret, mihique, ut adse-
dit, dixit se putare satis ab se etiam " de istis rebus "
esse responsum. Crassus posteaquam vidit illum ex-
cepisse laudem ex eo, quod suspicarentur homines ei
consulatum meum placere, surrexit ornatissimeque
de meo consulatu locutus est, cum ita diceret, " se,
quod esset senator, quod civis, quod liber, quod
viveret, mihi acceptum referre ; quotiens coniugem,
quotiens domum, quotiens patriam videret, toriens se
beneficium meum videre." Quid multa ? totum hunc
locum, quem ego varie meis orationibus, quarum tu
Aristarchus es, soleo pingere, de flamma, de ferro
(nosti illas ληκύθους), valde graviter pertexuit. Proximus Pompeio sedebam. Intellexi hominem moveri, utrum Crassum inire eam gratiam, quam ipse

needs trot out Pompey to deliver an harangue. This happened in the Circus Flaminius, where there was the usual market-day gathering of riff-raff. Fufius asked him whether he agreed with the proposal that the praetor should have the selection of the jury-men and then use them as his panel. That, of course, was the plan proposed by the Senate in Clodius' trial for sacrilege. To this Pompey replied *en grand seigneur* that he felt and always had felt the greatest respect for the Senate's authority; and very long-winded he was about it. Afterwards the consul Messalla asked Pompey in the Senate for his opinion on the sacrilege and the proposed bill. He delivered a speech eulogizing the Senate's measures *en bloc*, and said to me as he sat down at my side, that he thought he had given a sufficiently clear answer to "those questions." Crassus no sooner saw that he had won public appreciation, because people fancied that he approved of my consulship, than up he got and spoke of it in the most complimentary way. He said that he owed his seat in the House, his privileges as a citizen, his freedom, and his very life to me. He never saw his wife's face, or his home, or his native land, without recognizing the debt he owed to me. But enough. He worked up with great effect all that purple patch which I so often use here and there to adorn my speeches, to which you play Aristarchus [1]—the passage about fire and sword—you know the paints I have on my palette. I was sitting next to Pompey, and noticed that he was much affected, possibly at seeing Crassus

[1] An Alexandrine grammarian noted especially for his criticism of the Homeric poems, in which he detected many spurious lines.

praetermisisset, an esse tantas res nostras, quae tam
libenti senatu laudarentur, ab eo praesertim, qui
mihi laudem illam eo minus deberet, quod meis omnibus litteris in Pompeiana laude perstrictus esset.
Hic dies me valde Crasso adiunxit, et tamen ab illo
aperte tecte quicquid est datum, libenter accepi. Ego
autem ipse, di boni! quo modo ἐνεπερπερευσάμην
novo auditori Pompeio! Si umquam mihi περίοδοι,
si καμπαί, si ἐνθυμήματα, si κατασκευαί suppedita-
verunt, illo tempore. Quid multa? clamores. Etenim
haec erat ὑπόθεσις, de gravitate ordinis, de equestri
concordia, de consensione Italiae, de intermortuis
reliquiis coniurationis, de vilitate, de otio. Nosti iam
in hac materia sonitus nostros. Tanti fuerunt, ut
ego eo brevior sim, quod eos usque istinc exauditos
putem.

Romanae autem se res sic habent. Senatus Ἄρειος
πάγος; nihil constantius, nihil severius, nihil fortius.
Nam, cum dies venisset rogationi ex senatus consulto
ferendae, concursabant barbatuli iuvenes, totus ille
grex Catilinae, duce filiola Curionis et populum, ut
antiquaret, rogabant. Piso autem consul lator rogationis idem erat dissuasor. Operae Clodianae pontes
occuparant, tabellae ministrabantur ita, ut nulla daretur " VTI ROGAS." Hic tibi in rostra Cato advolat,

snap up the chance of winning popularity, which he had thrown away, and perhaps at realizing the importance of my achievements, when he saw that praise of them met with the Senate's entire approval, especially coming from one who had all the less necessity to praise me, because in every one of my works he has been censured for Pompey's benefit. To-day has done a great deal to cement my friendship with Crassus: but still I gladly received any crumbs Pompey let fall openly or covertly.[1] As for me, ye gods, how I showed off before my new listener Pompey! Then, if ever, my flow of rounded periods, my easy transitions, my antitheses, my constructive arguments stood me in good stead. In a word, loud applause! For the gist of it was the importance of the Senatorial order, its unison with the knights, the concord of all Italy, the paralysed remains of the conspiracy, peace and plenty. You know how I can thunder on a subject like that. This time my thunders were so loud that I forbear to say any more about them. I expect you heard them right over there.

Well, there you have the news of the town. The Senate is a perfect Areopagus, all seriousness, steadfastness, and firmness. For when the time came for passing the Senate's measure all those callow youths, Catiline's cubs, met under the leadership of Curio's feminine son and asked the people to reject it. The consul Piso had to propose the law, but spoke against it. Clodius' rowdies held the gangways; and the voting papers were so managed that no *placet* forms were given out. Then you have Cato flying to the

[1] Or " let fall with obvious covertness "; or " I openly received what he covertly gave."

commulcium Pisoni consuli mirificum facit, si id est
commulcium,[1] vox plena gravitatis, plena auctoritatis,
plena denique salutis. Accedit eodem etiam noster
Hortensius, multi praeterea boni; insignis vero opera
Favoni fuit. Hoc concursu optimatium comitia
dimittuntur, senatus vocatur. Cum decerneretur
frequenti senatu contra pugnante Pisone, ad pedes
omnium singillatim accidente Clodio, ut consules
populum cohortarentur ad rogationem accipiendam,
homines ad quindecim Curioni nullum senatus consultum facienti adsenserunt, ex altera parte facile
cccc fuerunt. Acta res est. Fufius tribunus tum
concessit. Clodius contiones miseras habebat, in
quibus Lucullum, Hortensium, C. Pisonem, Messallam consulem contumeliose laedebat; me tantum
"comperisse" omnia criminabatur. Senatus et de
provinciis praetorum et de legationibus et de ceteris
rebus decernebat, ut, antequam rogatio lata esset, ne
quid ageretur.

Habes res Romanas. Sed tamen etiam illud, quod
non speraram, audi. Messalla consul est egregius,
fortis, constans, diligens, nostri laudator, amator,
imitator. Ille alter uno vitio minus vitiosus, quod
iners, quod somni plenus, quod imperitus, quod
ἀπρακτότατος, sed voluntate ita κακέκτης, ut Pom-

---

[1] Commulticium *M*: convicium *M in the margin. But as
Schmidt points out*, commulcium, *which is the reading of Z
in the first case and of Z M in the second case, is probably a genuine
vulgar Latin word.*

rostrum and giving Piso a slap in the face, if one can say " slap in the face " of an utterance full of dignity, full of authority, and full of saving counsel. Our friend Hortensius joined him too, and many other loyalists, Favonius particularly distinguishing himself for his energy. This rally of the conservatives broke up the meeting, and the Senate was called together. In a full house a resolution was passed that persuasion should be used to induce the people to accept the measure, though Piso opposed it and Clodius went down on his knees to us one by one. Some fifteen supported Curio's rejection of the bill, while the opposite party numbered easily 400. That settled the matter. Fufius the tribune collapsed. Clodius delivered some pitiful harangues, in which he hurled reproaches at Lucullus, Hortensius, C. Piso, and the consul Messalla: me he only twitted with my sensational discoveries.[1] The Senate decided that no action was to be taken as to the distribution of provinces among the praetors, hearing of legations or anything else, till this measure was passed.

There you have the political situation. But there is one piece of news I must tell you, as it is better than I expected. Messalla is an excellent consul, resolute, reliable, and energetic: for me he expresses admiration and respect, and shows it by imitating me. That other fellow has only one redeeming vice, laziness, sleepiness, ignorance, and *fainéance*: but at heart he is such a *mauvais sujet* that he began to

---

[1] Cicero had contented himself at the time he unmasked Catiline with declaring that he had " discovered " (*comperisse*) full details without making them public. Hence the phrase was frequently cast in his teeth. Cf. *Fam.* v. 5, 2.

peium post illam contionem, in qua ab eo senatus
laudatus est, odisse coeperit. Itaque mirum in modum omnes a se bonos alienavit. Neque id magis
amicitia Clodi adductus fecit quam studio perditarum
rerum atque partium. Sed habet sui similem in
magistratibus praeter Fufium neminem. Bonis utimur tribunis pl., Cornuto vero Pseudocatone. Quid
quaeris?

Nunc ut ad privata redeam, Τεῦκρις promissa pa-
travit. Tu mandata effice, quae recepisti. Quintus
frater, qui Argiletani aedificii reliquum dodrantem
emit HS D̅C̅C̅X̅X̅V̅, Tusculanum venditat, ut, si possit,
emat Pacilianam domum. Cum Lucceio in gratiam
redii. Video hominem valde petiturire. Navabo operam. Tu quid agas, ubi sis, cuius modi istae res sint,
fac me quam diligentissime certiorem. Idibus Febr.

XV

CICERO ATTICO SAL.

Scr. Romae
Id. Mart. a.
693

Asiam Quinto, suavissimo fratri, obtigisse audisti.
Non enim dubito, quin celerius tibi hoc rumor quam
ullius nostrum litterae nuntiarint. Nunc, quoniam
et laudis avidissimi semper fuimus et praeter ceteros
φιλέλληνες et sumus et habemur et multorum odia
atque inimicitias rei publicae causa suscepimus,
παντοίης ἀρετῆς μιμνήσκεο curaque, effice, ut ab
omnibus et laudemur et amemur. His de rebus
plura ad te in ea epistula scribam, quam ipsi Quinto

46

detest Pompey after that speech of his in praise of the Senate. So he is at daggers drawn with all the patriotic party. It was not so much friendship for Clodius that induced him to act like this as a taste for knaves and knavery. But there are none of his kidney in office except Fufius. Our tribunes of the people are all sound men, and Cornutus is Cato's double. Can I say more?

Now for private affairs. Teucris has kept her promise. Do you carry out the commissions you received. My brother Quintus has bought the remaining three-quarters of his house on the Argiletum for £6,000,[1] and is selling his place at Tusculum to buy Pacilius' house, if he can. I have made it up with Lucceius. I see he's got the office-seeking complaint badly. I will do my best for him. Please keep me posted up in your doings, your address and the progress of our affairs. Feb. 13.

XV

CICERO TO ATTICUS, GREETING.

You have heard that that good brother of mine, *Rome,* Quintus, has Asia assigned him as his province. I *March 15,* have no doubt a rumour of it has reached you before B.C. *61* any of our letters. We have always had a keen regard for our reputation, and both are and are considered unusually Philhellenic, and our public services have won us a host of ill-wishers. So now is the time for you to " screw your courage to the sticking-place," *Iliad, xxii,8* and help us to secure universal applause and approval. I will write further about it in a letter which I shall

---

[1] 725,000 sesterces.

47

dabo. Tu me velim certiorem facias, quid de meis
mandatis egeris atque etiam quid de tuo negotio;
nam, ut Brundisio profectus es, nullae mihi abs te
sunt redditae litterae. Valde aveo scire, quid agas.
Idibus Martiis.

XVI

CICERO ATTICO SAL.

Scr. Romae
m. Quint. a.
693

Quaeris ex me, quid acciderit de iudicio, quod tam
praeter opinionem omnium factum sit, et simul vis
scire, quo modo ego minus, quam soleam, proeliatus
sim. Respondebo tibi ὕστερον πρότερον Ὁμηρικῶς.
Ego enim, quam diu senatus auctoritas mihi defen-
denda fuit, sic acriter et vehementer proeliatus sum,
ut clamor concursusque maxima cum mea laude
fierent. Quodsi tibi umquam sum visus in re publica
fortis, certe me in illa causa admiratus esses. Cum
enim ille ad contiones confugisset in iisque meo
nomine ad invidiam uteretur, di immortales! quas
ego pugnas et quantas strages edidi! quos impetus in
Pisonem, in Curionem, in totam illam manum feci!
quo modo sum insectatus levitatem senum, libidinem
iuventutis! Saepe, ita me di iuvent! te non solum
auctorem consiliorum meorum, verum etiam specta-
torem pugnarum mirificarum desideravi. Postea vero
quam Hortensius excogitavit, ut legem de religione
Fufius tribunus pl. ferret, in qua nihil aliud a consulari
rogatione differebat nisi iudicum genus (in eo autem
erant omnia), pugnavitque, ut ita fieret, quod et sibi
et aliis persuaserat nullis illum iudicibus effugere

give to Quintus himself. Please let me know which of my orders you have carried out and how your own affairs are getting on. I haven't had a single letter from you since you left Brundisium: and I badly want to know how you are. March 15.

XVI

CICERO TO ATTICUS, GREETING.

You ask what can have happened about the trial *Rome, June,* to give it such an unexpected ending, and you want B.C. *61* to know, too, why I showed less fight than usual. Well! In my answer I'll put the cart before the horse like Homer. So long as I had to defend the Senate's decree, I fought so fiercely and doughtily, that cheering crowds rallied round me enthusiastic in my applause. You would certainly have marvelled at my courage on this occasion, if ever you credited me with any courage in my country's defence. When Clodius fell back on speechifying and took my name in vain, didn't I just show fight, didn't I deal havoc! How I charged Piso, Curio, and all that crowd! Didn't I rate the old men for their frivolity, the young for their wanton passions! Heaven is my witness, I often wanted you not only to prompt my plans, but also to be a spectator of my doughty deeds. But when Hortensius had conceived the idea of letting Fufius bring in his bill about the sacrilege, which differed from the consular measure only in the method of choosing the jury—though that was the point on which everything turned—and fought for his own way, under the impression, which he had also conveyed to others, that no conceivable

49

posse, contraxi vela perspiciens inopiam iudicum,
neque dixi quicquam pro testimonio, nisi quod erat
ita notum atque testatum, ut non possem praeterire.
Itaque, si causam quaeris absolutionis, ut iam πρὸς τὸ
πρότερον revertar, egestas iudicum fuit et turpitudo.
Id autem ut accideret, commissum est Hortensi consilio, qui dum veritus est, ne Fufius ei legi inter-
cederet, quae ex senatus consulto ferebatur, non
vidit illud, satius esse illum in infamia relinqui ac
sordibus quam infirmo iudicio committi, sed ductus
odio properavit rem deducere in iudicium, cum illum
plumbeo gladio iugulatum iri tamen diceret.

Sed iudicium si quaeris quale fuerit, incredibili
exitu, sic uti nunc ex eventu ab aliis, a me tamen ex
ipso initio consilium Hortensi reprehendatur.   Nam,
ut reiectio facta est clamoribus maximis, cum accu-
sator tamquam censor bonus homines nequissimos
reiceret, reus tamquam clemens lanista frugalissimum
quemque secerneret, ut primum iudices consederunt,
valde diffidere boni coeperunt.   Non enim umquam
turpior in ludo talario consessus fuit, maculosi senatores, nudi equites, tribuni non tam aerati quam, ut
appellantur, aerarii.   Pauci tamen boni inerant, quos
reiectione fugare ille non potuerat, qui maesti inter
sui dissimiles et maerentes sedebant et contagione

jury could acquit Clodius, I drew in a reef or two, not being blind to the impecuniosity of the jurymen. I confined my testimony to points so thoroughly well known and attested that I could not omit them. So, to come at last to the " horse," if you want to know the reason for his acquittal, it lay in the jury's lack of pence and of conscience. But it was Hortensius' plan that made such a result possible. In his fright that Fufius might veto the Senate's measure, he overlooked the fact that it would be better for Clodius to be kept in disgrace with a trial hanging over his head than for the case to come before an unsound court. Spurred on by hatred, he rushed the matter into court, saying that a leaden sword was sharp enough to cut Clodius' throat.

If you want to know about the trial, the result of it was so incredible that now after the event everybody agrees with my forebodings and blames Hortensius. The challenging of the jury took place amidst an uproar, since the prosecutor, like a good censor, rejected all the knaves, and the defendant, like a kind-hearted trainer of gladiators, set aside all the respectable people. And as soon as the jury took their seats the patriotic party began to have grave misgivings : for never did a more disreputable set of people get together even in a gambling hell. Senators with a past, knights without a penny, tribunes whose only right to a title implying pay lay in their readiness to take it.[1] The few honest folk among them, that he had not managed to remove in his selection, sat as woe-begone as fish out of water,

---

[1] Or keeping the ordinary sense of " aerarii ": " cashiered rather than rich in cash." But the sense both of " aerati " and of " aerarii " here is very doubtful.

turpitudinis vehementer permovebantur. Hic, ut
quaeque res ad consilium primis postulationibus re-
ferebatur, incredibilis erat severitas nulla varietate
sententiarum. Nihil impetrabat reus, plus accusatori
debatur, quam postulabat; triumphabat (quid quaeris?) Hortensius se vidisse tantum; nemo erat, qui
illum reum ac non miliens condemnatum arbitraretur.
Me vero teste producto credo te ex acclamatione
Clodi advocatorum audisse quae consurrectio iudicum
facta sit, ut me circumsteterint, ut aperte iugula sua
pro meo capite P. Clodio ostentarint. Quae mihi res
multo honorificentior visa est quam aut illa, cum
iurare tui cives Xenocratem testimonium dicentem
prohibuerunt, aut cum tabulas Metelli Numidici,
cum eae, ut mos est, circumferrentur, nostri iudices
aspicere noluerunt. Multo haec, inquam, nostra res
maior. Itaque iudicum vocibus, cum ego sic ab iis
ut salus patriae defenderer, fractus reus et una patroni omnes conciderunt; ad me autem eadem frequentia postridie convenit, quacum abiens consulatu
sum domum reductus. Clamare praeclari Areopagi-
tae se non esse venturos nisi praesidio constituto. Re-
fertur ad consilium. Una sola sententia praesidium
non desideravit. Defertur res ad senatum. Gravis-
sime ornatissimeque decernitur; laudantur iudices;
datur negotium magistratibus. Responsurum hominem nemo arbitrabatur.

> Ἔσπετε νῦν μοι, Μοῦσαι —
> ὅππως δὴ πρῶτον πῦρ ἔμπεσε.

sadly upset and bemoaning their contact with infamy.
At the preliminary proceedings, as point after point
was put before the jury, their strict and unanimous
uprightness was extraordinary. The defendant never
won a point, and the prosecution were granted more
than they asked for. It goes without saying that
Hortensius was triumphant at his penetration; and
no one regarded Clodius so much as a man on his trial
as one that had been condemned a thousand times
over. You have no doubt heard how the jury rose in
a body to protect me when I stepped into the witness-
box and Clodius' supporters began to hoot: and how
they offered their throats to Clodius' sword in defence
of me. Thereby, to my mind, they paid me a far
higher compliment than your fellow-citizens paid
Xenocrates when they refused to let him take the
oath before giving his testimony, or our Roman jury
paid Metellus Numidicus when they would not look
at the accounts which he passed round as is usual in
such cases. I repeat, the honour shown me was far
greater. The shouts of the jury, proclaiming me as
the saviour of the country crushed and annihilated
the defendant and all his supporters. And on the
next day a crowd as great as that which conducted
me home at the end of my consulship gathered
round me. Our noble Areopagites declared they
would not come without a guard. The votes of the
court were taken, and there was only one person who
voted a guard unnecessary. The point was laid before the Senate, who passed a decree in the strongest
and most complimentary terms, thanking the jury
and referring the matter to the magistrates. No one
thought Clodius would defend his case. " Tell me Iliad xvi, 112
now, ye Muses, how first the fire fell."

Nosti Calvum ex Nanneianis illum, illum laudatorem meum, de cuius oratione erga me honorifica ad te scripseram. Biduo per unum servum et eum ex ludo gladiatorio confecit totum negotium; arcessivit ad se, promisit, intercessit, dedit. Iam vero (o di boni, rem perditam!) etiam noctes certarum mulierum atque adulescentulorum nobilium introductiones non nullis iudicibus pro mercedis cumulo fuerunt. Ita summo discessu bonorum, pleno foro servorum xxv iudices ita fortes tamen fuerunt, ut summo proposito periculo vel perire maluerint quam perdere omnia. xxxi fuerunt, quos fames magis quam fama commoverit. Quorum Catulus cum vidisset quendam, " Quid vos," inquit, " praesidium a nobis postulabatis? an, ne nummi vobis eriperentur, timebatis? " Habes, ut brevissime potui, genus iudicii et causam absolutionis.

Quaeris deinceps, qui nunc sit status rerum et qui meus. Rei publicae statum illum, quem tu meo consilio, ego divino confirmatum putabam, qui bonorum omnium coniunctione et auctoritate consulatus mei fixus et fundatus videbatur, nisi quis nos deus respexerit, elapsum scito esse de manibus uno hoc iudicio, si iudicium est triginta homines populi Ro-

You know Baldpate of Nanneian fame,[1] my late panegyrist, whose complimentary speech in my honour I have already mentioned in my letters; well, he managed the whole job in a couple of days with the help of one slave, and that an ex-prizefighter. He sent for everybody, made promises, gave security, paid money down. Good heavens, what a scandal there was! Even the favours of certain ladies and introductions to young men of good family were given to some of the jury to swell the bribe. All honest men withdrew entirely from the case, and the forum was full of slaves. Yet five and twenty of the jury were brave enough to risk their necks, preferring death to treachery: but there were thirty-one who were more influenced by famine than fame. Catulus, meeting one of these latter, remarked to him: "Why did you ask for a guard? For fear of having your pocket picked?" There you have as short a summary as possible of the trial and the reason for the acquittal.

You want to know next what is the present state of public affairs, and how I am getting on. We thought that the condition of the Republic had been set on a firm footing, you by my prudence, I by divine interposition; and that its preservation was secured and established by the combination of all patriots and by the influence of my consulship. But, let me tell you, unless some god remembers us, it has been dashed from our grasp by this one trial, if one can call it a trial, when thirty of the

---

[1] Crassus; but why *ex Nanneianis* is uncertain. Manutius says he bought up the property of Nanneius, who was among those proscribed by Sulla, and gave in his name as Licinius Calvus; but this is probably only a guess.

mani levissimos ac nequissimos nummulis acceptis
ius ac fas omne delere et, quod omnes non modo
homines, verum etiam pecudes factum esse sciant, id
Talnam et Plautum et Spongiam et ceteras huius
modi quisquilias statuere numquam esse factum. Sed
tamen, ut te de re publica consoler, non ita, ut spe-
rarunt mali, tanto imposito rei publicae vulnere,
alacris exsultat improbitas in victoria. Nam plane ita
putaverunt, cum religio, cum pudicitia, cum iudiciorum fides, cum senatus auctoritas concidisset, fore ut
aperte victrix nequitia ac libido poenas ab optimo
quoque peteret sui doloris, quem improbissimo cuique
inusserat severitas consulatus mei. Idem ego ille (non
enim mihi videor insolenter gloriari, cum de me apud
te loquor, in ea praesertim epistula, quam nolo aliis
legi) idem, inquam, ego recreavi adflictos animos
bonorum unum quemque confirmans, excitans; inse-
ctandis vero exagitandisque nummariis iudicibus omnem omnibus studiosis ac fautoribus illius victoriae
παρρησίαν eripui, Pisonem consulem nulla in re consistere umquam sum passus, desponsam homini iam
Syriam ademi, senatum ad pristinam suam severita-
tem revocavi atque abiectum excitavi, Clodium praesentem fregi in senatu cum oratione perpetua plenissima gravitatis tum altercatione huius modi; ex qua
licet pauca degustes; nam cetera non possunt habere
eandem neque vim neque venustatem remoto illo
studio contentionis, quem ἀγῶνα vos appellatis. Nam,
ut Idibus Maiis in senatum convenimus, rogatus ego
sententiam multa dixi de summa re publica, atque

most worthless scoundrels in Rome have blotted out
right and justice for filthy lucre, and when Hodge
and John a Nokes and Tom a Styles and all the riff-
raff of that description have declared a thing not to
have happened which every man—man did I say?—
nay, every beast of the field, knows for a fact. Still
—to give you some consolation about politics—the
country has not received so serious a blow as traitors
wished, nor is iniquity vaunting itself so rampantly
on its victory. For they clearly thought that, when
religious and moral scruples, judicial honour and the
Senate's authority had been destroyed, iniquity and
lust would triumph openly, and would wreak their
vengeance on all honest folk for the brand that had
been stamped on vice by my consulship. I was the
man—I don't think I am boasting unduly in saying
so to you privately, especially in a letter which I
would rather you didn't read to anyone—I was the
man who revived the fainting courage of the patriots,
encouraging and cheering them one by one. I
attacked and routed that venal jury; and I did not
leave the victorious party and its supporters a word
to say for themselves. The consul Piso I did not
leave an inch to stand on. Syria, which had been
promised him as his province, I wrested from him.
The Senate I aroused from its despondency, recalling
it to its former uprightness. Clodius I bearded and
crushed in the Senate with a set speech full of dignity,
and then with a cross-examination, of which I will
give you a taste. The rest would lose both its verve
and its wit, when the fire of battle is out, and the tug-
of-war, as you Greeks call it, past. When I entered
the House on the 15th of May, and was asked for
my opinion, I discussed politics at length, and by a

ille locus inductus a me est divinitus, ne una plaga
accepta patres conscripti conciderent, ne deficerent;
vulnus esse eius modi, quod mihi nec dissimulandum
nec pertimescendum videretur, ne aut ignorando
stultissimi aut metuendo ignavissimi iudicaremur;
bis absolutum esse Lentulum, bis Catilinam, hunc
tertium iam esse a iudicibus in rem publicam immis-
sum. "Erras, Clodi; non te iudices urbi, sed carceri
reservarunt, neque te retinere in civitate, sed exsilio
privare voluerunt. Quam ob rem, patres conscripti,
erigite animos, retinete vestram dignitatem. Manet
illa in re publica bonorum consensio; dolor accessit
bonis viris, virtus non est imminuta; nihil est damni
factum novi, sed, quod erat, inventum est. In unius
hominis perditi iudicio plures similes reperti sunt."
Sed quid ago? paene orationem in epistulam inclusi.
Redeo ad altercationem. Surgit pulchellus puer,
obicit mihi me ad Baias fuisse. Falsum, sed tamen
quid hoc? "Simile est," inquam, "quasi in operto
dicas fuisse." "Quid," inquit, "homini Arpinati cum
aquis calidis?" "Narra," inquam, "patrono tuo,
qui Arpinatis aquas concupivit"; nosti enim Mari-
nas.[1] "Quousque," inquit, "hunc regem feremus?"
"Regem appellas," inquam, "cum Rex tui mentionem nullam fecerit?"; ille autem Regis hereditatem

---

[1] Marianas *Rom. and many editors.*

happy inspiration introduced this passage: "The Senate must not be crushed by a single blow, they must not be faint-hearted. The wound is such that it cannot be disguised, yet it must not be feared, lest by our fear we prove ourselves abject cowards, or by ignoring it, very fools. Lentulus twice obtained an acquittal, and Catiline as often, and this is the third criminal let loose on the country by a jury. But you are mistaken, Clodius. The jury saved you for the gallows, not for public life: their object was not to keep you in the country, but to keep you from leaving it. Keep up your hearts, then, senators, and preserve your dignity. The feelings of all patriots are unchanged; they have suffered grief, but their courage is undiminished. It is no new disaster that has befallen us, we have merely discovered one that existed unnoticed. The trial of one villain has revealed many as guilty as himself." But there, I've nearly copied the whole speech. Now for our passage of arms. Up gets this pretty boy and reproaches me with spending my time at Baiae. It was a lie: and anyhow what did it matter? "One would think," said I, "you were accusing me of spending my time in hiding." "What need has a man of Arpinum to take the waters?" asks Clodius: and I answered: "You should talk like that to your patron [1] who wanted to take the waters of a man of Arpinum,"— you know about the sea-water baths. "How long are we going to let this man king it over us?" says he. "I wonder you mention the word king," I replied, "since King [2] did not mention you." He had

---

[1] C. Scribonius Curio the elder, who bought the villa of Marius at Baiae in the Sullan proscription.

[2] Q. Marcius Rex, brother-in-law to Clodius.

spe devorarat. " Domum," inquit, " emisti." " Putes," inquam, " dicere : Iudices emisti." " Iuranti,"
inquit, " tibi non crediderunt." " Mihi vero," inquam, " xxv iudices crediderunt, xxxi, quoniam nummos ante acceperunt, tibi nihil crediderunt." Magnis
clamoribus adflictus conticuit et concidit.

Noster autem status est hic. Apud bonos iidem
sumus, quos reliquisti, apud sordem urbis et faecem
multo melius nunc, quam reliquisti. Nam et illud
nobis non obest, videri nostrum testimonium non
valuisse; missus est sanguis invidiae sine dolore
atque etiam hoc magis, quod omnes illi fautores illius
flagitii rem manifestam illam redemptam esse a iudicibus confitentur. Accedit illud, quod illa contionalis
hirudo aerarii, misera ac ieiuna plebecula, me ab hoc
Magno unice diligi putat, et hercule multa et iucunda
consuetudine coniuncti inter nos sumus usque eo, ut
nostri isti comissatores coniurationis barbatuli iuvenes
illum in sermonibus " Cn. Ciceronem " appellent.
Itaque et ludis et gladiatoribus mirandas ἐπισημασίας
sine ulla pastoricia fistula auferebamus.

Nunc est exspectatio comitiorum ; in quae omnibus
invitis trudit noster Magnus Auli filium atque in eo
neque auctoritate neque gratia pugnat, sed quibus
Philippus omnia castella expugnari posse dicebat, in
quae modo asellus onustus auro posset ascendere.
Consul autem ille deterioris histrionis similis susce-

been dying to inherit King's money. "You have bought a house," he says. "You seem to think it is the same as buying a jury," I answer. "They did not credit you on your oath," he remarks. To which I answer: "Twenty-five jurymen credited me: the other thirty-one gave you no credit, but took care to get their money first." There was loud applause, and he collapsed without a word, utterly crushed.

My own position is this. I have retained the influence I had, when you left, over the conservative party, and have gained much more influence over the sordid dregs of the populace than I had then. That my testimony was not accepted does me no harm. My unpopularity has been tapped like a dropsy and painlessly reduced, and another thing has done me even more good: the supporters of that crime confess that that open scandal was due to bribery. Besides, that blood-sucker of the treasury, the wretched and starveling mob, thinks I am a prime favourite with the "great man" Pompey, and upon my soul we are upon terms of very pleasant intimacy —so much so indeed that these bottle-conspirators, these youths with budding beards in common table-talk call him Gnaeus Cicero. So both at the games and at the gladiatorial shows, I have been the object of extraordinary demonstrations without hisses or catcalls.

Now everyone is looking forward to the elections. Our "great" Pompey is pushing Aulus' son amidst general disapproval: and the means he is using are neither authority nor influence, but those which Philip said would storm any fort to which an ass laden with money could climb. Piso is said to be playing second fiddle to Pompey and to have bribery

pisse negotium dicitur et domi divisores habere;
quod ego non credo.   Sed senatus consulta duo iam
facta sunt odiosa, quod in consulem facta putantur,
Catone et Domitio postulante, unum, ut apud magistratus inquiri liceret, alterum, cuius domi divisores
habitarent, adversus rem publicam.   Lurco autem
tribunus pl., qui magistratum insimul cum [1] lege alia
iniit, solutus est et Aelia et Fufia, ut legem de ambitu
ferret, quam ille bono auspicio claudus homo promul-
gavit.   Ita comitia in a. d. vi Kal. Sext. dilata sunt.
Novi est in lege hoc, ut, qui nummos in tribu pro-
nuntiarit, si non dederit, impune sit, sin dederit, ut,
quoad vivat, singulis tribubus HS cɔ cɔ cɔ debeat.
Dixi hanc legem P. Clodium iam ante servasse; pro-
nuntiare enim solitum esse et non dare.   Sed heus
tu! videsne consulatum illum nostrum, quem Curio
antea ἀποθέωσιν vocabat, si hic factus erit, fabam [2]
mimum futurum?   Quare, ut opinor, φιλοσοφητέον,

---

[1] *Munro's suggestion* insimulatum " *impugned by* " *is perhaps the best of the many suggested emendations.*
[2] Fabam *or* Famam mimum *Orelli:* fabae hilum *Hoffmann:*
fabae midam *Brooks.*

agents in his house; but I don't believe it. But two decrees have been passed on the proposal of Cato and Domitius, which are unpopular because they are thought to be directed against the consul; one making it lawful to search the house of any magistrate, and the other making it a treasonable offence to have bribery agents in one's house. The tribune Lurco, who entered on his office under another law,[1] has been freed from the obligations of the Aelian and Fufian laws so that he may propose his law about bribery. He had luck in publishing it in spite of his deformity. Accordingly, the elections have been postponed till the 27th of July. The new point about this law is that a mere promise to bribe the tribesmen counts for nothing if it is not fulfilled; but if it is fulfilled the man who made it is liable for life to a fine of £27[2] per tribe. I remarked Clodius had kept this law before it was passed; for he is always promising and not paying. But, I say, if he[3] gets in, that consulship of mine which Curio used to call a deification will become an absolute farce.[4] So I suppose I must take to philosophy

---

[1] Lurco's proposal was irregular because it was made between the notice of the elections and the elections themselves, which was forbidden by the *leges Aelia et Fufia* (153 B.C.).

[2] 3,000 sesterces.

[3] Afranius.

[4] Supposed to allude to the election of a king by boys at the Saturnalia, using beans to vote with; but it is rather dubious Latin. In Seneca's *Apocolocyntosis* 9 the same proverbs seem to be referred to in the phrase " *olim* " *inquit* " *magna res erat deum fieri: iam famam mimum fecisti* ": whence it has been suggested that *Faba* or *Fama* was the name of some well-known farce. Cf. *Laserpiciarius mimus* (Petronius 33).

id quod tu facis, et istos consulatus non flocci facteon.

Quod ad me scribis te in Asiam statuisse non ire, equidem mallem, ut ires, ac vereor, ne quid in ista re minus commode fiat; sed tamen non possum reprehendere consilium tuum, praesertim cum egomet in provinciam non sim profectus.

Epigrammatis tuis, quae in Amaltheo posuisti, contenti erimus, praesertim cum et Thyillus nos reliquerit, et Archias nihil de me scripserit. Ac vereor, ne, Lucullis quoniam Graecum poema condidit, nunc ad Caecilianam fabulam spectet. Antonio tuo nomine gratias egi eamque epistulam Mallio dedi. Ad te ideo antea rarius scripsi, quod non habebam idoneum, cui darem, nec satis sciebam, quo darem. Valde te venditavi. Cincius si quid ad me tui negotii detulerit, suscipiam; sed nunc magis in suo est occupatus; in quo ego ei non desum. Tu, si uno in loco es futurus, crebras a nobis litteras exspecta; ast plures etiam ipse mittito. Velim ad me scribas, cuius modi sit ᾿Αμαλθεῖον tuum, quo ornatu, qua τοποθεσία, et, quae poemata quasque historias de ᾿Αμαλθεία habes, ad me mittas. Lubet mihi facere in Arpinati. Ego tibi aliquid de meis scriptis mittam. Nihil erat absoluti.

XVII

CICERO ATTICO SAL.

Scr. Romae
Non. Dec. a.
693
Magna mihi varietas voluntatis et dissimilitudo opinionis ac iudicii Quinti fratris mei demonstrata est ex litteris tuis, in quibus ad me epistularum illius exempla misisti. Qua ex re et molestia sum tanta

64

like yourself, and not give a button for consulships.

You write that you have made up your mind not to
go to Asia. I would rather you did go, and I am
afraid it may cause unpleasantness if you do not.
But I cannot blame your determination, especially
as I have refused to go to a province.

I shall be contented with the inscriptions you have
put in your Amaltheum, especially as Thyillus has
deserted me and Archias has not written anything
about me. I am afraid, now he has written his
Greek poem on the Luculli, he is turning to the
Caecilian drama. I have thanked Antonius on your
behalf and given that letter to Mallius. My letters
to you up to now have been fewer than they should
have been, as I had no trusty messenger nor any
certain address to send them to. I have sung your
praises loudly. If Cincius delegates any of your business to me I will undertake it. But just at present he
is more concerned with his own, in which I am ready
to assist him. Expect frequent letters from me, if
you are settled: and send me even more. Please
write me a description of your Amaltheum, its adornment and situation; and send me any poems and tales
you have about Amalthea. I should like to make one
too in my place at Arpinum. I will send you some of
my writings: but there is nothing finished.

XVII

CICERO TO ATTICUS, GREETING.

Your letter and the enclosed copy of one of my *Rome, Dec.*
brother Quintus' letters show me that he has con- *5, B.C. 61*
tinually changed his mind and wavered in his opinion
and judgement. I am exceedingly disturbed about

adfectus, quantam mihi meus amor summus erga
utrumque vestrum adferre debuit, et admiratione,
quidnam accidisset, quod adferret Quinto fratri meo
aut offensionem tam gravem aut commutationem
tantam voluntatis. Atque illud a me iam ante intel-
legebatur, quod te quoque ipsum discedentem a
nobis suspicari videbam, subesse nescio quid opinionis
incommodae sauciumque esse eius animum et inse-
disse quasdam odiosas suspiciones. Quibus ego
mederi cum cuperem antea saepe et vehementius
etiam post sortitionem provinciae, nec tantum intellegebam ei esse offensionis, quantum litterae tuae
declararant, nec tantum proficiebam, quantum volebam. Sed tamen hoc me ipse consolabar, quod non
dubitabam, quin te ille aut Dyrrachi aut in istis locis
uspiam visurus esset; quod cum accidisset, confidebam ac mihi persuaseram fore ut omnia placarentur
inter vos non modo sermone ac disputatione, sed
conspectu ipso congressuque vestro. Nam quanta sit
in Quinto fratre meo comitas, quanta iucunditas,
quam mollis animus et ad accipiendam et ad depo-
nendam offensionem, nihil attinet me ad te, qui ea
nosti, scribere. Sed accidit perincommode, quod
eum nusquam vidisti. Valuit enim plus, quod erat
illi non nullorum artificiis inculcatum, quam aut
officium aut necessitudo aut amor vester ille pristinus,
qui plurimum valere debuit. Atque huius incommodi
culpa ubi resideat, facilius possum existimare quam
scribere; vereor enim, ne, dum defendam meos, non
parcam tuis. Nam sic intellego, ut nihil a domesticis

it, as indeed I could not help being, considering my affection for both of you, and I wonder what can have happened to cause my brother Quintus such grave offence and to make him change his mind so extraordinarily. I grasped some time ago, what I think you were beginning to suspect when you left, that at the bottom of it must be some idea of an insult, and that his feelings were wounded and some unpleasant suspicions had taken deep root. Though I often before sought to heal the wound, and redoubled my efforts after the allotment of his province, I could neither find that he was as much annoyed as your letter makes out nor yet make as much headway with him as I wished. However, I used to console myself with the thought that he would be sure to see you either at Dyrrachium or somewhere thereabout. And I had quite made up my mind that when that occurred all the difficulties between you would be smoothed over as much by the mere sight of one another and the pleasure of meeting as by conversation and discussion. For I need not tell you, who know it yourself, how amiable and kindly my brother Quintus is, and how sensitive he is and ready both to take offence and to forget it. But it has happened most unfortunately that you have not seen him anywhere. For the impression he has received from some designing persons has had more weight with him than either his duty or your old intimacy and affection which ought to have had the greatest weight of all. Where the blame for this unpleasantness rests it is easier for me to imagine than to write. For I am afraid that in defending my relatives I may not spare yours. For my view is that, even if no wound was inflicted

vulneris factum sit, illud quidem, quod erat, eos certe
sanare potuisse. Sed huiusce rei totius vitium, quod
aliquanto etiam latius patet, quam videtur, praesenti
tibi commodius exponam. De iis litteris, quas ad te
Thessalonica misit, et de sermonibus, quos ab illo et
Romae apud amicos tuos et in itinere habitos putas,
ecquid tantum causae sit, ignoro, sed omnis in tua
posita est humanitate mihi spes huius levandae molestiae. Nam, si ita statueris, et irritabiles animos
esse optimorum saepe hominum et eosdem placabiles
et esse hanc agilitatem, ut ita dicam, mollitiamque
naturae plerumque bonitatis et, id quod caput est,
nobis inter nos nostra sive incommoda sive vitia sive
iniurias esse tolerandas, facile haec, quem ad modum
spero, mitigabuntur; quod ego ut facias te oro. Nam
ad me, qui te unice diligo, maxime pertinet neminem
esse meorum, qui aut te non amet aut abs te non
ametur.

Illa pars epistulae tuae minime fuit necessaria, in
qua exponis, quas facultates aut provincialium aut
urbanorum commodorum et aliis temporibus et me
ipso consule praetermiseris. Mihi enim perspecta est
et ingenuitas et magnitudo animi tui; neque ego
inter me atque te quicquam interesse umquam duxi
praeter voluntatem institutae vitae, quod me ambitio
quaedam ad honorum studium, te autem alia minime
reprehendenda ratio ad honestum otium duxit. Vera
quidem laude probitatis, diligentiae, religionis neque
me tibi neque quemquam antepono, amoris vero erga

by members of the family, they could certainly have healed the one which existed. But the real fault of the whole matter, which is of rather wider extent than it appears, I can explain to you more conveniently when we meet. As to the letter which he sent to you from Thessalonica and the language which you think he used about you both to your friends at Rome and on his journey, I cannot see any sufficient cause for them; but all my hope of removing this unpleasantness lies in your kindness. For if you can persuade yourself that the best of men are often those whose feelings are easy to arouse and easy to appease, and that this nimbleness, if I may use the word, and sensitiveness of disposition are generally signs of a good heart, and—what is the main point —that we must put up with one another's unpleasantnesses and faults and insults, then, as I hope, all this can be smoothed over easily. This I beg of you to do. For, as I hold you in such peculiar esteem, it is my dearest wish that there may not be any of my people who either does not love you or is not loved by you.

That part of your letter in which you mention the chances of preferment in the provinces or in town, which you neglected in my consulship and at other times, was most unnecessary, for I am thoroughly persuaded of your disinterestedness and magnanimity, and I have never thought that there was any difference between you and me, except our choice of a career. A touch of ambition led me to seek for distinction, while another perfectly laudable motive led you to honourable ease. But in the real glory which consists in uprightness, industry, and piety, there is no one I place above you, not even myself, and as

me, cum a fraterno amore domesticoque discessi, tibi primas defero. Vidi enim, vidi penitusque perspexi in meis variis temporibus et sollicitudines et laetitias tuas. Fuit mihi saepe et laudis nostrae gratulatio tua iucunda et timoris consolatio grata. Quin mihi nunc te absente non solum consilium, quo tu excellis, sed etiam sermonis communicatio, quae mihi suavissima tecum solet esse, maxime deest—quid dicam? in publicane re, quo in genere mihi neglegenti esse non licet, an in forensi labore, quem antea propter ambitionem sustinebam, nunc, ut dignitatem tueri gratia possim, an in ipsis domesticis negotiis, in quibus ego cum antea tum vero post discessum fratris te sermonesque nostros desidero? Postremo non labor meus, non requies, non negotium, non otium, non forenses res, non domesticae, non publicae, non privatae carere diutius tuo suavissimo atque amantissimo consilio ac sermone possunt.

Atque harum rerum commemorationem verecundia saepe impedivit utriusque nostrum; nunc autem ea fuit necessaria propter eam pártem epistulae tuae, per quam te ac mores tuos mihi purgatos ac probatos esse voluisti. Atque in ista incommoditate alienati illius animi et offensi illud inest tamen commodi, quod et mihi et ceteris amicis tuis nota fuit et abs te aliquanto ante testificata tua voluntas omittendae provinciae, ut, quod una non estis, non dissensione ac discidio vestro, sed voluntate ac iudicio tuo factum esse videatur. Quare et illa, quae violata, expiabun-

regards affection to myself, after my brother and my immediate connections, I give you the palm. For I have seen time after time, and have had thorough experience of your sorrow and your joy in my changing fortunes. I have often had the pleasure of your congratulations in times of triumph and the comfort of your consolation in hours of despondency. Nay, at this very moment your absence makes me feel the lack not only of your advice, which you excel in giving, but also of the interchange of speech, which I enjoy most with you. I hardly know if I miss it most in politics, where I dare not make a slip; or in my legal work, which I used to undertake for advancement's sake and now keep up to preserve my position through popularity; or in my private concerns. In all of them I have felt your loss all along and especially since my brother's departure. Finally, neither my work nor my recreation, neither my business nor my leisure, neither my legal affairs nor my domestic, my public life nor my private, can do without your most agreeable and affectionate advice and conversation any longer.

The modesty of both of us has often prevented me from mentioning these facts: but now it was forced upon me by that part of your letter in which you say you want yourself and your character cleared and vindicated in my eyes. There is one good thing as regards the unpleasantness caused by his alienation and anger, that your determination not to go to the province was known to me and other friends of yours, as you told us some time before; so the fact that you are not with him cannot be attributed to your quarrel and rupture, but to your choice and plans already fixed. So amends will be made for

tur, et haec nostra, quae sunt sanctissime conservata,
suam religionem obtinebunt.

Nos hic in re publica infirma, misera commutabili-
que versamur. Credo enim te audisse nostros equites
paene a senatu esse diiunctos; qui primum illud
valde graviter tulerunt, promulgatum ex senatus consulto fuisse, ut de eis, qui ob iudicandum accepissent,
quaereretur. Qua in re decernenda cum ego casu
non adfuissem, sensissemque id equestrem ordinem
ferre moleste neque aperte dicere, obiurgavi senatum,
ut mihi visus sum, summa cum auctoritate, et in causa
non verecunda admodum gravis et copiosus fui. Ecce
aliae deliciae equitum vix ferendae! quas ego non
solum tuli, sed etiam ornavi. Asiam qui de censoribus conduxerunt, questi sunt in senatu se cupiditate
prolapsos nimium magno conduxisse, ut induceretur
locatio, postulaverunt. Ego princeps in adiutoribus
atque adeo secundus; nam, ut illi auderent hos
postulare, Crassus eos impulit. Invidiosa res, turpis
postulatio et confessio temeritatis. Summum erat
periculum, ne, si nihil impetrassent, plane alienaren-
tur a senatu. Huic quoque rei subventum est maxime
a nobis perfectumque, ut frequentissimo senatu et
libentissimo uterentur multaque a me de ordinum
dignitate et concordia dicta sunt Kal. Decembr. et
postridie. Neque adhuc res confecta est, sed voluntas senatus perspecta; unus enim contra dixerat

the breach of friendship; and the ties between us, which have been so religiously preserved, will retain their inviolability.

The political position here is wretched, rotten, and unstable. I expect you have heard that our friends the knights have almost had a rupture with the Senate. The first point that seriously annoyed them was the publication of a senatorial decree for an investigation into any cases of bribery of jurymen. As I did not happen to be present when the decree was passed, and noticed that the knights were annoyed though they did not openly say so, I remonstrated with the Senate very impressively, I think, and spoke with great weight and fluency, considering how shameless the case was. Here is another intolerable piece of petulance on the part of the knights! Yet I have not only put up with it, but forwarded their cause. The people who farmed the province of Asia from the censors, complained in the Senate that their avariciousness had led them to pay too high a price for it, and requested to have the lease annulled. I was their chief supporter, or rather the second, for it was Crassus who encouraged them to venture on the demand. It is a scandalous affair, a disgraceful request, and a confession of foolhardiness. There was considerable danger that, if they met with a refusal, they might have severed their connection with the Senate entirely. In this case, too, I was the main person who came to the rescue, and obtained for them a hearing in a very full and friendly House, and discoursed freely on the dignity and harmony of the two orders both on the 1st of December and the following day. The matter is not yet settled; but the Senate's inclination is clear. For one person

Metellus consul designatus. Atqui erat [1] dicturus,
ad quem propter diei brevitatem perventum non est,
heros ille noster Cato. Sic ego conservans rationem
institutionemque nostram tueor, ut possum, illam a
me conglutinatam concordiam. Sed tamen, quoniam
ista sunt tam infirma, munitur quaedam nobis ad retinendas opes nostras tuta, ut spero, via; quam tibi
litteris satis explicare non possum, significatione parva
ostendam tamen. Utor Pompeio familiarissime. Video,
quid dicas. Cavebo, quae sunt cavenda, ac scribam alias
ad te de meis consiliis capessendae rei publicae plura.

Lucceium scito consulatum habere in animo statim
petere. Duo enim soli dicuntur petituri, Caesar
(cum eo coire per Arrium cogitat) et Bibulus (cum
hoc se putat per C. Pisonem posse coniungi). Rides?
Non sunt haec ridicula, mihi crede. Quid aliud scribam ad te, quid? Multa sunt, sed in aliud tempus.
† exspectare [2] velis, cures ut sciam. Iam illud modeste
rogo, quod maxime cupio, ut quam primum venias.
Nonis Decembribus.

XVIII

CICERO ATTICO SAL.

Scr. XI Kal. Nihil mihi nunc scito tam deesse quam hominem
Febr. a. 694 eum, quocum omnia, quae me cura aliqua adficiunt,
uno communicem, qui me amet, qui sapiat, quicum
ego cum loquar, nihil fingam, nihil dissimulem, nihil

[1] qui erat *MSS. Bosius' correction* quin erat *may well be
right. But I have ventured to suggest* atqui, *supposing that
the last two letters of* designatus *were written in an abbreviated
form, and the two* at's *came together.*

[2] *Tyrrell reads* Si exspectare velis, *following Klotz, with
the meaning* " *If you mean to remain absent from Rome till
you hear from me again.*" *Others suggest* Tu fac ut quando
nos te exspectare *or* Quo nos te tempore exspectare. *But
none of these is very convincing.*

only has opposed it, Metellus the consul elect. Our hero Cato was to have spoken, but the day was too short for it to come to his turn. So I am keeping to our policy and plan, and am preserving to the best of my ability that harmony which I have welded: but still, as that is now in such a shaky condition, I am, I hope, keeping a road open to preserve my position. I cannot explain fully in a letter; but I will give you a gentle hint. I am on the best of terms with Pompey. You know what I mean. I will take all reasonable precautions, and will write again at fuller length as to my plans for managing the republic.

Lucceius is thinking of standing for the consulship at once: for only two candidates are spoken of as likely to come forward. With Caesar he thinks he may come to terms through Arrius, and Bibulus' co-operation he hopes to win through C. Piso. You smile? There is nothing to laugh at, I assure you. Is there anything else I want to tell you? Anything else? Yes, lots of things, but another time . . . you wish to wait (?), let me know. At present I have one modest request to make, though it is my chief desire: that you come as soon as possible.

December 5th.

XVIII

CICERO TO ATTICUS, GREETING.

Believe me, there is nothing I want so much at the present time as a person with whom I can share *Jan. 20,* B.C. anything that causes me the least anxiety, a man of *60* affection and common sense, to whom I can speak without affectation, reserve, or concealment. My

obtegam. Abest enim frater ἀφελέστατος et aman-
tissimus. Metellus non homo, sed

" litus atque aer et solitudo mera."

Tu autem, qui saepissime curam et angorem animi
mei sermone et consilio levasti tuo, qui mihi et in
publica re socius et in privatis omnibus conscius et
omnium meorum sermonum et consiliorum particeps
esse soles, ubinam es? Ita sum ab omnibus destitu-
tus, ut tantum requietis habeam, quantum cum uxore
et filiola et mellito Cicerone consumitur. Nam illae
ambitiosae nostrae fucosaeque amicitiae sunt in quodam splendore forensi, fructum domesticum non habent. Itaque, cum bene completa domus est tempore matutino, cum ad forum stipati gregibus amicorum descendimus, reperire ex magna turba neminem
possumus, quocum aut iocari libere aut suspirare
familiariter possimus. Quare te exspectamus, te desideramus, te iam etiam arcessimus. Multa sunt
enim, quae me sollicitant anguntque; quae mihi
videor aures nactus tuas unius ambulationis sermone
exhaurire posse.

Ac domesticarum quidem sollicitudinum aculeos
omnes et scrupulos occultabo, neque ego huic epistulae atque ignoto tabellario committam. Atque hi
(nolo enim te permoveri) non sunt permolesti, sed
tamen insident et urgent et nullius amantis consilio
aut sermone requiescunt; in re publica vero, quamquam animus est praesens, tamen vulnus [1] etiam
atque etiam ipsa medicina efficit. Nam, ut ea breviter, quae post tuum discessum acta sunt, colligam,
iam exclames necesse est res Romanas diutius stare
non posse. Etenim post profectionem tuam primus,

---

[1] vulnus *Sternkopf, Leo:* voluntas *MSS.*

brother, who is the most unaffected of persons and
most affectionate, is away. Metellus is not a human
being, but "sea-shore and airy void and desert
waste."[1] And you whose conversation and advice
have so often lightened my load of care and anxiety,
who have aided me in my political life, been my con-
fidant in my family affairs, and shared my conversations and projects—where are you? So utterly am I
deserted, that the only moments of repose I have are
those which are spent with my wife, my little daughter, and darling boy. For my grand and showy
friendships bring some public *éclat*, but of private satisfaction they have none. And so, when my house has
been crowded with the morning *levée* and I have gone
down to the forum amid a throng of friends, I cannot
find in the whole company a single man with whom I
can jest freely or whisper familiarly. So I look forward with longing to your coming and in fact urge
you to hurry : for I have many cares and anxieties,
which I fancy would be banished by a single walk
and talk in your sympathetic hearing.

However, I will conceal the stings and pricks of
my private troubles, and will not entrust them to
this letter and an unknown messenger. They are
not very grievous—so don't alarm yourself—but still
they are persistent and worrying, and I have no
friend's advice and discussion to lull them to rest.
For the State, though there is still life in it, the very
cures that have been tried on it, have again and
again opened fresh wounds. If I were to give you
a brief summary of what has happened since you left
you would certainly exclaim that Rome cannot
possibly stand any longer. For it was after your

[1] Probably from Accius.

ut opinor, introitus fuit in causam fabulae Clodianae,
in qua ego nactus, ut mihi videbar, locum resecandae
libidinis et coercendae iuventutis; vehemens fui et
omnes profudi vires animi atque ingenii mei non odio
adductus alicuius, sed spe corrigendae et sanandae
civitatis. Adflicta res publica est empto constupra-
toque iudicio. Vide, quae sint postea consecuta.
Consul est impositus is nobis, quem nemo praeter nos
philosophos aspicere sine suspiritu posset. Quantum
hoc vulnus! facto senatus consulto de ambitu, de
iudiciis nulla lex perlata, exagitatus senatus, alienati
equites Romani. Sic ille annus duo firmamenta rei
publicae per me unum constituta evertit; nam et
senatus auctoritatem abiecit et ordinum concordiam
diiunxit. Instat hic nunc ille annus egregius. Eius
initium eius modi fuit, ut anniversaria sacra Iuventa-
tis non committerentur; nam M. Luculli uxorem
Memmius suis sacris initiavit; Menelaus aegre id
passus divortium fecit. Quamquam ille pastor Idaeus
Menelaum solum contempserat, hic noster Paris tam
Menelaum quam Agamemnonem liberum non pu-
tavit. Est autem C. Herennius quidam tribunus pl.,
quem tu fortasse ne nosti quidem; tametsi potes
nosse, tribulis enim tuus est, et Sextus, pater eius,
nummos vobis dividere solebat. Is ad plebem P.
Clodium traducit, idemque fert, ut universus populus
in campo Martio suffragium de re Clodi ferat. Hunc

---

[1] L. Lucullus, whose claim to a triumph Memmius opposed
as tribune in 66–65 B.C.

departure, I believe, that the opening scene of the Clodian drama became the topic of discussion. There I thought I had a chance of using the surgeon's knife on licentiousness and curbing youthful excesses: and I exerted myself, putting forth all the resources of my intellect and mind, not out of private spite, but in the hope of effecting a radical cure of the State. The corruption of the jury by bribery and debauchery dealt a crushing blow to the republic. See what has followed. We have had a consul forced on us, at whom no one except us philosophers can look without a sigh. That is a fatal stroke. Though a senatorial decree has been passed about the bribery of juries, no law has been carried; the Senate has been frightened out of it, and the knights have been estranged. So this one year has overturned two bulwarks of the State which had been erected by me alone: for it has destroyed the prestige of the Senate and broken up the harmony of the orders. Now comes this precious year. It was inaugurated by the suspension of the annual rites of the goddess of youth: for Memmius initiated M. Lucullus' wife into some rites of his own. Menelaus took it hard and divorced his wife. Unlike the shepherd of Ida, who only slighted Menelaus, our Modern Paris thought Agamemnon [1] as fitting an object for his contempt. There is one C. Herennius, a tribune—you may not even know him, though perhaps you do, as he is a member of the same tribe as yourself, and his father Sextus used to distribute money to your tribesmen—he is trying to transfer P. Clodius to the plebs, and even proposes that the whole people shall vote on the matter in the Campus Martius. I gave him my

ego accepi in senatu, ut soleo, sed nihil est illo
homine lentius. Metellus est consul egregius et nos
amat, sed imminuit auctoritatem suam, quod habet
dicis causa promulgatum illud idem de Clodio. Auli
autem filius, o di immortales! quam ignavus ac sine
animo miles! quam dignus, qui Palicano, sicut facit,
os ad male audiendum cotidie praebeat! Agraria
autem promulgata est a Flavio sane levis eadem fere,
quae fuit Plotia. Sed interea πολιτικὸς ἀνὴρ οὐδ᾽
ὄναρ quisquam inveniri potest; qui poterat, familiaris
noster (sic est enim; volo te hoc scire) Pompeius
togulam illam pictam silentio tuetur suam. Crassus
verbum nullum contra gratiam. Ceteros iam nosti;
qui ita sunt stulti, ut amissa re publica piscinas suas
fore salvas sperare videantur. Unus est, qui curet
constantia magis et integritate quam, ut mihi videtur,
consilio aut ingenio, Cato; qui miseros publicanos,
quos habuit amantissimos sui, tertium iam mensem
vexat neque iis a senatu responsum dari patitur. Ita
nos cogimur reliquis de rebus nihil decernere, antequam publicanis responsum sit. Quare etiam lega-
tiones reiectum iri puto.

Nunc vides quibus fluctibus iactemur, et, si ex iis,
quae scripsimus tanta, etiam a me non scripta perspicis, revise nos aliquando et, quamquam sunt haec

usual reception in the Senate; but he is the most phlegmatic of mortals. Metellus is an excellent consul and an admirer of mine; but he has lessened his influence by making, only for form's sake, the very same proposal about Clodius. But Aulus' son— heavens above! what a cowardly and spiritless wretch for a soldier! Just fit to be exposed, as he is, to the daily abuse of Palicanus. An agrarian law has been proposed by Flavius,—a very paltry production, almost identical with the Plotian law. And in the meantime not the ghost of a real statesman is to be found. The man who could be one, my intimate friend—for so he is, I would have you to know—Pompey, wraps that precious triumphal cloak of his around him in silence. Crassus never utters a word to risk his popularity. The others you know well enough— fools who seem to hope that their fish-ponds may be saved, though the country go to rack and ruin. There is one who can be said to take some pains, but, according to my view, with more constancy and honesty than judgement and ability—Cato. It is now three months that he has been worrying those wretched tax-collectors, who used to be great friends of his, and won't let the Senate give them an answer. So we are forced to suspend all decrees on other subjects until the tax-collectors have had an answer. And I suppose even the embassies[1] will have to be postponed for the same reason.

Now you see the storm we have to weather; and, as you can grasp from what I have written with such emphasis, something of what I have left unwritten, come and see me again, for it is high time. Though

[1] Foreign embassies were received in February.

fugienda, quo te voco, tamen fac ut amorem nostrum tanti aestimes, ut eo vel cum his molestiis perfrui velis. Nam, ne absens censeare, curabo edicendum et proponendum locis omnibus; sub lustrum autem censeri germani negotiatoris est. Quare cura, ut te quam primum videamus. Vale.

xi Kal. Febr. Q. Metello, L. Afranio coss.

XIX

CICERO ATTICO SAL.

Scr. Romae
Id. Mart. a.
694

Non modo si mihi tantum esset otii, quantum est tibi, verum etiam si tam breves epistulas vellem mittere, quam tu soles, facile te superarem et in scribendo multo essem crebrior quam tu. Sed ad summas atque incredibiles occupationes meas accedit, quod nullam a me volo [1] epistulam ad te sine argumento ac sententia pervenire. Et primum tibi, ut aequum est civi amanti patriam, quae sint in re publica, exponam; deinde, quoniam tibi amore nos proximi sumus, scribemus etiam de nobis ea, quae scire te non nolle arbitramur.

Atque in re publica nunc quidem maxime Gallici belli versatur metus. Nam Haedui fratres nostri pugnam nuper malam [2] pugnarunt, et Helvetii sine dubio sunt in armis excursionesque in provinciam faciunt. Senatus decrevit, ut consules duas Gallias sortirentur, delectus haberetur, vacationes ne valerent, legati cum auctoritate mitterentur, qui adirent Galliae civitates darentque operam, ne eae se cum Helvetiis coniungerent. Legati sunt Q. Metellus Creticus et L. Flaccus et, τὸ ἐπὶ τῇ φακῇ μύρον, Lentulus

---

[1] volo *Baiter:* solo *MSS.*
[2] pugnant pueri (*or* puer) malam (*or* in alam *or* male) *MSS.: the reading of the text is that of Boot.*

what I invite you to you might well avoid, let your affection for me conquer even your objection in such unpleasant circumstances. I will see to it that notice is given and posted up everywhere, that you may not be entered on the census list as absent. But to get put on the roll just before the census is too thoroughly tradesman-like. So let me see you as soon as possible. Farewell.

Jan. 20th in the consulship of C. Metellus and L. Afranius.

XIX

CICERO TO ATTICUS, GREETING.

If I had as much time as you have, or if I could *Rome,* bring myself to write such short letters as you gener- *March 15,* ally write, I could beat you hollow and write far B.C. *60* more frequently than you write. But on the top of my inconceivable stress of work, you have to add my habit of never sending you a letter without a theme and a moral. First, as one ought to a loyal citizen, I will give you a sketch of political events, and then, as I am the nearest in your affection, I will tell you any of my own affairs that I think you would not be disinclined to know.

In politics, then, at the present minute fears of war in Gaul are the main topic: for " our brothers " the Aedui have had a disastrous battle recently, and the Helvetii are undoubtedly in arms and making raids on our province. The Senate has decreed that the consuls should cast lots for the two Gauls, that levies should be made, furloughs cancelled, and ambassadors with full powers sent to visit the Gallic states and prevent them from joining the Aedui. The ambassadors are Quintus Metellus Creticus, and Lucius Flaccus, and—" the caper sauce on

83

Clodiani filius. Atque hoc loco illud non queo praeterire, quod, cum de consularibus mea prima sors
exisset, una voce senatus frequens retinendum me in
urbe censuit. Hoc idem post me Pompeio accidit,
ut nos duo quasi pignora rei publicae retineri videremur. Quid enim ego aliorum in me ἐπιφωνήματα
exspectem, cum haec domi nascantur?

Urbanae autem res sic se habent. Agraria lex a
Flavio tribuno pl. vehementer agitabatur auctore
Pompeio; quae nihil populare habebat praeter auctorem. Ex hac ego lege secunda contionis voluntate
omnia illa tollebam, quae ad privatorum incommodum
pertinebant, liberabam agrum eum, qui P. Mucio, L.
Calpurnio consulibus publicus fuisset, Sullanorum
hominum possessiones confirmabam, Volaterranos et
Arretinos, quorum agrum Sulla publicarat neque
diviserat, in sua possessione retinebam; unam
rationem non reiciebam, ut ager hac adventicia
pecunia emeretur, quae ex novis vectigalibus per
quinquennium reciperetur. Huic toti rationi agrariae
senatus adversabatur suspicans Pompeio novam quandam potentiam quaeri; Pompeius vero ad voluntatem
perferendae legis incubuerat. Ego autem magna cum
agrariorum gratia confirmabam omnium privatorum

lenten fare " [1]—Lentulus, son of Clodianus. And I cannot forbear adding here that when my lot came up first in the ballot among the ex-consuls, the Senate were unanimous in declaring that I should be kept in Rome. The same happened to Pompey after me, so that we two appear to be kept as pledges of the State. Why should I look for the " bravos " of strangers when these triumphs bloom for me at home ?

Well, this is the state of affairs in the city. The agrarian law was zealously pushed by the tribune Flavius with the support of Pompey, though its only claim to popularity was its supporter. My proposal to remove from the law any points which encroached on private rights was favourably received by a public meeting. I proposed to exempt from its action such land as was public in the consulship of P. Mucius and L. Calpurnius,[2] to confirm Sulla's veterans in their possessions, to allow the people of Volaterra and Arretium to retain in their holding their land which Sulla had made public land, but had not distributed : the only clause I did not reject was that land should be purchased by this wind-fall which will come in from the new foreign revenues in the next five years. The Senate was opposed to the whole agrarian scheme, suspecting that Pompey was aiming at getting some new powers. Pompey had set his heart on carrying the law through. I, on the other hand, with the full approval of the applicants for land, was for securing the holdings of all private

[1] Lit. " myrrh oil on lentils "; referring to a line in the *Phoenissae* of Strattis.

[2] 133 B.C., the year before the agrarian law of Tiberius Gracchus.

possessiones; is enim est noster exercitus, hominum,
ut tute scis, locupletium; populo autem et Pompeio
(nam id quoque volebam) satis faciebam emptione,
qua constituta diligenter et sentinam urbis exhauriri
et Italiae solitudinem frequentari posse arbitrabar.
Sed haec tota res interpellata bello refrixerat. Metellus est consul sane bonus et nos admodum diligit;
ille alter nihil ita est, ut plane, quid emerit, nesciat.
Haec sunt in re publica, nisi etiam illud ad rem publicam putas pertinere, Herennium quendam, tribunum pl., tribulem tuum sane hominem nequam atque
egentem, saepe iam de P. Clodio ad plebem tradu-
cendo agere coepisse. Huic frequenter interceditur.
Haec sunt, ut opinor, in re publica.

Ego autem, ut semel Nonarum illarum Decembri-
um iunctam invidia ac multorum inimicitiis eximiam
quandam atque immortalem gloriam consecutus sum,
non destiti eadem animi magnitudine in re publica
versari et illam institutam ac susceptam dignitatem
tueri, sed, posteaquam primum Clodi absolutione levitatem infirmitatemque iudiciorum perspexi, deinde
vidi nostros publicanos facile a senatu diiungi, quamquam a me ipso non divellerentur, tum autem beatos
homines, hos piscinarios dico amicos tuos, non obscure
nobis invidere, putavi mihi maiores quasdam opes et
firmiora praesidia esse quaerenda. Itaque primum,
eum qui nimium diu de rebus nostris tacuerat, Pom-

persons—for, as you know, the strength of our party consists in the rich landed gentry—while at the same time I fulfilled my desire to satisfy Pompey and the populace by supporting the purchase of land, thinking that, if that were thoroughly carried out, the city might be emptied of the dregs of the populace, and the deserted parts of Italy peopled. But the matter has cooled off now this war has interrupted it. Metellus is an excellent consul and a great admirer of mine. The other one is an utter nonentity and clearly bought a pig in a poke when he got the consulship. That is all my political news, unless you think this has a bearing on politics. One Herennius, a tribune and fellow tribesman of yours, and a man of no character or position, has begun frequently proposing the transference of P. Clodius from a patrician to a plebeian; and his proposals are vetoed by many of his colleagues. This, I think, is all the public news.

For myself, ever since that December day when I won such splendid and immortal glory, though it carried with it much envy and enmity, I have not ceased to employ the same high-minded policy and to keep the position I have won and taken up. But, as soon as the acquittal of Clodius showed me the uncertainty and instability of the law courts, and I saw, too, how easily our friends the tax-gatherers could be estranged from the Senate, though they might not sever their connection with me, while the well-to-do —your friends with the fish-ponds, I mean—took no pains to disguise their envy of me, I bethought me that I had better look out for some stronger support and more secure protection. So first I brought Pompey, the man who had held his peace too long

peium adduxi in eam voluntatem, ut in senatu non
semel, sed saepe multisque verbis huius mihi salutem
imperii atque orbis terrarum adiudicarit; quod non
tam interfuit mea (neque enim illae res aut ita sunt
obscurae, ut testimonium, aut ita dubiae, ut lauda-
tionem desiderent) quam rei publicae, quod erant
quidam improbi, qui contentionem fore aliquam mihi
cum Pompeio ex rerum illarum dissensione arbitra-
rentur. Cum hoc ego me tanta familiaritate coni-
unxi, ut uterque nostrum in sua ratione munitior et
in re publica firmior hac coniunctione esse possit.
Odia autem illa libidinosae et delicatae iuventutis,
quae erant in me incitata, sic mitigata sunt comitate
quadam mea, me unum ut omnes illi colant; nihil
iam denique a me asperum in quemquam fit nec
tamen quicquam populare ac dissolutum, sed ita tem-
perata tota ratio est, ut rei publicae constantiam
praestem, privatis meis rebus propter infirmitatem
bonorum, iniquitatem malevolorum, odium in me
improborum adhibeam quandam cautionem et diligentiam atque ita, tametsi his novis amicitiis impli-
cati sumus, ut crebro mihi vafer ille Siculus insusurret
Epicharmus cantilenam illam suam:

Νᾶφε καὶ μέμνασ' ἀπιστεῖν· ἄρθρα ταυτα τᾶν
φρενῶν.

Ac nostrae quidem rationis ac vitae quasi quandam
formam, ut opinor, vides.

De tuo autem negotio saepe ad me scribis. Cui
mederi nunc non possumus; est enim illud senatus
88

about my achievements, into a frame of mind for attributing to me the salvation of the empire and the world not once only, but time after time and with emphasis in the House. That was not so much for my own benefit—for my achievements were neither so obscure that they required evidence nor so dubious that they required puffing up—but for the State's sake, for there were some ill-natured persons who thought that there was a certain amount of disagreement between Pompey and myself, owing to a difference of opinion about those matters. With him I have formed such an intimate connection that both of us are strengthened in our policy and surer in our political position through our coalition. The dislike which had been aroused against me among our dissipated and dandified youths has been smoothed away by my affability, and now they pay me more attention than anyone. In short, I avoid hurting anyone's feelings, though I do not court popularity by relaxing my principles ; indeed, my whole conduct is regulated so, that, while I preserve my firmness in public life, in my private affairs the weakness of the loyal party, the prejudice of the disaffected, and the hostility of the disloyal makes me move with some care and caution, and, involved though I am in my new friendships, I frequently have the refrain of Epicharmus, that subtle Sicilian, ringing in my ears :

" Be sober of head, and mistrustful of friends ;
  Hinges are these on which wisdom depends."

There you have, I think, an outline sketch of my rule of life.

You keep writing about that business of yours ; but at present I have no remedy for it. The decree

consultum summa pedariorum voluntate nullius nostrum auctioritate factum. Nam, quod me esse ad scribendum vides, ex ipso senatus consulto intellegere potes aliam rem tum relatam, hoc autem de populis liberis sine causa additum. Et ita factum est a P. Servilio filio, qui in postremis sententiam dixit, sed immutari hoc tempore non potest. Itaque conventus, qui initio celebrabantur, iam diu fieri desierunt. Tu si tuis blanditiis tamen a Sicyoniis nummulorum aliquid expresseris, velim me facias certiorem.

Commentarium consulatus mei Graece compositum misi ad te. In quo si quid erit, quod homini Attico minus Graecum eruditumque videatur, non dicam, quod tibi, ut opinor, Panhormi Lucullus de suis historiis dixerat, se, quo facilius illas probaret Romani hominis esse, idcirco barbara quaedam et σόλοικα dispersisse; apud me si quid erit eius modi, me imprudente erit et invito. Latinum si perfecero, ad te mittam. Tertium poema exspectato, ne quod genus a me ipso laudis meae praetermittatur. Hic tu cave dicas: Τίς πατέρ αἰνήσει; Si est enim apud homines quicquam quod potius sit, laudetur, nos vituperemur, qui non potius alia laudemus; quamquam non ἐγκωμιαστικὰ sunt haec, sed ἱστορικά, quae scribimus.

Quintus frater purgat se mihi per litteras et adfirmat nihil a se cuiquam de te secus esse dictum.

---

[1] Members who did not speak, but only took part in the division (*pedibus ire in sententiam*).

was passed by the enthusiasm of the silent members [1] without any support from our party. For as to my signature which you find attached to it, you can see from the decree itself that it was quite a different matter which was brought forward, and this clause about the free peoples was added without rhyme or reason. It was the work of P. Servilius the younger, who was one of the last to speak: but it cannot be altered at the present time. So the meetings which at first were held about it have ceased long ago. If, however, you should manage to squeeze a few pence out of the Sicyonians, please let me know.

I have sent you a copy of my account of my consulship in Greek. If there is anything in it which to your Attic taste seems bad Greek or unscholarly, I will not say what Lucullus said to you—at Panhormus, I think—about his history, that he had interspersed a few barbarisms and solecisms as a clear proof that it was the work of a Roman. If there is anything of the kind in my work, it is there without my knowledge and against my will. When I have finished the Latin version I will send it to you. In the third place, you may expect a poem, not to let slip any method of singing my own praises. Please don't quote " Who will praise his sire? " [2] For if there is any more fitting subject for eulogy, then I am willing to be blamed for not choosing some other subject. However, my compositions are not panegyrics at all but histories.

My brother Quintus has written exculpating himself and declaring that he never said a word against

---

[2] The whole proverb is found in Plutarch's Life of Aratus, τίς πατέρ' αἰνήσει εἰ μὴ κακοδαίμονες υἱοί.

MARCUS TULLIUS CICERO

Verum haec nobis coram summa cura et diligentia
sunt agenda; tu modo nos revise aliquando. Cossinius hic, cui dedi litteras, valde mihi bonus homo et
non levis et amans tui visus est et talis, qualem esse
eum tuae mihi litterae nuntiarant. Idibus Martiis.

XX

CICERO ATTICO SAL.

*Scr. Romae
m. Maio a.
694*

Cum e Pompeiano me Romam recepissem a. d. IV
Idus Maias, Cincius noster eam mihi abs te epistulam
reddidit, quam tu Idibus Febr. dederas. Ei nunc
epistulae litteris his respondebo. Ac primum tibi
perspectum esse iudicium de te meum laetor, deinde
te in iis rebus, quae mihi asperius a nobis atque nostris
et iniucundius actae videbantur, moderatissimum
fuisse vehementissime gaudeo idque neque amoris
mediocris et ingenii summi ac sapientiae iudico. Qua
de re cum ad me ita suaviter, diligenter, officiose,
humaniter scripseris, ut non modo te hortari amplius
non debeam, sed ne exspectare quidem abs te aut ab
ullo homine tantum facilitatis ac mansuetudinis po-
tuerim, nihil duco esse commodius quam de his rebus
nihil iam amplius scribere. Cum erimus congressi,
tum, si quid res feret, coram inter nos conferemus.

Quod ad me de re publica scribis, disputas tu
quidem et amanter et prudenter, et a meis consiliis
ratio tua non abhorret; nam neque de statu nobis
nostrae dignitatis est recedendum neque sine nostris
copiis intra alterius praesidia veniendum, et is, de quo
scribis, nihil habet amplum, nihil excelsum, nihil non

you to anyone. But that is a point we have to discuss very carefully when we meet, if only you will come and see me some time. This Cossinius, to whom I have given the letter, seems to me a very good steady sort of fellow, and devoted to you, exactly as you described him in your letter. March 15.

XX

CICERO TO ATTICUS, GREETING.

On my return from my villa at Pompeii on the *Rome, May,* 12th of May, our friend Cincius passed on to me your B.C. *60* letter which was dated the 13th of February. That is the letter which I shall now answer. And first I must say how delighted I am that you fully understood my opinion of you: next how very glad I am that you showed such forbearance with regard to the slights and unkindness which in my opinion you had received from me and mine: and I count it a sign of affection more than ordinary and the highest sense and wisdom. Indeed, your answer is so charmingly worded and with such consideration and kindliness that not only have I no further right to press you, but I can never expect to experience such courtesy and forbearance from you or any other man. So I think it would be best for me to say no more about the matter in my letters. If any point arises, we will discuss it together when we meet.

Your remarks about politics are couched in friendly and prudent terms, and your view does not differ from my own—for I must not withdraw from my dignified position, nor must I enter another's lines without any forces of my own, and the man you mention has no broad-mindedness and no high-mindedness,

summissum atque populare. Verum tamen fuit ratio
mihi fortasse ad tranquillitatem meorum temporum
non inutilis, sed mehercule rei publicae multo etiam
utilior quam mihi civium improborum impetus in me
reprimi, cum hominis amplissima fortuna, auctoritate,
gratia fluctuantem sententiam confirmassem et a spe
malorum ad mearum rerum laudem convertissem.
Quod si cum aliqua levitate mihi faciendum fuisset,
nullam rem tanti aestimassem; sed tamen a me ita
sunt acta omnia, non ut ego illi adsentiens levior, sed
ut ille me probans gravior videretur. Reliqua sic a
me aguntur et agentur, ut non committamus, ut ea,
quae gessimus, fortuito gessisse videamur. Meos
bonos viros, illos quos significas, et, eam quam mihi
dicis obtigisse, Σπάρταν non modo numquam deseram,
sed etiam, si ego ab illa deserar, tamen in mea pris-
tina sententia permanebo. Illud tamen velim existimes, me hanc viam optimatem post Catuli mortem
nec praesidio ullo nec comitatu tenere. Nam, ut ait
Rhinton, ut opinor,

Οἱ μὲν παρ' οὐδέν εἰσι, τοῖς δ' οὐδὲν μέλει.

Mihi vero ut invideant piscinarii nostri, aut scribam
ad te alias aut in congressum nostrum reservabo. A
curia autem nulla me res divellet, vel quod ita rectum

nothing in him that is not low and time-serving. Well, perhaps the course I took was not opposed to my own advantage and peace of life, but I swear it was far more to the advantage of the State than to mine that I should be the means of suppressing the attacks of the disloyal, and of strengthening the wavering policy of a man of the highest position, influence, and popularity, and converting him from pandering to the disloyal to approval of my achievements. If I had had to make any sacrifice of principle in so doing, I should never have thought it justifiable : but I managed it so that he seemed to gain in principle by his approval of me more than I lost in bowing to him. I will take care that my actions now and in the future do not convey the impression that what I did in the past was done at haphazard. My honest comrades, at whom you hint, and the lot[1] which has fallen to me, as you say, I will never desert. Nay, even if I am deserted by it I will abide by my ancient principles. But I would have you please remember that, since the death of Catulus, I am holding the way for the conservative party without a garrison and without a comrade. For, as Rhinton, I think it is, says :

"Some are stark naught, and naught do others reck."

How our friends of the fish-ponds envy me, I will either tell you in another letter or keep it till we meet. But from the Senate house nothing shall tear me : either because that is the right course, or

---

[1] Σπάρταν ἔλαχες ταύταν κόσμει is quoted in full from Euripides' Telephus in Att. IV, 6, 2.

est, vel quod rebus meis maxime consentaneum, vel quod, a senatu quanti fiam, minime me paenitet.

De Sicyoniis, ut ad te scripsi antea, non multum spei est in senatu ; nemo est enim, idem qui queratur. Quare, si id exspectas, longum est; alia via, si qua potes, pugna. Cum est actum, neque animadversum est, ad quos pertineret, et raptim in eam sententiam pedarii cucurrerunt. Inducendi senatus consulti maturitas nondum est, quod neque sunt, qui querantur, et multi partim malevolentia, partim opinione aequitatis delectantur.

Metellus tuus est egregius consul; unum reprehendo, quod otium nuntiari e Gallia non magno opere gaudet. Cupit, credo, triumphare. Hoc vellem mediocrius; cetera egregia. Auli filius vero ita se gerit, ut eius consulatus non consulatus sit, sed Magni nostri ὑπώπιον.

De meis scriptis misi ad te Graece perfectum consulatum meum. Eum librum L. Cossinio dedi. Puto te Latinis meis delectari, huic autem Graeco Graecum invidere. Alii si scripserint, mittemus ad te; sed, mihi crede, simul atque hoc nostrum legerunt, nescio quo pacto retardantur.

Nunc, ut ad rem meam redeam, L. Papirius Paetus, vir bonus amatorque noster, mihi libros eos, quos Ser. Claudius reliquit, donavit. Cum mihi per legem Cinciam licere capere Cincius, amicus tuus, diceret,

because it is most consistent with my position, or because I am by no means dissatisfied with the Senate's estimation of me.

As regards the Sicyonians, there is very little hope to be placed in the Senate, as I wrote you before: for there is no one now to raise a complaint. It would be tedious to wait for them to move. Fight the point in some other way, if you can. When the law was passed, nobody noticed to whom it applied, and the dummy members plumped eagerly in its favour. The time has not yet come for rescinding the decree, because there is no one who complains about it, and some favour it, partly from spite and partly from an idea of its justness.

Your friend Metellus is an excellent consul: I have only one fault to find with him, he is not at all pleased with the news of peace from Gaul. I take it he wants a triumph. I wish he would moderate that desire: in every other way he is excellent. The behaviour of Aulus's son makes his consulship not a consulship, but a blot on the scutcheon [1] of our friend Pompey.

I have sent you one of my works, a history of my consulship in Greek. I have given it to L. Cossinius. I fancy you like my Latin work, but, being a Greek, envy this Greek one. If others write about it I will send you copies; but I assure you, as soon as they read mine, they somehow or other don't hurry themselves about it.

Now to return to business. L. Papirius Paetus, my good friend and admirer, has offered me the books left to him by Ser. Claudius: and, as your friend Cincius said I could take them without breaking the

---

[1] Lit. " a black eye."

libenter dixi me accepturum, si attulisset. Nunc, si me amas, si te a me amari scis, enitere per amicos, clientes, hospites, libertos denique ac servos tuos, ut scida ne qua depereat; nam et Graecis iis libris, quos suspicor, et Latinis, quos scio illum reliquisse, mihi vehementer opus est. Ego autem cotidie magis, quod mihi de forensi labore temporis datur, in iis studiis conquiesco. Per mihi, per, inquam, gratum feceris, si in hoc tam diligens fueris, quam soles in iis rebus, quas me valde velle arbitraris, ipsiusque Paeti tibi negotia commendo, de quibus tibi ille agit maximas gratias, et, ut iam invisas nos, non solum rogo, sed etiam suadeo.

Cincian law,[1] I said I would very willingly accept, if he brought them here. Now, as you love me, as you know I love you, stir up all your friends, clients, guests, freedmen, nay even your slaves, to see that not a leaf is lost. For I have urgent necessity for the Greek works, which I suspect, and the Latin books, which I am sure, he left. Every day I seek my recreation, in such time as is left me from my legal labours, more and more in such studies. You will do me the greatest of favours if you will show the same zeal in this as you generally do in matters about which you think I am really keen. Paetus' own affairs I recommend to your notice too, and he expresses his deepest gratitude. And I do more than ask you, I urge you, to pay me a visit soon.

[1] The *lex Cincia de donis et muneribus* (204 B.C.), which forbade taking presents for pleading causes.

M. TULLI CICERONIS
EPISTULARUM AD ATTICUM
LIBER SECUNDUS

I

CICERO ATTICO SAL.

Scr. Romae
m. Iun. a.
694

Kal. Iuniis eunti mihi Antium, et gladiatores M. Metelli cupide relinquenti, venit obviam tuus puer. Is mihi litteras abs te et commentarium consulatus mei Graece scriptum reddidit. In quo laetatus sum me aliquanto ante de isdem rebus Graece item scriptum librum L. Cossinio ad te perferundum dedisse, nam, si ego tuum ante legissem, furatum me abs te esse diceres. Quamquam tua illa (legi enim libenter) horridula mihi atque incompta visa sunt, sed tamen erant ornata hoc ipso, quod ornamenta neglexerant, et ut mulieres ideo bene olere, quia nihil olebant, videbantur. Meus autem liber totum Isocratis myrothecium atque omnes eius discipulorum arculas ac non nihil etiam Aristotelia pigmenta consumpsit. Quem tu Corcyrae, ut mihi aliis litteris significas, strictim attigisti, post autem, ut arbitror, a Cossinio accepisti. Quem tibi ego non essem ausus mittere, nisi eum lente ac fastidiose probavissem. Quamquam ad me scripsit iam Rhodo Posidonius se, nostrum illud ὑπόμνημα cum legeret, quod ego ad eum, ut ornatius de isdem rebus scriberet, miseram, non modo non excitatum esse ad scribendum, sed etiam plane deterritum. Quid quaeris? conturbavi Graecam nationem. Ita, vulgo qui instabant, ut darem sibi, quod ornarent, iam exhibere mihi molestiam destiterunt. Tu, si tibi placuerit

CICERO'S LETTERS
TO ATTICUS
BOOK II

I

CICERO TO ATTICUS, GREETING.

On the 1st of June I met your boy as I was on my way to Antium and glad to get away from M. Metellus's gladiatorial exhibition. He delivered your letter, and a memorial of my consulship written in Greek. I felt very glad that I gave L. Cossinius the book I had written in Greek on the same subject to take to you some time ago. For, if I had read yours first you would say that I had plagiarized from you. Though yours (which I read with pleasure) seemed to me a trifle rough and unadorned, yet its very lack of ornament is an ornament in itself, just as women were thought to have the best scent who used no scent. My book, on the other hand, has exhausted all the scent box of Isocrates, and all the rouge-pots of his pupils, and some of Aristotle's colours too. You scanned it through, as you tell me in another letter, at Corcyra, before you had received it from Cossinius, I suppose. I should never have dared to send it to you, if I had not revised it with leisure and care. I sent the memoir to Posidonius too, asking him to write something more elaborate on the same subject; but he tells me that, far from being inspired to write by the perusal of it, he was decidedly put off. In fact, I have flabbergasted the whole Greek nation: so I have ceased to be plagued by the people who were always hanging about asking me to give them something of mine to polish up. If you like the

liber, curabis, ut et Athenis sit et in ceteris oppidis
Graeciae; videtur enim posse aliquid nostris rebus
lucis adferre. Oratiunculas autem, et quas postulas,
et plures etiam mittam, quoniam quidem ea, quae nos
scribimus adulescentulorum studiis excitati, te etiam
delectant. Fuit enim mihi commodum, quod in eis
orationibus, quae Philippicae nominantur, enituerat
civis ille tuus Demosthenes, et quod se ab hoc refra-
ctariolo iudiciali dicendi genere abiunxerat, ut σεμνό-
τερός τις καὶ πολιτικώτερος videretur, curare, ut meae
quoque essent orationes, quae consulares nominaren-
tur. Quarum una est in senatu Kal. Ianuariis, altera
ad populum de lege agraria, tertia de Othone, quarta
pro Rabirio, quinta de proscriptorum filiis, sexta, cum
provinciam in contione deposui, septima, cum Catilinam emisi, octava, quam habui ad populum, postridie
quam Catilina profugit, nona in contione, quo die
Allobroges indicarunt, decima in senatu Nonis Decembribus. Sunt praeterea duae breves, quasi ἀποσπα-
σμάτια legis agrariae. Hoc totum σῶμα curabo ut
habeas; et, quoniam te cum scripta tum res meae
delectant, isdem ex libris perspicies, et quae gesserim
et quae dixerim; aut ne poposcisses; ego enim tibi
me non offerebam.

Quod quaeris, quid sit, quo te arcessam, ac simul
impeditum te negotiis esse significas neque recusas,
quin, non modo si opus sit, sed etiam si velim, accurras, nihil sane est necesse, verum tamen videbare
mihi tempora peregrinationis commodius posse discri-
bere. Nimis abes diu, praesertim cum sis in propin-

book you will see to it that Athens and other Greek towns have it in stock; for I think it may add some lustre to my achievements. I will send you the bits of speeches you ask for and some more too, as you find some interest in things which I write to satisfy young admirers. Your fellow-citizen, Demosthenes, gained a reputation by the speeches called the Philippics, in which he departed from the quibbling style of pleading we use in the law-courts, and appeared in the role of a serious politician. So I took a fancy to leave behind me also some speeches which may be called consular. One was delivered in the House on the 1st of January, another to the people on the agrarian law, the third on Otho, the fourth for Rabirius, the fifth for the sons of the proscribed, the sixth when I declined a province in a public assembly, the seventh when I drove Catiline out, the eighth before the people the day after Catiline fled, the ninth in an assembly on the day when the Allobroges gave their information, the tenth in the House on the 5th of December. There are two more short ones, mere scraps of the agrarian law. I will see that you have the whole *corpus*; and, since both my writing and my achievements interest you, you will see from them what I have done, and what I have written. Or else you should not have asked for them: I was not the one to obtrude them.

You inquire why I ask you to come back, and hint that you are hindered by business. Still you don't refuse to come, if there is any need, or even if I wish it. There is no real necessity; but it does seem to me that you could arrange your times for going away more conveniently. You are away too long, especially when you are quite near, and so I

quis locis, neque nos te fruimur, et tu nobis cares. Ac nunc quidem otium est, sed, si paulo plus furor Pulchelli progredi posset, valde ego te istim excitarem. Verum praeclare Metellus impedit et impediet. Quid quaeris? est consul φιλόπατρις et, ut semper iudicavi, natura bonus. Ille autem non simulat, sed plane tribunus pl. fieri cupit. Qua de re cum in senatu ageretur, fregi hominem et inconstantiam eius reprehendi, qui Romae tribunatum pl. peteret, cum in Sicilia hereditatem se petere dictitasset, neque magno opere dixi esse nobis laborandum, quod nihilo magis ei liciturum esset plebeio rem publicam perdere, quam similibus eius me consule patriciis esset licitum. Iam, cum se ille septimo die venisse a freto, neque sibi obviam quemquam prodire potuisse, et noctu se introisse dixisset, in eoque se in contione iactasset, nihil ei novi dixi accidisse. "Ex Sicilia septimo die Romam; ante tribus horis Roma Interamnam. Noctu introisse; idem ante. Non est itum obviam; ne tum quidem, cum iri maxime debuit." Quid quaeris? hominem petulantem modestum reddo non solum perpetua gravitate orationis, sed etiam hoc genere dictorum. Itaque iam familiariter cum ipso cavillor ac iocor; quin etiam, cum candidatum deduceremus, quaerit ex me, num consuessem Siculis locum gladiatoribus dare. Negavi. "At ego,"

have no chance of enjoying your society and you lack mine. Just at present things are peaceful: but if that little beauty [1] should be strong enough to indulge in any wilder freaks I should certainly be routing you out of your retreat. However, Metellus is holding him in nobly and will continue to do so. Most assuredly he is a thoroughly patriotic consul, and, as I always thought, an excellent fellow. Clodius does not beat about the bush, he is quite plainly aiming at the tribunate. When the point was discussed in the Senate I sat on him, accusing him of inconsistency, for seeking the tribunate now in Rome, when in Sicily he did nothing but repeat that what he wanted was an inheritance. However, I added, we need not put ourselves about on that point, as he would not be allowed to ruin the country if he becomes a plebeian any more than patricians of his kidney were allowed to in my consulship. Then, when he said he had come from the straits in a week, so that no one could go to meet him, and had entered the city at night, and boasted of the fact in a public speech, I said there was nothing new in that. " Seven days from Sicily to Rome: the other time three hours from Rome to Interamna. He came in at night: so he did before. No one met him now: nor did anyone meet him last time, when they certainly ought to have done so." In fact, I am taking the cheek out of him, not only by serious set speeches, but by quips of this kind too. So nowadays I bandy jests and banter with him quite familiarly. For instance, when we were escorting a candidate he asked me whether I used to give the Sicilians seats at the gladiatorial shows. I said, " No." " Well," said he,

[1] P. Clodius Pulcher.

inquit, " novus patronus instituam ; sed soror, quae
tantum habeat consularis loci, unum mihi solum pe-
dem dat." " Noli," inquam " de uno pede sororis
queri ; licet etiam alterum tollas." Non consulare,
inquies, dictum. Fateor ; sed ego illam odi male consularem. " Ea est enim seditiosa, ea cum viro bellum
gerit " neque solum cum Metello, sed etiam cum
Fabio, quod eos [1] in hoc esse moleste fert.

Quod de agraria lege quaeris, sane iam videtur
refrixisse. Quod me quodam modo molli brachio de
Pompei familiaritate obiurgas, nolim ita existimes,
me mei praesidii causa cum illo coniunctum esse, sed
ita res erat instituta, ut, si inter nos esset aliqua forte
dissensio, maximas in re publica discordias versari
esset necesse. Quod a me ita praecautum atque
provisum est, non ut ego de optima illa mea ratione
decederem, sed ut ille esset melior et aliquid de
populari levitate deponeret. Quem de meis rebus,
in quas eum multi incitarant, multo scito gloriosius
quam de suis praedicare ; sibi enim bene gestae,
mihi conservatae rei publicae dat testimonium. Hoc
facere illum mihi quam prosit, nescio ; rei publicae
certe prodest. Quid ? si etiam Caesarem, cuius nunc
venti valde sunt secundi, reddo meliorem, num tantum obsum rei publicae ? Quin etiam, si mihi nemo
invideret, si omnes, ut erat aequum, faverent, tamen
non minus esset probanda medicina, quae sanaret
vitiosas partes rei publicae, quam quae exsecaret.
Nunc vero, cum equitatus ille, quem ego in clivo

---

[1] eos esse in hoc esse *MSS*.

" now I am their new patron, I intend to begin the practice : though my sister, who, as the consul's wife, has such a lot of room, will not give me more than standing room." " Oh, don't grumble about standing room with your sister," I answered. " You can always lie with her." You will say it was not the remark for a consular to make. I confess it was not; but I hate the woman, so unworthy of a consul. " For she's a shrew and wrangles with her mate," and not only with Metellus, but with Fabius too, because she is annoyed at their interference in this affair.

You ask about the agrarian law. Interest in it seems to have cooled down. You give me a gentle fillip for my familiarity with Pompey. Please don't imagine I have allied myself to him solely to save my skin : the position of affairs is such that, if we had had any disagreement, there would of necessity have been great discord in the State. Against that I have taken precautions and made provision without wavering from my own excellent policy, while making him more loyal and less the people's weathercock. He speaks, I may tell you, far more glowingly about my achievements than about his own, though many have tried to set him against me, saying that he did his duty to the country, but I saved it. What good his statements will do me, I fail to see : but they will certainly do the country good. Well! If I can make Caesar, who is now sailing gaily before the breeze, a better patriot too, shall I be doing so poor a service to the country? And, even if none were to envy me and all supported me, as they ought, still a remedy which cures the diseased parts of the State should be preferable to one which amputates them. But as it is, when the knights, whom I once stationed

Capitolino te signifero ac principe collocaram, senatum deseruerit, nostri autem principes digito se
caelum putent attingere, si mulli barbati in piscinis
sint, qui ad manum accedant, alia autem neglegant,
nonne tibi satis prodesse videor, si perficio, ut nolint
obesse, qui possunt? Nam Catonem nostrum non tu
amas plus quam ego; sed tamen ille optimo animo
utens et summa fide nocet interdum rei publicae;
dicit enim tamquam in Platonis πολιτείᾳ, non tamquam in Romuli faece sententiam. Quid verius quam
in iudicium venire, qui ob rem iudicandam pecuniam
acceperit? Censuit hoc Cato, adsensit senatus;
equites curiae bellum, non mihi; nam ego dissensi.
Quid impudentius publicanis renuntiantibus? fuit
tamen retinendi ordinis causa faciunda iactura. Re-
stitit et pervicit Cato. Itaque nunc consule in car-
cere incluso, saepe item seditione commota aspiravit
nemo eorum, quorum ego concursu itemque ii consules, qui post me fuerunt, rem publicam defendere
solebant. " Quid ergo? istos," inquies, " mercede
conductos habebimus? " Quid faciemus, si aliter
non possumus? An libertinis atque etiam servis
serviamus? Sed, ut tu ais, ἅλις σπουδῆς.

on the Capitoline hill with you as their standard-bearer and leader, have deserted the Senate, and our great men think themselves in the seventh heaven if they have bearded mullet in their fish-ponds that will feed from their hand, and don't care about anything else, surely you must allow that I have done my best, if I manage to take the will to do harm from those who have the power to do it. For our friend Cato is not more to you than to me : but still with the best of intentions and unimpeachable honesty at times he does harm to the country : for the opinions he delivers would be more in place in Plato's Republic than among the dregs of humanity collected by Romulus.[1] That a man who accepts a bribe for the verdict he returns at a trial should be put on trial himself is as fair a principle as one could wish. Cato voted for it and won the House's assent. Result, a war of the knights with the Senate, but not with me. I was against it. That the tax-collectors should repudiate their bargain was a most shameless proceeding. But we ought to have put up with the loss in order to keep their goodwill. Cato resisted and carried the day. Result, though we've had a consul in prison, and frequent riots, not a breath of encouragement from one of those, who in my own consulship and that of my successors used to rally round us to defend the country. " Must we, then, bribe them for their support ? " you will ask. What help is there, if we cannot get it otherwise ? Are we to be slaves of freedmen and slaves ? But, as you say, enough of the *grand sérieux*.

[1] Possibly " among the dregs of [the city] of Romulus "; but Plutarch, who translates it ἐν Ῥωμύλου ὑποστάθμῃ (*Phoc.* 3), is against that rendering.

Favonius meam tribum tulit honestius quam suam, Luccei perdidit. Accusavit Nasicam inhoneste ac modeste tamen. Dixit ita, ut Rhodi videretur molis potius quam Moloni operam dedisse. Mihi, quod defendissem, leviter suscensuit. Nunc tamen petit iterum rei publicae causa. Lucceius quid agat, scribam ad te, cum Caesarem videro, qui aderit biduo. Quod Sicyonii te laedunt, Catoni et eius aemulatori attribuis Servilio. Quid? ea plaga nonne ad multos bonos viros pertinet? Sed, si ita placuit, laudemus, deinde in discessionibus soli relinquamur.

Amalthea mea te exspectat et indiget tui. Tusculanum et Pompeianum valde me delectant, nisi quod me, illum ipsum vindicem aeris alieni, aere non Corinthio, sed hoc circumforaneo obruerunt. In Gallia speramus esse otium. Prognostica mea cum oratiunculis prope diem exspecta et tamen, quid cogites de adventu tuo, scribe ad nos. Nam mihi Pomponia nuntiari iussit te mense Quintili Romae fore. Id a tuis litteris, quas ad me de censu tuo miseras, discrepabat.

Paetus, ut antea ad te scripsi, omnes libros, quos frater suus reliquisset, mihi donavit. Hoc illius munus in tua diligentia positum est. Si me amas, cura, ut conserventur et ad me perferantur; hoc mihi nihil potest esse gratius. Et cum Graecos tum vero

Favonius carried my tribe with even more credit than his own, but lost that of Lucceius. His accusation of Nasica was nothing to be proud of; however, he conducted it very moderately. He spoke so badly that one would think he devoted more time at Rhodes to grinding in the mills than at Molo's lectures. I got into his bad books for undertaking the defence; however, he is standing again now on public grounds. How Lucceius is getting on I will write and tell you when I have seen Caesar, who will be here in a couple of days' time. The wrong the Sicyonians have done you you attribute to Cato and his imitator Servilius. But does not the blow affect many good citizens? However, if it so pleases them, let us acquiesce, and be utterly deserted at the next question put to the vote.

My Amalthea is waiting and longing for you. I am delighted with my places at Tusculum and Pompeii, except that, champion of creditors as I am, they have overwhelmed me not so much with Corinthian bronze as with debts in the common copper coin of the realm. We hope things have settled down in Gaul. Expect my Prognostics [1] and my bits of speeches very shortly: but for all that write and tell me your plans about coming. Pomponia has sent a message that you will be in Rome in July: but that disagrees with the letter you sent to me about placing your name on the census list.

Paetus, as I have already mentioned, has given me the books left him by his brother: but this gift depends on your kind services. As you love me, see that they are preserved and brought to me. You could do me no greater favour: and I should like the

---

[1] A translation of Aratus' Διοσημεῖα.

diligenter Latinos ut conserves velim. Tuum esse hoc munusculum putabo. Ad Octavium dedi litteras; cum ipso nihil eram locutus; neque enim ista tua negotia provincialia esse putabam neque te in tocullionibus habebam. Sed scripsi, ut debui, diligenter.

II

CICERO ATTICO SAL.

Scr. ad.
villam m.
Dec., ut
videtur, a.
694

Cura, amabo te, Ciceronem nostrum. Ei nos συννοσεῖν videmur. Πελληναίων in manibus tenebam et hercule magnum acervum Dicaearchi mihi ante pedes exstruxeram. O magnum hominem, et unde multo plura didiceris quam de Procilio! Κορινθίων et Ἀθηναίων puto me Romae habere. Mihi crede, si leges haec, dices [1]: mirabilis vir est. Ἡρώδης, si homo esset, eum potius legeret quam unam litteram scriberet. Qui me epistula petivit, ad te, ut video, comminus accessit. Coniurasse mallem quam restitisse coniurationi, si illum mihi audiendum putassem. De lolio [2] sanus non es; de vino laudo.

Sed heus tu, ecquid vides Kalendas venire, Antonium non venire? iudices cogi? Nam ita ad me mittunt, Nigidium minari in contione se iudicem, qui non adfuerit, compellaturum. Velim tamen, si quid est,

---

[1] crede, si leges haec, dices *Boot:* credes leges haec doceo *Z:* hredes lege hec doceo *M.*

[2] *The MSS. read* Lollio; *but* lolio, *the reading of the ed. Jensoniana (Venice, 1470) is supported by Reid with a reference to Pliny H.N.* xxii, 160, *where* lolium *is recommended for gout.*

Latin books kept as well as the Greek. I shall count them a present from yourself. I have written to Octavius, but not spoken to him about it: for I did not know that your business extended to the provinces, nor did I count you among the Shylocks. But I have written as punctiliously as duty bade.

II

CICERO TO ATTICUS, GREETING.

Look well after my little namesake. I am ill with him by sympathy. I have in hand my treatise on the constitution of Pellene, and you should see the huge heap of Dicaearchus that I have piled at my feet. What a great man! You could learn a lot more from him than from Procilius. I believe I have got his works on the constitutions of Corinth and Athens at Rome: and you may take my word for it that, if you read them, you will exclaim, "The man is a wonder." If Herodes had any sense in him he would spend his time reading him and never write a single letter of the alphabet. He has attacked me by post, and you, as I see, in person. I would far rather have joined in the conspiracy than opposed it, if I had thought I should have to pay for it by listening to him. As regards the darnel, you must be losing your senses: but about the wine I quite agree with you.

But, I say, have you noticed the Kalends are coming, and there is no Antonius? Though the jury is being empanelled,—at least they tell me so, and that Nigidius is threatening in a public meeting to serve a summons on any juror who does not attend.

At his country house, Dec. (?), B.C. 60

de Antoni adventu quod audieris, scribas ad me et,
quoniam huc non venis, cenes apud nos utique pridie
Kal. Cave aliter facias. Cura, ut valeas.

III

CICERO ATTICO SAL.

Scr. ad
villam m.
Dec. a. 694
Primum, ut opinor, εὐαγγέλια. Valerius absolutus
est Hortensio defendente. Id iudicium Auli filio
condonatum putabatur; et Iphicratem [1] suspicor, ut
scribis, lascivum fuisse. Etenim mihi caligae eius et
fasciae cretatae non placebant. Quid sit, sciemus,
cum veneris.

Fenestrarum angustias quod reprehendis, scito te
Κύρου παιδείαν reprehendere. Nam, cum ego idem
istuc dicerem, Cyrus aiebat viridariorum διαφάσεις
latis luminibus non tam esse suaves; etenim ἔστω
ὄψις μὲν ἡ ᾱ, τὸ δὲ ὁρώμενον β̄, γ̄, ἀκτῖνες δὲ δ̄ καὶ ε̄.
Vides enim cetera. Nam, si κατ᾽ εἰδώλων ἐμπτώσεις
videremus, valde laborarent εἴδωλα in angustiis.
Nunc fit lepide illa ἔκχυσις radiorum. Cetera si re-
prehenderis, non feres tacitum, nisi si quid erit eius
modi, quod sine sumptu corrigi possit.

[1] Epicrates *MSS.*: Iphicrates *Tyrrell.*

---

[1] Obviously a nickname for Pompey, and, in view of the
next sentence, the name of Iphicrates, who invented a military boot, seems more likely than Epicrates, which would
mean " our influential friend."

If you should happen to get any news of Antonius' coming, please let me know : and, as you won't come here, dine with me anyhow on the 29th at my town house. Be sure you do; and take care of yourself.

III

CICERO TO ATTICUS, GREETING.

First a trifle, please, for good news. Valerius has been acquitted, with Hortensius as his advocate. The verdict is generally thought to be a concession to Aulus' son; and I expect Iphicrates [1] has been up to some tricks, as you suggest. I didn't like the look of his military boots and puttees. We shall know what it was when you arrive.

In finding fault with the narrowness of my windows, let me tell you, you are finding fault with the Education of Cyrus [2] : for, when I made the same remark to Cyrus, he said that the view of gardens was not so pleasant if the windows were broad. For, let *a* be the point of vision, and *b*, *c* the object, and *d*, *e* the rays,—you see what follows. If our sight resulted from the impact of images [3] the images would be horribly squeezed in the narrow space : but, as it is, the emission of rays goes on merrily. If you have any other faults to find you will find me ready with an answer, unless they are such as can be put to rights without expense.

At his country house, Dec. (?), *B.C. 60*

[2] A play on the title of Xenophon's book the *Cyropaedeia* and the name of Cicero's architect.

[3] Democritus and the Epicureans held that sight resulted from the incidence of images cast by external things upon the eyes. The view supported by Cicero, that it resulted from rays sent out from the eyes, was that held by Plato.

Venio nunc ad mensem Ianuarium et ad ὑπόστασιν
nostram ac πολιτείαν, in qua Σωκρατικῶς εἰς ἑκάτε-
ρον, sed tamen ad extremum, ut illi solebant, τὴν ἀρέσ-
κουσαν. Est res sane magni consilii; nam aut fortiter
resistendum est legi agrariae, in quo est quaedam
dimicatio, sed plena laudis, aut quiescendum, quod est
non dissimile atque ire in Solonium aut Antium, aut
etiam adiuvandum, quod a me aiunt Caesarem sic
exspectare, ut non dubitet. Nam fuit apud me Cornelius, hunc dico Balbum, Caesaris familiarem. Is
adfirmabat illum omnibus in rebus meo et Pompei
consilio usurum daturumque operam, ut cum Pompeio
Crassum coniungeret. Hic sunt haec, coniunctio
mihi summa cum Pompeio, si placet, etiam cum
Caesare, reditus in gratiam cum inimicis, pax cum
multitudine, senectutis otium. Sed me κατακλεὶς
mea illa commovet, quae est in libro tertio:

" Interea cursus, quos prima a parte iuventae
  Quosque adeo consul virtute animoque petisti,
  Hos retine atque auge famam laudesque bonorum."

Haec mihi cum in eo libro, in quo multa sunt scripta
ἀριστοκρατικῶς, Calliope ipsa praescripserit, non opinor esse dubitandum, quin semper nobis videatur

$$εἷς οἰωνὸς ἄριστος ἀμύνεσθαι περὶ πάτρης.$$

Sed haec ambulationibus Compitaliciis reservemus.
Tu pridie Compitalia memento. Balineum calfieri
iubebo. Et Pomponiam Terentia rogat; matrem

---

[1] On his consulship.

Now I come to January and my political attitude; and I shall follow the fashion of the Socratic schools in giving both sides of the question, ending, however, as they do, with the one which I prefer. It really is a point that requires much consideration. For either I have got to resist the agrarian measure strongly, which would mean something of a fight, though I should gain prestige by it; or I must hold my peace, which is equivalent to retiring to Solonium or Antium; or else I must assist the measure, and that is what they say Caesar expects me to do beyond a doubt. For Cornelius paid me a visit—I mean Balbus, Caesar's great friend. He assured me that Caesar will take my own and Pompey's opinion on everything, and that he will make an effort to reconcile Pompey and Crassus. On this side of the sheet may be placed an intimate connection with Pompey and, if I like, with Caesar too, reconciliation with my enemies, peace with the populace, and ease in my old age. But my blood is still stirred by the *finale* I laid down for myself in the 3rd book of my poem : [1]

" Meantime the course you chose in youth's first spring
    And held to, heart and soul, 'mid civic strife
    Keep still, with growing fame and report."

Since Calliope herself dictated those verses to me in a book full of passages in lordly vein, I ought not to have the least hesitation in holding " no omen, better ^Iliad xii, 243 than to right one's country's wrongs."

But this point must be reserved for our strolls at the Compitalia. Do you remember the day before the festival. I will order the bath to be heated, and Terentia is going to invite Pomponia. We will make

adiungemus. Θεοφράστου περὶ φιλοτιμίας adfer mihi de libris Quinti fratris.

IV

CICERO ATTICO SAL.

Scr. Antium.
Aprili a.
695

Fecisti mihi pergratum, quod Serapionis librum ad me misisti; ex quo quidem ego, quod inter nos liceat dicere, millesimam partem vix intellego. Pro eo tibi praesentem pecuniam solvi imperavi, ne tu expensum muneribus ferres. Sed, quoniam nummorum mentio facta est, amabo te, cura, ut cum Titinio, quoquo modo poteris, transigas. Si in eo, quod ostenderat, non stat, mihi maxime placet ea, quae male empta sunt, reddi, si voluntate Pomponiae fieri poterit; si ne id quidem, nummi potius reddantur, quam ullus sit scrupulus. Valde hoc velim, antequam proficiscare, amanter, ut soles, diligenterque conficias.

Clodius ergo, ut ais, ad Tigranem! Velim Scepsii condicione; sed facile patior. Accommodatius enim nobis est ad liberam legationem tempus illud, cum et Quintus noster iam, ut speramus, in otio consederit, et, iste sacerdos Bonae Deae cuius modi futurus sit, scierimus. Interea quidem cum Musis nos delecta-

118

your mother one of the party. Bring me from my brother Quintus' library Theophrastus' " Hints for office-seekers."

IV

CICERO TO ATTICUS, GREETING.

I am much obliged to you for sending me Serapio's *Antium,* book, though between you and me I hardly under- *Apr.,* stand a thousandth part of it. I have given orders B.C. *59* for you to be paid ready money for it, to prevent your entering it among presentation copies. Since I am mentioning money matters, please settle up with Titinius as best you can. If he won't stand by his agreement, the best plan, so far as I can see, will be to return the goods for which he made a bad bargain, if Pomponia will consent to that course; if even that won't work, then give him his money back rather than have a fuss. I should be very glad if you would finish the business before you leave, with your usual kindness and carefulness.

So Clodius is going to Tigranes you say! I wish it were on the same terms as that Scepsian.[1] But I don't envy him. It will be a much more convenient time for me to get a free travelling pass when my brother Quintus has settled down in peace, as I hope he will, and when I know the intentions of that priest of Bona Dea.[2] Meantime I shall settle down to the enjoyment of the Muses with resignation,

[1] Metrodorus of Scepsus was sent by Mithridates to urge Tigranes to wage war with Rome, but privately spoke against it. He was therefore put to death by Mithridates.

[2] Clodius, on account of his intrusion into the mysteries of Bona Dea.

bimus animo aequo, immo vero etiam gaudenti ac libenti, neque mihi umquam veniet in mentem Crasso invidere neque paenitere, quod a me ipse non desciverim.

Deo geographia dabo operam ut tibi satis faciam; sed nihil certi polliceor. Magnum opus est, sed tamen, ut iubes, curabo, ut huius peregrinationis aliquod tibi opus exstet. Tu quicquid indagaris de re publica, et maxime quos consules futuros putes, facito ut sciam. Tametsi minus sum curiosus; statui enim nihil iam de re publica cogitare.

Terentiae saltum perspeximus. Quid quaeris? praeter quercum Dodonaeam nihil desideramus, quo minus Epirum ipsam possidere videamur. Nos circiter Kal. aut in Formiano erimus aut in Pompeiano. Tu, si in Formiano non erimus, si nos amas, in Pompeianum venito. Id et nobis erit periucundum et tibi non sane devium. De muro imperavi Philotimo ne impediret, quo minus id fieret, quod tibi videretur. Tu censeo tamen adhibeas Vettium. His temporibus tam dubia vita optimi cuiusque magni aestimo unius aestatis fructum palaestrae Palatinae, sed ita tamen, ut nihil minus velim quam Pomponiam et puerum versari in timore ruinae.

V

CICERO ATTICO SAL.

Scr. Anti m. Apr. a. 695 Cupio equidem et iam pridem cupio Alexandream reliquamque Aegyptum visere et simul ab hac hominum satietate nostri discedere et cum aliquo

Indeed with hearty goodwill and delight, for it will never enter my head to envy Crassus or to repent of not having turned traitor to myself.

For the geography I will endeavour to satisfy you, but I won't make any definite promise. It is a big piece of work: still I will do as I am told and see to it that this little tour is not entirely unproductive for you. Let me have any political news you may worm out, especially who you think are likely to be consuls. However, I am not very anxious. I have made up my mind to forget politics for the time.

I have had a good look at Terentia's woodlands, and can only say that if there was a Dodonaean oak there I should feel as though I possessed the whole of Epirus. About the first of the month I shall be either in my place at Formiae or at Pompeii. If I am not at Formiae, as you love me, come to Pompeii. I shall be delighted to see you, and it won't be far out of your way. With regard to the wall, I have given orders to Philotimus to let you do anything you like: but I think you ought to call in Vettius. In these days, when every honest man's life hangs in the balance, I set high store by the enjoyment of my Palatine palaestra for a summer, but not to the extent of wishing Pomponia and her boy to live in terror of a tottering ruin.

V

CICERO TO ATTICUS, GREETING.

I am eager, and have long been eager to pay a visit to Alexandria and the rest of Egypt, and also to get away from here, where people are sick of seeing me, and return when they miss me a little: but

Antium,
Apr.,
B.C. *59*

121

desiderio reverti; sed hoc tempore et his mittentibus

αἰδέομαι Τρῶας καὶ Τρωάδας ἑλκεσιπέπλους.

Quid enim nostri optimates, si qui reliqui sunt, lo-
quentur? an me aliquo praemio de sententia esse
deductum?

Πουλυδάμας μοι πρῶτος ἐλεγχείην ἀναθήσει,

Cato ille noster, qui mihi unus est pro centum milibus. Quid vero historiae de nobis ad annos D C
praedicarint? Quas quidem ego multo magis vereor
quam eorum hominum, qui hodie vivunt, rumusculos.
Sed, opinor, excipiamus et exspectemus. Si enim
deferetur, erit quaedam nostra potestas, et tum deliberabimus. Etiam hercule est in non accipiendo
non nulla gloria. Quare, si quid Θεοφάνης tecum
forte contulerit, ne omnino repudiaris.

De istis rebus exspecto tuas litteras, quid Arrius
narret, quo animo se destitutum ferat, et qui consules parentur, utrum, ut populi sermo, Pompeius et
Crassus an, ut mihi scribitur, cum Gabinio Servius
Sulpicius, et num quae novae leges et num quid novi
omnino, et, quoniam Nepos proficiscitur, cuinam auguratus deferatur; quo quidem uno ego ab istis capi
possum. Videte vilitatem [1] meam. Sed quid ego
haec, quae cupio deponere et toto animo atque omni
cura φιλοσοφεῖν? Sic, inquam, in animo est; vellem
ab initio, nunc vero, quoniam, quae putavi esse prae-

---

[1] vilitatem *Meuntz:* civitatem *M:* vitam *Z.*

considering the circumstances, and the people who
are sending me

" I fear the men and long-gowned dames of Troy." Iliad vi, 442

What will our conservative friends say, if there are
any of them left? That I have been bribed out of
my opinions?

" The first to chide will be Polydamas," Iliad xxii, 100

that friend of ours, Cato, who alone outweighs a
hundred thousand in my eyes. What would history
be saying of me six hundred years hence? And that
is a thing I fear much more than the petty gossip of
those who are alive to-day. But I suppose I can
only lie low and see what turns up. If an offer is
made to me the decision will to some extent rest in
my own hands, and then I will consider the question.
Upon my word, there is some little glory even in
refusing: so if Theophanes should happen to consult
you don't decline point blank.

This is what I am hoping to hear from you in your
letter: what Arrius has to say for himself, and how
he takes Caesar's desertion of him, whether popular
report is right in speaking of Pompey and Crassus as
the favourites for the consulship or a correspondent
of mine who mentions Gabinius and Servius Sulpicius,
whether there are any new laws or any news at all,
and to whom the augurship will be offered, now that
Nepos is going away. That is the only bait with
which they could catch me. You see how cheap I
am going. But this is a forbidden subject. I mean
to forget it, and devote myself heart and soul to
philosophy. That, I assure you, is my intention;
and I only wish I had always practised it. Now that
I have sampled the vanity of what I once thought

clara, expertus sum quam essent inania, cum omnibus
Musis rationem habere cogito. Tu tamen de Curtio
ad me rescribe certius, et nunc quis in eius locum
paretur, et quid de P. Clodio fiat, et omnia, quem ad
modum polliceris, ἐπὶ σχολῆς scribe, et, quo die Roma
te exiturum putes, velim ad me scribas, ut certiorem
te faciam, quibus in locis futurus sim, epistulamque
statim des de iis rebus, de quibus ad te scripsi.
Valde enim exspecto tuas litteras.

VI

CICERO ATTICO SAL.

Scr. Anti m.
Apr. a. 695

Quod tibi superioribus litteris promiseram, fore ut
opus exstaret huius peregrinationis, nihil iam magno
opere confirmo; sic enim sum complexus otium, ut
ab eo divelli non queam. Itaque aut libris me de-
lecto, quorum habeo Anti festivam copiam, aut fluctus
numero (nam ad lacertas captandas tempestates non
sunt idoneae); a scribendo prorsus abhorret animus.
Etenim γεωγραφικά, quae constitueram, magnum
opus est. Ita valde Eratosthenes, quem mihi proposue-
ram, a Serapione et ab Hipparcho reprehenditur. Quid
censes, si Tyrannio accesserit? Et hercule sunt res
difficiles ad explicandum et ὁμοειδεῖς nec tam possunt
ἀνθηρογραφεῖσθαι, quam videbantur, et, quod caput
est, mihi quaevis satis iusta causa cessandi est, qui
etiam dubitem, an hic Anti considam et hoc tempus
omne consumam, ubi quidem ego mallem duumvirum

glory, I am thinking of confining my attention exclusively to the Muses. For all that, you must post me up in news of Curtius and who will succeed to his position, and what is happening about P. Clodius. Take your time, and write fully about things in general, as you promise. Please let me know on what day you are leaving Rome, so that I can tell you where I shall be: and let me have a letter at once on the points I have mentioned, for I look forward to your letters very eagerly.

VI

CICERO TO ATTICUS, GREETING.

I am not so certain now about fulfilling the promises I made in former letters to produce some work in this tour: for I have fallen so in love with idleness that I can't tear myself from it. So I either enjoy myself with my books, of which I have a jolly good lot at Antium, or else count the waves —the rough weather won't allow me to catch shads. At writing my soul rebels utterly. The geographical work I had planned is a big undertaking. Eratosthenes, whom I had taken as my authority, is severely criticized by Serapion and Hipparchus; and, if I take Tyrannio's views too, there is no telling what the result would be. Besides, the subject is confoundedly hard to explain and monotonous, nor does it give one as many opportunities for flowers of fancy as I imagined; besides—and this is the chief point—I find any excuse for idleness good enough. I am even debating settling down at Antium and spending the rest of my life here: and I really wish I had been a magistrate here rather

Antium,
Apr., B.C.
59

quam Romae fuisse. Tu vero sapientior Buthroti domum parasti. Sed, mihi crede, proxima est illi municipio haec Antiatium civitas. Esse locum tam prope Romam, ubi multi sint, qui Vatinium numquam viderint, ubi nemo sit praeter me, qui quemquam ex viginti viris vivum et salvum velit, ubi me interpellet nemo, diligant omnes! Hic, hic nimirum πολιτευτέον; nam istic non solum non licet, sed etiam taedet. Itaque ἀνέκδοτα, quae tibi uni legamus, Theopompio genere aut etiam asperiore multo pangentur. Neque aliud iam quicquam πολιτεύομαι nisi odisse improbos et id ipsum nullo cum stomacho, sed potius cum aliqua scribendi voluptate.

Sed ut ad rem, scripsi ad quaestores urbanos de Quinti fratris negotio. Vide, quid narrent, ecquae spes sit denarii, an cistophoro Pompeiano iaceamus. Praeterea de muro statue quid faciendum sit. Aliud quid? Etiam. Quando te proficisci istinc putes, fac ut sciam.

than in Rome. You have been wiser in your generation and made a home for yourself at Buthrotum: but you may take my word for it that this township of Antium runs your borough very close. To think of there being a place so near Rome where there are lots of people who have never seen Vatinius, where there is not a single soul save myself who cares whether any of our new commissioners are alive or dead, where no one intrudes upon me, though everyone is fond of me. This, this is the very place for me to play the politician: for there in Rome, besides being shut out of politics, I am sick of them. So I will compose a private memoir, which I will read only to you, in the style of Theopompus, or even a still bitterer vein. My only policy now is hatred of the radicals: and that without rancour, indeed with some pleasure in expressing it.

But to return to business, I have written to the city quaestors about my brother Quintus' affairs. See what they have to say, and whether there is any hope of our getting current coin, or whether we must put up with Pompey's pice.[1] Also decide what is to be done with the wall. Is there anything else I meant to say? Yes. Let me know when you think of going away.

[1] The *cistophorus* was an Asiatic coin, of which Pompey had deposited a large quantity in the treasury. Apparently there was some idea of using them for paying Quintus during his proconsulship.

MARCUS TULLIUS CICERO

VII

CICERO ATTICO SAL.

Scr. Anti m. De geographia etiam atque etiam deliberabimus.
Apr. a. 695 Orationes autem a me duas postulas; quarum alteram non libebat mihi scribere, quia abscideram,[1] alteram, ne laudarem eum, quem non amabam. Sed id quoque videbimus. Denique aliquid exstabit, ne tibi plane cessasse videamur.

De Publio quae ad me scribis sane mihi iucunda sunt, eaque etiam velim omnibus vestigiis indagata ad me adferas, cum venies, et interea scribas, si quid intelleges aut suspicabere, et maxime de legatione quid sit acturus. Equidem, antequam tuas legi litteras, hominem[2] ire cupiebam, non mehercule ut differrem cum eo vadimonium (nam mira sum alacritate ad litigandum), sed videbatur mihi, si quid esset in eo populare, quod plebeius factus esset, id amissurus. " Quid enim? ad plebem transisti, ut Tigranem ires salutatum? Narra mihi, reges Armenii patricios resalutare non solent? " Quid quaeris? acueram me ad exagitandam hanc eius legationem. Quam si ille contemnit, et si, ut scribis, bilem id commovet et latoribus et auspicibus legis curiatae, spectaculum egregium. Hercule, verum ut loquamur, subcontumeliose tractatur noster Publius, primum qui, cum

---

[1] quia abscideram *most editors*: qui absciram *M*.
[2] hominem *Lambinus*, in hominem *M.R.I.*

VII

CICERO TO ATTICUS, GREETING.

I will give the geography further consideration. *Antium,*
As to the two speeches you ask for, one I did not *Apr.*, B.C. 59
want to write down, because I had broken off in the
middle, the other, because I had no desire to praise
a man whom I did not like. But that, too, I will see
about. Something shall appear anyhow, to convince
you that I have not idled all my time away.

I am highly delighted with the news about Publius, please investigate all the details thoroughly,
and bring a full account with you when you come.
Meantime, if you pick up any hints, or draw any
inferences, write to me, especially as to what he is
going to do about the embassy. For my part, before
I read your letter, I wished the man would go, not,
I assure you, through any desire to postpone his
impeachment—for I am extraordinarily anxious to
conduct the case—but because I thought that he
would lose any popularity he had gained by turning
plebeian. "Why did you transfer yourself to the
plebs? Was it to pay a visit to Tigranes? Pray tell
me : don't the kings of Armenia return the visit of a
patrician?" As you see, I had sharpened my wits
up to rally him on the subject of his embassy. But
if he rejects it with scorn, and, as you say, thereby
rouses the indignation of the proposers and augurs
of the bill of adoption, it will be a grand sight. To
speak the honest truth, you know, our friend Publius
is being treated with very scant courtesy. In the
first place, though he was once the only man in

129

domi Caesaris quondam unus vir fuerit, nunc ne in
viginti quidem esse potuerit; deinde alia legatio dicta
erat, alia data est. Illa opima ad exigendas pecunias
Druso, ut opinor, Pisaurensi an epuloni Vatinio reservatur; haec ieiuna tabellarii legatio datur ei, cuius
tribunatus ad istorum tempora reservatur. Incende
hominem, amabo te, quod potes. Una spes est salutis istorum inter ipsos dissensio; cuius ego quaedam
initia sensi ex Curione. Iam vero Arrius consulatum
sibi ereptum fremit; Megabocchus et haec sangui-
naria iuventus inimicissima est. Accedat vero, accedat etiam ista rixa auguratus. Spero me praeclaras
de istis rebus epistulas ad te saepe missurum.

Sed illud quid sit, scire cupio, quod iacis obscure
iam etiam ex ipsis quinque viris loqui quosdam.
Quidnam id est? Si est enim aliquid, plus est boni,
quam putaram. Atque haec sic velim existimes non
me abs te κατὰ τὸ πρακτικὸν quaerere, quod gestiat
animus aliquid agere in re publica. Iam pridem
gubernare me taedebat, etiam cum licebat; nunc
vero cum cogar exire de navi non abiectis, sed ereptis
gubernaculis, cupio istorum naufragia ex terra
intueri, cupio, ut ait tuus amicus Sophocles,

> κἂν ὑπὸ στέγῃ
> πυκνῆς ἀκούειν ψακάδος εὑδούσῃ φρενί.

De muro quid opus sit, videbis. Castricianum

Caesar's house, now he has not a footing even among twenty; and in the second place, one embassy is talked of, and another is given to him. That fat post for levying money is reserved for Drusus of Pisaurum, I suppose, or for the gourmand Vatinius, while this barren messenger's job is given to him, and his tribunate, too, has to wait their convenience. Fire the fellow's resentment please, as much as you can. My one hope of safety lies in their mutual disagreement: and from Curio I gather that there is a hint of such a thing. Arrius is beginning to rage at being robbed of his consulship: Megabocchus and the rest of that bloodthirsty band of youths are at daggers drawn with them. And God grant there may come a dispute about this augurship on the top. I hope I shall have occasion to send you some of my very best letters, and plenty of them on these topics.

But I am anxious to know the meaning of that dark hint of yours, that even some of the board of five commissioners are speaking their minds. What on earth can it be? If there really is anything in it, things are in a better way than I thought. Please don't imagine that I ask the question with a view to action, because my soul is yearning to take part in politics. I have long been sick of holding the helm, even when I was allowed to do so: and now, when I have been marooned and the helm torn from my grasp without waiting for me to surrender it, my only desire is to watch their shipwreck from the dry land. I could wish, as your friend Sophocles says,

" In peaceful slumber sunk
To hear the pattering raindrops on the roof."

About the wall you will see what is necessary. I

mendum nos corrigemus, et tamen ad me Quintus
HS ccioo ioo scripserat, nunc[1] ad sororem tuam
HS $\overline{\text{xxx}}$. Terentia tibi salutem dicit. Cicero tibi
mandat, ut Aristodemo idem de se respondeas, quod
de fratre suo, sororis tuae filio, respondisti. De
Ἀμαλθείᾳ quod me admones, non neglegemus. Cura,
ut valeas.

VIII

CICERO ATTICO SAL.

*Scr. Anti
medio m.
Apr. a. 695*

Epistulam cum a te avide exspectarem ad vespe-
rum, ut soleo, ecce tibi nuntius pueros venisse Roma!
Voco, quaero, ecquid litterarum. Negant. " Quid
ais ? " inquam, " nihilne a Pomponio ? " Perterriti
voce et vultu confessi sunt se accepisse, sed excidisse
in via. Quid quaeris ? permoleste tuli ; nulla enim
abs te per hos dies epistula inanis aliqua re utili et
suavi venerat. Nunc, si quid in ea epistula, quam
ante diem xvi Kal. Maias dedisti, fuit historia dignum, scribe quam primum, ne ignoremus ; sin nihil
praeter iocationem, redde id ipsum.

Et scito Curionem adulescentem venisse ad me
salutatum. Valde eius sermo de Publio cum tuis
litteris congruebat ; ipse vero mirandum in modum
" reges odisse superbos." Peraeque narrabat incen-

[1] non *M.*

will set the mistake about Castricius right; and yet
Quintus wrote about £130 [1] to me, though now to
your sister he makes it nearly £260. [2] Terentia sends
her love; and my little boy commissions you to give
Aristodemus the same answer for him as you gave
for his cousin, your sister's son. I won't forget your
reminder about your Amalthea. Take care of yourself.

VIII

CICERO TO ATTICUS, GREETING.

When I was looking forward eagerly to a letter of *Antium,*
yours towards evening, as usual, lo and behold a *Apr.,* B.C. *59*
message that some slaves had come from Rome. I
called them, and inquired if they had any letters.
" No," they said. " What's that," said I, " nothing
from Pomponius? " Frightened to death by my
voice and look, they confessed they had been given
one, but it had been lost on the way. As you may
suppose, I was wild with annoyance. For every letter
you have sent me these last few days has contained
something of importance or entertainment. So, if
there was anything worth saying in the letter of the
15th of April, write at once and let me know it: if
there was nothing but nonsense you owe me a repeti-
tion of it.

Let me tell you that young Curio has come and
paid his respects to me: and what he said about
Publius agreed very closely with your letter. It is
astonishing, too, how he " holds proud kings in hate,"
and he tells me that the younger generation in

[1] 15,000 sesterces.
[2] 30,000 sesterces.

sam esse iuventutem neque ferre haec posse. Bene
habemus. Nos, si in his spes est, opinor, aliud agamus. Ego me do historiae. Quamquam licet me
Saufeium putes esse, nihil me est inertius.

Sed cognosce itinera nostra, ut statuas, ubi nos
visurus sis. In Formianum volumus venire Parilibus;
inde, quoniam putas praetermittendum nobis esse hoc
tempore Cratera illum delicatum, Kal. Maiis de Formiano proficiscemur, ut Anti simus a. d. v Nonas
Maias. Ludi enim Anti futuri sunt a iiii ad pr. Nonas Maias. Eos Tullia spectare vult. Inde cogito
in Tusculanum, deinde Arpinum, Romam ad Kal.
Iunias. Te aut in Formiano aut Anti aut in Tusculano cura ut videamus. Epistulam superiorem re-
stitue nobis et adpinge aliquid novi.

IX

CICERO ATTICO SAL.

*Scr. Anti
medio m.
Apr. a. 695*

Subito cum mihi dixisset Caecilius quaestor puerum
se Romam mittere, haec scripsi raptim, ut tuos eli-
cerem mirificos cum Publio dialogos cum eos, de quibus scribis, tum illum, quem abdis et ais longum
esse, quae ad ea responderis, perscribere; illum vero,
qui nondum habitus est, quem illa βοῶπις, cum e
Solonio redierit, ad te est relatura. Sic velim putes,
nihil hoc posse mihi esse iucundius. Si vero, quae

---

[1] The bay of Naples, where Cicero's Pompeian villa was.
[2] Clodia.

general holds equally strong views, and cannot put up with the present state of affairs. We are all right. If we can put our trust in them we need not trouble ourselves, so far as I can see. I am devoting myself to history. But, though you think me as energetic as Saufeius, I am the laziest mortal alive.

But get clear about my journeys so that you may settle where you will see me. I am intending to get to my place at Formiae on the feast of Pales; and then, since you think I ought not to stop at the delightful Crater[1] on this occasion, I shall leave Formiae on the 1st of May, so as to reach Antium on the 3rd. There are games at Antium from the 4th to the 6th of May, and Tullia wants to see them. Then I am thinking of going to Tusculum, and from there to Arpinum, reaching Rome on the 1st of June. Be sure you pay me a visit either at Formiae or at Antium, or at my place at Tusculum. Reproduce your former letter for me, and add something new to it.

IX

CICERO TO ATTICUS, GREETING.

Caecilius the quaestor having suddenly told me that he was sending a man to Rome, I write this note in haste to extract from you all your wonderful dialogues with Publius, those you mention in your note, and the one you keep dark, saying that your answers were too long to write; and besides the one which has not yet been held, but which that Juno[2] is going to report to you when she returns from Solonium. Pray believe me when I say there is nothing that would please me more. If the compact about

Antium, Apr., B.C. *59*

de mc pacta sunt, ea non servantur, in caelo sum, ut
sciat hic noster Hierosolymarius traductor ad plebem,
quam bonam meis putissimis orationibus gratiam ret-
tulerit. Quarum exspecta divinam παλινῳδίαν. Etenim, quantum coniectura auguramur, si erit nebulo
iste cum his dynastis in gratia, non modo de cynico
consulari, sed ne de istis quidem piscinarum Tritoni-
bus poterit se iactare. Non enim poterimus ulla esse
invidia spoliati opibus et illa senatoria potentia. Sin
autem ab iis dissentiet erit absurdum in nos invehi.
Verum tamen invehatur.

Festive, mihi crede, et minore sonitu, quam putaram, orbis hic in re publica est conversus; citius
omnino, quam potuit, idque [1] culpa Catonis, sed rursus
improbitate istorum, qui auspicia, qui Aeliam legem,
qui Iuniam et Liciniam, qui Caeciliam et Didiam
neglexerunt, qui omnia remedia rei publicae effude-
runt, qui regna quasi praedia tetrarchis, qui immanes
pecunias paucis dederunt. Video iam, quo invidia
transeat et ubi sit habitatura. Nihil me existimaris
neque usu neque a Theophrasto didicisse, nisi brevi
tempore desiderari nostra illa tempora videris. Etenim, si fuit invidiosa senatus potentia, cum ea non ad
populum, sed ad tres homines immoderatos redacta
sit, quid iam censes fore? Proinde isti licet faciant,

---

[1] idque *Wesenberg:* id *M.*

me is not kept I am in the seventh heaven with delight at thinking how that Jerusalemite plebeian-monger will learn what a pretty return he has made for all my choicest panegyrics : and you may expect recantation of eclipsing brilliancy ; for, so far as I can see, if that good-for-nothing is in favour with our sovereigns, he will have to give up crowing over the " ex-consul with a cynic's tongue " and those " Tritons of the fish-ponds " together : for there will be nothing to envy me for when I have been robbed of my power and my influence in the Senate. If, on the other hand, he quarrels with them, then any attack on me would be absurd. However, let him attack, if he likes.

Upon my word, the wheel of State has turned round gaily and with less noise than I had expected : more quickly to be sure than it might have done. That is Cato's fault, but it is still more through the villainy of those who have disregarded auspices and the Aelian law, the Iunian and Licinian law, and the Caecilian and Didian law, who have thrown out of the window all the physic for the State, who have given kingdoms to tetrarchs as though they were farms and immense sums of money to one or two people. I can see already which way jealousy is tending and where it will come home to roost. Count me too big a dunce to have learned anything by experience or from Theophrastus if you do not see very shortly men mourning for the days of my government. For if the power of the Senate was unpopular, you can imagine what things will be like now, when the power has been transferred not to the people, but to three unbridled men. So let them make anyone they like consuls and tribunes,

quos volent, consules, tribunos pl., denique etiam
Vatini strumam sacerdotii διβάφῳ vestiant, videbis
brevi tempore magnos non modo eos, qui nihil titu-
barunt, sed etiam illum ipsum, qui peccavit, Catonem.
Nam nos quidem, si per istum tuum sodalem Publium
licebit, σοφιστεύειν cogitamus, si ille cogit, tum[1]
dumtaxat nos defendere, et, quod est proprium artis
huius, ἐπαγγέλλομαι

ἄνδρ' ἀπαμύνεσθαι, ὅτε τις πρότερος χαλεπήνῃ.

Patria propitia sit.   Habet a nobis, etiamsi non plus,
quam debitum est, plus certe, quam postulatum est.
Male vehi malo alio gubernante quam tam ingratis
vectoribus bene gubernare.   Sed haec coram commodius.

Nunc audi, quod quaeris.   Antium me ex Formiano
recipere cogito a. d. v Nonas Maias; Antio volo Nonis
Maiis proficisci in Tusculanum.   Sed, cum e Formiano
rediero (ibi esse usque ad pr. K. Maias volo), faciam
statim te certiorem.   Terentia tibi salutem, καὶ Κικέρων ὁ μικρὸς ἀσπάζεται Τίτον Ἀθηναῖον.

X

CICERO ATTICO SAL.

Scr. in Appi
Foro XII K.
Apr. a. 695
Volo ames meam constantiam.   Ludos Anti spectare non placet; est enim ὑποσόλοικον, cum velim
vitare omnium deliciarum suspiconem, repente
ἀναφαίνεσθαι non solum delicate, sed etiam inepte

[1] cogit, tum *Orelli:* cogitat tantium *M.*

let them cloak Vatinius' wen with the double-dyed purple gown of the augur, you will see very soon not only those who have made no slip, but even Cato himself, for all his mistakes, exalted to the skies. As for me, I am thinking of playing the sophist if your comrade Publius will allow me: I shall defend myself only if he compels me. Using the ordinary trick of the trade, I shall put up a notice that I am ready to

> Give blow for blow, if any rouse me first. Iliad xxiv, 369

If only the country will be on my side. Certainly it has had from me more than it ever asked for, if not more than I owe to it. I would rather have a bad passage with another at the helm than steer safely myself for such ungrateful passengers. But of this we can talk better when we meet.

Now listen to my answer to your question. I am thinking of betaking myself to Antium from Formiae on May the 3rd: and I hope to start from Antium for Tusculum on May the 7th. But, as soon as I have returned from Formiae—and I intend to stay there till the last of April—I will send you definite news. Terentia sends her love, and little Cicero his greeting to Titus the Athenian.

X

CICERO TO ATTICUS, GREETING.

I hope you will admire my consistency. I have decided not to see the games at Antium. For it would be rather noticeably inconsistent at a time when I am trying to avoid the suspicion of taking a pleasure trip suddenly to appear in the character of one travelling not only for pleasure, but for very

Appi Forum,
March 21,
B.C. *59*

peregrinantem. Quare usque ad Nonas Maias te in
Formiano exspectabo. Nunc fac ut sciam, quo die
te visuri simus. Ab Appi Foro hora quarta. Dederam aliam paulo ante a Tribus Tabernis.

XI

CICERO ATTICO SAL.

*Scr. in
Formiano m.
Apr. a. 695*
Narro tibi, plane relegatus mihi videor, posteaquam in Formiano sum.   Dies enim nullus erat, Anti
cum essem, quo die non melius scirem, Romae quid
ageretur, quam ii, qui erant Romae.   Etenim litterae
tuae, non solum quid Romae, sed etiam quid in re
publica, neque solum quid fieret, verum etiam quid
futurum esset, indicabant.   Nunc, nisi si quid ex
praetereunte viatore exceptum est, scire nihil possumus.   Quare, quamquam iam te ipsum exspecto,
tamen isti puero, quem ad me statim iussi recurrere,
da ponderosam aliquam epistulam plenam omnium
non modo actorum, sed etiam opinionum tuarum, ac
diem, quo Roma sis exiturus, cura ut sciam.   Nos in
Formiano esse volumus usque ad prid. Nonas Maias.
Eo si ante eam diem non veneris, Romae te fortasse
videbo; nam Arpinum quid ego te invitem?

Τρηχεῖ’, ἀλλ’ ἀγαθὴ κουροτρόφος, οὔτ’ ἄρ’ ἔγωγε
ἧς γαίης δύναμαι γλυκερώτερον ἄλλο ἰδέσθαι.

Haec igitur.   Cura, ut valeas.

foolish pleasure too. So I shall wait for you till the 7th of May at Formiae. Now let me know what day I shall see you. From Appi Forum at ten o'clock. I sent another letter a little earlier from the Three Taverns.

XI

CICERO TO ATTICUS, GREETING.

I assure you I feel an absolute exile since I have been at Formiae. There never was a day when I was at Antium that I was not better up in the news of Rome than those who were living there. The fact is your letters used to set before me not only the city news but all the political news, and not only what was happening but what was going to happen too. Now I can't get to know anything unless I pick up chance news from a passing traveller. So, although I am expecting you here very soon, give this man of mine, who is under orders to return at once, a bulky missive, full of news of all that has happened and what you think about it: and don't forget to say what day you are leaving Rome. I intend to stay at Formiae till the 6th of May. If you can't get here before that date, perhaps I shall see you at Rome, for I can hardly invite you to Arpinum.

Formiae,
Apr., B.C. *59*

My rugged native land, good nurse for men ;   Odyssey ix, 27
None other would mine eyes so gladly see.

That is all, then. Take care of yourself.

XII

CICERO ATTICO SAL.

Scr. Tribus Tabernis XIII K. Mai. a. 695

Negent illi Publium plebeium factum esse? Hoc vero regnum est et ferri nullo pacto potest. Emittat ad me Publius, qui obsignent; iurabo Gnaeum nostrum, collegam Balbi, Anti mihi narrasse se in auspicio fuisse.

O suaves epistulas tuas uno tempore mihi datas duas! Quibus εὐαγγέλια quae reddam, nescio; deberi quidem plane fateor. Sed vide συγκύρημα. Emerseram commodum ex Antiati in Appiam ad Tris Tabernas ipsis Cerialibus, cum in me incurrit Roma veniens Curio meus. Ibidem ilico puer abs te cum epistulis. Ille ex me, nihilne audissem novi. Ego negare. "Publius," inquit, "tribunatum pl. petit." "Quid ais?" "Et inimicissimus quidem Caesaris, et ut omnia," inquit, "ista rescindat." "Quid Caesar?" inquam. "Negat se quicquam de illius adoptione tulisse." Deinde suum, Memmi, Metelli Nepotis exprompsit odium. Complexus iuvenem dimisi properans ad epistulas. Ubi sunt, qui aiunt "ζώσης φωνῆς"? quanto magis vidi ex tuis litteris quam ex illius sermone, quid ageretur, de ruminatione cotidiana, de cogitatione Publi, de lituis βοώπιδος, de signifero Athenione, de litteris missis ad Gnaeum, de

XII

CICERO TO ATTICUS, GREETING.

So they deny that Publius has been made a ple- *Tres* beian, do they? This is certainly sheer tyranny and *Tabernae,* not to be borne. Let Publius send someone to wit- *Apr. 18,* B.C. ness my affidavit. I will take my oath that my friend *59* Gnaeus, Balbus' colleague, told me at Antium that he had himself assisted at taking the auspices.

Fancy two such delightful letters of yours being delivered at one and the same time! I don't know how to pay you back for your good news, though I candidly confess my debt. Here's a coincidence. I had just taken the turn off the road to Antium on to the Appian Way at the Three Taverns on the very day of the Cerealia, when my friend Curio met me, fresh from Rome: and at the very same moment your man with a letter. Curio inquired whether I hadn't heard the news. " No," said I. " Publius is stand- ing for the tribuneship," says he. " You don't say so!" "And he is at deadly enmity with Caesar," he replies, " and wants to annul all those laws of his." "And what is Caesar doing?" I inquired. " He is denying that he ever proposed Clodius' adoption." Then he emptied the vials of his own wrath and that of Memmius and Metellus Nepos. I embraced the youth and said good-bye, being in a hurry to get to your letters. What a lot of nonsense is talked about " viva vox "? Why, I learned a dozen times as much about affairs from your letter as from his talk—the daily chit-chat, the designs of Publius, Juno's war- cries, how Athenio [1] is raising the standard, his letter

---

[1] *Juno* = Clodia, while it is probably Sex. Clodius who is referred to as *Athenio.* Athenio was one of the leaders in the insurrection of slaves in Sicily 103–101 B.C.

Theophanis Memmique sermone; quantam porro mihi exspectationem dedisti convivii istius ἀσελγοῦς! Sum in curiositate ὀξύπεινος, sed tamen facile patior te id ad me συμπόσιον non scribere; praesentem audire malo.

Quod me, ut scribam aliquid, hortaris, crescit mihi quidem materies, ut dicis, sed tota res etiam nunc fluctuat, κατ᾽ ὀπώρην τρύξ. Quae si desederit, magis erunt iam liquata,[1] quae scribam. Quae si statim a me ferre non potueris, primus habebis tamen et aliquamdiu solus. Dicaearchum recte amas; luculentus homo est et civis haud paulo melior quam isti nostri ἀδικαίαρχοι. Litteras scripsi hora decima Cerialibus, statim ut tuas legeram, sed eas eram daturus, ut putaram, postridie ei, qui mihi primus obviam venisset. Terentia delectata est tuis litteris; impertit tibi multam salutem, καὶ Κικέρων ὁ φιλόσοφος τὸν πολιτικὸν Τίτον ἀσπάζεται.

XIII

CICERO ATTICO SAL.

Scr. in Formiano m. Apr. circ. a. d. VIII K. Mai. a. 695

Facinus indignum! epistulam αὐθωρεὶ tibi a Tribus Tabernis rescriptam ad tuas suavissimas epistulas neminem reddidisse! At scito eum fasciculum, quo illam conieceram, domum eo ipso die latum esse, quo ego dederam, et ad me in Formianum relatum esse. Itaque tibi tuam epistulam iussi referri, ex qua intellegeres, quam mihi tum illae gratae fuissent. Romae

---

[1] iudicata *MSS.;* liquata *Orelli;* iam liquata *Kayser.*

144

to Gnaeus, the conversation with Theophanes and Memmius: and you have made me wild with inquisitiveness about that " fast " dinner. My curiosity is insatiable: but I have no grievance at your omitting to write an account of the dinner. I would much rather hear it by word of mouth.

As for your exhortations to write something, my material certainly is increasing, as you say; but everything is still in a state of ferment, like must in autumn. When things have settled down my writing will be more clarified. Though you may not get anything from me at once, you shall be the first to have it, however, and no one else for a long time. You are right in admiring Dicaearchus. He is a splendid fellow and a far better patriot than any of these great men of ours to whom his name would certainly not apply.[1] I write this on the day of the Cerealia at four o'clock, as soon as I read yours: but I am thinking of giving it to the first person I meet tomorrow. Terentia is delighted with your letters. She sends you her warmest greetings, and Cicero in his new rôle of philosopher salutes Titus the politician.

XIII

CICERO TO ATTICUS, GREETING.

What a shame! The letter I wrote on the spur *Formiae,* of the moment at the Three Taverns in answer to *circa Apr.* your delightful notes never reached you! The reason *23,* B.C. *59* was that the packet in which I had put it was taken to my town house the same day and brought back to me at Formiae. So I have had the letter sent back to show you how pleased I was with yours.

---

[1] Cicero puns on the name Dicaearchus (="just ruler").

quod scribis sileri, ita putabam; at hercule in agris
non siletur, nec iam ipsi agri regnum vestrum ferre
possunt. Si vero in hanc Τηλέπυλον veneris Λαιστρυ-
γονίην, Formias dico, qui fremitus hominum! quam
irati animi? quanto in odio noster amicus Magnus!
cuius cognomen una cum Crassi Divitis cognomine
consenescit. Credas mihi velim, neminem adhuc of-
fendi, qui haec tam lente, quam ego fero, ferret.
Quare, mihi crede, φιλοσοφῶμεν. Iuratus tibi possum
dicere nihil esse tanti. Tu si litteras ad Sicyonios
habes, advola in Formianum, unde nos pridie Nonas
Maias cogitamus.

XIV

CICERO ATTICO SAL.

*Scr. in
Formiano
inter XI et
III K. Mai.
a. 695*

Quantam tu mihi moves exspectationem de sermone Bibuli, quantam de colloquio βοώπιδος, quantam etiam de illo delicato convivio! Proinde ita fac
venias ut ad sitientes aures. Quamquam nihil est
iam, quod magis timendum nobis putem, quam ne
ille noster Sampsiceramus, cum se omnium sermonibus sentiet vapulare, et cum has actiones εὐανατρέ-
πτους videbit, ruere incipiat. Ego autem usque eo
sum enervatus, ut hoc otio, quo nunc tabescimus,
malim ἐντυραννεῖσθαι quam cum optima spe dimicare.

De pangendo quod me crebro adhortaris, fieri nihil
potest. Basilicam habeo, non villam, frequentia For-

Your news that the uproar has died down in Rome does not surprise me : but I can assure you it has not died down in the country, and the very country cannot endure that despotism you endure. If you come to this " Laestrygonia of the far gates,"—Formiae I mean—you will find the people raging with indignation, and our friend Magnus—a name which is now growing as obsolete as Crassus' surname Dives—held in the deepest abhorrence. You may not believe me, but I have not met anyone here who takes the matter as coolly as myself. So follow my advice and let us stick to philosophy. I can take my oath there is nothing like it. If you have a letter to send to the Sicyonians, hasten to Formiae. I am thinking of leaving on the 6th of May.

Odyssey, x, 81.

XIV

CICERO TO ATTICUS, GREETING.

You have aroused the liveliest curiosity in me as to your talk with Bibulus and your conversation with Juno, and about that " fast " dinner too. So remember my ears are thirsting for news, and come quickly. However, the thing I am most afraid of at the present moment is that our friend the Pasha may run amuck as soon as he realizes that everyone is railing at him and laying it on to him, and that these new measures are quite easy to upset. For myself, however, I have grown so slack that I should prefer to waste my life in my present ease under a despotism than to take part in the struggle, however bright the prospect of success. As for the writing, for which you so incessantly clamour, it is impossible. My house is so crowded with the townsfolk that it is a

Formiae, between Apr. 20 and 28, B.C. 59

mianorum atque imparem basilica tribui Aemiliae.[1]
Sed omitto vulgus; post horam quartam molesti
ceteri non sunt. C. Arrius proximus est vicinus,
immo ille quidem iam contubernalis, qui etiam se
idcirco Romam ire negat, ut hic mecum totos dies
philosophetur. Ecce ex altera parte Sebosus, ille
Catuli familiaris. Quo me vertam? Statim mehercule Arpinum irem, ni te in Formiano commodissime
exspectari viderem dumtaxat ad pr. Nonas Maias;
vides enim, quibus hominibus aures sint deditae meae.
O occasionem mirificam, si qui nunc, dum hi apud me
sunt, emere de me fundum Formianum velit! Et
tamen illud probem: " Magnum quid aggrediamur
et multae cogitationis atque otii "? Sed tamen satis
fiet a nobis, neque parcetur labori.

XV

CICERO ATTICO SAL.

*Scr. in
Formiano
inter XI et
III K. Mai.
a. 695*

Ut scribis, ita video non minus incerta in re publica quam in epistula tua, sed tamen ista ipsa me
varietas sermonum opinionumque delectat. Romae
enim videor esse, cum tuas litteras lego, et, ut fit in
tantis rebus, modo hoc, modo illud audire. Illud
tamen explicare non possum, quidnam invenire possit
nullo recusante ad facultatem agrariam. Bibuli
autem ista magnitudo animi in comitiorum dilatione
quid habet nisi ipsius iudicium sine ulla correctione

[1] ad quam partem basilicae tribum Aemiliam *M: the text
follows Boot's emendation.*

public hall rather than a private house: and too
small at that for the Aemilian tribe. But—to omit
the common herd, for others don't bother me after
ten o'clock—C. Arrius is my next-door neighbour,
or rather he lives with me, declaring that he has
forborne to go to Rome, expressly for the purpose of
spending his whole day philosophizing with me here.
Then on the other side there is Sebosus, Catulus'
intimate friend. Which way can I turn? Upon
my word, I would go to Arpinum straight away if I
did not see that Formiae is the most convenient
place to wait for your visit: but only up to the 6th
of May, for you see what bores my ears are condemned to endure. Now's the time to bid for my
Formian estate, while these people are pestering me.
And in spite of this am I to make good my promise
" Let me attempt something great, requiring much
thought and leisure "? Still I will satisfy you and
not spare my labour.

XV

CICERO TO ATTICUS, GREETING.

I fully realize that, as you say, your letter only *Formiae,*
reflects the general uncertainty of public affairs : but *between*
still that very variety of talk and opinion has its *Apr. 20 and*
charm : for I feel as though I was at Rome when *28*, B.C. *59*
I read your letter and was hearing first one thing
and then another, as one does on questions of importance. But what I can't make out is how Caesar can
possibly find any solution of the land question that
will not meet with opposition. As to Bibulus' firmness in impeding the comitia, it amounts to nothing
but an expression of his opinion and does not improve

rei publicae? Nimirum in Publio spes est. Fiat, fiat tribunus pl., si nihil aliud, ut eo citius tu ex Epiro revertare; nam, ut illo tu careas, non video posse fieri, praesertim si mecum aliquid volet disputare. Sed id quidem non dubium est, quin, si quid erit eius modi, sis advolaturus. Verum, ut hoc non sit, tamen, sive ruet sive eriget [1] rem publicam, praeclarum spectaculum mihi propono, modo te consessore spectare liceat.

Cum haec maxime scriberem, ecce tibi Sebosus! Nondum plane ingemueram, " salve," inquit Arrius. Hoc est Roma decedere! Quos ego homines effugi cum in hos incidi! Ego vero

" In montes patrios et ad incunabula nostra "

pergam. Denique, si solus non potuero, cum rusticis potius quam cum his perurbanis, ita tamen, ut, quoniam tu certi nihil scribis, in Formiano tibi praestoler usque ad III Nonas Maias.

Terentiae pergrata est adsiduitas tua et diligentia in controversia Mulviana. Nescit omnino te communem causam defendere eorum, qui agros publicos possideant; sed tamen tu aliquid publicanis pendis, haec etiam id recusat. Ea tibi igitur et Κικέρων, ἀριστοκρατικώτατος παῖς, salutem dicunt.

[1] sive eriget *Corradus:* get *CZ:* ΔΣ. *omit the word.*

the position of affairs at all. Upon my word, our only hope rests in Publius. Let him by all means become tribune; if for no other reason, to make you return all the sooner from Epirus. For I don't see how you can possibly keep away from him, especially if he should choose to quarrel with me. But of course I have no doubt that you would fly to my side if anything of the kind were to happen. But, even if this does not happen, I am looking forward to a sight worth seeing, whether he runs amuck or saves the State, if I can watch it with you sitting by my side.

Just as I was writing these words in comes Sebosus: and I had hardly fetched a sigh when there was Arrius saying, " Good day." This is going out of town! Is it escaping from society to run into people like this? I shall certainly be off to " My native hills, the cradle of my youth." To put it shortly, if I can't be alone I would rather be with country-folk than with these ultra-city men. However, as you send no definite date, I will wait for you at Formiae till the 5th of May.

Terentia is much gratified by the attention and care you have bestowed on her dispute with Mulvius. She has not the least idea that you are supporting the common cause of all the owners of public land. However, you do pay something to the tax-collectors; while she refuses to pay a penny. Accordingly, she and my boy, a most conservative lad, send their respects.

MARCUS TULLIUS CICERO

XVI

CICERO ATTICO SAL.

Scr. in Formiano in. m. Maio a. 695

Cenato mihi et iam dormitanti pridie K. Maias epistula est illa reddita, in qua de agro Campano scribis. Quid quaeris? primo ita me pupugit, ut somnum mihi ademerit, sed id cogitatione magis quam molestia; cogitanti autem haec fere succurrebant. Primum ex eo, quod superioribus litteris scripseras, ex familiari te illius audisse prolatum iri aliquid, quod nemo improbaret, maius aliquid timueram. Hoc mihi eius modi non videbatur. Deinde, ut me egomet consoler, omnis exspectatio largitionis agrariae in agrum Campanum videtur esse derivata, qui ager, ut dena iugera sint, non amplius hominum quinque milia potest sustinere; reliqua omnis multitudo ab illis abalienetur necesse est. Praeterea si ulla res est, quae bonorum animos, quos iam video esse commotos, vehementius possit incendere, haec certe est et eo magis, quod portoriis Italiae sublatis, agro Campano diviso quod vectigal superest domesticum praeter vicensimam? quae mihi videtur una contiuncula clamore pedisequorum nostrorum esse peritura. Gnaeus quidem noster iam plane quid cogitet nescio;

φυσᾷ γὰρ οὐ σμικροῖσιν αὐλίσκοις ἔτι,
ἀλλ' ἀγρίαις φύσαισι φορβειᾶς ἄτερ.

qui quidem etiam istuc adduci potuerit. Nam adhuc

XVI

CICERO TO ATTICUS, GREETING.

As I was taking a nap after dinner on the last of *Formiae,* April your letter about the Campanian land arrived. *May,* B.C. *59* Well, at first it startled me so that it banished all desire to sleep, though it was thought rather than uneasiness that kept me awake. The result of my cogitations was something of this sort. First, when you said in your last letter you had heard from a great friend of Caesar's that some proposal was going to be made to which no one could object I had feared some sweeping measure; but this I don't consider anything of the kind. Secondly—and that is some consolation to me—all hope of agrarian distribution seems to have been diverted to the Campanian land. Supposing that the allotments are about 6 acres apiece, that land will not hold more than 5,000 people; so they have to offend all the rest of the masses. Besides, if anything is calculated to arouse a fiercer pitch of indignation in the minds of the conservatives, who are obviously getting roused already, this is the very thing that will; all the more so because there won't be any home tax left except the 5 per cent,[1] now that the customs duties have been abolished, if the Campanian land is distributed: and that, I fancy, it would take only one petty harangue assisted by the cheers of our lacqueys to abolish. What on earth our friend Gnaeus is thinking of in letting himself be carried so far, I cannot tell:

He blows no more on slender pipe of reed,
But fierce unmodulated trumpet-blasts.

[1] On manumitted slaves.

haec ἐσοφίζετο, se leges Caesaris probare, actiones ipsum praestare debere; agrariam legem sibi placuisse, potuerit intercedi necne, nihil ad se pertinere; de rege Alexandrino placuisse sibi aliquando confici, Bibulus de caelo tum servasset necne, sibi quaerendum non fuisse; de publicanis voluisse se illi ordini commodare, quid futurum fuerit, si Bibulus tum in forum descendisset, se divinare non potuisse. Nunc vero, Sampsicerame, quid dices? vectigal te nobis in monte Antilibano constituisse, agri Campani abstulisse? Quid? hoc quem ad modum obtinebis? " Oppressos vos," inquit, " tenebo exercitu Caesaris." Non mehercule me tu quidem tam isto exercitu quam ingratis animis eorum hominum, qui appellantur boni, qui mihi non modo praemiorum, sed ne sermonum quidem umquam fructum ullum aut gratiam rettulerunt. Quodsi in eam me partem incitarem, profecto iam aliquam reperirem resistendi viam. Nunc prorsus hoc statui, ut, quoniam tanta controversia est Dicaearcho, familiari tuo, cum Theophrasto, amico meo, ut ille tuus τὸν πρακτικὸν βίον longe omnibus anteponat, hic autem τὸν θεωρητικόν, utrique a me mos gestus esse videatur. Puto enim me Dicaearcho adfatim satis fecisse; respicio nunc ad hanc familiam, quae mihi non modo, ut requiescam, permittit, sed reprehendit, quia non semper quierim. Quare incumbamus, o noster Tite, ad illa praeclara studia et

For up to now he has chopped logic about the matter, saying that he approved of Caesar's laws, but it was for Caesar to see to their passing : that the agrarian law was sound enough to his mind, but whether it could be vetoed by a tribune or not did not matter to him : he thought it was high time the question was settled with the king of Alexandria : whether Bibulus had been watching for omens or not at that particular moment was no business of his : as for the tax-gatherers, they were a class that he wished to oblige : what was going to happen if Bibulus came down to the forum on that occasion he could not have prophesied. But now what has the Pasha got to say for himself ? That he imposed a tax on Antilibanus and took it off the Campanian land ? Well, I don't see how he will make it good. " I will keep you in check with Caesar's army," he says. No, not me at least ; that army will not restrain me so much as the ungrateful minds of the so-called constitutionalists, who have not repaid my services even by thanks, much less by more substantial rewards. But if I were really to rouse myself to energy against that party I would certainly find some means of resisting them. As it is, since there is such an endless controversy between your intimate Dicaearchus and my friend Theophrastus, Dicaearchus giving the preference to a practical life, Theophrastus to a contemplative, I have set my mind on making it clear that I have humoured them both. I take it I have fully satisfied Dicaearchus : now I am turning my eye to the other school, which not only gives me permission to take my ease now, but blames me for ever having done anything else. So, my dear Titus, let me throw myself heart and soul into those excellent studies,

eo, unde discedere non oportuit, aliquando revertamur.

Quod de Quinti fratris epistula scribis, ad me
quoque fuit πρόσθε λέων, ὄπιθεν δὲ —[1] quid dicam,
nescio; nam ita deplorat primis versibus mansionem
suam, ut quemvis movere possit, ita rursus remittit,
ut me roget, ut annales suos emendem et edam.
Illud tamen, quod scribis, animadvertas velim de por-
torio circumvectionis; ait se de consilii sententia rem
ad senatum reiecisse. Nondum videlicet meas litteras legerat, quibus ad eum re consulta et explorata
perscripseram non deberi. Velim, si qui Graeci iam
Romam ex Asia ea causa venerunt, videas et, si
tibi videbitur, iis demonstres, quid ego de ea re sen-
tiam. Si possum discedere, ne causa optuma in
senatu pereat, ego satis faciam publicanis; εἰ δὲ μή
(vere tecum loquar), in hac re malo universae Asiae
et negotiatoribus; nam eorum quoque vehementer
interest. Hoc ego sentio valde nobis opus esse. Sed
tu id videbis. Quaestores autem, quaeso, num etiam
de cistophoro dubitant? Nam, si aliud nihil erit,
cum erimus omnia experti, ego ne illud quidem
contemnam, quod extremum est. Te in Arpinati
videbimus et hospitio agresti accipiemus, quoniam
maritumum hoc contempsisti.

[1] Iliad vi, 181, ending δράκων, μέσση δε χίμαιρα.

and at length seek the home that I ought never to have left.

As for your complaints about my brother Quintus' letter, to me, too, it seemed " a lion before, behind " —heaven knows what. For the groans in the first lines about his long absence would touch anybody's heart: then afterwards he calms down sufficiently to ask me to touch up and edit his journal. Please pay some attention to the point you mention about the dues on goods transferred from port to port. He says he referred it to the Senate by the advice of his assessors. Evidently he had not read my letter, in which I told him after careful consideration and re-search that no tax was legally due. If any Greeks have come from Asia to Rome about it please see them and, if you think fit, tell them my opinion. If I can recant I will do as the tax-collectors wish, rather than see the good cause worsted in the House: but if not I candidly confess I prefer the interests of the whole of Asia and the merchants, for I feel it is really a matter of great importance to them. I think, however, it is a case of necessity for us. But you will see to it. Are the quaestors, then, still debating about the currency? If there is no escape from it in spite of all our efforts I shouldn't turn up my nose at the Asiatic coins as the last resource. I shall see you at Arpinum and give you a country welcome, since you have despised this at the seaside.

MARCUS TULLIUS CICERO

XVII

CICERO ATTICO SAL.

*Scr. in
Formiano
in m. Mai.
a. 695*

Prorsus, ut scribis, ita sentio, turbatur Sampsiceramus. Nihil est, quod non timendum sit; ὁμολογουμένως τυραννίδα συσκευάζεται. Quid enim ista repentina adfinitatis coniunctio, quid ager Campanus, quid effusio pecuniae significant? Quae si essent extrema, tamen esset nimium mali, sed ea natura rei est, ut haec extrema esse non possint. Quid enim? eos haec ipsa per se delectare possunt? Numquam huc venissent, nisi ad alias res pestiferas aditus sibi compararent. Verum, ut scribis, haec in Arpinati a. d. vi circiter Idus Maias non deflebimus, ne et opera et oleum philologiae nostrae perierit; sed conferemus tranquillo animo. Di immortales neque tam me εὐελπιστία consolatur ut antea quam ἀδιαφορία, qua nulla in re tam utor quam in hac civili et publica. Quin etiam, quod est subinane in nobis et non ἀφιλόδοξον (bellum est enim sua vitia nosse), id adficitur quadam delectatione. Solebat enim me pungere, ne Sampsicerami merita in patriam ad annos sescentos maiora viderentur quam nostra. Hac quidem cura certe iam vacuus sum; iacet enim ille sic, ut πτῶσις [1] Curiana stare videatur. Sed haec coram. Tu tamen videris mihi Romae fore ad nostrum adventum, quod sane facile patiar, si tuo commodo fieri possit; sin, ut scribis, ita venies, velim ex Theo-

---

[1] πτῶσις *Bosius:* phocis *codd.*

XVII

CICERO TO ATTICUS, GREETING.

I agree entirely with what you say in your letter. *Formiae,* The Pasha is running amuck. We may anticipate *May,* B.C. *59* anything: he is quite clearly setting up a tyranny. What else is the meaning of this sudden marriage-contract,[1] of the proposals about the Campanian land, of this reckless expenditure of money? If that were the end of it, it would be disastrous enough: but the nature of the case makes it impossible that this should be the end. These things in themselves cannot possibly give them any pleasure: and they would never have taken this step except as the first to other pernicious acts. But, as you say, we will discuss these questions rationally at Arpinum about the 10th of May, and not prove all the labour and the midnight oil we have spent on our studies wasted by weeping over them. Heaven help us! I derive consolation not so much from hope, as I did formerly, as from a spirit of indifference, which I call to my service especially in civic and political matters. Nay more, the little strain of vanity and thirst for fame that there is in me—it is a good thing to recognize one's own faults—even experiences a pleasurable sensation. For the thought that the Pasha's services to the country might in the dim future be reckoned higher than mine, used to prick me to the heart: but now I rest quite easy on that score. He has fallen so low that the fallen Curius in comparison seems to stand erect. But of this when we meet. It seems now as though you will be at Rome when I arrive: for which I shall not be at all sorry, if it is

---

[1] Of Pompey with Caesar's daughter.

MARCUS TULLIUS CICERO

phane expiscere, quonam in me animo sit Arabarches. Quaeres scilicet κατὰ τὸ κηδεμονικόν et ad me ab eo quasi ὑποθήκας adferes, quem ad modum me geram. Aliquid ex eius sermone poterimus περὶ τῶν ὅλων suspicari.

XVIII

CICERO ATTICO SAL.

Scr. Romae m. Iun. aut in. Quint. a. 695

Accepi aliquot epistulas tuas; ex quibus intellexi, quam suspenso animo et sollicito scire averes, quid esset novi. Tenemur undique neque iam, quo minus serviamus, recusamus, sed mortem et eiectionem quasi maiora timemus, quae multo sunt minora. Atque hic status, quasi [1] una voce omnium gemitur neque verbo cuiusquam sublevatur. Σκοπός est, ut suspicor, illis, qui tenent, nullam cuiquam largitionem relinquere. Unus loquitur et palam adversatur adulescens Curio. Huic plausus maximi, consalutatio forensis perhonorifica, signa praeterea benevolentiae permulta a bonis impertiuntur. Fufium clamoribus et conviciis et sibilis consectantur. His ex rebus non spes, sed dolor est maior, cum videas civitatis voluntatem solutam, virtutem alligatam. Ac, ne forte quaeras κατὰ λεπτὸν de singulis rebus, universa res eo est deducta, spes ut nulla sit aliquando non modo privatos, verum etiam magistratus liberos fore. Hac tamen in oppressione sermo in circulis dumtaxat

---

[1] quasi *Schiche:* qui *codd.*

convenient to you. But if you come to see me, as you promise in your note, I wish you would fish out of Theophanes how the Sheikh is disposed to me. You will, of course, use your usual care in inquiring, and will deliver to me a kind of Whole Duty by which to regulate my conduct. From his conversation we shall be able to get an inkling of the entire situation.

XVIII

CICERO TO ATTICUS, GREETING.

I have received several letters of yours, and from them I see with what tense anxiety you are looking forward to news. We are hemmed in on every side; yet we do not rebel at servitude, fearing death and exile as though they were greater evils, whereas they are really far lesser evils. Yes, that is the position, and though everyone groans about it, not a voice is raised to relieve it. The object, I presume, of those who hold the reins is to leave nothing for anyone else to give away. One man only opens his mouth and opposes them publicly, and that is young Curio. The loyal party cheers him loudly, greets him in the forum with the highest respect, and shows its goodwill to him in many other ways, while Fufius is pursued with shouts and jeers and hisses. But this raises not one's hope so much as one's disgust at seeing the people's will so free and their courage so enslaved. And, not to enter into details with you, affairs have come to such a pass that there is no hope of ever again having free magistrates, let alone a free people. But in the midst of this tyranny speech is freer than ever, at any rate in clubs and over our

Rome, June or July, B.C. *59*

et in conviviis est liberior quam fuit. Vincere incipit timorem dolor, sed ita, ut omnia sint plenissima desperationis. Habet etiam Campana lex exsecrationem candidatorum, si mentionem in contione fecerint, quo aliter ager possideatur atque ut ex legibus Iuliis. Non dubitant iurare ceteri; Laterensis existimatur laute fecisse, quod tribunatum pl. petere destitit, ne iuraret.

Sed de re publica non libet plura scribere. Displiceo mihi nec sine summo scribo dolore. Me tueor ut oppressis omnibus non demisse, ut tantis rebus gestis parum fortiter. A Caesare valde liberaliter invitor in legationem illam, sibi ut sim legatus, atque etiam libera legatio voti causa datur. Sed haec et praesidii apud pudorem Pulchelli non habet satis et a fratris adventu me ablegat, illa et munitior est et non impedit, quo minus adsim, cum velim. Hanc ego teneo, sed usurum me non puto, neque tamen scit quisquam. Non lubet fugere, aveo pugnare. Magna sunt hominum studia. Sed nihil adfirmo; tu hoc silebis.

De Statio manu misso et non nullis aliis rebus angor equidem, sed iam prorsus occallui. Tu vellem

cups. Disgust is beginning to conquer fear, though it still leaves the blankest despair everywhere. The Campanian law goes so far as to impose upon candidates a formula of execration upon themselves if they propose any different occupation of the land to that laid down by the Julian laws, to be used by them in their speech as candidates. The others showed no compunction in taking the oath: but Laterensis is thought a hero because he threw up his candidature for the tribunate rather than take it.

I have no heart to write more about politics. I am disgusted with myself, and it is agony to me to write. I stand my ground without losing self-respect considering the universal servility, but with less courage than I could wish considering my past record. Caesar most liberally invites me to take a place on his personal staff: and I even have an offer of a free travelling pass nominally to fulfil a vow.[1] But it is hardly safe to trust to that Beauty's delicacy to that extent. Besides, it would mean that I should not be here for my brother's return. The other post is much safer, and does not prevent me from being here when I wish. The free pass I have, but I don't think I shall use it. No one knows of it, however. I don't want to run away; I long to fight. I have plenty of ardent admirers. But I won't take my oath on anything, and please don't mention what I've said.

I am much distressed about the manumission of Statius and some other things, but I've become thick-skinned by now. I wish you were here, I long for

[1] The *libera legatio* was a pseudo-embassy at state expense, granted to senators who wished to pay a vow, receive an inheritance, or exact a debt.

ego vel cuperem adesses; nec mihi consilium nec consolatio deesset. Sed ita te para, ut, si inclamaro, advoles.

XIX

CICERO ATTICO SAL.

*Scr. Romae
m. Quint. a.
695*
Multa me sollicitant et ex rei publicae tanto motu et ex iis periculis, quae mihi ipsi intenduntur et sescenta sunt; sed mihi nihil est molestius quam Statium manu missum:

" Nec meum imperium, ac mitto imperium, non
  simultatem meam
Revereri saltem! "

Nec, quid faciam, scio, neque tantum est in re, quantus est sermo. Ego autem ne irasci possum quidem iis, quos valde amo; tantum doleo ac mirifice quidem. Cetera in magnis rebus. Minae Clodi contentionesque, quae mihi proponuntur, modice me tangunt; etenim vel subire eas videor mihi summa cum dignitate vel declinare nulla cum molestia posse. Dices fortasse: " Dignitatis ἅλις tamquam δρυός, saluti, si me amas, consule." Me miserum! cur non ades? nihil profecto te praeteriret. Ego fortasse τυφλώττω et nimium τῷ καλῷ προσπέπονθα. Scito nihil umquam fuisse tam infame, tam turpe, tam peraeque omnibus generibus, ordinibus, aetatibus offensum quam hunc statum, qui nunc est, magis mehercule, quam vellem, non modo quam putarem. Populares isti iam etiam

it. I should no longer feel the lack of advice or consolation. However, hold yourself ready to come
quickly if I call for you.

XIX

CICERO TO ATTICUS, GREETING.

I have many causes for anxiety, both from the Rome, July,
troubled state of the constitution and from the in- B.C. 59
numerable personal dangers which threaten me. But
nothing annoys me more than Statius' manumission:

That my authority—nay, I let that be—   Terence, *Phorm*
That my displeasure should be counted nought!   232

But what I am to do, I don't know; and the matter
is more talk than anything. I can never be angry
with those I really love: I can only feel sorrow, and
very deep sorrow too. My other cares are for important matters. Clodius' threats and the struggle
I have to face do not affect me much: for I think I
can face the music with dignity or avoid the danger
without unpleasantness. Perhaps you will say:
" Hang dignity. It's prehistoric.[1] For mercy's sake
look after your safety." Alas! Why aren't you
here? You would notice everything: while I perhaps am blinded by my passion for high ideals. Nothing was ever so scandalous, so disgraceful, and so
objectionable to every rank and class of men young
or old as this present state of affairs, far more so than
I expected, nay, upon my soul it is more so than I
could wish. The popular party have taught even

---

[1] Lit. " enough of the oak," a proverb alluding to a supposed acorn diet in the days before the use of corn was
discovered.

modestos homines sibilare docuerunt. Bibulus in caelo est, nec, quare, scio, sed ita laudatur, quasi

" Unus homo nobis cunctando restituit rem."

Pompeius, nostri amores, quod mihi summo dolori est, ipse se adflixit. Neminem tenent voluntate; ne metu necesse sit iis uti, vereor. Ego autem neque pugno cum illa causa propter illam amicitiam neque approbo, ne omnia improbem, quae antea gessi; utor via. Populi sensus maxime theatro et spectaculis perspectus est; nam gladiatoribus qua dominus qua advocati sibilis conscissi; ludis Apollinaribus Diphilus tragoedus in nostrum Pompeium petulanter invectus est:

" Nostra miseria tu es magnus—"

miliens coactus est dicere;

" Eandem virtutem istam veniet tempus cum graviter gemes "

totius theatri clamore dixit itemque cetera. Nam et eius modi sunt ii versus, uti in tempus ab inimico Pompei scripti esse videantur:

" Si neque leges neque mores cogunt—,"

et cetera magno cum fremitu et clamore sunt dicta. Caesar cum venisset mortuo plausu, Curio filius est insecutus. Huic ita plausum est, ut salva re publica Pompeio plaudi solebat. Tulit Caesar graviter. Litterae Capuam ad Pompeium volare dicebantur. Ini-

the moderate men to hiss. Bibulus is exalted to the sky, though I don't know why. However, he is as much bepraised as though

> " His wise delay alone did save the State." [1]

To my infinite sorrow, my pet, Pompey, has shattered his own reputation. They have no hold on anyone by affection : and I am afraid they may find it necessary to try the effect of fear. I do not quarrel with them on account of my friendship for him, though I refrain from showing approval not to stultify all my previous actions. I keep to the high-road. The popular feeling can be seen best in the theatre and at public exhibitions. For at the gladiatorial show both the leader [2] and his associates were overwhelmed with hisses : at the games in honour of Apollo the actor Diphilus made an impertinent attack on Pompey, " By our misfortunes thou art Great," which was encored again and again. " A time will come when thou wilt rue that might " he declaimed amid the cheers of the whole audience, and so on with the rest. For indeed the verses do look as though they had been written for the occasion by an enemy of Pompey : " If neither law nor custom can constrain," etc., was received with a tremendous uproar and outcry. At Caesar's entry the applause dwindled away ; but young Curio, who followed, was applauded as Pompey used to be when the constitution was still sound. Caesar was much annoyed : and it is said a letter flew post haste to Pompey at Capua.

---

[1] So Ennius speaking of Q. Fabius Maximus.
[2] Probably Pompey, Caesar being the chief of the *socii*, though some take it to refer to Gabinius, who gave the show, or to Caesar.

mici erant equitibus, qui Curioni stantes plauserant,
hostes omnibus; Rosciae legi, etiam frumentariae
minitabantur. Sane res erat perturbata. Equidem
malueram, quod erat susceptum ab illis, silentio
transiri, sed vereor, ne non liceat. Non ferunt homines, quod videtur esse tamen ferendum; sed est
iam una vox omnium magis odio firmata quam praesidio.

Noster autem Publius mihi minitatur, inimicus est.
Impendet negotium, ad quod tu scilicet advolabis.
Videor mihi nostrum illum consularem exercitum bonorum omnium, etiam satis bonorum habere firmissi-
mum. Pompeius significat studium erga me non me-
diocre; idem adfirmat verbum de me illum non esse
facturum; in quo non me ille fallit, sed ipse fallitur.
Cosconio mortuo sum in eius locum invitatus. Id
erat vocari in locum mortui. Nihil me turpius apud
homines fuisset neque vero ad istam ipsam ἀσφάλειαν
quicquam alienius. Sunt enim illi apud bonos in-
vidiosi, ego apud improbos meam retinuissem invidiam,
alienam adsumpsissem. Caesar me sibi vult esse
legatum. Honestior declinatio haec periculi; sed
ego hoc non repudio. Quid ergo est? pugnare
malo. Nihil tamen certi. Iterum dico "utinam
adesses!" Sed tamen, si erit necesse, arcessemus.

They are annoyed with the knights who stood up and clapped Curio, and their hand is against every man's. They are threatening the Roscian law and even the corn law. Things are in a most disturbed condition. I used to think it would be best silently to ignore their doings, but I am afraid that will be impossible. The public cannot put up with things, and yet it looks as though they would have to put up with them. The whole people speak now with one voice, but the unanimity has no foundation but common hate.

Anyhow, our friend Publius is threatening me and making hostile advances: there is trouble ahead, and you must fly to the rescue. I think I have at my back the same firm bodyguard of all the sound men, and even the moderately sound, as I had in my consulship. The affection Pompey shows me is more than ordinary. He declares Clodius will not say a word against me: but there he is deceiving himself not me. I have been asked to fill Cosconius' place [1] now he is dead. That would be stepping into a dead man's shoes, with a vengeance! I should disgrace myself utterly in the world's eyes: and nothing could be more opposed to the state of safety you keep talking of. For that board is unpopular with the loyal party, and so I should keep my unpopularity with the disloyal and take up another's burden too. Caesar wants me to go as his lieutenant. That would be a more honourable way of getting out of danger. But I don't want to shirk it, for the very good reason that I prefer fighting. However, nothing is settled. I repeat, I wish you were here. However,

[1] As one of the twenty commissioners for the distribution of public land.

Quid aliud? quid? Hoc opinor. Certi sumus perisse omnia; quid enim ἀκκιζόμεθα tam diu?

Sed haec scripsi properans et mehercule timide. Posthac ad te aut, si perfidelem habebo, cui dem, scribam plane omnia, aut, si obscure scribam, tu tamen intelleges. In iis epistulis me Laelium, te Furium faciam; cetera erunt ἐν αἰνιγμοῖς. Hic Caecilium colimus et observamus diligenter. Edicta Bibuli audio ad te missa. Iis ardet dolore et ira noster Pompeius.

XX

CICERO ATTICO SAL.

Scr. Romae
m. Quint. a.
695

Anicato, ut te velle intellexeram, nullo loco defui. Numestium ex litteris tuis studiose scriptis libenter in amicitiam recepi. Caecilium, quibus rebus possum, tueor diligenter. Varro satis facit nobis. Pompeius amat nos carosque habet. " Credis? " inquies. Credo; prorsus mihi persuadet; sed, quia volgo pragmatici homines omnibus historiis, praeceptis, versibus denique cavere iubent et vetant credere, alterum facio, ut caveam, alterum, ut non credam, facere non possum. Clodius adhuc mihi denuntiat periculum. Pompeius adfirmat non esse periculum, adiurat; addit etiam se prius occisum iri ab eo quam me violatum iri. Tracta-

if it is necessary I will send for you. Anything
else? One thing, I think: I am sure the country is
lost. It is no use mincing matters [1] any longer.

However, I have written this in a hurry, and, I may
say, in a fright too. Some time I will give you a clear
account if I find a very trusty messenger; or if I
veil my meaning you will manage to understand it.
In these letters I will call myself Laelius and you
Furius: and convey the rest in riddles. Here I am
cultivating Caecilius and paying him elaborate attention. I hear Bibulus' edicts have been sent to you.
Pompey is blazing with wrath and indignation at
them.

XX

CICERO TO ATTICUS, GREETING.

I have done all I could for Anicatus, knowing *Rome, July,*
you wanted me to do so, and have willingly adopted *B.C. 59*
Numestius as a friend on the strength of the earnest
recommendation in your letter. To Caecilius I take
care to pay every suitable attention. Varro is as
good as I can expect; and Pompey shows me friendship and affection. Can I believe him, you ask. I
do believe him: he quite convinces me. But since
men of the world are always advising one in their histories and precepts and even in their verses to beware
and forbidding one to believe, I do the one and beware, but to the other—not to believe—I cannot
persuade myself. Clodius is still threatening me with
danger, while Pompey asserts that there is no danger.
He swears it, adding even that he will not see me
injured if it costs him his life. The point is under

[1] Lit. " to be coy," or " to coquet."

tur res. Simul et quid erit certi, scribam ad te. Si
erit pugnandum, arcessam ad societatem laboris; si
quies dabitur, ab Amalthea te non commovebo.

De re publica breviter ad te scribam; iam enim,
charta ipsa ne nos prodat, pertimesco. Itaque posthac, si erunt mihi plura ad te scribenda, ἀλληγορίαις
obscurabo. Nunc quidem novo quodam morbo civitas moritur, ut, cum omnes ea, quae sunt acta,
improbent, querantur, doleant, varietas nulla in re
sit, aperteque loquantur et iam clare gemant, tamen
medicina nulla adferatur. Neque enim resisti sine
internecione posse arbitramur nec videmus, qui finis
cedendi praeter exitium futurus sit. Bibulus hominum admiratione et benevolentia in caelo est; edicta
eius et contiones describunt et legunt. Novo quodam genere in summam gloriam venit. Populare
nunc nihil tam est quam odium popularium. Haec
quo sint eruptura, timeo; sed, si dispicere quid
coepero, scribam ad te apertius. Tu, si me amas tantum, quantum profecto amas, expeditus facito ut sis,
si inclamaro, ut accurras; sed do operam et dabo, ne
sit necesse. Quod scripseram me tibi ut [1] Furio
scripturum, nihil necesse est tuum nomen mutare;
me faciam Laelium et te Atticum neque utar meo
chirographo neque signo, sit modo erunt eius modi
litterae, quas in alienum incidere nolim.

[1] me tibi ut *Wesenberg:* et *M.*

negotiation: as soon as any certain conclusion is reached, I will write to you. If I have to fight I will summon you to share my labour: but if I am left in peace I will not rout you out of your Amalthea.

Political matters I shall touch on only briefly: for I am beginning to be afraid that the very paper may betray me. So in future if I have to write in fuller detail to you I shall hide my meaning under covert language. Now the State is dying of a new disease. The measures that have been passed cause universal discontent and grumbling and indignation: there is no disagreement on the point, and people are now venting their opinion and their disapproval openly and loudly, yet no remedy is applied. Resistance seems impossible without bloodshed: nor can we see any other end to concession except destruction. Bibulus is exalted to the skies amid universal admiration and popularity. His edicts and speeches are copied out and read. He has attained the height of glory in quite a novel way. Nothing is so popular now as hatred of the popular party. I have my fears about the issue of all this. But I will write more clearly if I get any definite views. Do you, if your affection for me is as real as I know it to be, hold yourself ready to run to my call when it comes. But I am doing my best, and will continue to do it, to prevent any necessity. I said I would call you Furius in my letters, but there is no need to alter your name. I will call myself Laelius and you Atticus, and I won't use my own handwriting or seal, at any rate if the letters are such that I should not like them to fall into a stranger's hands.

Diodotus mortuus est; reliquit nobis HS fortasse centiens. Comitia Bibulus cum Archilochio edicto in ante diem xv Kal. Novembr. distulit. A Vibio libros accepi. Poeta ineptus et tamen scit nihil, sed est non inutilis. Describo et remitto.

XXI

CICERO ATTICO SAL.

Scr. Romae post VIII K. Sext., ante XV K. Nov. a. 695

De re publica quid ego tibi subtiliter? Tota periit atque hoc est miserior, quam reliquisti, quod tum videbatur eius modi dominatio civitatem oppressisse, quae iucunda esset multitudini, bonis autem ita molesta, ut tamen sine pernicie, nunc repente tanto in odio est omnibus, ut, quorsus eruptura sit, horreamus. Nam iracundiam atque intemperantiam illorum sumus experti, qui Catoni irati omnia perdiderunt, sed ita lenibus uti videbantur venenis, ut posse videremur sine dolore interire; nunc vero sibilis volgi, sermonibus honestorum, fremitu Italiae vereor ne exarserint. Equidem sperabam, ut saepe etiam loqui tecum solebam, sic orbem rei publicae esse conversum, ut vix

---

[1] 10,000,000 sesterces. But it seems too large a sum for Diodotus, a stoic who lived in Cicero's house for some time,

Diodotus is dead: he left me about £88,000.[1]
Bibulus has written a scathing edict putting off the
elections till the 18th of October. I have received
the books from Vibius: he[2] is a wretched poet, and
indeed has nothing in him; still he is of some use to
me. I am going to copy the work out and send it
back.

XXI

CICERO TO ATTICUS, GREETING.

To enter into details about politics would be super-
fluous. The whole country has gone to rack and
ruin: and affairs are in one respect worse than when
you left. Then it looked as though we were op-
pressed with a tyranny which was popular with the
lower classes, and, though annoying to the upper, still
comparatively harmless: but now it has become suddenly so universally detested that I tremble for the
issue. For we have had an experience of the wrath
and recklessness of the Triumvirs, and in their indignation with Cato they have ruined the State. The
poisons they used seemed to be so slow that I thought
we could die painlessly. But now I am afraid they
have been roused to energy by the hisses of the crowd,
the talk of the loyalists, and the murmurs of Italy.
I had hopes, as I used often to say to you, that the
wheel of State had turned so smoothly that we could

*Rome,
between
July 25 and
Oct. 18,
B.C. 59*

to have left. Tyrrell therefore suggests *centum*, i.e. 100,000
sesterces, about £880.

[2] Not Vibius himself, but Alexander of Ephesus, author of
a Cosmographia; cf. Att. ii, 22, 7.

sonitum audire, vix impressam orbitam videre possemus; et fuisset ita, si homines transitum tempestatis
exspectare potuissent. Sed, cum diu occulte suspi-
rassent, postea iam gemere, ad extremum vero loqui
omnes et clamare coeperunt. Itaque ille amicus
noster insolens infamiae, semper in laude versatus,
circumfluens gloria, deformatus corpore, fractus animo, quo se conferat, nescit; progressum praecipitem,
inconstantem reditum videt; bonos inimicos habet,
improbos ipsos non amicos.

Ac vide mollitiem animi. Non tenui lacrimas, cum
illum a. d. viii Kal. Sextiles vidi de edictis Bibuli con-
tionantem. Qui antea solitus esset iactare se magni-
ficentissime illo in loco summo cum amore populi,
cunctis faventibus, ut ille tum humilis, ut demissus
erat, ut ipse etiam sibi, non iis solum, qui aderant,
displicebat! O spectaculum uni Crasso iucundum,
ceteris non item! Nam, quia deciderat ex astris,
lapsus quam progressus potius videbatur, et, ut Apelles, si Venerem, aut Protogenes, si Ialysum illum
suum caeno oblitum videret, magnum, credo, acciperet dolorem, sic ego hunc omnibus a me pictum et
politum artis coloribus subito deformatum non sine
magno dolore vidi. Quamquam nemo putabat propter Clodianum negotium me illi amicum esse debere,
tamen tantus fuit amor, ut exhauriri nulla posset

scarcely catch the sound of its motion, and scarcely see the track of its path: and that is what would have happened if people could only have waited for the storm to pass. But for a while they stifled their sighs; then they began to groan aloud; and finally all set about airing their grievances at the top of their voices. And so our friend, being unused to unpopularity, and having always lived in an atmosphere of flattery and glory, disfigured in person and broken in spirit, does not know what to do with himself: he sees that to advance is dangerous, to retreat a confession of weakness: the respectable parties are his enemies, the very riff-raff not his friends.

Yet see how soft-hearted I am. I could not restrain my tears when I saw him on the 25th of July delivering a speech on the subject of the edicts of Bibulus. He used to carry himself with such a lofty bearing, enjoying unbounded popularity and universal respect: and now, how humble he was, how cast down, and what discontent he aroused in himself as well as in his hearers! What a sight! Crassus may have enjoyed it, but no one else. For seeing that he had fallen from the stars, one could not but attribute his swift descent to accident rather than to voluntary motion. And, just as Apelles or Protogenes, if they had seen their Venus or Ialysus smeared with mud, would, I imagine, have been cut to the heart, so I myself could not but feel poignant grief at seeing the idol on whose adornment I had lavished all the colours of my art suddenly disfigured. For though no one looked on it as my duty to retain my friendship with him after the Clodian affair, my affection for him was such that no slight could extinguish

iniuria. Itaque Archilochia in illum edicta Bibuli populo ita sunt iucunda, ut eum locum, ubi proponuntur, prae multitudine eorum, qui legunt, transire nequeamus, ipsi ita acerba, ut tabescat dolore, mihi mehercule molesta, quod et eum, quem semper dilexi, nimis excruciant, et timeo, tam vehemens vir tamque acer in ferro et tam insuetus contumeliae ne omni animi impetu dolori et iracundiae pareat.

Bibuli qui sit exitus futurus, nescio. Ut nunc res se habet, admirabili gloria est. Qui cum comitia in mensem Octobrem distulisset, quod solet ea res populi voluntatem offendere, putarat Caesar oratione sua posse impelli contionem, ut iret ad Bibulum; multa cum seditiosissime diceret, vocem exprimere non potuit. Quid quaeris? sentiunt se nullam ullius partis voluntatem tenere. Eo magis vis nobis est timenda.

Clodius inimicus est nobis. Pompeius confirmat eum nihil esse facturum contra me. Mihi periculosum est credere, ad resistendum me paro. Studia spero me summa habiturum omnium ordinum. Te cum ego desidero, tum vero res ad tempus illud vocat. Plurimum consilii, animi, praesidii denique mihi, si te ad tempus videro, accesserit. Varro mihi satis facit. Pompeius loquitur divinitus. Spero nos aut certe cum summa gloria aut etiam sine molestia discessuros. Tu quid agas, quem ad modum te oblectes, quid cum Sicyoniis egeris, ut sciam, cura.

---

[1] Archilochus was a Greek poet of Paros, who wrote scathing iambic verses.

it. The result is that now Bibulus' scathing [1] edicts against him are so popular, that one can't pass the place where they are posted up for the crowd of people reading them. Pompey finds them so distressing that he is wasting away with grief; and I myself am much annoyed with them, partly because they cause so much pain to a man whom I have always loved, and partly for fear that being so impulsive and ready to draw the sword, as well as so unused to abuse, he may give full reins to his indignation and wrath.

I don't know what will be the end of Bibulus. As things stand at present, his reputation is extraordinarily high. When he put off the elections till October, which generally annoys the populace, Caesar thought he could induce the people by a speech to attack Bibulus : but in spite of all his seditious talk, he could not force a word out of anybody. In short, they feel that they have lost the goodwill of all parties : and so violent action on their part is all the more to be feared.

Clodius is hostile to me. Pompey assures me he will do nothing against me : but I am afraid to trust him and am getting ready for resistance. I hope I shall have very strong support from all classes. For your presence I have a longing myself, and circumstances call for it to meet the crisis. If I see you in time I shall feel it a great accession to my policy, my courage, and my safety. Varro is very obliging; and Pompey talks like an angel. I hope that in the end I shall either be certain of a glorious victory or even escape unmolested. Let me know what you are doing, how you are enjoying yourself, and what has happened as regards the Sicyonians.

179

XXII

CICERO ATTICO SAL.

Scr. Romae post VIII K. Sext., ante XV K. Nov. a. 695

Quam vellem Romae! Mansisses profecto, si haec fore putassemus. Nam Pulchellum nostrum facillime teneremus aut certe, quid esset facturus, scire possemus. Nunc se res sic habet. Volitat, furit; nihil habet certi, multis denuntiat, quod fors obtulerit, id acturus videtur; cum videt, quo sit in odio status hic rerum, in eos, qui haec egerunt, impetum facturus videtur; cum autem rursus opes eorum et vim et exercitus recordatur, convertit se in bonos, nobis autem ipsis tum vim, tum iudicium minatur. Cum hoc Pompeius egit et, ut ad me ipse referebat (alium enim habeo neminem testem), vehementer egit, cum diceret in summa se perfidiae et sceleris infamia fore, si mihi periculum crearetur ab eo, quem ipse armasset, cum plebeium fieri passus esset. Fidem recepisse sibi et ipsum et Appium de me. Hanc si ille non servaret, ita laturum, ut omnes intellegerent nihil sibi antiquius amicitia nostra fuisse. Haec et in eam sententiam cum multa dixisset, aiebat illum primo sane diu multa contra, ad extremum

180

XXII

CICERO TO ATTICUS, GREETING.

How I wish you were in town! You would cer- *Rome,* tainly have stayed if we had thought this was going *between July* to happen. For then we could have easily kept that *25 and* little Beauty in order, or at any rate should have *Oct. 18,* B.C. known what he was going to do. As it is he flits *59* about in a frenzy and doesn't know what he is doing; he threatens lots of people, but will probably do whatever turns up. When he sees the general abhorrence of the present state of affairs he seems to meditate an attack on the authors of it; but when he remembers the armed force behind them he turns his wrath against the loyalists. As for me, he threatens me now with brute force, and now with a prosecution. Pompey spoke to him about it, and according to his own account—for he is the only witness I have —he remonstrated strongly with him, saying that he would become a byword for treachery and underhandedness if my life were threatened by one whose weapons he himself had forged by acquiescing in his transference to the plebs: that both he and Appius had pledged their word for me: and that, unless Clodius respected their promise, he would be so annoyed that he would make it plain to the world that he prized my friendship beyond everything. He declared that after he had said this and much more to the same effect, Clodius at first persisted in arguing the point at length, but finally gave way and

autem manus dedisse et adfirmasse nihil se contra eius
voluntatem esse facturum. Sed postea tamen ille
non destitit de nobis asperrime loqui. Quodsi non
faceret, tamen ei nihil crederemus atque omnia, sicut
facimus, pararemus.

Nunc ita nos gerimus, ut in dies singulos et studia
in nos hominum et opes nostrae augeantur; rem
publicam nulla ex parte attingimus, in causis atque
in illa opera nostra forensi summa industria versamur; quod egregie non modo iis, qui utuntur opera,
sed etiam in vulgus gratum esse sentimus. Domus
celebratur, occurritur, renovatur memoria consulatus,
studia significantur; in eam spem adducimur, ut
nobis ea contentio, quae impendet, interdum non
fugienda videatur.

Nunc mihi et consiliis opus est tuis et amore et
fide. Quare advola. Expedita mihi erunt omnia, si
te habebo. Multa per Varronem nostrum agi possunt, quae te urgente erunt firmiora, multa ab ipso
Publio elici, multa cognosci, quae tibi occulta esse non
poterunt, multa etiam—sed absurdum est singula
explicare, cum ego requiram te ad omnia. Unum
illud tibi persuadeas velim, omnia mihi fore explicata,
si te videro; sed totum est in eo, si ante, quam ille
ineat magistratum. Puto Pompeium Crasso urgente,
si tu aderis, qui per βοῶπιν ex ipso intellegere possis,
qua fide ab illis agatur, nos aut sine molestia aut certe

promised he would not do anything to offend him. Since then, however, he has not ceased to speak very unpleasantly about me : but, even if he did not, I should not believe him and should continue the preparations which I am making.

At the present time I am managing things so that my popularity and the strength of my position increases daily. Politics I am not touching at all, but am busily engaged in the law courts and in my other forensic work : and thereby I find I win extraordinary favour not only with those who enjoy my services, but with the people in general too. My house is thronged with folk ; processions meet me ; the days of my consulship are recalled ; friendships are not disguised : and my hopes are so raised that I often think there is no reason for me to shrink from the struggle which threatens.

What I want now is your advice and your affection and loyalty : so fly to me. It will simplify everything if I have you with me. Varro can render me many services, but they would be far surer if you were here to support them : a great deal of information can be extracted from Publius himself, and a great deal found out, which could not possibly be kept from your ears : besides a great deal more—but it is absurd to specify details when I want you for everything. The one point I want you to grasp is that the mere sight of you would simplify everything for me ; but it all depends on your coming before he enters on his office. I think that, though Crassus is egging on Pompey, if you were here and could find out from the enemy through Juno how far the great men are to be trusted I should either escape molestation altogether or at any rate I should no longer be

sine errore futuros. Precibus nostris et cohortatione
non indiges; quid mea voluntas, quid tempus, quid
rei magnitudo postulet, intellegis.

De re publica nihil habeo ad te scribere nisi summum odium omnium hominum in eos, qui tenent
omnia. Mutationis tamen spes nulla. Sed, quod
facile sentias, taedet ipsum Pompeium vehementer-
que paenitet. Non provideo satis, quem exitum
futurum putem; sed certe videntur haec aliquo eruptura.

Libros Alexandri, neglegentis hominis et non boni
poetae, sed tamen non inutilis, tibi remisi. Nume-
rium Numestium libenter accepi in amicitiam et
hominem gravem et prudentem et dignum tua com-
mendatione cognovi.

XXIII

CICERO ATTICO SAL.

Scr. Romae
ante XV K.
Nov. a. 695
Numquam ante arbitror te epistulam meam legisse
nisi mea manu scriptam. Ex eo colligere poteris,
quanta occupatione distinear. Nam, cum vacui temporis nihil haberem, et cum recreandae voculae causa
necesse esset mihi ambulare, haec dictavi ambulans.
Primum igitur illud te scire volo, Sampsiceramum,
nostrum amicum, vehementer sui status paenitere
restituique in eum locum cupere, ex quo decidit,
doloremque suum impertire nobis et medicinam interdum aperte quaerere, quam ego possum invenire
nullam; deinde omnes illius partis auctores ac socios
nullo adversario consenescere, consensionem univer-

in a fog. There is no need of prayers and exhortations between you and me: you know what I wish and what the gravity of the occasion demands.

I have no political news except that the present masters of the world have the world's hatred: and yet there is no hope of a change. But, as you can easily imagine, Pompey is disgusted and heartily sick of it all. I can't see what the end of it will be, but I am pretty sure there will be an explosion of some sort.

I have sent back the works of Alexander, who is a careless writer and not much of a poet: still there is some use in him. Numerius Numestius I have admitted to my friendship with pleasure and find he has plenty of sober good sense and is quite worthy of your recommendation.

XXIII

CICERO TO ATTICUS, GREETING.

I don't think you ever before read a letter of mine which I had not written myself. That will show you how I am plagued to death by business. As I haven't a moment to spare, and must take some exercise to refresh my poor voice, I am dictating this as I walk.

Rome, before Oct. 18, B.C. *59*

Well, the first thing I have to tell you is that our friend the Pasha is heartily sick of his position and wants to be restored to the place from which he fell. He confides his sorrows to me, and at times openly looks for a remedy; but for the life of me I cannot find any. Secondly, the whole of that party, both the principals and their followers, are losing their strength, though no one opposes them; and there

sorum nec voluntatis nec sermonis maiorem umquam fuisse.

Nos autem (nam id te scire cupere certo scio) publicis consiliis nullis intersumus totosque nos ad forensem operam laboremque contulimus. Ex quo, quod facile intellegi possit, in multa commemoratione earum rerum, quas gessimus, desiderioque versamur. Sed βοώπιδος nostrae consanguineus non mediocres terrores iacit atque denuntiat et Sampsiceramo negat, ceteris prae se fert et ostentat. Quam ob rem, si me amas tantum, quantum profecto amas, si dormis, expergiscere, si stas, ingredere, si ingrederis, curre, si curris, advola. Credibile non est, quantum ego in consiliis et prudentia tua, quodque maximum est, quantum in amore et fide ponam. Magnitudo rei longam orationem fortasse desiderat, coniunctio vero nostrorum animorum brevitate contenta est. Permagni nostra interest te, si comitiis non potueris, at declarato illo esse Romae. Cura, ut valeas.

XXIV

CICERO ATTICO SAL.

Scr. Romae ante XV K. Nov. a. 695

Quas Numestio litteras dedi, sic te iis evocabam, ut nihil acrius neque incitatius fieri posset. Ad illam celeritatem adde etiam, si quid potes. Ac ne sis perturbatus (novi enim te et non ignoro, " quam sit amor omnis sollicitus atque anxius ")—sed res est, ut

never was a greater unanimity of sentiment or of the popular expression of it than there is now.

As for me—for I am sure you want to hear about myself—I take no part in public deliberations and devote myself entirely to my law-court practice, which arouses, as you can easily conceive, many a memory of my past achievements and much regret for them. But our dear Juno's brother is venting most alarming threats and, though he denies them to the Pasha, he openly parades them to others. So, if your affection is as real as I know it is, wake up if you are sleeping, start moving if you are standing still, run if you are moving, and fly if you are running. I set greater store than you can possibly believe by your advice and your wisdom, and, what is still more, by your love and your loyalty. The importance of the theme would perhaps demand a long disquisition; but our hearts are so united that a word is enough. It is of the highest importance to me that you should be in Rome after the elections if you can't get here before them. Take care of yourself.

XXIV

CICERO TO ATTICUS, GREETING.

In the letter I gave to Numestius I made a most *Rome, before* urgent and pressing appeal to you to come. To the *Oct. 18,* speed I then enjoined add something if you possibly B.C. *59* can. And don't be alarmed (for I know you and don't forget that to love " It is to be all made of sighs and tears "[1]): the matter, I hope, is one that

---

[1] *quam . . . anxius* seems to be a quotation from some drama; and Jeans happily translates by this verse from Shakespeare's *As You Like It*.

spero, non tam exitu molesta quam aditu. Vettius ille, ille noster index, Caesari, ut perspicimus, pollicitus est sese curaturum, ut in aliquam suspicionem facinoris Curio filius adduceretur. Itaque insinuavit in familiaritatem adulescentis et cum eo, ut res indicat, saepe congressus rem in eum locum deduxit, ut diceret sibi certum esse cum suis servis in Pompeium impetum facere eumque occidere. Hoc Curio ad patrem detulit, ille ad Pompeium. Res delata ad senatum est. Introductus Vettius primo negabat se umquam cum Curione constitisse, neque id sane diu; nam statim fidem publicam postulavit. Reclamatum est. Tum exposuit manum fuisse iuventutis duce Curione, in qua Paulus initio fuisset et Q. Caepio hic Brutus et Lentulus, flaminis filius, conscio patre; postea C. Septimium, scribam Bibuli, pugionem sibi a Bibulo attulisse. Quod totum irrisum est, Vettio pugionem defuisse, nisi ei consul dedisset, eoque magis id eiectum est, quod a. d. III Idus Mai. Bibulus Pompeium fecerat certiorem, ut caveret insidias; in quo ei Pompeius gratias egerat.

Introductus Curio filius dixit ad ea, quae Vettius dixerat, maximeque in eo tum quidem Vettius est reprehensus, quod dixerat id fuisse adulescentium consilium, ut in foro gladiatoribus Gabini Pompeium adorirentur; in eo principem Paulum fuisse, quem constabat eo tempore in Macedonia fuisse. Fit sena-

will not be so troublesome at the end as at the beginning. That fellow Vettius, my famous informer, promised Caesar, so far as we can see, that he would get some criminal suspicion thrown on young Curio. So he wormed his way into intimacy with the young man, and after meeting him often, as events prove, he went so far as to declare that he was determined to make an attack on Pompey with the assistance of his slaves, and to slay him. Curio told his father of this, and he told Pompey. The affair was reported to the Senate. Vettius was summoned before them and at first denied that he had ever had an appointment with Curio. However, he did not stick to that tale long; but at once claimed the privilege of king's evidence. Amid cries of " no," he began to explain that there had been a confederacy of the younger men under the leadership of Curio, to which Paulus at first belonged and Q. Caepio, Brutus I mean, and Lentulus, the flamen's son, with his father's consent; and then that C. Septimius, Bibulus' secretary, had brought him a dagger from Bibulus. The idea of Vettius not having a dagger, unless the consul gave him one, and the rest of it, was too much for anybody's gravity : and the charge was scouted the more because Bibulus had warned Pompey on the 13th of May to be on his guard against plots; and Pompey had thanked him for the advice.

Young Curio was brought in and repelled Vettius' assertions : and the point for which Vettius was especially jumped on was saying that the young men's intention was to attack Pompey in the forum at the gladiatorial show which Gabinius gave, and that Paulus was to be the leader, when it was well known that he was in Macedonia at the time. The House

tus consultum, ut Vettius, quod confessus esset se cum
telo fuisse, in vincula coniceretur; qui emisisset, eum
contra rem publicam esse facturum. Res erat in ea
opinione, ut putarent id esse actum, ut Vettius in foro
cum pugione et item servi eius comprehenderentur
cum telis, deinde ille se diceret indicaturum. Idque
ita factum esset, nisi Cuirones rem ante ad Pompeium
detulissent. Tum senatus consultum in contione
recitatum est. Postero autem die Caesar, is qui olim,
praetor cum esset, Q. Catulum ex inferiore loco ius-
serat dicere, Vettium in rostra produxit eumque in
eo loco constituit, quo Bibulo consuli adspirare non
liceret. Hic ille omnia, quae voluit de re publica,
dixit, et qui illuc factus institutusque venisset, primum Caepionem de oratione sua sustulit, quem in
senatu acerrime nominarat, ut appareret noctem et
nocturnam deprecationem intercessisse. Deinde,
quos in senatu ne tenuissima quidem suspicione atti-
gerat, eos nominavit, L. Lucullum, a quo solitum
esse ad se mitti C. Fannium, illum qui in P. Clodium
subscripserat, L. Domitium, cuius domum constitu-
tam fuisse, unde eruptio fieret. Me non nominavit,
sed dixit consularem disertum vicinum consulis sibi
dixisse Ahalam Servilium aliquem aut Brutum opus
esse reperiri. Addidit ad extremum, cum iam di-
missa contione revocatus a Vatinio fuisset, se audisse
a Curione his de rebus conscium esse Pisonem, generum meum, et M. Laterensem.

Nunc reus erat apud Crassum Divitem Vettius de
vi et, cum esset damnatus, erat indicium postulaturus.

decreed that Vettius should be committed on his own confession of having carried a weapon; and that it should be high treason to release him. The view most generally held is that it was a put-up job: Vettius was to be discovered in the forum with a dagger and his slaves round him with weapons, and then he was to turn king's evidence: and it would have come off if the Curios had not reported the matter to Pompey. Then the senatorial decree was read aloud to an assembly. On the next day, however, Caesar, the man who as praetor some years ago had bidden Q. Catulus speak from the floor, brought Vettius out on the rostra and set him in a place which was beyond Bibulus' aspiration, though a consul. Here he said anything he liked about public affairs; and, as he had come ready primed and tutored, he omitted all mention of Caepio, though he had named him most emphatically in the House: so it was obvious that a night and a nocturnal appeal had intervened. Then he mentioned people on whom he had not cast the slightest suspicion in the House,—L. Lucullus, who, he said, generally used to send to him C. Fannius, the man who once supported a prosecution of P. Clodius, and L. Domitius, whose house was to be the basis of operations. My name he did not mention, but he said that an eloquent ex-consul, a neighbour of the consul, had remarked to him that we stood in need of a Servilius Ahala or a Brutus. He added at the end, when he had been called back by Vatinius after the assembly was dismissed, that he had heard from Curio that Piso, my son-in-law, was in the plot, and M. Laterensis too.

Now Vettius is on trial for violence before Crassus Dives, and when he is condemned he will claim to

Quod si impetrasset, iudicia fore videbantur. Ea nos, utpote qui nihil contemnere soleremus, non perti- mescebamus. Hominum quidem summa erga nos studia significabantur; sed prorsus vitae taedet; ita sunt omnia omnium miseriarum plenissima. Modo caedem timueramus quam oratio fortissimi senis, Q. Considi, discusserat: ea, ea, inquam, quam [1] cotidie timere potueramus, subito exorta est. Quid quaeris? nihil me infortunatius, nihil fortunatius est Catulo cum splendore vitae tum mortis tempore. Nos tamen in his miseriis erecto animo et minime perturbato sumus honestissimeque et dignitatem et auctoritatem nostram magna cura tuemur.

Pompeius de Clodio iubet nos esse sine cura et summam in nos benevolentiam omni oratione signi- ficat. Te habere consiliorum auctorem, sollicitudi- num socium, omni in cogitatione coniunctum cupio. Quare, ut Numestio mandavi, tecum ut ageret, item atque eo, si potest, acrius, te rogo, ut plane ad nos advoles. Respiraro, si te videro.

XXV

CICERO ATTICO SAL.

Scr. Romae ante K. Nov. a. 695

Cum aliquem apud te laudaro tuorum familiarium, volam illum scire ex te me id fecisse, ut nuper me scis scripsisse ad te de Varronis erga me officio, te ad me rescripsisse eam rem summae tibi voluptati esse. Sed ego mallem ad illum scripsisses mihi illum

---

[1] ea inquam M^1; eam quam M^2; ea, ea inquam, quam *Tyrrell.*

turn king's evidence. If he is successful there may very well be some prosecutions. Of that—though to be sure I never despise anything—I'm not much afraid. Everybody is showing me the greatest kindness; but I am sick of life; the whole world is so thoroughly out of joint. Just lately we were afraid of a massacre, but it was averted by a speech of that gallant old man Q. Considius: and now the disaster of which we had been in daily fear has suddenly happened. In fact, nothing could be more deplorable than my situation, nothing more enviable than that of Catulus, considering his glorious life and his timely end. However, I keep up my heart in spite of my miseries, and don't show the white feather, and, with an exercise of caution, I maintain my position and authority with honour.

Pompey tells me to have no fear of Clodius, and shows me the greatest goodwill whenever he speaks. I am longing to have you to advise my actions, to be the partner of my anxieties, to share my every thought. So I have commissioned Numestius to plead with you, and now add, if possible, even more urgent prayers of my own, that you literally fly to me. I shall breathe again when I see you.

XXV

CICERO TO ATTICUS, GREETING.

When I write to you praising any of your friends *Rome,* I wish you would let them know I have done so. *before Nov.* For example, I mentioned in a letter lately Varro's *1,* B.C. *59* kindness to me, and you answered that you were delighted to hear it. But I had much rather you had written to him saying he was doing all I wished

satis facere, non quo faceret, sed ut faceret; mirabiliter enim moratus est, sicut nosti, ἑλικτὰ καὶ οὐδέν—
Sed nos tenemus praeceptum illud τὰς τῶν κρατούντων—— At hercule alter tuus familiaris, Hortalus,
quam plena manu, quam ingenue, quam ornate nostras laudes in astra sustulit, cum de Flacci praetura
et de illo tempore Allobrogum diceret! Sic habeto,
nec amantius nec honorificentius nec copiosius potuisse dici. Ei te hoc scribere a me tibi esse missum
sane volo. Sed quid tu scribas? quem iam ego venire
atque adesse arbitror; ita enim egi tecum superioribus litteris. Valde te exspecto, valde desidero neque
ego magis, quam ipsa res et tempus poscit.

His de negotiis quid scribam ad te nisi idem quod
saepe? re publica nihil desperatius, iis, quorum opera,
nihil maiore odio. Nos, ut opinio et spes et coniectura nostra fert, firmissima benevolentia hominum
muniti sumus. Quare advola; aut expedies nos
omni molestia aut eris particeps. Ideo sum brevior,
quod, ut spero, coram brevi tempore conferre, quae
volumus, licebit. Cura, ut valeas.

—not that he was, but to make him do it. For, as you know, he is an odd creature, " all tortuous thoughts and no——" [1] But I hold to the maxim, "A great man's follies." [2] However, your other friend, Hortalus, most certainly lauded me to the skies in the most liberal, open-hearted, and elaborate manner when he was delivering a speech on Flaccus' praetorship and that incident of the Allobroges. You may take my word for it that he could not have expressed himself in more affectionate and laudatory terms, nor more fully. I should much like you to write and tell him that I sent you word of it. But I hope you won't have to write, and are now on your way and quite close after the appeals in my former letter. I am eagerly looking out for you, and in sore need of you: and circumstances and the times call for you as much as I do.

On these affairs I have nothing new to say: the country is in the most desperate position possible, and nothing could exceed the unpopularity of those who are responsible for it. I myself, as I think, hope, and imagine, am safeguarded by the staunchest support. So hasten your coming: you will either relieve all my cares or share them with me. If I am rather brief it is because I hope that I may soon be able to discuss anything I wish with you face to face. Take care of yourself.

---

[1] Euripides, And. 448 ἑλικτὰ κοὐδὲν ὑγιὲς ἀλλὰ πᾶν πέριξ φρονοῦντες: " Thinking tortuous thoughts, naught honest, but all roundabout."

[2] Euripides, Phoen. 393, τὰς τῶν κρατούντων ἀμαθίας φέρειν χρεών. " One needs must bear the follies of those in power."

M. TULLI CICERONIS
EPISTULARUM AD ATTICUM
LIBER TERTIUS

I

CICERO ATTICO SAL.

Scr. in itinere in. m. Apr. a. 696

Cum antea maxime nostra interesse arbitrabar te esse nobiscum, tum vero, ut legi rogationem, intellexi ad iter id, quod constitui, nihil mihi optatius cadere posse, quam ut tu me quam primum consequerere, ut, cum ex Italia profecti essemus, sive per Epirum iter esset faciendum, tuo tuorumque praesidio uteremur, sive aliud quid agendum esset, certum consilium de tua sententia capere possemus. Quam ob rem te oro, des operam, ut me statim consequare. Facilius potes, quoniam de provincia Macedonia perlata lex est. Pluribus verbis tecum agerem, nisi pro me apud te res ipsa loqueretur.

II

CICERO ATTICO SAL.

Scr. in itinere VI Id. Apr. a. 696

Itineris nostri causa fuit, quod non habebam locum, ubi pro meo iure diutius esse possem quam in fundo Siccae, praesertim nondum rogatione correcta, et simul intellegebam ex eo loco, si te haberem, posse me Brundisium referre, sine te autem non esse nobis illas partes tenendas propter Autronium. Nunc, ut ad te antea scripsi, si ad nos veneris, consilium totius rei capiemus. Iter esse molestum scio, sed tota calamitas omnes molestias habet. Plura scribere non possum; ita sum animo perculso et abiecto. Cura, ut valeas. Data VI Idus Apriles Narib. Luc.

CICERO'S LETTERS
TO ATTICUS
BOOK III

I

CICERO TO ATTICUS, GREETING.

I had been thinking that it would be of the greatest *On a* service to me to have you with me, but when I read *journey,* the bill [1] I saw at once that the most desirable thing in *Apr.,* B.C. view of the journey I have undertaken would be that *58* you should join me as soon as possible.   Then I should have the benefit of your own and your friends' protection if I passed through Epirus after leaving Italy; and if I chose any other course I could lay down fixed plans on your advice.   So please be quick and join me. You can the more easily do so, as the bill about the province of Macedonia has been passed. I would say more if facts themselves did not speak for me with you.

II

CICERO TO ATTICUS, GREETING.

The reason why I moved was that there was no- *On a* where where I could remain unmolested except on *journey,* Sicca's estate, especially as the bill has not been *Apr. 8,* emended.   Besides, I noticed that I could get back to B.C. *58* Brundisium from there if I had you with me.   Without you I could not stay in those districts on account of Autronius.   Now, as I said in my last letter, if you will come I can take your advice on the whole matter. I know the journey is an annoyance : but the whole of this miserable business is full of annoyances.   I can't write any more, I am so down-hearted and wretched. Take care of yourself.   April 8, Nares in Lucania.

[1] Clodius' bill interdicting from fire and water anyone who had put to death a Roman citizen uncondemned.

MARCUS TULLIUS CICERO

III

CICERO ATTICO SAL.

Scr. in itinere circ. Non. Apr. a. 696

Utinam illum diem videam, cum tibi agam gratias, quod me vivere coegisti! adhuc quidem valde me paenitet. Sed te oro, ut ad me Vibonem statim venias, quo ego multis de causis converti iter meum. Sed, eo si veneris, de toto itinere ac fuga mea consilium capere potero. Si id non feceris, mirabor; sed confido te esse facturum.

IV

CICERO ATTICO SAL.

Scr. in itinere inter Vibonem et Brundisium Id. Apr. a. 696

Miseriae nostrae potius velim quam inconstantiae tribuas, quod a Vibone, quo te arcessebamus, subito discessimus. Allata est enim nobis rogatio de pernicie mea; in qua quod correctum esse audieramus, erat eius modi, ut mihi ultra quadringenta milia liceret esse, illo pervenire non liceret. Statim iter Brundisium versus contuli ante diem rogationis, ne et Sicca, apud quem eram, periret, et quod Melitae esse non licebat. Nunc tu propera, ut nos consequare, si modo recipiemur. Adhuc invitamur benigne, sed, quod superest, timemus. Me, mi Pomponi, valde paenitet vivere; qua in re apud me tu plurimum valuisti. Sed haec coram. Fac modo, ut venias.

III

CICERO TO ATTICUS, GREETING.

Pray God that the day may come when I shall be *On a* able to thank you for compelling me to go on living. *journey,* At present I am heartily sorry for it. Please come *about* to me at once at Vibo. For several reasons I've made *Apr. 5,* my way thither. If you come I shall be able to lay *B.C. 58* plans for my whole journey in exile. If you do not I shall be surprised: but I trust you will.

IV

CICERO TO ATTICUS, GREETING.

Please attribute my sudden departure from Vibo *Between* after asking you to join me there to my misery rather *Vibo and* than to caprice. I received a copy of the bill for my *Brundisium* destruction, and found that the alteration of which I *Apr. 13,* had heard took the form of banishment beyond four *B.C. 58* hundred miles. Since I could not go where I wished, I went straight to Brundisium before the bill was passed, for fear of involving my host Sicca in my destruction and because I am not permitted to stay at Malta. Now make haste and join me if I can find anyone to take me in. At present I receive kind invitations: but I fear the future. I indeed, Pomponius, am heartily sick of life: and it is mainly for your sake that I consented to live. But of this when we meet. Please do come.

MARCUS TULLIUS CICERO

V

CICERO ATTICO SAL.

Scr. Thuriis
IIII Id.
Apr., ut vide-
tur, a. 696
Terentia tibi et saepe et maximas agit gratias. Id
est mihi gratissimum. Ego vivo miserrimus et maximo dolore conficior. Ad te quid scribam, nescio.
Si enim es Romae, iam me adsequi non potes, sin es
in via, cum eris me adsecutus, coram agemus, quae
erunt agenda. Tantum te oro, ut, quoniam me ipsum
semper amasti, ut nunc eodem amore sis; ego enim
idem sum. Inimici mei mea mihi, non me ipsum
ademerunt. Cura, ut valeas.

Data IIII Idus April. Thurii.

VI

CICERO ATTICO SAL.

Scr. in
Tarentino
XIV K.
Mai. a 696.
Non fuerat mihi dubium, quin te Tarenti aut
Brundisi visurus essem, idque ad multa pertinuit, in
eis, et ut in Epiro consisteremus et de reliquis rebus
tuo consilio uteremur. Quoniam id non contigit, erit
hoc quoque in magno numero nostrorum malorum.
Nobis iter est in Asiam, maxime Cyzicum. Meos tibi
commendo. Me vix misereque sustento.

Data XIIII K. Maias de Tarentino.

V

CICERO TO ATTICUS, GREETING.

Terentia continually expresses the deepest grati- *Thurii, Apr.* tude to you: and I am very glad of it. My life is *10* (?), B.C. one long misery, and I am crushed with the weight *58* of my sorrows. What to write I don't know. If you are in Rome you will be too late to catch me: but if you are already on the way we will discuss all that has to be discussed when you join me. One thing only I beg of you, since you have always loved me for myself, to preserve your affection for me. I am still the same. My enemies have robbed me of all I had; but they have not robbed me of myself. Take care of your health.

At Thurium, April 10.

VI

CICERO TO ATTICUS, GREETING.

I quite expected to see you at Tarentum or Brun- *Tarentum,* disium, and it was important that I should for many *Apr. 17,* reasons, among others for my stay in Epirus and for B.C. *58* the advantage of your advice in other matters. That it did not happen I shall count among my many other misfortunes. I am starting for Asia, for Cyzi- cus in particular. I entrust my dear ones to you. It is with difficulty that I prolong my miserable existence.

From the neighbourhood of Tarentum, April 17.

VII

CICERO ATTICO SAL.

Scr. Brundisi
pr. K. Mai.
a. 696

Brundisium veni a. d. XIIII Kal. Maias. Eo die pueri tui mihi a te litteras reddiderunt, et alii pueri post diem tertium eius diei alias litteras attulerunt. Quod me rogas et hortaris, ut apud te in Epiro sim, voluntas tua mihi valde grata est et minime nova. Esset consilium mihi quidem optatum, si liceret ibi omne tempus consumere; odi enim celebritatem, fugio homines, lucem aspicere vix possum, esset mihi ista solitudo, praesertim tam familiari in loco, non amara; sed, itineris causa ut deverterer, primum est devium, deinde ab Autronio et ceteris quadridui, deinde sine te. Nam castellum munitum habitanti mihi prodesset, transeunti non est necessarium. Quod si auderem, Athenas peterem. Sane ita cadebat, ut vellem. Nunc et nostri hostes ibi sunt, et te non habemus et veremur ne interpretentur illud quoque oppidum ab Italia non satis abesse, nec scribis quam ad diem te exspectemus.

Quod me ad vitam vocas, unum efficis, ut a me manus abstineam, alterum non potes, ut me non nostri consilii vitaeque paeniteat. Quid enim est, quod me retineat, praesertim si spes ea non est quae nos proficiscentes prosequebatur? Non faciam ut enumerem miserias omnes, in quas incidi per summam iniuriam et scelus non tam inimicorum meorum

VII

CICERO TO ATTICUS, GREETING.

I arrived at Brundisium on April the 17th, and on *Brundisium,* the same day your men delivered a letter from you. *Apr. 29,* B.C. The next day but one some others brought me 58 another letter. I am very grateful for your kind invitation to stay at your place in Epirus, though I expected it. It is a plan which would have just suited me if I could have stayed there all the time. I hate a crowd, I shun my fellow-men, I can hardly bear to look upon the light: so the solitude there, especially as I am so at home there, would have been far from unpleasant. But for stopping on the route it is too far out of the way: moreover, I should be only four days' march from Autronius and the rest; moreover you would not be there yourself. Yes, a fortified place would be useful to me if I were settling there, but it is unnecessary when I am merely passing. If I dared I should make for Athens; and things were turning out right for it: but now my enemies are there, you have not joined me, and I am afraid that town, too, may not be counted far enough away from Italy. Nor have you let me know when I may expect you.

Your pleas to me not to think of suicide have one result that I refrain from laying violent hands on myself; but you cannot make me cease to regret our decision and my existence. What is there for me to live for, especially if I have lost even that hope I had when I set out? I will forbear to mention all the miseries into which I have fallen through the villainous machinations not so much of my enemies as of

quam invidorum, ne et meum maerorem exagitem et
te in eundem luctum vocem; hoc adfirmo, neminem
umquam tanta calamitate esse adfectum, nemini
mortem magis optandam fuisse. Cuius oppetendae
tempus honestissimum praetermissum est; reliqua
tempora sunt non iam ad medicinam, sed ad finem
doloris.

De re publica video te colligere omnia quae putes
aliquam spem mihi posse adferre mutandarum rerum.
Quae quamquam exigua sunt, tamen, quoniam placet,
exspectemus. Tu nihilo minus, si properaris, nos
consequere; nam aut accedemus in Epirum aut tarde
per Candaviam ibimus. Dubitationem autem de
Epiro non inconstantia nostra adferebat, sed quod de
fratre, ubi eum visuri essemus, nesciebamus; quem
quidem ego nec quo modo visurus nec ut dimissurus
sim, scio. Id est maximum et miserrimum mearum
omnium miseriarum. Ego et saepius ad te et plura
scriberem, nisi mihi dolor meus cum omnes partes
mentis tum maxime huius generis facultatem ademis-
set. Videre te cupio. Cura ut valeas.

Data pr. Kal. Mai. Brundisii.

VIII

CICERO ATTICO SAL.

*Scr. Thessa-
lonicae IV
K. Iun. a.
696*

Brundisio[1] proficiscens scripseram ad te, quas ob
causas in Epirum non essemus profecti, quod et
Achaia prope esset plena audacissimorum inimicorum
et exitus difficiles haberet, cum inde proficisceremur.
Accessit, cum Dyrrachi essemus, ut duo nuntii ad-
ferrentur, unus classe fratrem Epheso Athenas, alter

---

[1] Brundisio *added by Graevius.*

those who envy me, for fear of arousing my grief again, and provoking you to share it by sympathy. But this I will say, that no one has ever suffered such a misfortune, and no one ever had more right to wish for death. But I have missed the time when I could have died with honour. At any other time death will only end my pain, not heal it.

I notice you collect everything which you think can raise any hopes in me of a change in affairs. That " everything " is very little: still, since you so decide, I will await the issue. Though you have not started, you will catch me yet, if you hurry. I shall either go to Epirus or proceed slowly through Candavia. My hesitation about Epirus does not arise from my changefulness, but from doubts as to where I shall see my brother. I don't know where I shall see him, nor how I shall tear myself from him. That is the chief and most pitiful of all my miseries. I would write to you oftener and fuller if grief had not robbed me of all my wits and especially of that particular faculty. I long to see you. Take care of yourself.

At Brundisium, April 29th.

VIII

CICERO TO ATTICUS, GREETING.

As I was setting out from Brundisium I wrote to you, explaining why I could not go to Epirus, because it is close to Achaia, which is full of my most virulent enemies, and it is a hard place to get out of when I want to start. My decision was confirmed by the receipt of two messages at Dyrrachium, one saying that my brother was coming by sea from Ephesus to

Thessalonica, May 29, B.C. 58

pedibus per Macedoniam venire. Itaque illi obviam
misimus Athenas, ut inde Thessalonicam veniret.
Ipsi processimus et Thessalonicam a. d. x Kal. Iunias
venimus, neque de illius itinere quicquam certi habebamus nisi eum ab Epheso ante aliquanto profectum.
Nunc, istic quid agatur, magno opere timeo; quamquam tu altera epistula scribis Idibus Maiis audire te
fore ut acrius postularetur, altera iam esse mitiora.
Sed haec est pridie data quam illa, quo conturber
magis. Itaque cum meus me maeror cotidianus lace-
rat et conficit, tum vero haec addita cura vix mihi
vitam reliquam facit. Sed et navigatio perdifficilis
fuit, et ille, incertus ubi ego essem, fortasse alium
cursum petivit. Nam Phaetho libertus eum non
vidit. Vento reiectus ab Ilio in Macedoniam Pellae
mihi praesto fuit. Reliqua quam mihi timenda sint
video, nec quid scribam habeo et omnia timeo, nec
tam miserum est quicquam, quod non in nostram
fortunam cadere videatur. Equidem adhuc miser in
maximis meis aerumnis et luctibus hoc metu adiecto
maneo Thessalonicae suspensus nec audeo quicquam.

Nunc ad ea, quae scripsisti. Tryphonem Caecilium
non vidi. Sermonem tuum et Pompei cognovi ex
tuis litteris. Motum in re publica non tantum ego
impendere video, quantum tu aut vides aut ad me
consolandum adfers. Tigrane enim neglecto sublata
sunt omnia. Varroni me iubes agere gratias.
Faciam; item Hypsaeo. Quod suades, ne longius

Athens, the other that he was coming by land through Macedonia. So I sent a note to catch him at Athens, asking him to come on to Thessalonica, and I myself set off and arrived at Thessalonica on the 23rd of May. The only certain news about him that I have had is that he started a short time ago from Ephesus. Now I am in great anxiety to know what is happening at Rome. It is true that in one letter dated May the 15th you say you have heard that Quintus will be rigorously called in question, and in another that things are calming down: but the latter is dated a day before the former, to increase my perplexity. So, what between my own personal grief, which racks and tortures me daily, and this additional anxiety, I have hardly any life left in me. But the passage was very bad, and perhaps, not knowing where I was, he took some other direction. My freedman Phaetho has seen nothing of him. Phaetho was driven back by wind from Ilium to Macedonia and came to me at Pella. I see how threatening the future is, though I have not the heart to write. I am afraid of everything: there is no misfortune that does not seem to fall to my lot. I am still staying in suspense at Thessalonica, with this new fear added to the woes and sorrows that oppress me; and I do not dare to make a move of any kind.

Now for the things you mention in your letter. Caecilius Trypho I have not seen. Of your talk with Pompey I have heard from your letter. I cannot see such signs of a political change as you either see or invent to comfort me: for if they take no notice of the Tigranes episode all hope is lost. You bid me pay my thanks to Varro. I will, and to Hypsaeus too. I think I will follow your advice not to go any

discedamus, dum acta mensis Maii ad nos perferantur, puto me ita esse facturum, sed, ubi, nondum statui; atque ita perturbato sum animo de Quinto, ut
nihil queam statuere, sed tamen statim te faciam
certiorem.

Ex epistularum mearum inconstantia puto te mentis meae motum videre, qui, etsi incredibili et singulari calamitate adflictus sum, tamen non tam est ex
miseria quam ex culpae nostrae recordatione commotus. Cuius enim scelere impulsi ac proditi simus,
iam profecto vides, atque utinam iam ante vidisses
neque totum animum tuum errori mecum simul de-
disses! Quare, cum me adflictum et confectum luctu
audies, existimato me stultitiae meae poenam ferre
gravius quam eventi, quod ei crediderim, quem esse
nefarium non putarim. Me et meorum malorum memoria et metus de fratre in scribendo impedit. Tu
ista omnia vide et guberna. Terentia tibi maximas
gratias agit. Litterarum exemplum, quas ad Pompeium scripsi, misi tibi.

Data iiii Kal. Iunias Thessalonicae.

IX

CICERO ATTICO SAL.

*Scr. Thessa-
lonicae Id.
Iun. a. 696*
Quintus frater cum ex Asia discessisset ante Kal.
Maias et Athenas venisset Idibus, valde fuit ei pro-
perandum, ne quid absens acciperet calamitatis, si
quis forte fuisset, qui contentus nostris malis non
esset. Itaque eum malui properare Romam quam
ad me venire et simul (dicam enim, quod verum, est,

208

farther away until I receive the parliamentary news for May. But where to stop I have not yet made up my mind; and I am so anxious about Quintus that I can't make up my mind to anything. But I will soon let you know.

From these rambling notes of mine, you can see the perturbed state of my wits. Yet, though I have been crushed by an incredible and unparalleled misfortune, it is not so much my misery as the remembrance of my own mistake that affects me. For now surely you see whose treachery egged me on and betrayed me. Would to heaven you had seen it before, and had not let a mistake dominate your mind as I did. So when you hear that I am crushed and overwhelmed with grief be assured that the sense of my folly in trusting one whose treachery I had not suspected is a heavier penalty than all the consequences. The thought of my misfortunes and my fears for my brother prevent me from writing. Keep your eye on events and your hand at the helm. Terentia expresses the deepest gratitude to you. I have sent you a copy of the letter I wrote to Pompey.

At Thessalonica, May 29th.

IX

CICERO TO ATTICUS, GREETING.

My brother Quintus left Asia at the end of April *Thessa-* and reached Athens on May the 15th: and he had *lonica, June* to hurry, for fear anything disastrous might happen *13, B.C. 58* in his absence, if there were anyone who was not yet contented with the measure of our woes. So I preferred him to hurry on to Rome rather than to come to me: and besides—I will confess the

ex quo magnitudinem miseriarum mearum perspicere possis) animum inducere non potui, ut aut illum amantissimum mei, mollissimo animo tanto in maerore aspicerem aut meas miserias luctu adflictus [1] et perditam fortunam illi offerrem aut ab illo aspici paterer. Atque etiam illud timebam, quod profecto accidisset, ne a me digredi non posset. Versabatur mihi tempus illud ante oculos, cum ille aut lictores dimitteret aut vi avelleretur ex complexu meo. Huius acerbitatis eventum altera acerbitate non videndi fratris vitavi. In hunc me casum vos vivendi auctores impulistis. Itaque mei peccati luo poenas. Quamquam me tuae litterae sustentant, ex quibus, quantum tu ipse speres, facile perspicio; quae quidem tamen aliquid habebant solacii, antequam eo venisti a Pompeio, " Nunc Hortensium allice et eius modi viros." Obsecro, mi Pomponi, nondum perspicis, quorum opera, quorum insidiis, quorum scelere perierimus? Sed tecum haec omnia coram agemus; tantum dico, quod scire te puto, nos non inimici, sed invidi perdiderunt. Nunc, si ita sunt, quae speras, sustinebimus nos et spe, qua iubes, nitemur; sin, ut mihi videntur, infirma sunt, quod optimo tempore facere non licuit, minus idoneo fiet.

Terentia tibi saepe agit gratias. Mihi etiam unum de malis in metu est, fratris miseri negotium; quod si sciam cuius modi sit, sciam, quid agendum mihi sit.

[1] adflictus *Reid*; adflictas *MSS*.

truth and it will show you the depth of my misery—
I could not bear in my great distress to look on one
so devoted to me and so tender-hearted, nor could I
thrust upon him the misery of my affliction and my
fallen fortune, or suffer him to see me. Besides I
was afraid of what would have been sure to happen
—that he would not be able to part from me. The
picture of the moment when he would have had to
dismiss his lictors or to be torn by force from my arms
was ever before me. The bitterness of parting I have
avoided by the bitterness of not seeing my brother.
That is the kind of dilemma into which you who are
responsible for my survival have forced me; and so
I have to pay the penalty for my mistake. Your
letter, however, cheers me, though I can easily see
from it how little hope you have yourself. Still it
offered some little consolation till you passed from
your mention of Pompey to the passage: " Now
try to win over Hortensius and such people." In
heaven's name, my dear Pomponius, have you not
yet grasped whose agency, whose villainy, and whose
treachery have ruined me? But that I will discuss when I meet you. Now I will only say, what
you must surely know, that it is not so much my
enemies as my enviers who have ruined me. If
there is any real foundation for your hopes I will
bear up and rely on the hope you suggest. But if,
as seems probable to me, your hopes are ill-founded,
then I will do now what you would not let me do
before, though the time is far less appropriate.

Terentia often expresses her gratitude to you.
The thing I most fear among all my misfortunes is
my poor brother's business: if I knew the exact state
of affairs I might know what to do about it. I am

Me etiam nunc istorum beneficiorum et litterarum
exspectatio, ut tibi placet, Thessalonicae tenet. Si
quid erit novi allatum, sciam, de reliquo quid agendum sit. Tu si, ut scribis, Kal. Iuniis Roma profectus es, prope diem nos videbis. Litteras, quas ad
Pompeium scripsi, tibi misi.

Data Id. Iun. Thessalonicae.

X

Scr. Thessa-
lonicae XIV
K. Quint. a.
696

Acta quae essent usque ad VIII Kal. Iunias, cognovi
ex tuis litteris; reliqua exspectabam, ut tibi placebat,
Thessalonicae. Quibus adlatis facilius statuere potero, ubi sim. Nam, si erit causa, si quid agetur, si
spem videro, aut ibidem opperiar aut me ad te
conferam; sin, ut tu scribis, ista evanuerint, aliquid
aliud videbimus. Omnino adhuc nihil mihi significa-
tis nisi discordiam istorum; quae tamen inter eos de
omnibus potius rebus est quam de me. Itaque, quid
ea mihi prosit, nescio, sed tamen, quoad me vos sperare vultis, vobis obtemperabo. Nam, quod me tam
saepe et tam vehementer obiurgas et animo infirmo
esse dicis, quaeso, ecquod tantum malum est, quod in
mea calamitate non sit? ecquis umquam tam ex amplo
statu, tam in bona causa, tantis facultatibus ingenii,
consilii, gratiae, tantis praesidiis bonorum omnium
concidit? Possum oblivisci, qui fuerim, non sentire,
qui sim, quo caream honore, qua gloria, quibus liberis,
quibus fortunis, quo fratre? Quem ego, ut novum
calamitatis genus attendas, cum pluris facerem quam

following your advice and still staying at Thessalonica in hope of the advantages you mention and of letters. When I get some news I shall be able to shape my course of action. If you started from Rome on the 1st of June, as you say, I shall very soon see you. I have sent you the letter I wrote to Pompey.

Thessalonica, June 13th.

X

CICERO TO ATTICUS, GREETING.

Your letter has posted me up in political news to May 25: and I am awaiting the course of events at Thessalonica, as you suggest. When I hear more I shall know where to be. For if there is any excuse, if anything is being done, if I see a ray of hope, I shall either wait here or pay you a visit: but if, as you say in your letter, those hopes have vanished into air I shall look for something else. At present you do not give me the least hint of anything except the disagreement of those friends of yours: and they are quarrelling about anything rather than me, so I do not see what good it will do me. But, as long as you wish me to hope, I will bow to your wishes. You frequently reproach me strongly for weak-heartedness: but I should like to know if I have been spared any hardship in my misfortune. Did anyone ever fall from such a high estate in such a good cause, especially when he was so well endowed with genius and good sense, so popular, and so strongly supported by all honest men? Can I forget what I was? Can I help feeling what I am? Can I help missing my honour and fame, my children, my fortune, and my brother? That is a fresh misfortune for you to con-

Thessa-
lonica, June
17, B.C. 58

213

me ipsum semperque fecissem, vitavi ne viderem, ne
aut illius luctum squaloremque aspicerem aut me,
quem ille florentissimum reliquerat, perditum illi
adflictumque offerrem. Mitto cetera intolerabilia;
etenim fleta impedior. Hic utrum tandem sum ac-
cusandus, quod doleo, an quod commisi, ut haec aut
non retinerem, quod facile fuisset, nisi intra parietes
meos de mea pernicie consilia inirentur, aut certe
vivus non amitterem?

Haec eo scripsi, ut potius relevares me, quod facis,
quam ut castigatione aut obiurgatione dignum putares, eoque ad te minus multa scribo, quod et
maerore impedior et, quod exspectem istinc, magis
habeo, quam quod ipse scribam. Quae si erunt
allata, faciam te consilii nostri certiorem. Tu, ut
adhuc fecisti, quam plurimis de rebus ad me velim
scribas, ut prorsus ne quid ignorem.

Data xiiii Kal. Quintiles Thessalonicae.

XI

CICERO ATTICO SAL.

Scr. Thessa-
lonicae IV
K. Quint. a.
696

Me et tuae litterae et quidam boni nuntii, non
optimis tamen auctoribus, et exspectatio vestrarum
litterarum, et quod tibi ita placuerat, adhuc Thessalonicae tenebat. Si accepero litteras, quas exspecto,
si spes erit ea, quae rumoribus adferebatur, ad te me
conferam; si non erit faciam te certiorem, quid

template. I have avoided seeing my brother, though I love him and always have loved him better than myself, for fear that I should see him in his grief and misery, or that I, from whom he had parted in the height of prosperity, should present myself to him in ruin and humiliation. Of other things too hard to bear, I will say nothing: my tears prevent me. And what pray is it that calls for reproof? My grief, or my sin in not retaining my position,—which would have been easy enough if there had not been a conspiracy for my ruin within my own walls,—or that I should not have lost it without losing life too?

My object in writing thus is to call for your ready sympathy, instead of seeming to deserve your reproaches and reproofs, and the reason why I write less than usual is partly that my sorrow prevents me, and partly that I have more reason to expect news from you than to write to you. When I get your news I will give you a clearer idea of my plans. Please continue to write fully about things as you have at present, that no detail may escape me.

Thessalonica, June 17th.

XI

CICERO TO ATTICUS, GREETING.

At present I am kept at Thessalonica by your letter and by some good news, which, however, has not the best authority. Besides, I am waiting for your note, and you expressed your desire that I should stay here. As soon as I receive the note I am waiting for, I will come to you, if the hope which has reached me by rumour is confirmed. If not, I will let you know my movements. Please continue to

Thessalonica, June 27, B.C. 58

egerim. Tu me, ut facis, opera, consilio, gratia iuva ;
consolari iam desine, obiurgare vero noli ; quod cum
facis, ut ego tuum amorem et dolorem desidero !
Quem ita adfectum mea aerumna esse arbitror, ut te
ipsum consolari nemo possit. Quintum fratrem optimum humanissimumque sustenta. Ad me obsecro
te ut omnia certa perscribas.

Data iiii Kal. Quintiles.

XII

CICERO ATTICO SAL.

Scr. Thessa-
lonicae XVI
Kal. Sext. a.
696

Tu quidem sedulo argumentaris, quid sit speran-
dum et maxime per senatum, idemque caput rogationis proponi scribis, quare in senatu dici nihil liceat.
Itaque siletur. Hic tu me accusas, quod me adfli-
ctem, cum ita sim adflictus ut nemo umquam, quod
tute intellegis. Spem ostendis secundum comitia.
Quae ista est eodem tribuno pl. et inimico consule
designato? Percussisti autem me etiam de oratione
prolata. Cui vulneri, ut scribis, medere, si quid
potes. Scripsi equidem olim ei iratus, quod ille prior
scripserat, sed ita compresseram, ut numquam ema-
naturam putarem. Quo modo exciderit, nescio.
Sed, quia numquam accidit, ut cum eo verbo uno
concertarem, et quia scripta mihi videtur neglegentius quam ceterae, puto posse probari non esse meam.

exert your energy, your wits, and your influence on my behalf. I don't ask for encouragement: but please don't find fault with me; for when you do that I feel as though I had lost your affection and your sympathy, though I am sure you take my misfortune so to heart, that you yourself are inconsolable. Lend a helping hand to Quintus, the best and kindest of brothers, and for mercy's sake let me have all the definite news there is.

June 27th.

XII

CICERO TO ATTICUS, GREETING.

You lay great stress on the hopes I may entertain, *Thessa-*especially of action on the part of the Senate; yet at *lonica, July* the same time you write that the clause forbidding *17,* B.C. *58* any mention of my case in the House is being posted up. So no one opens his mouth. Then you accuse me of distressing myself, though, as you know quite well, I have more reason for distress than ever mortal had. You hold out hopes to me on the results of the elections. What hope is there, if the same tribune is re-elected and a consul elect is my enemy? Your news too that my speech [1] has been published is a blow to me. Heal the wound, if possible, as you propose. In my indignation I paid him back in his own coin: but I had suppressed it so carefully that I thought it would never leak out. How it has, I can't imagine. But since it so happens that I have never said a word against him, and this appears to me to be more carelessly written than my other speeches, I should think it could be passed off as someone else's work. If you think my case is not hopeless,

[1] A speech against Curio, not extant.

Id, si putas me posse sanari, cures velim; sin plane perii, minus laboro.

Ego etiam nunc eodem in loco iaceo sine sermone ullo, sine cogitatione ulla. Licet tibi, ut scribis, significaram, ut ad me venires, dudum tamen [1] intellego te istic prodesse, hic ne verbo quidem levare me posse. Non queo plura scribere, nec est, quod scribam; vestra magis exspecto.

Data xvi Kal. Sextiles Thessalonicae.

XIII

CICERO ATTICO SAL.

Scr. Thessalonicae Non. Sext. a. 696

Quod ad te scripseram me in Epiro futurum, posteaquam extenuari spem nostram et evanescere vidi, mutavi consilium nec me Thessalonica commovi, ubi esse statueram, quoad aliquid ad me de eo scriberes, quod proximis litteris scripseras, fore uti secundum comitia aliquid de nobis in senatu ageretur; id tibi Pompeium dixisse. Qua de re, quoniam comitia habita sunt, tuque nihil ad me scribis, proinde habebo, ac si scripsisses nihil esse, meque temporis non longinqui spe ductum esse non [2] moleste feram. Quem autem motum te videre scripseras, qui nobis utilis fore videretur, eum nuntiant, qui veniunt, nullum fore. In tribunis pl. designatis reliqua spes est. Quam si exspectaro, non erit, quod putes me causae meae, voluntati meorum defuisse.

[1] dudum tamen *Koch*; si donatum ut *M*.
[2] non *added by Tyrrell*.

please give your attention to the matter; but if I am past praying for, then I don't much mind about it.

I am still lying dormant at the same place, and neither speak nor think. Though, as you say, I did suggest that you should come to me, I see now that you are useful to me where you are, while here you could not find even a word of comfort to lighten my sorrows. I cannot write more, nor have I anything to say. Therefore, I am all the more anxious for your news.

Thessalonica, July 17th.

XIII

CICERO TO ATTICUS, GREETING.

I changed my mind about the proposed journey to Epirus when I saw my hope growing less and less and finally vanishing, and have not moved from Thessalonica, where I proposed to stay till you should send me some news of what you mentioned on Pompey's authority in your last letter, that my case might come before the House after the elections. And so, now the elections are over and I get no news from you, I shall take that as equivalent to your writing and saying that nothing has come of it, nor shall I regret that the hope which buoyed me up has not lasted long. As for the movement that appeared to be in my favour, which you said you foresaw, new arrivals here assure me that it won't come off. The only hope left is in the tribunes elect : and if I wait till that is settled you will have no right to regard me as a traitor to my own cause and to my friends' wishes.

Thessalonica, Aug. 5, B.C. 58

MARCUS TULLIUS CICERO

Quod me saepe accusas, cur hunc meum casum
tam graviter feram, debes ignoscere, cum ita me adflictum videas, ut neminem umquam nec videris nec
audieris. Nam, quod scribis te audire me etiam mentis errore ex dolore adfici, mihi vero mens integra
est. Atque utinam tam in periculo fuisset! cum ego
iis, quibus meam salutem carissimam esse arbitrabar,
inimicissimis crudelissimisque usus sum; qui, ut me
paulum inclinari timore viderunt, sic impulerunt, ut
omni suo scelere et perfidia abuterentur ad exitium
meum. Nunc, quoniam est Cyzicum nobis eundum,
quo rarius ad me litterae perferentur, hoc velim diligentius omnia, quae putaris me scire opus esse, perscribas. Quintum fratrem meum fac diligas; quem
ego miser si incolumem relinquo, non me totum
perisse arbitror.

Data Nonis Sextilibus.

XIV

CICERO ATTICO SAL.

*Scr. Thessa-
lonicae XII
K. Sext. a.
696*
Ex tuis litteris plenus sum exspectatione de Pompeio, quidnam de nobis velit aut ostendat. Comitia
enim credo esse habita; quibus absolutis scribis illi
placuisse agi de nobis. Si tibi stultus esse videor,
qui sperem, facio tuo iussu, et scio te me iis epistulis
potius et meas spes solitum esse remorari. Nunc
velim mihi plane perscribas, quid videas. Scio nos
nostris multis peccatis in hanc aerumnam incidisse.
Ea si qui casus aliqua ex parte correxerit, minus
moleste feremus nos vixisse et adhuc vivere.

Instead of blaming me so often for taking my troubles so seriously, you ought to pardon me, as you see that my afflictions surpass all that you have ever seen or heard of. You say you have heard that my mind is becoming unhinged with grief: my mind is sound enough. Would that it had been as sound in the hour of danger, when I found those my cruelest enemies who I thought had my salvation most at heart. As soon as they saw I had lost my balance a little through fear, they used all their malice and treachery to thrust me to my doom. Now that I have to go to Cyzicus, where your letters will reach me less frequently, please be all the more careful to give me a thorough account of everything you think I ought to know. Be a good friend to my brother Quintus, for if I leave him unharmed by my fall I shall not regard myself as utterly overwhelmed.

August 5th.

XIV

CICERO TO ATTICUS, GREETING.

Your letter has filled me with hopes of Pompey's intentions or professed intentions as regards me. *Thessalonica, July 21, B.C. 58* For I think the elections have been held, and it is when they are over you say he has decided to have my affair brought forward. If you think me foolish for hoping, I only do what you bid me to do, and I know your letters generally are more inclined to restrain me and my hopes than to encourage them. Now please tell me plainly and fully what you see. I know it is through many faults of my own that I have fallen into this misery: and if fate mends my faults even partially, I shall be less disgusted both with my past and my present existence.

Ego propter viae celebritatem et cotidianam exspectationem rerum novarum non commovi me adhuc
Thessalonica. Sed iam extrudimur non a Plancio
(nam is quidem retinet), verum ab ipso loco minime
apposito ad tolerandam in tanto luctu calamitatem.
In Epirum ideo, ut scripseram, non ii, quod subito
mihi universi nuntii venerant et litterae, quare nihil
esset necesse quam proxime Italiam esse. Hinc, si
aliquid a comitiis audierimus, nos in Asiam converte-
mus; neque adhuc stabat quo potissimum, sed scies.
Data xii Sextiles Thessalonicae.

XV

CICERO ATTICO SAL.

*Scr. Thessa-
lonicae XIV
K. Sept. a.
696*

Accepi Idibus Sextilibus quattuor epistulas a te
missas, unam, qua me obiurgas et rogas, ut sim firmior, alteram, qua Crassi libertum ais tibi de mea sollicitudine macieque narrasse, tertiam, qua demonstras
acta in senatu, quartam de eo, quod a Varrone scribis
tibi esse confirmatum de voluntate Pompei. Ad primam tibi hoc scribo, me ita dolere, ut non modo a
mente non deserar, sed id ipsum doleam, me tam
firma mente ubi utar et quibuscum non habere.
Nam, si tu me uno non sine maerore cares, quid me
censes, qui et te et omnibus? et, si tu incolumis me
requiris, quo modo a me ipsam incolumitatem desiderari putas? Nolo commemorare, quibus rebus

The amount of traffic on the roads and the daily expectation of a change of government have prevented me from leaving Thessalonica at present. But now I am forced to quit, not by Plancius—who wants me to stop—but by the nature of the place, which is not at all suitable to help one to bear such distress and misfortune. I did not go to Epirus as I said I should, since all the news and all the letters that have reached me lately have shown me that there was no necessity to remain very near Italy. If I get any important news from the scene of the elections I shall betake myself to Asia when I leave here. Where exactly, is not yet fixed : but I will let you know.

Thessalonica, July 21st.

XV

CICERO TO ATTICUS, GREETING.

On August 13 I received four letters from you,— one in terms of reproof, urging me to firmness, another telling me of Crassus' freedman's account of my careworn appearance, a third relating the doings in the House, and a fourth containing Varro's confirmation of your opinion as to Pompey's wishes. My answer to the first is that though I am distressed, it has not unhinged my mind : nay, I am even distressed that, though my mind is so sound, I have neither place nor opportunity for using it. For, if you feel the loss of a single friend like myself, what do you suppose my feelings are, when I have lost you and everyone else ? And if you, on whom no ban of outlawry has fallen, miss my presence, you can imagine the aching void outlawry leaves in me. I will not mention all that I

Thessalonica, Aug. 17, B.C. *58*

sim spoliatus, non solum quia non ignoras, sed etiam
ne rescindam ipse dolorem meum; hoc confirmo,
neque tantis bonis esse privatum quemquam neque
in tantas miserias incidisse. Dies autem non modo
non levat luctum hunc, sed etiam auget. Nam ceteri
dolores mitigantur vetustate, hic non potest non et
sensu praesentis miseriae et recordatione praeteritae
vitae cotidie augeri. Desidero enim non mea solum
neque meos, sed me ipsum. Quid enim sum? Sed
non faciam, ut aut tuum animum angam querelis aut
meis vulneribus saepius manus adferam.

Nam, quod purgas eos, quos ego mihi scripsi invi-
disse, et in eis Catonem, ego vero tantum illum puto
ab isto scelere afuisse, ut maxime doleam plus apud
me simulationem aliorum quam istius fidem valuisse.
Ceteros quos purgas, debent mihi probati esse, tibi si
sunt. Sed haec sero agimus.

Crassi libertum nihil puto sincere locutum. In
senatu rem probe scribis actam. Sed quid Curio? an
illam orationem non legit? quae unde sit prolata, nescio. Sed Axius eiusdem diei scribens ad me acta
non ita laudat Curionem. At potest ille aliquid
praetermittere, tu, nisi quod erat, profecto non scripsisti. Varronis sermo facit exspectationem Caesaris.
Atque utinam ipse Varro incumbat in causam! quod
profecto cum sua sponte tum te instante faciet.

Ego, si me aliquando vestri et patriae compotem
fortuna fecerit, certe efficiam, ut maxime laetere
unus ex omnibus amicis, meaque officia et studia,
quae parum antea luxerunt (fatendum est enim), sic

have lost,—you know it well enough, and it would only open my wound again. But this I do assert that no one has ever lost so much and no one has ever fallen into such a depth of misery. Time too, instead of lightening my grief, can but add to it: for other sorrows lose their sting as time passes, but my sorrow can but grow daily, as I feel my present misery and think on my past happiness. I mourn the loss not only of my wealth and my friends but of my old self. For what am I now? But I will not wring your soul with my complaints nor keep fingering my sore.

You write in defence of those who, I said, envied me and among them Cato. Of him I have not the least suspicion: indeed, I am sorry that the false friendship of others had more weight with me than his loyalty. As to the others, I suppose I should acquit them if you do. But it is too late to matter now.

I don't think Crassus' freedman meant what he said. You say things went well in the House. But what about Curio? Hasn't he read that speech? Goodness knows how it got published. Axius, however, writing on the same day an account of the meeting, has less to say for Curio. Still he might well miss something, while you would certainly not have written what was not true. Varro's talk with you gives me hopes of Caesar. I only wish Varro himself would throw his weight into my cause; and I think he will with a little pressing from you, if not of his own accord.

If ever I have the fortune to see you and my country again I will not fail to give you more cause for joy at my recall than all my other friends: and, though I must confess that up to now my friendly attentions have not been as conspicuous as they

exsequar, ut me aeque tibi ac fratri et liberis nostris restitutum putes. Si quid in te peccavi ac potius quoniam peccavi, ignosce; in me enim ipsum peccavi vehementius. Neque haec eo scribo, quo te non meo casu maximo dolore esse adfectum sciam, sed profecto, si, quantum me amas et amasti, tantum amare deberes ac debuisses, numquam esses passus me, quo tu abundabas, egere consilio nec esses passus mihi persuaderi utile nobis esse legem de collegiis perferri. Sed tu tantum lacrimas praebuisti dolori meo, quod erat amoris, tamquam ipse ego; quod meritis meis perfectum potuit, ut dies et noctes, quid mihi faciendum esset, cogitares, id abs te meo, non tuo scelere praetermissum est. Quodsi non modo tu, sed quisquam fuisset, qui me Pompei minus liberali responso perterritum a turpissimo consilio revocaret, quod unus tu facere maxime potuisti, aut occubuissem honeste, aut victores hodie viveremus. Hic mihi ignosces; me enim ipsum multo magis accuso, deinde te quasi me alterum et simul meae culpae socium quaero. Ac, si restituor, etiam minus videbimur deliquisse abs teque certe, quoniam nullo nostro, tuo ipsius beneficio diligemur.

should have been, I will be so persistent with them that you shall feel that I have been restored to you quite as much as to my brother and children. If ever I have wronged you, or rather for the wrongs that I have done you, forgive me. I have wronged myself far more deeply. I do not write this in ignorance of your great grief at my misfortune, but because, if I had earned a right to all the affection you lavish and have lavished on me, you would never have suffered me to stand in need of that sound common sense of yours, and you would not have let me be persuaded that it was to my interest to let the bill about the guilds [1] be passed. But you, like myself, only gave your tears to my distress, as a tribute of affection: and it was my fault, not yours, that you did not devote day and night to pondering on the course I should take, as you might have done if my claims on you had been stronger. If you or anyone had dissuaded me from the disgraceful resolve I formed in my alarm at Pompey's ungenerous reply—and you were the person best qualified to do so—I should either have died with honour or should to-day be living in triumph. You will pardon what I have said. I am blaming myself far more than you, and you only as my second self, and because I want a companion in my guilt. If I am restored, our common guilt will seem far less, and you, at any rate, will hold me dear for services rendered, not received, by you.

[1] The *Collegia* were guilds for social, mercantile, or religious purposes. A decree had declared some of them illegal in 64 B.C.; but this was counteracted by a bill passed by Clodius in 58 B.C. The result was many new guilds were formed, which he used for political purposes.

MARCUS TULLIUS CICERO

Quod te cum Culleone scribis de privilegio locutum, est aliquid, sed multo est melius abrogari. Si
enim nemo impediet, sic est firmius; sin erit, qui
ferri non sinat, idem senatus consulto intercedet.
Nec quicquam aliud opus est abrogari; nam prior
lex nos nihil laedebat. Quam si, ut est promulgata,
laudare voluissemus, aut, ut erat neglegenda, negle-
gere, nocere omnino nobis non potuisset. Hic mihi
primum meum consilium defuit, sed etiam obfuit.
Caeci, caeci, inquam, fuimus in vestitu mutando, in
populo rogando, quod, nisi nominatim mecum agi
coeptum esset, fieri perniciosum fuit. Sed pergo
praeterita, verum tamen ob hanc causam, ut, si quid
agetur, legem illam, in qua popularia multa sunt, ne
tangatis. Verum est stultum me praecipere, quid
agatis aut quo modo. Utinam modo agatur aliquid!
In quo ipso multa occultant tuae litterae, credo, ne
vehementius desperatione perturber. Quid enim
vides agi posse aut quo modo? per senatumne? At
tute scripsisti ad me quoddam caput legis Clodium in
curiae poste fixisse, NE REFERRI NEVE DICI LICERET.
Quo modo igitur Domitius se dixit relaturum? quo
modo autem iis, quos tu scribis, et de re dicentibus
et, ut referretur, postulantibus Clodius tacuit? Ac,

You mention talking to Culleo about this bill being directed against an individual.[1] There is something in that point: but it is much better to have it repealed. If no one vetoes it, it is by far the surest course. If, on the other hand, anyone is opposed to it he will veto the Senate's decree too. There is no necessity to repeal anything else as well: the former law did not touch me. If we had had the sense to support it when it was brought forward, or to take no notice of it, which was all it deserved, it never would have done us any harm. It was then I first lost the use of my wits, or rather used them to my own destruction. It was blind, absolutely blind of us to put on mourning, to appeal to the crowd—a fatal thing to do before I was attacked personally. But I keep harping on what is over and done with. My point, however, is to urge you, when you do make a move, not to touch that law on account of its claims to popularity. But it is absurd of me to law down what you should do or how. If only something could be done! And on that very point I am afraid your letters keep back a good deal, to save me from giving way to even deeper despair. What course of action do you suppose can be taken and how? Through the Senate? But you yourself have told me that a clause of Clodius' bill, forbidding any motion or reference to my case, has been posted up in the House. How, then, does Domitius propose to make a motion? And how is it that Clodius holds his tongue, when the men you mention talk about the case and ask for a motion? And, if you think

[1] A *privilegium* was a law passed for or against some particular person, which was expressly forbidden by the Twelve Tables.

si per populum, poteritne nisi de omnium tribunorum
pl. sententia? Quid de bonis? quid de domo? poteritne restitui? aut, si non poterit, egomet quo
modo potero? Haec nisi vides expediri, quam in
spem me vocas? sin autem spei nihil est, quae est
mihi vita? Itaque exspecto Thessalonicae acta Kal.
Sext., ex quibus statuam, in tuosne agros confugiam,
ut neque videam homines, quos nolim, et te, ut
scribis, videam et propius sim, si quid agatur, id
quod intellexi cum tibi tum Quinto fratri placere,
an abeam Cyzicum.

Nunc, Pomponi, quoniam nihil impertisti tuae pru-
dentiae ad salutem meam, quod aut in me ipso satis
esse consilii decreras aut te nihil plus mihi debere,
quam ut praesto esses, quoniamque ego proditus,
inductus, coniectus in fraudem omnia mea praesidia
neglexi, totam Italiam mire erectam ad me defendendum destitui et reliqui, me, meos, mea tradidi
inimicis inspectante et tacente te, qui, si non plus
ingenio valebas quam ego, certe timebas minus, si
potes, erige adflictos et in eo nos iuva ; sin omnia sunt
obstructa, id ipsum fac ut sciamus et nos aliquando
aut obiurgare aut communiter consolari desine. Ego
si tuam fidem accusarem, non me potissimum tuis

of acting through the people, can it be managed without the consent of all the tribunes? What about my goods and chattels? What about my house? Will they be restored? If not, how can I be? If you don't see your way to managing that, what is it you want me to hope for? And if there is nothing to hope for, what sort of life can I lead? Under these circumstances I am awaiting the gazette for August the 1st at Thessalonica before I make up my mind whether to take refuge on your estate, where I can avoid seeing those I don't want to see, and see you, as you point out in your letter, and be nearer at hand if any action is being taken, or whether I shall go to Cyzicus. I believe you and Quintus want me to keep at hand.

Now, Pomponius, you used none of your wisdom in saving me from ruin—either because you thought I had enough common sense myself or because you thought you owed me nothing but the support of your presence : while I, basely betrayed and hurried to my ruin, threw down my arms and fled, deserting my country, though all Italy would have stood up and defended me with enthusiasm. You looked on in silence, while I betrayed myself, my family, and my possessions to my enemies, though, even if you had not more sense than I had, you certainly had less cause for panic. Now, if you can, raise me from my fall, and in that render me assistance. But if all ways are blocked let me know of the fact, and do not keep on either reproaching me or offering us [1] your sympathy. If I had any fault to find with your loyalty I should not trust myself to your house in

---

[1] *Communiter* must apparently = me and my family. Some, however, read *comiter*.

tectis crederem ; meam amentiam accuso, quod me a
te tantum amari, quantum ego vellem, putavi. Quod
si fuisset, fidem eandem, curam maiorem adhibuisses,
me certe ad exitium praecipitantem retinuisses, istos
labores, quos nunc in naufragiis nostris suscipis, non
subisses. Quare fac, ut omnia ad me perspecta et
explorata perscribas meque, ut facis, velis esse aliquem, quoniam, qui fui, et qui esse potui, iam esse
non possum, et ut his litteris non te, sed me ipsum
a me esse accusatum putes. Si qui erunt, quibus
putes opus esse meo nomine litteras dari, velim con-
scribas curesque dandas.

Data xiiii Kal. Sept.

XVI

CICERO ATTICO SAL.

Scr. Thessa-
lonicae XII
K. Sept. a.
696
Totum iter mihi incertum facit exspectatio litterarum vestrarum Kal. Sextil. datarum. Nam, si spes
erit, Epirum, si minus, Cyzicum aut aliud aliquid
sequemur. Tuae quidem litterae quo saepius a me
leguntur, hoc spem faciunt mihi minorem ; quae cum
laetae sunt, tum id, quod attulerunt ad spem, infirmant, ut facile appareat te et consolationi servire et
veritati. Itaque te rogo, plane ut ad me, quae scies,
ut erunt, quae putabis, ita scribas.

Data xii Kal.

preference to all others. It is my own folly in thinking that your affection for me was as great as I wished it to be that I am finding fault with. If it had been so you would not have shown more loyalty, but you would have taken more trouble, and you would certainly have prevented me from rushing to my fate, and would not have had all the trouble you are now taking to repair the shipwreck. So please let me know all that you can ascertain for certain, and continue to wish to see me a somebody again, even if I cannot regain the position I once held and might have held. I hope you won't think it is you and not myself I am blaming in this letter. If there is anyone to whom you think a letter ought to be sent in my name, please write one and see that it is sent.

August 17th.

XVI

CICERO TO ATTICUS, GREETING.

I am waiting for your letters of the first of August *Thessa-* before I can decide at all where I shall go. If there *lonica, Aug.* is any hope I shall go to Epirus: if not, I shall make *19,* B.C. *58* for Cyzicus, or take some other direction. The more often I read your letters, the less hope I have: for, though they are cheerful, they tone down any hope they raise, so that one can easily see that your allegiance wavers between consolation of me and truth. I must therefore beg you to report facts just as they are, and what you really think of them.

August 19th.

XVII

CICERO ATTICO SAL.

Scr. Thessa-
lonicae
pr. Non.
Sept. a. 696

De Quinto fratre nuntii nobis tristes nec varii venerant ex ante diem III Non. Iun. usque ad prid. Kal.
Sept. Eo autem die Livineius, L. Reguli libertus,
ad me a Regulo missus venit. Is omnino mentionem
nullam factam esse nuntiavit, sed fuisse tamen sermonem de C. Clodi filio, isque mihi a Q. fratre litteras
attulit. Sed postridie Sesti pueri venerunt, qui a te
litteras attulerunt non tam exploratas a timore, quam
sermo Livinei fuerat. Sane sum in meo infinito
maerore sollicitus et eo magis, quod Appi quaestio est.

Cetera, quae ad me eisdem litteris scribis de nostra
spe, intellego esse languidiora, quam alii ostendunt.
Ego autem, quoniam non longe ab eo tempore absu-
mus, in quo res diiudicabitur, aut ad te conferam me
aut etiam nunc circum haec loca commorabor.

Scribit ad me frater omnia sua per te unum susti-
neri. Quid te aut horter, quod facis, aut agam
gratias, quod non exspectas? Tantum velim fortuna
det nobis potestatem, ut incolumes amore nostro per-
fruamur. Tuas litteras semper maxime exspecto; in
quibus cave vereare ne aut diligentia tua mihi molesta
aut veritas acerba sit.

Data pr. Nonas Sept.

XVII

CICERO TO ATTICUS, GREETING.

All the news I have had about my brother Quintus *Thessa-* from June the 3rd to the end of August has been *lonica, Sept.* bad news without exception. But on the last of *4*, B.C. *58* August Livineius, who had been sent by his former master, L. Regulus, came to me. He assured me that no notice whatever had been given of a prosecution, though there was some talk of C. Clodius' son under-taking one : and he brought me letters from Quintus himself. But on the next day came some of Sestius' men, with some letters of yours which are not so positive and alarming as Livineius' conversation was. My own unending distress, of course, renders me anxious, all the more so, as Appius would preside at the trial.

From the rest of your remarks in the same letter as to my own chances, I infer that our hopes are fainter than others make out. But since it will not be long now before the matter is settled, I will either remove to your house or still stay somewhere round here.

My brother writes that you alone are his support. I need not urge you to efforts, which you make of your own accord, nor will I offer my thanks, since you do not expect them. I only hope fate may allow us to enjoy our affection in safety. I am always looking eagerly for your letters : and please don't be afraid either of boring me with your minuteness or paining me by telling the truth.

September 4th.

XVIII

CICERO ATTICO SAL.

Scr. Thessa-
lonicae
medio m.
Sept. a. 696
Exspectationem nobis non parvam attuleras, cum scripseras Varronem tibi pro amicitia confirmasse causam nostram Pompeium certe suscepturum et, simul a Caesare ei litterae, quas exspectaret, remissae essent, actorem etiam daturum. Utrum id nihil fuit, an adversatae sunt Caesaris litterae, an est aliquid in spe? Etiam illud scripseras eundem " secundum comitia " dixisse.

Fac, si vides, quantis in malis iaceam, et si putas esse humanitatis tuae, me fac de tota causa nostra certiorem. Nam Quintus frater, homo mirus, qui me tam valde amat, omnia mittit spei plena metuens, credo, defectionem animi mei; tuae autem litterae sunt variae; neque enim me desperare vis nec temere sperare. Fac, obsecro te, ut omnia quae perspici a te possunt, sciamus.

XIX

CICERO ATTICO SAL.

Scr. Thessa-
lonicae XVI
K. Oct. a.
696
Quoad eius modi mihi litterae a vobis adferebantur, ut aliquid ex iis esset exspectandum, spe et cupiditate Thessalonicae retentus sum; posteaquam omnis actio huius anni confecta nobis videbatur, in Asiam ire nolui, quod et celebritas mihi odio est, et, si fieret aliquid a novis magistratibus, abesse longe nolebam. Itaque in Epirum ad te statui me conferre, non quo

XVIII

CICERO TO ATTICUS, GREETING.

You raised my hopes considerably by writing that *Thessa-* Varro had assured you as a friend that Pompey was *lonica, Sept.,* going to take up my case, and that he would appoint B.C. *58* an agent as soon as he had received a letter which he was expecting from Caesar. Did it come to nothing? Or was Caesar's letter hostile? Or is there still room for hope? You mentioned too that he used the words " after the elections."

Please do let me have full information as to the state of my case,—you know the anxiety I am in and how kind it would be of you. For my brother, a dear good fellow and very fond of me, sends me nothing but hopeful news, for fear, I suppose, that I should entirely lose heart. Whereas your letters vary in tone; for your intention is neither to cast me into despondency nor to raise rash hopes in me. Pray do let me know everything you may succeed in discovering.

XIX

CICERO TO ATTICUS, GREETING.

So long as your letters afforded me any ground for *Thessalo-* it, my hopes and my longings kept me at Thessalo- *nica, Sept.* nica: but, as soon as I saw that all political business *15,* B.C. *58* for this year had come to an end, I made up my mind not to go to Asia, because I cannot put up with society and I do not want to be far away in case the new magistrates should make a move. So I deter- mined to go to your house in Epirus, not that the

mea interesset loci natura, qui lucem omnino fugerem,
sed et ad salutem lubentissime ex tuo portu proficiscar, et, si ea praecisa erit, nusquam facilius hanc
miserrimam vitam vel sustentabo vel, quod multo
est melius, abiecero. Ero cum paucis, multitudinem
dimittam.

Me tuae litterae numquam in tantam spem addu-
xerunt quantam aliorum; ac tamen mea spes etiam
tenuior semper fuit quam tuae litterae. Sed tamen,
quoniam coeptum est agi, quoquo modo coeptum est
et quacumque de causa, non deseram neque optumi
atque unici fratris miseras ac luctuosas preces, nec
Sesti ceterorumque promissa, nec spem aerumnosis-
simae mulieris Terentiae, nec miserrimae mulieris
Tulliolae obsecrationem et fideles litteras tuas. Mihi
Epirus aut iter ad salutem dabit, aut quod scripsi
supra.

Te oro et obsecro, T. Pomponi, si me omnibus
amplissimis, carissimis iucundissimisque rebus perfidia
hominum spoliatum, si me a meis consiliariis proditum
et proiectum vides, si intellegis me coactum, ut ipse
me et meos perderem, ut me tua misericordia iuves
et Quintum fratrem, qui potest esse salvus, sustentes,
Terentiam liberosque meos tueare, me, si putas te
istic visurum, exspectes, si minus, invisas, si potes,
mihique ex agro tuo tantum adsignes, quantum meo
corpore occupari potest, et pueros ad me cum litteris
quam primum et quam saepissime mittas.

Data XVI Kal. Octobres.

features of the place make any difference to me now that I shun the light of day entirely, but I should like to sail back to freedom from a port of yours, and if that hope is cut off I could not find a better place either to drag on my miserable existence or, what is preferable, to end it. I shall have few people about me, and shall get free from society.

Your letters never aroused my hopes as much as other people's : and yet my hopes were always fainter than your letters. However, since some kind of a move has been made in the matter, whatever kind it may be and whatsoever its cause, I will not disappoint either my dear and only brother's sad and touching entreaties, or the promises of Sestius and others, or the appeals of my wife in her deep affliction and my little Tullia in her misery, or your own true-hearted letters. Epirus shall be my road back to freedom or to what I mentioned before.

I beg and beseech you, Pomponius, as you see how I have been robbed of my honours and of my dearest and fondest possessions by men's treachery, as you see how I was betrayed and cast aside by those on whose advice I relied, as you know how I was forced into betraying myself and my family, of your pity help me, and support my brother Quintus, who is not past salvation : guard Terentia and my children; as for me, wait for me in Rome if you think there is any chance of seeing me there. If not, come to see me, if you can, and allot me of your land enough for my body to rest in; and send a man with letters as soon and as often as possible.

September 15th.

XX

CICERO S. D. Q. CAECILIO Q. F. POMPONIANO ATTICO,

Scr. Thessalonicae IV Non. Oct. a. 696 quod quidem ita esse et avunculum tuum functum esse officio vehementissime probo, gaudere me tum dicam, si mihi hoc verbo licebit uti. Me miserum! quam omnia essent ex sententia, si nobis animus, si consilium, si fides eorum, quibus credidimus, non defuisset! Quae colligere nolo, ne augeam maerorem; sed tibi venire in mentem certo scio, quae vita esset nostra, quae suavitas, quae dignitas. Ad quae recuperanda, per fortunas! incumbe, ut facis, diemque natalem reditus mei cura ut in tuis aedibus amoenissimis agam tecum et cum meis. Ego huic spei et exspectationi, quae nobis proponitur maxima, tamen volui praestolari apud te in Epiro, sed ita ad me scribitur, ut putem esse commodius non eisdem in locis esse.

De domo et Curionis oratione, ut scribis, ita est. In universa salute, si ea modo nobis restituetur, inerunt omnia; ex quibus nihil malo quam domum. Sed tibi nihil mando nominatim, totum me tuo amori fideique commendo.

Quod te in tanta hereditate ab omni occupatione expedisti, valde mihi gratum est. Quod facultates

XX

MY DEAR QUINTUS CAECILIUS POMPONIANUS ATTICUS, SON
OF QUINTUS,

that this name is now yours and that your uncle *Thessalo-* has done his duty by you meets with my heartiest *nica, Oct. 4,* approval; I will reserve the phrase " I am glad " for B.C. *58* a time when circumstances may permit of my using the word. Poor devil that I am! Everything would be going as right as possible with me if my own courage and judgement and the loyalty of those in whom I trusted had not failed me. But I will not piece my misfortunes together, for fear of increasing my misery. I am sure you must recollect my former life and its charm and dignity. In the name of good luck and bad, do not let the efforts you are making to recover my position relax; and let me celebrate the birthday of my return in your delightful house with you and my family. Though my hopes and expectations of return have been roused to the highest pitch, I still thought of awaiting their fulfilment at your house in Epirus: but from letters I infer it would be more convenient for me not to be in the same neighbourhood.

You are quite right about my house and Curio's speech. If only restoration is promised in general terms, everything else is comprised in that word: and of all things I am most anxious about my house. But I won't enter into details: I trust myself entirely to your affection and loyalty.

That you have freed yourself from all embarrassments in taking over your large inheritance is exceedingly pleasant news to me; and I fully realize

tuas ad meam salutem polliceris, ut omnibus rebus a
te praeter ceteros iuver, id quantum sit praesidium,
video intellegoque te multas partes meae salutis et
suscipere et posse sustinere, neque, ut ita facias,
rogandum esse. Quod me vetas quicquam suspicari
accidisse ad animum tuum, quod secus a me erga te
commissum aut praetermissum videretur, geram tibi
morem et liberabor ista cura, tibi tamen eo plus
debebo, quo tua in me humanitas fuerit excelsior
quam in te mea. Velim, quid videas, quid intellegas,
quid agatur, ad me scribas tuosque omnes ad nostram
salutem adhortere.

Rogatio Sesti neque dignitatis satis habet nec
cautionis. Nam et nominatim ferri oportet et de
bonis diligentius scribi, et id animadvertas velim.

Data iiii Nonas Octobres Thessalonicae.

XXI

CICERO ATTICO SAL.

*Scr. Thessa-
lonicae V K.
Nov. a. 696*
Triginta dies erant ipsi, cum has dabam litteras,
per quos nullas a vobis acceperam. Mihi autem erat
in animo iam, ut antea ad te scripsi, ire in Epirum
et ibi omnem casum potissimum exspectare. Te oro,
ut, si quid erit, quod perspicias quamcumque in partem, quam planissime ad me scribas et meo nomine,
ut scribis, litteras, quibus putabis opus esse, ut des.

Data v Kal. Novembres.

what an assistance to me is your promise to devote all your resources to my restoration, that I need not call on anyone else for help. I know too that you are taking on your shoulders several men's burdens on my behalf, and that you are quite capable of bearing them, and will not require asking to do so. You forbid me to imagine that it has ever entered your head that I have done what I ought not or left undone what I ought to have done in my dealings with you—well, I will humour you and free my heart from that anxiety, but I shall count myself still deeper in your debt, because your kindness to me has far exceeded mine to you. Please send me news of everything you see or gather and of all that is being done; and urge all your friends to support my return.

Sestius' bill does not pay sufficient regard to dignity or caution. The proposal should mention me by name, and contain a carefully worded clause about my property. Please pay attention to that point.

Thessalonica, October 4th.

XXI

CICERO TO ATTICUS, GREETING.

It is just thirty days from the date of this letter since I had any news from you. My intentions are, as I have said before, to go to Epirus, and to await my fate there rather than anywhere else. I must beg you to inform me quite openly of anything you notice, whether for good or for bad, and, as you suggest, to send letters in my name to everyone to whom you think it necessary. *Thessalonica, Oct. 28, B.C. 58*

October 28th.

XXII

CICERO ATTICO SAL.

Scr. partim Thessalonicae, partim Dyrrachi VI K. Dec. a. 696

Etsi diligenter ad me Quintus frater et Piso, quae essent acta, scripserant, tamen vellem tua te occupatio non impedisset, quo minus, ut consuesti, ad me, quid ageretur, et quid intellegeres, perscriberes. Me adhuc Plancius liberalitate sua retinet iam aliquotiens conatum ire in Epirum. Spes homini est iniecta non eadem quae mihi, posse nos una decedere; quam rem sibi magno honori sperat fore. Sed iam, cum adventare milites dicentur, faciendum nobis erit, ut ab eo discedamus. Quod cum faciemus, ad te statim mittemus, ut scias, ubi simus. Lentulus suo in nos officio, quod et re et promissis et litteris declarat, spem nobis non nullam adfert Pompei voluntatis; saepe enim tu ad me scripsisti eum totum esse in illius potestate. De Metello scripsit ad me frater quantum speraret profectum esse per te. Mi Pomponi, pugna, ut tecum et cum meis mihi liceat vivere, et scribe ad me omnia. Premor luctu, desiderio cum omnium rerum tum meorum, qui mihi me cariores semper fuerunt. Cura, ut valeas.

Ego quod, per Thessaliam si irem in Epirum, perdiu nihil eram auditurus, et quod mei studiosos habeo Dyrrachinos, ad eos perrexi, cum illa superiora Thessalonicae scripsissem. Inde cum ad te me convertam, faciam, ut scias, tuque ad me velim omnia quam diligentissime, cuicuimodi sunt, scribas. Ego iam aut rem aut ne spem quidem exspecto.

Data vi Kal. Decembr. Dyrrachi.

XXII

CICERO TO ATTICUS, GREETING.

Though my brother Quintus and Piso have sent me careful accounts of what has been done, I am sorry you were too busy to write your usual full description of events and of your surmises. Plancius' kindness keeps me here still, though I have several times tried to go to Epirus. He is inspired with a hope, which I do not share, that we may return together: which he hopes would redound to his honour. But now, as soon as news arrives of the approach of the soldiers, I shall have to make an effort to leave him. When I do, I will send word to you at once and let you know where I am. The courtesy which Lentulus shows in his actions, his promises, and his letters gives me some hope of Pompey's goodwill: for you have often mentioned that he would do anything for him. With Metellus, my brother tells me, you have had as much success as he hoped. My dear Pomponius, fight hard for me to be allowed to live with you and with my family; and send me all the news. I am bowed down with grief through my longing for all my dear ones, who have always been dearer to me than myself. Take care of yourself.

Knowing that I should be a very long time without any news if I went to Epirus through Thessaly, and that the people of Dyrrachium were warm friends of mine, I have come to them, after writing the first part of this letter at Thessalonica. As soon as I leave here and go to your house, I will let you know; and please write me every detail of whatsoever kind. Now I look either for the fulfilment of my hopes or for blank despair.

Dyrrachium, November 25th.

Partly at Thessalonica, partly at Dyrrachium, Nov. 25, B.C. 58

MARCUS TULLIUS CICERO

XXIII

CICERO ATTICO SAL.

Scr.
Dyrrachi
pr. K. Dec.
a. 696

A. d. v Kal. Decembr. tres epistulas a te accepi, unam datam a. d. viii Kal. Novembres, in qua me hortaris, ut forti animo mensem Ianuarium exspectem, eaque, quae ad spem putas pertinere de Lentuli studio, de Metelli voluntate, de tota Pompei ratione, perscribis. In altera epistula praeter consuetudinem tuam diem non adscribis, sed satis significas tempus; lege enim ab octo tribunis pl. promulgata scribis te eas litteras eo ipso die dedisse, id est a. d. iiii Kal. Novembres, et, quid putes utilitatis eam promulgationem attulisse, perscribis. In quo si iam nostra salus cum hac lege desperata erit, velim pro tuo in me amore hanc inanem meam diligentiam miserabilem potius quam ineptam putes, sin est aliquid spei, des operam, ut maiore diligentia posthac a nostris magistratibus defendamur. Nam ea veterum tribunorum pl. rogatio tria capita habuit, unum de reditu meo scriptum incaute; nihil enim restituitur praeter civitatem et ordinem, quod mihi pro meo casu satis est; sed, quae cavenda fuerint et quo modo, te non fugit. Alterum caput est tralaticium de impunitate, SI QVID CONTRA ALIAS LEGES EIVS LEGIS ERGO FACTVM SIT.

Tertium caput, mi Pomponi, quo consilio et a quo sit inculcatum, vide. Scis enim Clodium sanxisse, ut vix aut ut omnino non posset nec per senatum nec per populum infirmari sua lex. Sed vides numquam

XXIII

On the 26th of November I received three letters *Dyrrachium,* from you. In one of them, posted on the 25th of *Nov. 29,* B.C. October, you exhort me to keep up my courage and *58* wait for January, and you give a full list of all the hopeful signs, Lentulus' zeal for my cause, Metellus' goodwill, and Pompey's policy. One of the others is undated, which is unlike you; but you give a clear clue to the time, for you say you were writing it on the very day that the bill was published by the eight tribunes, that is to say the 29th of October : and you state the advantages you think have resulted from the publication of the law. If my restoration and this law together are long past praying for, I hope your affection will make you regard the trouble I am taking about it with pity rather than amusement. But if there is still some hope, please see to it that our new magistrates set up a more careful case. For the old tribunes' bill had three sections, and the one about my return was carelessly worded ; it does not provide for the restitution of anything but my citizenship and my position. In my fallen fortunes that is enough for me, but you cannot fail to see what ought to have been stipulated and how. The second clause is the usual form of indemnity : " If in virtue of this law there be any breach of other laws," etc.

But it is the third clause, Pomponius, to which I would call your attention. What is its object, and who put it in ? You know that Clodius had so provided that it was almost, if not quite, impossible for either the Senate or the people to annul his law ;

esse observatas sanctiones earum legum, quae abro-
garentur. Nam, si id esset, nulla fere abrogari posset;
neque enim ulla est, quae non ipsa se saepiat difficul-
tate abrogationis. Sed, cum lex abrogatur, illud ipsum abrogatur, quo modo eam abrogari oporteat.
Hoc cum et re vera ita sit, et cum semper ita habitum
observatumque sit, octo nostri tribuni pl. caput
posuerunt hoc: SI QVID IN HAC ROGATIONE SCRIPTVM
EST, QVOD PER LEGES PLEBISVE SCITA, hoc est quod per
legem Clodiam, PROMVLGARE, ABROGARE, DEROGARE,
OBROGARE SINE FRAVDE SVA NON LICEAT, NON LICVERIT,
QVODVE EI, QVI PROMVLGAVIT, ABROGAVIT, DEROGAVIT,
OBROGAVIT, OB EAM REM POENAE MVLTAEVE SIT, E. H. L.
N. R. Atque hoc in illis tribunis pl. non laedebat;
lege enim collegii sui non tenebantur. Quo maior
est suspicio malitiae alicuius, cum id, quod ad ipsos
nihil pertinebat, erat autem contra me, scripserunt,
ut novi tribuni pl., si essent timidiores, multo magis
sibi eo capite utendum putarent. Neque id a Clodio
praetermissum est; dixit enim in contione a. d. III
Nonas Novembres hoc capite designatis tribunis pl.
praescriptum esse, quid liceret. Tamen in lege nulla
esse eius modi caput te non fallit, quod si opus esset,
omnes in abrogando uterentur. Ut Ninnium aut
ceteros fugerit, investiges velim, et quis attulerit, et
quare octo tribuni pl. ad senatum de me referre non
dubitarint, scilicet[1] quod observandum illud caput non

---

[1] scilicet *Lallemand;* sive *MSS.*

but, you see, the imprecations [1] attached to laws which are repealed are never regarded, otherwise hardly any law ever would be repealed; for there never is a law which did not hedge itself in with obstacles against its repeal. But when a law is repealed the provisions against repeal are repealed likewise. Though this is the case, and always has been in theory and in practice, our eight tribunes have thought fit to insert a clause: " If there be anything contained in this bill, which by law or popular decree," that is by Clodius' law, " cannot now or hereafter be brought forward, whether by way of proposal, repeal, amendment, or modification, without penalty, or without involving the author of the proposal or amendment in a penalty or fine, no such proposal is made in this law." And yet these tribunes did not run any risks; as a law made by one of their own body was not binding on them. That increases my suspicion that there is some trickery about it, as they have inserted a clause which does not apply to themselves, but is against my interest; and as a result the new tribunes, if they should happen to be rather timid, would suppose that clause still more indispensable. Nor did Clodius overlook the point: for in the meeting on November the third he said that this clause defined the powers of the tribunes elect. Yet you know quite well that no such clause is ever inserted in a law: and if it were necessary everybody would use it when repealing a law. Please try to find out how this clause escaped the notice of Ninnius and the rest, also who inserted it, and why the eight tribunes, after showing no hesitation about bringing my case before the House—which proves they did not think

[1] Against anyone who should seek to repeal the law.

putabant, eidem in abrogando tam cauti fuerint, ut
id metuerent, soluti cum essent, quod ne iis quidem,
qui lege tenentur, est curandum. Id caput sane
nolim novos tribunos pl. ferre; sed perferant modo
quidlubet; uno capite, quo revocabor, modo res con-
ficiatur, ero contentus. Iam dudum pudet tam multa
scribere; vereor enim, ne re iam desperata legas, ut
haec mea diligentia miserabilis tibi, aliis irridenda
videatur. Sed, si est aliquid in spe, vide legem, quam
T. Fadio scripsit Visellius. Ea mihi perplacet; nam
Sesti nostri, quam tu tibi probari scribis, mihi non
placet.

Tertia est epistula pridie Idus Novembr. data, in
qua exponis prudenter et diligenter, quae sint, quae
rem distinere videantur, de Crasso, de Pompeio, de
ceteris. Quare oro te, ut, si qua spes erit posse studiis bonorum, auctoritate, multitudine comparata rem
confici, des operam, ut uno impetu perfringantur, in
eam rem incumbas ceterosque excites. Sin, ut ego
perspicio cum tua coniectura tum etiam mea, spei
nihil est, oro obtestorque te, ut Quintum fratrem
ames, quem ego miserum misere perdidi, neve quid
eum patiare gravius consulere de se, quam expediat
sororis tuae filio, meum Ciceronem, cui nihil misello
relinquo praeter invidiam et ignominiam nominis
mei, tueare, quoad poteris, Terentiam, unam omnium

that section need be taken seriously—yet when it came to repealing the law, became so cautious that they feared a rule, which even those who are bound by the law do not regard, though they themselves were not bound by it. That clause I would rather the new tribunes did not propose; but do let them pass something—anything. I shall be quite contented with a single clause of recall, if only the matter can be settled. For some time past I have been ashamed of writing such long letters. For by the time you read this I am afraid that there may be no hope left, and that all my trouble may serve only to make you pity and others laugh. But, if there is any hope left, look at the bill which Visellius has drawn up for Fadius: it takes my fancy very much, whereas our friend Sestius' proposal, which you say has your approval, does not please me at all.

The third letter is dated November the 12th, and in it you go through the reasons which you think are causing delay in my case, thoughtfully and carefully, mentioning Crassus, Pompey, and the rest. Now if there is the least chance of getting the matter settled by the good offices and authority of the conservatives and by getting a large mass of supporters, for heaven's sake try to break the barrier down at a rush: devote yourself to it and incite others to join. But if, as I infer from your guesses as well as mine, there is no hope left, then I beg and pray you to cherish my poor brother Quintus, whom I have involved in my own ruin, and not to let him pursue any rash course which would endanger your sister's son. Watch over my poor little boy, to whom I leave nothing but the hatred and the disgrace of my name, so far as you can, and support Terentia with your kindness in her

aerumnosissimam, sustentes tuis officiis. Ego in Epirum proficiscar, cum primorum dierum nuntios excepero. Tu ad me velim proximis litteris, ut se initia dederint, perscribas.

Data pridie Kal. Decembr.

XXIV

CICERO ATTICO SAL.

Scr. Dyrra-chi IV Id. Dec. a. 696

Antea, cum ad me scripsissetis vestro consensu consulum provincias ornatas esse, etsi verebar, quorsum id casurum esset, tamen sperabam vos aliquid aliquando vidisse prudentius; postea quam mihi et dictum est et scriptum vehementer consilium vestrum reprehendi, sum graviter commotus, quod illa ipsa spes exigua, quae erat, videretur esse sublata. Nam, si tribuni pl. nobis suscensent, quae potest spes esse? Ac videntur iure suscensere, cum et expertes consilii fuerint ei, qui causam nostram susceperant, et nostra concessione omnem vim sui iuris amiserint, praesertim cum ita dicant, se nostra causa voluisse suam potestatem esse de consulibus ornandis, non ut eos impedirent, sed ut ad nostram causam adiungerent; nunc, si consules a nobis alieniores esse velint, posse id libere facere; sin velint nostra causa, nihil posse se invitis. Nam, quod scribis, ni ita vobis placuisset,

unparalleled misfortune. I shall start for Epirus as soon as I have news about the first few days of the new tribunate. Please let me know in your next letter how the beginning has turned out.

November 29th.

XXIV

CICERO TO ATTICUS, GREETING.

When you wrote to me some time ago that the estimates for the consular provinces [1] were passed with your consent, I hoped you saw some good reason or other for that course, though I was afraid of the result: but now that I have been told by word of mouth and by letter that your policy was severely criticized, I am much disturbed at seeing the faint hope I had apparently taken from me. For if the tribunes are annoyed with us, what hope is left? And they seem to me to have every reason for annoyance, when they were left out of the plan, though they had espoused my cause, and by our concession they have lost all use of their just right, especially as they assert that it was for my sake they wished to exercise their powers in fitting out the consuls, with a view not to oppose them but to attach them to my cause. But now if the consuls choose to stand aloof from me they are perfectly free to do so, while if they take my part they can do nothing against the tribunes' will. As for your writing that if you had

Dyrrachium, Dec. 10, B.C. 58

---

[1] *Ornare consules* or *provincias* is the phrase used of the arrangement of the number of troops, the staff, and the amount of money to be granted to each consul, when going he went to his province. It generally took place after they came into office; but for some reason it had been arranged earlier on this occasion.

illos hoc idem per populum adsecuturos fuisse, invitis
tribunis pl. fieri nullo modo potuit. Ita vereor ne et
studia tribunorum amiserimus et, si studia maneant,
vinclum illud adiungendorum consulum amissum sit.

Accedit aliud non parvum incommodum, quod gravis illa opinio, ut quidem ad nos perferebatur, senatum nihil decernere, antequam de nobis actum esset,
amissa est, praesertim in ea causa, quae non modo
necessaria non fuit, sed etiam inusitata ac nova (neque enim umquam arbitror ornatas esse provincias
designatorum), ut, cum in hoc illa constantia, quae
erat mea causa suscepta, imminuta sit, nihil iam possit non decerni. Iis, ad quos relatum est, amicis
placuisse non mirum est; erat enim difficile reperire,
qui contra tanta commoda duorum consulum palam
sententiam diceret. Fuit omnino difficile non obse-
qui vel amicissimo homini, Lentulo, vel Metello, qui
simultatem humanissime deponeret; sed vereor, ne
hos tamen tenere potuerimus, tribunos pl. amiserimus. Haec res quem ad modum ceciderit, et tota res
quo loco sit, velim ad me scribas et ita, ut instituisti.
Nam ista veritas, etiamsi iucunda non est, mihi tamen
grata est.

Data iiii Id. Decembr.

not assented they would have got their way all the same through the people, that could never have happened if the tribunes opposed it. So I am afraid that I have lost the tribunes' favour, and that, if it is still retained, the bond which should have united the consuls with them has been lost.

There is another considerable disadvantage too. There was a strong opinion, or so at least it was reported to me, that the Senate would not pass any measure until my case was settled. That is now lost, and in a case where there was no necessity whatever; indeed, the proceeding was unusual and unprecedented. For I do not think the estimates for the provinces were ever passed before the consuls entered on their office. The result is that, now that the firm resolution formed in favour of my case has been broken for this one occasion, there is no reason why any decree should not be passed. I don't wonder that those friends to whom the question was referred agreed to it: it would, of course, have been difficult to find anyone who would openly oppose a measure so favourable to the two consuls. It would have been very difficult, too, not to oblige so good a friend as Lentulus, or Metellus, considering his kindness in laying aside his quarrel with me. But I am afraid that, while we could have retained their friendship in any case, we have thrown away that of the tribunes. Please write and tell me what the result has been, and how my whole case stands, as freely as you have before. For, however unpleasant the truth may be, I am grateful for it.

December 10th.

MARCUS TULLIUS CICERO

XXV

CICERO ATTICO SAL.

Scr. Dyrrachi m. Dec. a. 696, post IV Id., ante II K. Ian.

Post tuum a me discessum litterae mihi Roma allatae sunt, ex quibus perspicio nobis in hac calamitate tabescendum esse. Neque enim (sed bonam in partem accipies), si ulla spes salutis nostrae subesset, tu pro tuo amore in me hoc tempore discessisses. Sed, ne ingrati aut ne omnia velle nobiscum una interire videamur, hoc omitto; illud abs te peto des operam, id quod mihi adfirmasti, ut te ante Kalendas Ianuarias ubicumque erimus, sistas.

XXVI

CICERO ATTICO SAL.

Scr. Dyrrachi m. Ianuario a. 697

Litterae mihi a Quinto fratre cum senatus consulto, quod de me est factum, allatae sunt. Mihi in animo est legum lationem exspectare, et, si obtrectabitur, utar auctoritate senatus et potius vita quam patria carebo. Tu, quaeso, festina ad nos venire.

XXVII

CICERO ATTICO SAL.

Scr. Dyrrachi ex. m. Ian. a. 697

Ex tuis litteris et ex re ipsa nos funditus perisse video. Te oro, ut, quibus in rebus tui mei indigebunt, nostris miseriis ne desis. Ego te, ut scribis, cito videbo.

XXV

CICERO TO ATTICUS, GREETING.

After your departure from me I received a letter *Dyrrachium,* from Rome, from which I can see that I shall have *between Dec.* to waste away in my present misery. For (you must *10 and 29,* take it in good part) if there had been any hopes of B.C. *58* my salvation, I am sure your affection would not have permitted you to go away at such a time. But about that I will say no more, lest I appear ungrateful and seem to want to involve the whole world in my ruin. One thing I do beg of you; keep your promise to present yourself, wherever I am, before the New Year.

XXVI

CICERO TO ATTICUS, GREETING.

A letter from my brother Quintus has come, con- *Dyrrachium,* taining the decree which the Senate passed about *Jan.,* B.C. *57* me. I am thinking of waiting till the bill is brought forward; and then if it meets with opposition I will avail myself of the Senate's expressed opinion, pre- ferring to be deprived of my life rather than of my native land. Please make haste and come to me.

XXVII

CICERO TO ATTICUS, GREETING.

Your letter shows me that I am ruined beyond *Dyrrachium,* redemption; the facts speak for themselves. I im- *Jan.,* B.C. *57* plore you to stand by us in our misfortune, and not to let my family want for your assistance in anything. As you say, I myself shall see you soon.

257

M. TULLI CICERONIS
EPISTULARUM AD ATTICUM
LIBER QUARTUS

I

CICERO ATTICO SAL.

Scr. Romae
med. m. Sept.
a. 697

Cum primum Romam veni, fuitque cui recte ad te litteras darem, nihil prius faciendum mihi putavi, quam ut tibi absenti de reditu nostro gratularer. Cognoram enim, ut vere scribam, te in consiliis mihi dandis nec fortiorem nec prudentiorem quam me ipsum nec etiam pro praeterita mea in te observantia[1] nimium in custodia salutis meae diligentem, eundemque te, qui primis temporibus erroris nostri aut potius furoris particeps et falsi timoris socius fuisses, acerbissime discidium nostrum tulisse, plurimumque operae, studii, diligentiae, laboris ad conficiendum reditum meum contulisse. Itaque hoc tibi vere adfirmo, in maxima laetitia et exoptatissima gratulatione unum ad cumulandum gaudium conspectum aut potius complexum mihi tuum defuisse. Quem semel nactus si umquam dimisero ac nisi etiam praetermissos fructus tuae suavitatis praeteriti temporis omnes exegero, profecto hac restitutione fortunae me ipse non satis dignum iudicabo.

Nos adhuc, in nostro statu quod difficillime recuperari posse arbitrati sumus, splendorem nostrum illum forensem et in senatu auctoritatem et apud viros bonos gratiam, magis, quam optamus, consecuti sumus; in re autem familiari, quae quem ad modum

---

[1] propter (*or* propterea) meam in te observantiam. *MSS.* *Corrected by Bosius.*

CICERO'S LETTERS
TO ATTICUS
BOOK IV

I

CICERO TO ATTICUS, GREETING.

As soon as I reached Rome and there was anyone Rome, Sept., to whom I could safely entrust a letter to you, my B.C. 57 first thought was to write and thank you for my return, since you are not here to receive my thanks. For I grasped, to tell you the truth, that though in the advice you gave me you showed yourself no wiser and no braver than myself, and indeed, considering my past attentions to you, you were none too energetic in defence of my honour, still, though at first you shared my mistake or rather my madness and my unnecessary fright, it was you who took my exile most to heart and contributed most energy, zeal, and perseverance in bringing about my return. And so I can assure you that in the midst of great rejoicing and the most gratifying congratulations, one thing was lacking to fill the cup of my happiness, the sight of your or rather your embrace. When once I have obtained that, I shall certainly think myself undeserving of this renewal of good fortune, if ever I let you go again, and if I do not exact to the full all arrears in the enjoyment of your pleasant society.

As regards my political position, I have attained what I thought would be the hardest thing to recover —my distinction at the Bar, my authority in the House, and more popularity with the sound party than I desire. But you know how my private property has been crippled, dissipated, plundered. I

fracta, dissipata, direpta sit, non ignoras, valde laboramus tuarumque non tam facultatum, quas ego nostras
esse iudico, quam consiliorum ad colligendas et con-
stituendas reliquias nostras indigemus.

Nunc, etsi omnia aut scripta esse a tuis arbitror
aut etiam nuntiis ac rumore perlata, tamen ea scribam
brevi, quae te puto potissimum ex meis litteris velle
cognoscere. Pr. Nonas Sextiles Dyrrachio sum profectus ipso illo die, quo lex est lata de nobis. Brundisium veni Nonis Sextilibus. Ibi mihi Tulliola mea
fuit praesto, natali suo ipso die, qui casu idem natalis
erat et Brundisinae coloniae et tuae vicinae Salutis;
quae res animadversa a multitudine summa Brundisi-
norum gratulatione celebrata est. Ante diem vi Idus
Sextiles cognovi, cum Brundisi essem, litteris Quinti
mirifico studio omnium aetatum atque ordinum, incredibili concursu Italiae legem comitiis centuriatis esse
perlatam. Inde a Brundisinis honestissimis ornatus,
iter ita feci, ut undique ad me cum gratulatione legati
convenerint. Ad urbem ita veni, ut nemo ullius
ordinis homo nomenclatori notus fuerit, qui mihi
obviam non venerit, praeter eos inimicos, quibus id
ipsum, se inimicos esse, non liceret aut dissimulare
aut negare. Cum venissem ad portam Capenam,
gradus templorum ab infima plebe completi erant. A
qua plausu maximo cum esset mihi gratulatio signi-
ficata, similis et frequentia et plausus me usque ad
Capitolium celebravit, in foroque et in ipso Capitolio
miranda multitudo fuit.

am in great difficulties with it and stand in need not so much of your means, which I know I can look upon as my own, as of your advice to gather the fragments together and arrange matters.

Now, though I suppose you have had all the news from your family or from messengers and rumours, I will give you a short account of everything I think you would rather learn from my letters. On the 4th of August, the very day the law about me was proposed, I started from Dyrrachium, and arrived at Brundisium on the 5th. There my little Tullia was waiting for me, on her own birthday, which, as it happened, was the commemoration day of Brundisium and of the temple of Safety near your house too. The coincidence was noticed and the people of Brundisium held great celebrations. On the 8th of August, while I was still at Brundisium, I heard from Quintus that the law had been passed in the Comitia Centuriata with extraordinary enthusiasm of all ages and ranks in Italy who had flocked to Rome in thousands. Then I started on my journey amid the rejoicings of all the loyal folk of Brundisium, and was met everywhere by deputations offering congratulations. When I came near the city there was not a soul of any class known to my attendant [1] who did not come to meet me, except those enemies who could neither hide nor deny their enmity. When I reached the Capenan Gate the steps of the temples were thronged with the populace. Their joy was exhibited in loud applause : a similar crowd accompanied me with like applause to the Capitol, and in the Forum and on the very Capitol there was an extraordinary gathering.

[1] A *nomenclator* attended canvassers and others to tell them the names of persons they met.

MARCUS TULLIUS CICERO

Postridie in senatu, qui fuit dies Nonarum Septembr., senatui gratias egimus. Eo biduo cum esset annonae summa caritas, et homines ad theatrum primo, deinde ad senatum concurrissent, impulsu Clodi mea opera frumenti inopiam esse clamarent, cum per eos dies senatus de annona haberetur, et ad eius procurationem sermone non solum plebis, verum etiam bonorum Pompeius vocaretur, idque ipse cuperet, multitudoque a me nominatim, ut id decernerem, postularet, feci et accurate sententiam dixi. Cum abessent consulares, quod tuto se negarent posse sententiam dicere, praeter Messallam et Afranium, factum est senatus consultum in meam sententiam, ut cum Pompeio ageretur, ut eam rem susciperet, lexque ferretur. Quo senatus consulto recitato cum more hoc insulso et novo populus[1] plausum meo nomine recitando dedisset, habui contionem. Omnes magistratus praesentes praeter unum praetorem et duos tribunos pl. dederunt. Postridie senatus frequens et omnes consulares nihil Pompeio postulanti negarunt. Ille legatos quindecim cum postularet, me principem nominavit et ad omnia me alterum se fore dixit. Legem consules conscripserunt, qua Pompeio per quinquennium omnis potestas rei frumentariae toto orbe terrarum daretur, alteram Messius, qui omnis pecuniae dat potestatem et adiungit classem et exercitum et maius imperium in provinciis, quam sit eorum, qui eas obtineant. Illa nostra lex consularis nunc modesta videtur, haec

---

[1] populus *added by Boot.*

Next day, on the 5th of September, I returned thanks to the Senate [1] in the House. On those two days bread was very dear and crowds ran first to the theatre and then to the House, crying out at Clodius' instigation that the dearth of corn was my fault. On the same days there were meetings of the House about the corn supply, and Pompey was called upon by poor and rich alike to take the matter in hand. He was more than willing; and the people asked me by name to propose it: so I delivered my opinion carefully. As the ex-consuls, except Messalla and Afranius, were absent, thinking it was not safe to record a vote, a decree was passed in accordance with my proposal that Pompey should be appealed to take the matter in hand and a law should be passed. When this bill was read out the people received the mention of my name with applause after the new silly fashion: and I delivered an harangue, with the permission of all the magistrates present, except one praetor and two tribunes. On the next day there was a full House and all the ex-consuls were willing to grant Pompey anything. He asked for a committee of fifteen, naming me at the head of them and saying that I should count as his second self in everything. The consuls drew up a law giving Pompey the direction of the whole corn supply in the world for five years: Messius another granting him the control of the treasury, and adding an army and a fleet and higher powers than those of the local officials in the provinces. The law we ex-consuls proposed is regarded now as quite moderate, this

[1] This the *Oratio cum senatui gratias egit,* and a few lines lower down he refers to another extant speech, the *Oratio cum populo gratias egit.*

Messi non ferenda. Pompeius illam velle se dicit,
familiares hanc. Consulares duce Favonio fremunt;
nos tacemus et eo magis, quod de domo nostra nihil
adhuc pontifices responderunt. Qui si sustulerint
religionem, aream praeclaram habebimus; superficiem consules ex senatus consulto aestimabunt;
sin aliter, demolientur, suo nomine locabunt, rem
totam aestimabunt.

Ita sunt res nostrae,

" Ut in secundis fluxae, ut in advorsis bonae."

In re familiari valde sumus, ut scis, perturbati. Praeterea sunt quaedam domestica, quae litteris non com-
mitto. Quintum fratrem insigni pietate, virtute, fide
praeditum sic amo, ut debeo. Te exspecto et oro, ut
matures venire eoque animo venias, ut me tuo consilio
egere non sinas. Alterius vitae quoddam initium
ordimur. Iam quidam, qui nos absentes defenderunt,
incipiunt praesentibus occulte irasci, aperte invidere.
Vehementer te requirimus.

II

CICERO ATTICO SAL.

*Scr. Romae
in. m. Oct. a.
697*
Si forte rarius tibi a me quam a ceteris litterae
redduntur, peto a te, ut id non modo neglegentiae
meae, sed ne occupationi quidem tribuas; quae etsi

264

of Messius as perfectly intolerable. Pompey says he prefers the former; his friends that he prefers the latter. Favonius is leading the consular party, who rebel against it, while I hold my peace, especially as the pontifices at present have given no answer about my house. If they annul the consecration I shall have a splendid site. The consuls will value the building according to the decree of the Senate; if not, they will pull it down, lease it out in their own name, and reckon up the whole cost.

So my affairs are,

" For happy though but ill, for ill not worst." [1]

My monetary affairs, as you know, are in an awful muddle: and there are some private matters which I won't commit to writing. I am devoted to my brother Quintus as his extraordinary affection, virtue, and loyalty deserve. I am looking forward to your coming and beg you to come soon, and to come resolved to give me the full benefit of your advice. I am standing at the threshold of a new life. Already those who took my part in my exile are beginning to feel annoyance at my presence, though they disguise it, and to envy me without even taking the trouble to disguise that. I really stand in urgent need of you.

II

CICERO TO ATTICUS, GREETING.

If I am a less-regular correspondent than others, *Rome, Oct.,* please do not lay it to my carelessness or to my B.C. *657* business either; for, though I am extraordinarily

---

[1] Shuckburgh aptly borrows this line from Milton, *P.L.,* II, 224.

summa est, tamen nulla esse potest tanta, ut inter-
rumpat iter amoris nostri et officii mei. Nam, ut
veni Romam, iterum nunc sum certior factus esse
cui darem litteras; itaque has alteras dedi.

Prioribus tibi declaravi, adventus noster qualis
fuisset, et quis esset status, atque omnes res nostrae
quem ad modum essent,

" Ut in secundis fluxae, ut in advorsis bonae."

Post illas datas litteras secuta est summa contentio
de domo. Diximus apud pontifices pr. Kal. Octobres.
Acta res est accurate a nobis, et, si umquam in dicendo fuimus aliquid, aut etiam si numquam alias
fuimus, tum profecto doloris magnitudo vim quandam
nobis dicendi dedit. Itaque oratio iuventuti nostrae
deberi non potest; quam tibi, etiamsi non desideras,
tamen mittam cito. Cum pontifices decressent ita,
SI NEQVE POPVLI IVSSV NEQVE PLEBIS SCITV IS, QVI SE DE-
DICASSE DICERET, NOMINATIM EI REI PRAEFECTVS ESSET
NEQVE POPVLI IVSSV AVT PLEBIS SCITU ID FACERE IVSSVS
ESSET, VIDERI POSSE SINE RELIGIONE EAM PARTEM AREAE
MIHI RESTITVI, mihi facta statim est gratulatio; nemo
enim dubitabat, quin domus nobis esset adiudicata:
cum subito ille in contionem escendit, quam Appius
ei dedit. Nuntiat iam populo pontifices secundum se
decrevisse, me autem vi conari in possessionem
venire; hortatur, ut se et Appium sequantur et suam
Libertatem vi defendant. Hic cum etiam illi infirmi
partim admirarentur, partim irriderent hominis
amentiam, ego statueram illuc non accedere, nisi

busy, no press of work could be sufficient to break the course of our affection or of my duty to you. Since I have come to Rome, this is the second time that I have heard of a messenger, and so this is the second letter I send.

In my former I described the sort of return I had, my position, and the state of all my affairs:

" For happy though but ill, for ill not worst."

After I sent that letter there followed a great fight about my house. I delivered a speech [1] before the pontifices on the 29th of September. I bestowed great pains on the matter, and, if ever I had any oratorical ability, or even if I never had before, on that occasion at any rate, my great indignation lent some vigour to my style. So its publication is a debt which I must not leave unpaid to the rising generation: and to you I will send it very soon, whether you want it or not. The pontifices decreed that " if the party alleging that he had dedicated had not been appointed by name either by order of the people or vote of the plebs, and if he had not been commanded to do so, either by order of the people or by vote of the plebs then it appeared that that part of the site might be restored to me without sacrilege." I was congratulated at once, everybody thinking that the house had been adjudged to me. But all of a sudden up gets a man to speak, at Appius' invitation, and announces that the pontifices have decided in his favour and I am trying to take possession by force: he exhorts them to follow him and Appius and defend their shrine of Liberty. Thereupon, though even those pliable persons were partly lost in wonder and partly laughing at the man's folly, I determined

[1] *De domo sua ad pontifices.*

cum consules ex senatus consulto porticum Catuli restituendam locassent. Kal. Octobr. habetur senatus frequens. Adhibentur omnes pontifices, qui erant senatores. A quibus Marcellinus, qui erat cupidissimus mei, sententiam primus rogatus quaesivit, quid essent in decernendo secuti. Tum M. Lucullus de omnium collegarum sententia respondit religionis iudices pontifices fuisse, legis esse senatum; se et collegas suos de religione statuisse, in senatu de lege statuturos cum senatu. Itaque suo quisque horum loco sententiam rogatus multa secundum causam nostram disputavit. Cum ad Clodium ventum est, cupiit diem consumere, neque ei finis est factus, sed tamen, cum horas tres fere dixisset, odio et strepitu senatus coactus est aliquando perorare. Cum fieret senatus consultum in sententiam Marcellini omnibus praeter unum adsentientibus, Serranus intercessit. De intercessione statim ambo consules referre coeperunt. Cum sententiae gravissimae dicerentur, senatui placere mihi domum restitui, porticum Catuli locari, auctoritatem ordinis ab omnibus magistratibus defendi, si quae vis esset facta, senatum existimaturum eius opera factum esse, qui senatus consulto intercessisset, Serranus pertimuit, et Cornicinus ad suam veterem fabulam rediit; abiecta toga se ad generi pedes abiecit. Ille noctem sibi postulavit. Non concedebant, reminiscebantur enim Kal. Ianuar. Vix

not to go near the place until the consuls by decree of the Senate had given out the contract for restoring the porch of Catulus. On the first of October there was a full meeting of the Senate. All the pontifices who were senators were summoned: and Marcellinus, a strong partisan of mine, being called upon first for his opinion, asked them what was the purport of their decree. Then M. Lucullus, speaking for all his colleagues, answered that the pontifices had to decide points of religion and the Senate points of law: he and his colleagues had settled the religious point and now in the Senate they would join the other senators in settling the legal point. Accordingly, as each of them was called upon in his turn, he delivered a long speech in my favour. When it came to Clodius he wanted to waste the whole day and spoke on endlessly, but at last, after speaking for nearly three hours, he was forced by the indignant outcry of the Senate to wind up his speech. A decree was passed in accordance with Marcellinus' proposal with only one dissentient voice: and then Serranus put his veto on it. Both consuls at once referred the veto to the Senate, and many resolute speeches were delivered: " that the Senate approved of the restitution of my house," " that a contract should be drawn up for the portico of Catulus," " that the Senate's resolution should be supported by all the magistrates," " that if any violence occurred, the Senate would hold him responsible who had vetoed its decree." Serranus showed the white feather and Cornicinus played the same old farce: he threw off his toga and flung himself at his son-in-law's feet. Serranus demanded a night to think it over. They would not grant it, remembering the first of January. At last with my

tamen tibi de mea voluntate concessum est. Postridie senatus consultum factum est id, quod ad te misi. Deinde consules porticum Catuli restituendam locarunt; illam porticum redemptores statim sunt demoliti libentissimis omnibus. Nobis superficiem aedium consules de consilii sententia aestimarunt sestertio viciens, cetera valde inliberaliter, Tusculanam villam quingentis milibus, Formianum HS ducentis quinquaginta milibus. Quae aestimatio non modo vehementer ab optimo quoque, sed etiam a plebe reprenditur. Dices: " Quid igitur causae fuit? " Dicunt illi quidem pudorem meum, quod neque negarim neque vehementius postularim; sed non est id: nam hoc quidem etiam profuisset. Verum iidem, mi T. Pomponi, iidem, inquam, illi, quos ne tu quidem ignoras, qui mihi pinnas inciderant, nolunt easdem renasci. Sed, ut spero, iam renascuntur. Tu modo ad nos veni; quod vereor ne tardius interventu Varronis tui nostrique facias.

Quoniam, acta quae sint, habes, de reliqua nostra cogitatione cognosce. Ego me a Pompeio legari ita sum passus, ut nulla re impedirer. Quod nisi vellem mihi esset integrum, ut, si comitia censorum proximi consules haberent, petere possem, votivam legationem sumpsissem prope omnium fanorum, lucorum; sic enim nostrae rationes utilitatis meae postulabant. Sed volui meam potestatem esse vel petendi vel

consent the concession was unwillingly made. On the next day the decree which I send was passed. Then the consuls gave out the contract for the restoration of the portico of Catulus; and the contractors immediately pulled down that portico of his to everybody's satisfaction. The consuls valued my house at nearly £18,000 [1] at their assessor's advice: and the other things very stingily—my Tusculan villa at £4,400 and my Formian at £2,200.[2] This estimate was violently decried not only by all the conservative party, but by the people too. If you ask me the reason, they say it was my bashfulness, as I did not refuse or make pressing demands. But that is not the reason; for that in itself would have counted for me. But the fact is, my dear Pomponius, those very same men—you know quite well who I mean—who cut my wings, do not wish them to grow again. But I hope they are growing. Do you only come to me. But I fear you may be delayed by the visit of your and my friend Varro.

There you have all that has happened. Now you shall dip into my thoughts. I have let myself be appointed legate to Pompey with a reservation that it should not hamper me at all. If I did not want to have a free hand to stand for the censorship, if the next consuls hold a censorial election, I would have taken a votive commission [3] to nearly any shrines or groves. For that was what suited my idea of my interests best. But I wanted to be free either to stand for election or to quit the city at the beginning of summer, and meanwhile I thought it good policy

---

[1] 2,000,000 sesterces.   [2] 500,000 and 250,000 sesterces.
[2] Cf. p. 163 footnote.

ineunte aestate exeundi et interea me esse in oculis
civium de me optime meritorum non alienum putavi.

Ac forensium quidem rerum haec nostra consilia
sunt, domesticarum autem valde impedita. Domus
aedificatur, scis, quo sumptu, qua molestia; reficitur
Formianum, quod ego nec relinquere possum nec
videre; Tusculanum proscripsi; suburbano facile
careo. Amicorum benignitas exhausta est in ea re,
quae nihil habuit praeter dedecus, quod sensisti tu
absens, nos [1] praesentes; quorum studiis ego et
copiis, si esset per meos defensores licitum, facile
essem omnia consecutus. Quo in genere nunc vehementer laboratur. Cetera, quae me sollicitant,
μυστικώτερα sunt. Amamur a fratre et a filia. Te
exspectamus.

III

CICERO ATTICO SAL.

*Scr. Romae
VIIIK.Dec.
a. 697*
Avere te certo scio cum scire, quid hic agatur, tum
ea a me scire, non quo certiora sint ea, quae in oculis
omnium geruntur, si a me scribantur, quam cum ab
aliis aut scribantur tibi aut nuntientur, sed ut perspicias ex meis litteris, quo animo ea feram, quae
geruntur, et qui sit hoc tempore aut mentis meae
sensus aut omnino vitae status.

Armatis hominibus ante diem tertium Nonas Novembres expulsi sunt fabri de area nostra, disturbata
porticus Catuli, quae ex senatus consulto consulum

---

[1] nos *added by Madvig.*

to keep myself before the eyes of the citizens who have treated me well.

As regards public affairs those are my plans: but my private affairs are in a horrible muddle. My house is being built and you know the expense and the bother it entails: my Formian villa is being restored, though I cannot bring myself either to abandon it or to look at it. My house at Tusculum I have put up for sale: I can easily do without a suburban residence. My friends' benevolence has been exhausted in what has brought nothing but dishonour: this you saw, though you were absent, and so do I who am on the spot: and I might have obtained all I wanted easily from their efforts and their wealth, if my champions had allowed it. In this respect I am now in sore straits. My other anxieties may not be rashly mentioned. My brother and daughter are devoted to me. I am looking forward to your coming.

III

CICERO TO ATTICUS, GREETING.

I am sure you are wanting to know what is going *Rome, Nov.* on here and to know it from me too, not that there *23*, B.C. *57* is any more certainty about events which take place before the eyes of the whole world, if I write to you about them, than if others either write or tell you of them: but that you may see from my letters how I am taking events and what are my feelings and my general state of existence.

On the 3rd of November the workmen were driven out of my building-ground by armed assault: the porch of Catulus, which was being repaired on a contract made by the consuls in accordance with a decree

locatione reficiebatur et ad tectum paene pervenerat,
Quinti fratris domus primo fracta coniectu lapidum
ex area nostra, deinde inflammata iussu Clodi inspectante urbe coniectis ignibus, magna querela et gemitu
non dicam bonorum, qui nescio an nulli sint, sed plane
hominum omnium. Ille demens ruere, post hunc
vero furorem nihil nisi caedem inimicorum cogitare,
vicatim ambire, servis aperte spem libertatis osten-
dere. Etenim antea, cum iudicium nolebat, habebat
ille quidem difficilem manifestamque causam, sed
tamen causam; poterat infitiari, poterat in alios
derivare, poterat etiam aliquid iure factum defendere; post has ruinas, incendia, rapinas desertus a
suis vix iam Decimum designatorem, vix Gellium
retinet, servorum consiliis utitur, videt, si omnes, quos
vult, palam occiderit, nihilo suam causam difficilio-
rem, quam adhuc sit, in iudicio futuram. Itaque ante
diem tertium Idus Novembres, cum Sacra via descen-
derem, insecutus est me cum suis. Clamor, lapides,
fustes, gladii, haec improvisa omnia. Discessimus
in vestibulum Tetti Damionis. Qui erant mecum,
facile operas aditu prohibuerunt. Ipse occidi potuit,
sed ego diaeta curare incipio, chirurgiae taedet. Ille
omnium vocibus cum se non ad iudicium, sed ad
supplicium praesens trudi videret, omnes Catilinas

of the Senate, and had nearly got as high as the roof, was knocked down: my brother Quintus' house was first smashed by a discharge of stones from my plot, and then set on fire under Clodius' orders by firebrands hurled before the eyes of the whole city, amidst the groans and growls—I will not say of the loyal party, which seems to have vanished out of existence—but simply of every human creature. He was rushing about in a frenzy, thinking of nothing but the slaughter of his enemies after this mad freak, and canvassing the city quarter by quarter, openly promising liberation to slaves. Before this, when he was trying to shirk his trial, he had a case hard indeed to support and obviously wrongful, but still it was a case: he could deny things, he could put the blame on others, he could even plead that he had the right on his side in some respects. But after this wreckage, arson, and pillage, his own supporters have left him in the lurch and he hardly has a hold now even on Decimus the marshal, or Gellius: he has to take slaves into his confidence and sees that if he openly commits all the murders he wishes to commit his case before the court will not be one whit worse than it is now. So, on the 11th of November, as I was going down the Sacred Way, he followed me with his gang. There were shouts, stones, clubs, swords, all without a moment's warning. We stepped aside into Tettius Damio's hall: and those who were with me easily prevented his roughs from entering. He might have been killed himself: but I have got tired of surgery and am beginning a regime cure. He realized that there was a universal outcry not for his prosecution but for his execution, and has since behaved in such a way that a Catiline looks ultra-

275

Acidinos postea reddidit.   Nam Milonis domum, eam
quae est in Cermalo, pr. Idus Novembr. expugnare
et incendere ita conatus est, ut palam hora quinta
cum scutis homines eductis gladiis, alios cum accensis
facibus adduxerit.   Ipse domum P. Sullae pro castris
sibi ad eam impugnationem sumpserat.   Tum ex
Anniana Milonis domo Q. Flaccus eduxit viros acris ;
occidit homines ex omni latrocinio Clodiano notissi-
mos, ipsum cupivit, sed ille se in interiora [1] aedium
Sullae.   Exin senatus postridie Idus.   Domi Clodius.
Egregius Marcellinus, omnes acres.   Metellus calu-
mnia dicendi tempus exemit adiuvante Appio, etiam
hercule familiari tuo, de cuius constantia virtute tuae
verissimae litterae.   Sestius furere.   Ille postea, si
comitia sua non fierent, urbi minari.   Milo, proposita
Marcellini sententia, quam ille de scripto ita dixerat,
ut totam nostram causam areae, incendiorum, periculi
mei iudicio complecteretur eaque omnia comitiis
anteferret, proscripsit se per omnes dies comitiales
de caelo servaturum.

Contiones turbulentae Metelli, temerariae Appi,
furiosissimae Publi.   Haec tamen summa, nisi Milo
in campo obnuntiasset, comitia futura.   Ante diem
XII Kal. Decembr.   Milo ante mediam noctem cum
magna manu in campum venit.   Clodius, cum habe-

---

[1] in interiora *Orelli :* ex interiorem *M.*

conservative beside him. For on the 12th of November he attempted to storm and burn Milo's house— the one on the Cermalus—openly bringing men with shields and drawn swords and others with lighted torches to the spot at eleven o'clock in the morning. His own headquarters during the assault were P. Sulla's house. Then Q. Flaccus led forth a gallant band from Milo's family house and slew the most notorious of Clodius' troop of ruffians. He wanted to slay Clodius himself: but he was skulking in the recesses of Sulla's house. There followed a meeting of the Senate on the 14th: Clodius stayed at home: Marcellinus behaved splendidly: and everybody was enthusiastic. Metellus with the assistance of Appius and, mark you, your great friend [1] of whose constancy you sent me such a veracious account, tried the ruse of talking the time away. Sestius was furious. Clodius afterwards vowed vengeance on the city if his election did not take place. Marcellinus posted up his resolution, which he had in writing when he delivered it—it provided that my entire case should be included in the trial, the attack on my building ground, the arson, and the assault on my person, and that all these should precede the election—and Milo gave notice that he intended to watch the sky for omens on all the election days.

Disorderly meetings were held by Metellus, wild meetings by Appius, and raging mad meetings by Publius. But the end of it all was that the elections would have taken place, if Milo had not reported evil omens in the Campus Martius. On the 19th of November Milo took up his position in the Campus before midnight with a large force; while Clodius in

[1] Hortensius.

ret fugitivorum delectas copias, in campum ire non
est ausus. Milo permansit ad meridiem mirifica
hominum laetitia summa cum gloria. Contentio
fratrum trium turpis, fracta vis, contemptus furor.
Metellus tamen postulat, ut sibi postero die in
foro obnuntietur; nihil esse, quod in campum nocte
veniretur; se hora prima in comitio fore. Itaque
ante diem xi Kal. in comitium Milo de nocte venit.
Metellus cum prima luce futim in campum itineribus
prope deviis currebat: adsequitur inter lucos hominem Milo, obnuntiat. Ille se recepit magno et turpi
Q. Flacci convicio. Ante diem x Kal. nundinae.
Contio biduo nulla.

Ante diem viii Kal. haec ego scribebam hora no-
ctis nona. Milo campum iam tenebat. Marcellus
candidatus ita stertebat, ut ego vicinus audirem.
Clodi vestibulum vacuum sane mihi nuntiabatur:
pauci pannosi linea lanterna. Meo consilio omnia
illi fieri querebantur ignari quantum in illo heroe
esset animi, quantum etiam consilii. Miranda virtus
est. Nova quaedam divina mitto; sed haec summa
est. Comitia fore non arbitror; reum Publium, nisi
ante occisus erit, fore a Milone puto; si se in turba
ei iam [1] obtulerit, occisum iri ab ipso Milone video.
Non dubitat facere, prae se fert; casum illum nostrum non extimescit. Numquam enim cuiusquam

[1] se in turba ei iam *Klotz:* se uti turbae iam *NCZ*[b] *:* si
sentitur veiam *M.*

spite of his picked gangs of runaway slaves did not venture to show himself. Milo to the huge delight of everybody and to his own great credit stayed there till midday : and the three brethren's struggle ended in disgrace, their strength broken and their mad pride humbled. Metellus, however, demands that the prohibition should be repeated in the forum on the next day. There was no necessity, he said, for Milo to come to the Campus at night; he would be in the Comitium at six in the morning. So on the 20th Milo went to the Comitium in the early hours of the morning. At daybreak Metellus came sneaking into the Campus by something like byepaths. Milo catches the fellow up " between the groves "[1] and serves his notice : and he retired amid loud jeers and insults from Q. Flaccus. The 21st was a market-day, and for two days there were no meetings.

It is now three o'clock on the morning of the 23rd as I am writing. Milo has already taken possession of the Campus. Marcellus, the candidate, is snoring loud enough for me to hear him next door. I have just had news that Clodius' hall is utterly deserted, save for a few rag and bob tails with a canvas lantern. His side are complaining that I am at the bottom of it all : but they little know the courage and wisdom of that hero. His valour is marvellous. I can't stop to mention some of his new strokes of genius. But this is the upshot : I believe the elections will not be held, and Milo will bring Publius before the bar, unless he kills him first. If he gives him a chance in a riot I can see Milo will kill him with his own hands. He has got no scruples

[1] A spot between the Capitol and the Campus Martius where Romulus founded his Asylum.

279

invidi et perfidi consilio est usus, nec inerti nobili crediturus.

Nos animo dumtaxat vigemus, etiam magis, quam cum florebamus, re familiari comminuti sumus. Quinti fratris tamen liberalitati pro facultatibus nostris, ne omnino exhaustus essem, illo recusante subsidiis amicorum respondemus. Quid consilii de omni nostro statu capiamus, te absente nescimus. Quare adpropera.

IV

CICERO ATTICO SAL.

Scr. Romae III K. Febr. a. 698 Periucundus mihi Cincius fuit ante diem III Kal. Febr. ante lucem; dixit enim mihi te esse in Italia seseque ad te pueros mittere. Quos sine meis litteris ire nolui, non quo haberem, quod tibi, praesertim iam prope praesenti, scriberem, sed ut hoc ipsum significarem, mihi tuum adventum suavissimum exspectatissimumque esse. Quare advola ad nos eo animo, ut nos ames, te amari scias. Cetera coram agemus. Haec properantes scripsimus. Quo die venies, utique cum tuis apud me eris.

IVa

CICERO ATTICO SAL.

Scr. in Antiati m. Apr. aut Mai. a. 698 Perbelle feceris, si ad nos veneris. Offendes designationem Tyrannionis mirificam in librorum meorum bibliotheca, quorum reliquiae multo meliores sunt, quam putaram. Et velim mihi mittas de tuis

about it and avows his intentions, undeterred by my downfall: for he has never followed the advice of a jealous and treacherous friend, nor trusted in a weak aristocrat.

So far as my mind is concerned, I am as strong as ever I was even in my most palmy days, if not stronger; but my circumstances are straitened. My brother Quintus' liberality I shall repay, in spite of his protests, as the state of my finances compels me—by the aid of friends, so as not entirely to beggar myself. What general course of action to adopt I cannot make up my mind without your assistance; so make haste.

IV

CICERO TO ATTICUS, GREETING.

I was charmed by Cincius' visit on the 28th of January before daybreak: for he told me you were in Italy and he was sending some men to you. I did not like them to go without a letter from me—not that I had anything to write, especially when you are so near, but that I might express my delight at your arrival and how I have longed for it. So fly to me with the assurance that your love for me is fully reciprocated. The rest we will discuss when we meet. I am writing in haste. The day you arrive, mind, you and your party are to accept my hospitality.

Rome, Jan. 28, B.C. 56

IVa

CICERO TO ATTICUS, GREETING.

I shall be delighted if you can pay me a visit. You will be surprised at Tyrannio's excellent arrangement in my library. What is left of it is much better than I expected: still I should be glad if you would

Antium, Apr. or May, B.C. 56

librariolis duos aliquos, quibus Tyrannio utatur glu-
tinatoribus, ad cetera administris, iisque imperes, ut
sumant membranulam, ex qua indices fiant, quos vos
Graeci, ut opinor, σιλλύβους appellatis. Sed haec, si
tibi erit commodum. Ipse vero utique fac venias, si
potes in his locis adhaerescere et Piliam adducere.
Ita enim et aequum est et cupit Tullia. Medius
fidius ne tu emisti λόχον [1] praeclarum. Gladiatores
audio pugnare mirifice. Si locare voluisses, duobus
his muneribus liber esses.[2] Sed haec posterius. Tu
fac venias et de librariis, si me amas, diligenter.

V

CICERO ATTICO SAL.

*Scr. in
Antiati m.
Apr. aut
Mai. a. 698*

    Ain tu? an me existimas ab ullo malle mea legi
probarique quam a te? Cur igitur cuiquam misi
prius? Urgebar ab eo, ad quem misi, et non habebam exemplar. Quid? Etiam (dudum enim cir-
cumrodo, quod devorandum est) subturpicula mihi
videbatur esse παλινῳδία. Sed valeant recta, vera,
honesta consilia. Non est credibile, quae sit perfidia
in istis principibus, ut volunt esse et ut essent, si
quicquam haberent fidei. Senseram, noram inductus, relictus, proiectus ab iis. Tamen hoc eram animo, ut cum iis in re publica consentirem. Idem erant
qui fuerant. Vix aliquando te auctore resipui.
Dices ea te monuisse, suasisse, quae facerem, non
etiam ut scriberem. Ego mehercule mihi necessita-

---

[1] λόχον *Bosius*; locum *M.*; ludum *Ernesti.*
[2] liber esses *Pius*; liberasses *M.*

send me two of your library slaves to Tyrannio to employ to glue pages together and assist in general, and would tell them to get some bits of parchment to make title-pieces, which I think you Greeks call " sillybi." That is only if it is convenient to you. In any case mind you come yourself, if you can stick in such a place, and bring Pilia with you. For that is only right and Tullia wishes her to come. My word! you have bought a fine troop. I hear your gladiators are fighting splendidly. If you had cared to let them out you would have cleared your expenses on these two shows. But of that later. Be sure you come, and, as you love me, remember the library slaves.

V

CICERO TO ATTICUS, GREETING.

Come now, do you really imagine I prefer my things to be read and criticized by anyone but you? Then why did I send them to anyone else first? The man I sent them to was very pressing and I had not a copy. Anything else? Well, yes—though I keep mouthing the pill instead of swallowing it—I was a bit ashamed of my palinode. But good-bye to honesty, straightforwardness, and uprightness! You would hardly believe the treachery of our leaders, as they want to be and would be, if they had any honour. I knew full well how they had taken me in, abandoned me, and cast me off. Still I resolved to stick to them in politics. But they have proved the same as ever: and at last I have come to my senses under your guidance. You will say your advice applied exclusively to my actions and did not include writing too. The fact is,

Antium,
Apr. or
May, B.C. *56*

tem volui imponere huius novae coniunctionis, ne qua
mihi liceret labi ad illos, qui etiam tum, cum misereri
mei debent, non desinunt invidere. Sed tamen
modici fuimus ὑποθέσει, ut scripsi. Erimus uberiores, si et ille libenter accipiet, et ii subringentur, qui
villam me moleste ferunt habere, quae Catuli fuerat,
a Vettio emisse non cogitant; qui domum negant
oportuisse me aedificare, vendere aiunt oportuisse.
Sed quid ad hoc, si, quibus sententiis dixi, quod et
ipsi probarent, laetati sunt tamen me contra Pompei
voluntatem dixisse? Finis sit. Quoniam, qui nihil
possunt, ii me nolunt amare, demus operam, ut ab iis,
qui possunt, diligamur. Dices: "Vellem iam pridem." Scio te voluisse et me asinum germanum
fuisse. Sed iam tempus est me ipsum a me amari,
quando ab illis nullo modo possum.

Domum meam quod crebro invisis est mihi valde
gratum. Viaticum Crassipes praeripit. Tu "de via
recta in hortos." Videtur commodius ad te: postridie scilicet; quid enim tua? Sed viderimus. Bibliothecam mihi tui pinxerunt constructione et sillybis.
Eos velim laudes.

VI

CICERO ATTICO SAL.

*Scr. in villa
m. Apr. aut
Mai. a. 698* De Lentulo scilicet sic fero, ut debeo. Virum bonum et magnum hominem et in summa magnitudine
animi multa humanitate temperatum perdidimus nos-

I wanted to tie myself down to this new alliance so as to leave myself no chance of slipping back to those who do not cease to envy me, even when they ought to pity me. However, I was quite moderate in my treatment of the subject, as I have said. I will let myself go more, if he takes it well, and those make wry faces who are annoyed to see me occupy a villa which used to belong to Catulus, forgetting that I bought it from Vettius; and who declare I ought not to have built a house, but ought to have sold the site. That, however, is nothing compared with their unholy joy when the very speeches I delivered in support of their views were alienating me from Pompey. Let us have an end of it. Since those who have no influence refuse me their affection, I may as well try to win that of those who have some influence. You will say you wish I had before. I know you wished it, and I was a downright ass. But now is the time to show affection for myself, since I cannot get any from them anyhow.

I am very grateful to you for going to see my house so often. Crassipes is swallowing all my travelling money. You say I must go straight to your country house. It seems to me more convenient to go to your town house, and on the next day. It can't make any difference to you. But we shall see. Your men have beautified my library by binding the books and affixing title-slips. Please thank them.

VI

CICERO TO ATTICUS, GREETING.

The news about Lentulus I feel of course as I ought: we have lost a good man and a fine fellow, and one who combined a remarkable strength of character with great courtesy. Still I find some con- *At his country house, Apr. or May,* B.C. *56*

que malo solacio, sed non nullo tamen, consolamur,
quod ipsius vicem minime dolemus, non ut Saufeius
et vestri, sed mehercule quia sic amabat patriam, ut
mihi aliquo deorum beneficio videatur ex eius incendio esse ereptus. Nam quid foedius nostra vita,
praecipue mea? Nam tu quidem, etsi es natura
πολιτικός, tamen nullam habes propriam servitutem,
communi frueris nomine [1]; ego vero, qui, si loquor de
re publica, quod oportet, insanus, si, quod opus est,
servus existimor, si taceo, oppressus et captus, quo
dolore esse debeo? Quo sum scilicet, hoc etiam
acriore, quod ne dolere quidem possum, ut non in-
gratus videar. Quid, si cessare libeat et in otii por-
tum confugere? Nequiquam. Immo etiam in bellum et in castra. Ergo erimus ὀπαδοί, qui ταγοὶ esse
noluimus? Sic faciendum est, tibi enim ipsi (cui
utinam semper paruissem!) sic video placere. Reliquum iam [2] est

> Σπάρταν ἔλαχες, ταύταν κόσμει.

Non mehercule possum et Philoxeno ignosco, qui
reduci in carcerem maluit. Verum tamen id ipsum
mecum in his locis commentor, ut ista improbem,
idque tu, cum una erimus, confirmabis.

A te litteras crebro ad me scribi video, sed omnes
uno tempore accepi. Quae res etiam auxit dolorem

---

[1] frueris nomine *Pius*; fueris nonne M.
[2] reliquum iam *Orelli*; reliquia *M*.

solation, though a poor one, in the thought that I need not grieve for him—not for the same reason as Saufeius and your Epicurean friends, but because he was so true a patriot that it seems as though a merciful providence had snatched him from his country's fiery ruin. For what could be more shameful than the life we are all leading, especially myself? You, in spite of a political bent, have avoided wearing any special yoke; but you share the universal bondage. But think of the sufferings I undergo when I am taken for a lunatic if I say what I ought about the State, for a slave if I say what expediency dictates, and for a cowed and helpless bondsman if I hold my tongue. I suffer, as you may suppose, with the added bitterness that I cannot show my grief without seeming ungrateful. Well! why shouldn't I take a rest, and flee to the haven of retirement? I haven't the chance. Then be it war and camp. And so I must be a subaltern, after refusing to be a captain. So be it. That, I see, is your opinion, and I wish I had always followed your advice. Hobson's choice [1] is all that is left to me. But upon my soul I can't stomach it, and have a fellow feeling for Philoxenus, who preferred to go back to his prison.[2] However, I am spending my time here devising a way of confounding their policy, and when we meet you will strengthen my purpose.

I see your letters were written at several times, but I received them all together, and that increased

[1] Lit. " Sparta has fallen to your lot, do it credit," a phrase denoting that one has no choice. Cf. p. 95.

[2] Philoxenus of Cythera, a dithyrambic poet, was condemned to the quarries for criticizing the literary compositions of Dionysius of Syracuse. He was given a chance of freedom, if he altered his opinion; but preferred to return to the quarries.

meum. Casu enim trinas ante legeram, quibus meliuscule Lentulo esse scriptum erat. Ecce quartae fulmen! Sed ille, ut scripsi, non miser, nos vero ferrei.

Quod me admones, ut scribam illa Hortensiana, in alia incidi non immemor istius mandati tui; sed mehercule in incipiendo refugi, ne, qui videor stulte illius amici intemperiem non tulisse, rursus stulte iniuriam illius faciam inlustrem, si quid scripsero, et simul ne βαθύτης mea, quae in agendo apparuit, in scribendo sit occultior, et aliquid satisfactio levitatis habere videatur. Sed viderimus; tu modo quam saepissime ad me aliquid. Epistulam, Lucceio nunc quam misi, qua, meas res ut scribat, rogo, fac ut ab eo sumas (valde bella est) eumque, ut adproperet, adhorteris et, quod mihi se ita facturum rescripsit, agas gratias, domum nostram, quoad poteris, invisas, Vestorio aliquid significes. Valde enim est in me liberalis.

VII

CICERO ATTICO SAL.

Scr. in
Arpinati m.
Apr. aut
Mai. a. 698

Nihil εὐκαιρότερον epistula tua, quae me sollicitum de Quinto nostro, puero optimo, valde levavit. Venerat horis duabus ante Chaerippus; mera monstra nuntiarat. De Apollonio quod scribis, qui illi di irati! homini Graeco, qui conturbat atque idem putat

288

my sorrow; for, as it happened, I first read the three
in which you said Lentulus was a little better; and
then, lo and behold, a thunderbolt in the fourth.
Still, as I said, he is out of misery, while we live on
in an Iron Age.[1]

I have not forgotten your advice to write that
attack on Hortensius, though I have drifted into
other things. But upon my word, I jibbed at the
very beginning. I look foolish enough for not sub-
mitting to his conduct, outrageous though it was,
from a friend, and if I were to write about it I fear
I should enhance my folly by advertising his insult,
while at the same time the self-restraint which I
showed in my actions might not be so apparent in
writing, and this way of taking satisfaction might
seem rather weak. But we will see. Be sure you
send me a line as often as you can, and take care you
get from Lucceius the letter I sent asking him to
write my biography. It is a very pretty bit of writing. Urge him to be quick about it, and give him my
thanks for his answer undertaking it. Have a look
at my house as often as possible. Say something to
Vestorius: he is behaving most liberally to me.

VII

CICERO TO ATTICUS, GREETING.

Nothing could be more à propos than your letter, *Arpinum,*
which has relieved me about the dear child Quintus *Apr. or May,*
very greatly. Chaerippus had come two hours earlier B.C. *56*
with the wildest tales. As to your news about Apollonius, confound him! A Greek to go bankrupt and

---

[1] *Ferrei,* according to Kayser, contains an allusion to
Hesiod's Iron Age: but others take it as simply " callous."

sibi licere quod equitibus Romanis.   Nam Terentius
suo iure.   De Metello

Odyssey xxii
412

οὐχ ὁσίη φθιμένοισιν,

sed tamen multis annis civis nemo erat mortuus qui
quidem. . . . Tibi nummi meo periculo sint.   Quid
enim vereris quemcumque [1] heredem fecit, nisi Publium fecit.   Verum fecit non improbiorem, quam fuit
ipse.[2]   Quare in hoc thecam nummariam non rete-
xeris, in aliis eris cautior.

Mea mandata de domo curabis, praesidia locabis,
Milonem admonebis.   Arpinatium fremitus est incredibilis de Laterio.   Quid quaeris ? equidem dolui ;

Odyssey, i, 271

ὁ δὲ οὐκ ἐμπάζετο μύθων.

Quod superest, etiam puerum Ciceronem curabis et
amabis, ut facis.

VIII

CICERO ATTICO SAL.

Scr. Anti m.
Apr. aut
Mai. a. 698

Multa me in epistula tua delectarunt, sed nihil
magis quam patina tyrotarichi.   Nam de rausculo
quod scribis,

μήπω μέγ᾽ εἴπῃς, πρὶν τελευτήσαντ᾽ ἴδῃς.

Aedificati tibi in agris nihil reperio.   In oppido est
quiddam, de quo est dubium, sitne venale, ac proximum quidem nostris aedibus.   Hoc scito, Antium
Buthrotum esse Romae, ut Corcyrae illud tuum.
Nihil quietius, nihil alsius, nihil amoenius.

Εἴη μοὶ οὗτος φίλος οἶκος.[3]

---

[1] quemcumque *editors:* quaecunque *M.*
[2] improbiorem quam *Müller:* improve (*corr. to* improbi)
quemquam *M.   The reading of the whole passage from* qui
quidem *is very uncertain.*
[3] Εἴη—οἶκος *Peerlkamp:* ΕΙΜΗΙΣΗΤΩ ΦΙΛΟ͞Ο ΚΟΣ *M.*

think he has the same privilege as a Roman knight!
For of course Terentius was within his rights. As to
Metellus " de mortuis nil nisi bonum," still for years
no citizen has died who—— For your money I will go
bail. Why should you fear, whoever he has appointed
his heir, unless it was Publius? However, he has
chosen an heir no worse than himself : so you won't
have to open your coffers over this business, and you
will be more careful another time.

You will attend to my instructions about the house,
hire some guards and give Milo a hint. There is a
tremendous outcry here at Arpinum about Laterium.[1]
Of course I am much distressed about it : but " little
he recked my rede." For the rest, look after little
Quintus with the affection you always show towards
him.

VIII

CICERO TO ATTICUS, GREETING.

*Antium, Apr.
or May,* B.C.
56

Your letter contained many delightful passages,
but nothing to beat the " plate of red herrings." For
as to what you say about the little debt, " don't
holloa till you are out of the wood." [2]

I can't find anything like a country house for you.
In the town there is something, and quite close to
me too, but it is not certain if it is for sale. Let me
tell you that Antium is the Buthrotum of Rome, and
just what your Buthrotum is to Corcyra. Nothing
could be quieter or fresher or prettier : " this be my

---

[1] An estate of Q. Cicero in Arpinum. He seems to have
diverted a watercourse to the annoyance of his neighbours.

[2] Lit. " Do not boast till you see your enemy dead." From
a lost play of Sophocles.

MARCUS TULLIUS CICERO

Postea vero quam Tyrannio mihi libros disposuit, mens addita videtur meis aedibus. Qua quidem in re mirifica opera Dionysi et Menophili tui fuit. Nihil venustius quam illa tua pegmata, postquam mi silly- bis [1] libros illustrarunt. Vale. Et scribas ad me velim de gladiatoribus, sed ita, bene si rem gerunt; non quaero, male si se gessere.

VIIIa

CICERO ATTICO SAL.

Scr. auctu- mno anni 698

Apenas vix discesserat, cum epistula. Quid ais? Putasne fore ut legem non ferat? Dic, oro te, clarius; vix enim mihi exaudisse videor. Verum statim fac ut sciam, si modo tibi est commodum. Ludis quidem quoniam dies est additus, eo etiam melius hic eum diem cum Dionysio conteremus.

De Trebonio prorsus tibi adsentior. De Domitio

σύκῳ, μὰ τὴν Δήμητρα, σῦκον οὐδὲ ἕν
οὕτως ὅμοιον γέγονεν,

quam est ista περίστασις nostrae, vel quod ab isdem, vel quod praeter opinionem, vel quod viri boni nus- quam; unum dissimile, quod huic merito. Nam de ipso casu nescio an illud melius. Quid enim hoc miserius, quam eum, qui tot annos, quot habet, de- signatus consul fuerit, fieri consulem non posse, praesertim cum aut solus aut certe non plus quam cum altero petat? Si vero id est, quod nescio an sit ut non minus longas iam in codicillorum fastis futu- rorum consulum paginulas habeat quam factorum,

[1] mi sillybis *editors*: misit *M*: sit tibi *NP*: sit tibae *Z*[1].

292

own sweet home." Since Tyrannio has arranged my
books, the house seems to have acquired a soul: and
your Dionysius and Menophilus were of extraordinary
service. Nothing could be more charming than those
bookcases of yours now that the books are adorned
with title-slips. Farewell. Please let me know
about the gladiators: but only if they are behaving
well; if not, I don't want to know.

VIIIa

CICERO TO ATTICUS, GREETING.

Apenas had hardly gone when your letter came. *Autumn,*
Really? Do you think he won't propose his law? B.C. *56*
Pray speak a little more clearly, I hardly think I
caught your meaning. But let me know at once, if
you possibly can. Well, as they have given an extra
day to the games, I shall be all the better contented
to spend that day here with Dionysius.

About Trebonius I heartily agree with you. As
for Domitius, his *dénouement* was as like mine as two
peas; the same persons had a hand in it, it was
equally unexpected, and the conservative party deserted us both. There is only one point of difference:
he deserved his fate. Perhaps my fall was the less
hard to bear. For what could be more humiliating
than for one who all his life long has looked forward
to the consulship as his birth-right to fail to obtain
it—and that, too, when there is no one or at most
only one other candidate standing against him? But
if it is true that our friend [1] has in his note-books as
many pages of names of future consuls as of past, then

---

[1] Pompey.

quid illo miserius nisi res publica, in qua ne speratur quidem melius quicquam?

De Natta ex tuis primum scivi litteris; oderam hominem. De poëmate quod quaeris, quid, si cupiat effugere? quid? sinas? De Fabio Lusco quod eram exorsus, homo peramans semper nostri fuit nec mihi umquam odio. Satis enim acutus et permodestus ac bonae frugi. Eum, quia non videbam, abesse putabam: audivi ex Gavio hoc Firmano Romae esse hominem et fuisse adsiduum. Percussit animum. Dices: "Tantulane causa?" Permulta ad me detulerat non dubia de Firmanis fratribus. Quid sit, quod se a me removit, si modo removit, ignoro.

De eo, quod me mones, ut et πολιτικῶς me geram et τὴν ἔξω [1] γραμμὴν teneam, ita faciam. Sed opus est maiore prudentia. Quam a te, ut soleo, petam. Tu velim ex Fabio, si quem habes aditum, odorere et istum convivam tuum degustes et ad me de his rebus et de omnibus cotidie scribas. Ubi nihil erit, quod scribas, id ipsum scribito. Cura ut valeas.

IX

CICERO ATTICO SAL.

Scr. Neapoli
IV K. Mai.
a. 699

Sane velim scire, num censum impediant tribuni diebus vitiandis (est enim hic rumor) totaque de censura quid agant, quid cogitent. Nos hic cum

---

[1] ἔξω *Manutius:* εω *M.*

Domitius has only one rival in his misfortunes—the country which has given up even hoping for better days.

Your letter was the first to give me information about Natta: I could never abide the man. You ask about my poem. Well, what if it wants to take wing? Will you let it? I had begun to mention Fabius Luscus: he was always a great admirer of mine, and I never disliked him, for he was intelligent enough and very worthy and unassuming. As I had not seen him for a long time, I thought he was away: but I hear from this fellow Gavius of Firmum that the man is in Rome and has been here all along. It struck me as odd. You will say it is an insignificant trifle. But he had told me a good many things, of which there was no doubt, about those brothers from Firmum: and what has made him shun me, if he has shunned me, I cannot imagine.

Your advice to act diplomatically and not to steer too close to the wind [1] I will follow: but I shall want more than my own stock of wisdom; so, as usual, I shall draw on you. Please scent out anything you can from Fabius, if you can get at him, and suck that guest of yours dry, and write to me every day about these points and anything else. When you have nothing to write, write and say so. Look after yourself.

IX

CICERO TO ATTICUS, GREETING.

I should much like to know whether the tribunes *Naples,* are hindering the census by declaring days void—for *Apr. 27,* there is a rumour to that effect—and what is happen- B.C. *55* ing about the census in general and what people are

---

[1] Lit. " Keep the outside course " in a chariot race.

Pompeio fuimus. Multa mecum de re publica sane
sibi displicens, ut loquebatur (sic est enim in hoc
homine dicendum), Syriam spernens, Hispaniam iactans, hic quoque, ut loquebatur; et, opinor, usque-
quaque, de hoc cum dicemus, sit hoc quasi καὶ τόδε
Φωκυλίδου. Tibi etiam gratias agebat, quod signa
componenda suscepisses; in nos vero suavissime hercule est effusus. Venit etiam ad me in Cumanum a
se. Nihil minus velle mihi visus est quam Messallam
consulatum petere. De quo ipso si quid scis, velim
scire.

Quod Lucceio scribis te nostram gloriam commen-
daturum, et aedificium nostrum quod crebro invisis,
gratum. Quintus frater ad me scripsit se, quoniam
Ciceronem suavissimum tecum haberes, ad te Nonis
Maiis venturum. Ego me de Cumano movi ante
diem v Kal. Maias. Eo die Neapoli apud Paetum.
Ante diem iiii Kal. Maias iens in Pompeianum bene
mane haec scripsi.

X

CICERO ATTICO SAL.

*Scr. in
Cumano* IX
*K. Mai. a.
699*
Puteolis magnus est rumor Ptolomaeum esse in
regno. Si quid habes certius, velim scire. Ego hic
pascor bibliotheca Fausti. Fortasse tu putabas his

thinking. I met Pompey here; and he told me a lot
of political news. He was very dissatisfied with himself, as he said—for that is a necessary proviso in
his case. Of Syria he expressed a very low opinion,
while he runs down [1] Spain—with the same proviso
" as he said," which I think must be inserted everywhere when he is mentioned, like the tag " this
too is by Phocylides." To you he expressed his
thanks for undertaking the arrangement of the statues, and he laid himself out to be most uncommonly
pleasant to me. He even came to visit me in my
house at Cumae. The last thing he seemed to wish
was that Messalla should stand for the consulship :
and if you have any information on that point I should
like to know it.

I am most grateful to you for saying that you will
recommend me as a subject for a panegyric to Lucceius and for your frequent visits to my house. My
brother Quintus has written that he will pay you a
visit on the 7th of May since you have his dear child
with you. I left my villa at Cumae on the 26th of
April, spent that night with Paetus at Naples, and
am writing this very early in the morning of the 27th
on my way to my place at Pompeii.

X

CICERO TO ATTICUS, GREETING.

Puteoli is full of the report that Ptolemy is restored. If you have more definite news I should
like to know it. Here I am feasting on Faustus'

*Cumae, Apr.
22, B.C. 55*

---

[1] Following Manutius and Tyrrell. Others, however, trans-
late *iactans* as " extolling."

rebus Puteolanis et Lucrinensibus. Ne ista quidem
desunt. Sed mehercule a ceteris oblectationibus
deseror et voluptatibus propter rem publicam. Sic
litteris sustentor et recreor maloque in illa tua sede-
cula, quam habes sub imagine Aristotelis, sedere
quam in istorum sella curuli tecumque apud te ambulare quam cum eo, quocum video esse ambulandum.
Sed de illa ambulatione fors viderit, aut si qui est, qui
curet, deus; nostram ambulationem et Laconicum
eaque, quae Cyrea sint, velim, quod poterit, invisas et
urgeas Philotimum, ut properet, ut possim tibi aliquid
in eo genere respondere. Pompeius in Cumanum
Parilibus venit. Misit ad me statim, qui salutem
nuntiaret. Ad eum postridie mane vadebam, cum
haec scripsi.

XI

CICERO ATTICO SAL.

Scr. in
Cumano ex.
m. Mai. a.
699

Delectarunt me epistulae tuae, quas accepi uno
tempore duas ante diem v Kal. Perge reliqua.
Gestio scire ista omnia. Etiam illud cuius modi sit,
velim perspicias; potes a Demetrio. Dixit mihi
Pompeius Crassum a se in Albano exspectari ante
diem iiii Kal.; is cum venisset, Romam eum [1] et se
statim venturos, ut rationes cum publicanis putarent.
Quaesivi, gladiatoribusne. Respondit, antequam in-
ducerentur. Id cuius modi sit, aut nunc, si scies, aut
cum is Romam venerit, ad me mittas velim.

[1] eum *added by Lehmann.*

library. Perhaps you thought it was on the attractions of Puteoli and the Lucrine lakes. Well, I have them too. But upon my word the more I am deprived of other enjoyments and pleasures on account of the state of politics, the more support and recreation do I find in literature. And I would rather be in that niche of yours under Aristotle's statue than in their curule chair, and take a walk with you at home than have the company which I see will be with me on my path. But my path I leave to fate or god, if there be any god that looks after these things. Please have a look at my garden path and my Spartan bath and the other things which are in Cyrus' province when you can, and urge Philotimus to make haste, so that I may have something in that line to match yours. Pompey came to his place at Cumae on the Parilia: and at once sent a man to me with his compliments. I am going to call on him on the morning following, as soon as I have written this letter.

XI

CICERO TO ATTICUS, GREETING.

I was delighted with your two letters which I *Cumae,* received together on the 26th. Go on with the *May,* B.C. *55* story. I am longing to hear the whole of it. I should also like you to look into the meaning of this: you can find out from Demetrius. Pompey told me he was expecting Crassus at his house at Alba on the 27th: and as soon as he arrived they were going to Rome together to settle accounts with the tax-gatherers. I asked, " During the show of gladiators? " And he answered, " Before it begins." Please let me know what this means, either at once, if you know, or when he gets to Rome.

Nos hic voramus litteras cum homine mirifico (ita mehercule sentio) Dionysio, qui te omnesque vos salutat.

Οὐδὲν γλυκύτερον ἢ πάντ᾽ εἰδέναι. Quare ut homini curioso ita perscribe ad me, quid primus dies, quid secundus, quid censores, quid Appius, quid illa populi Appuleia; denique etiam, quid a te fiat, ad me velim scribas. Non enim, ut vere loquamur, tam rebus novis quam tuis litteris delector.

Ego mecum praeter Dionysium eduxi neminem, nec metuo tamen, ne mihi sermo desit: ita ab isto puero [1] delector. Tu Lucceio nostrum librum dabis. Demetri Magnetis tibi mitto, statim ut sit, qui a te mihi epistulam referat.

XII

CICERO ATTICO SAL.

Scr. m. Mai. a. 699 Egnatius Romae est. Sed ego cum eo de re Halimeti vehementer Anti egi. Graviter se acturum cum Aquilio confirmavit. Videbis ergo hominem, si voles. Macroni vix videor praesto esse posse; Idibus enim auctionem Larini video et biduum praeterea. Id tu, quoniam Macronem tanti facis, ignoscas mihi velim. Sed, si me diligis, postridie Kal. cena apud me cum Pilia. Prorsus id facies. Kalendis cogito in hortis Crassipedis quasi in deversorio cenare. Facio fraudem senatus consulto. Inde domum cenatus, ut sim

---

[1] ita ab isto puero *Madvig:* abs te opere *codd.*

I am devouring literature here with that extraordinary person—for upon my soul I really think he
is extraordinary—Dionysius, who sends his respects
to you and all your family.

"Than universal knowing nought more sweet."
So satisfy my curiosity by describing to me all about
the first and second days of the show, the censors,
Appius, and that unsexed Appuleius [1] of the populace: and finally, please let me know what you are
doing yourself. For to tell you the truth your
letters are as exciting to me as a revolution.

I did not bring anyone away with me except Dionysius; yet I have no fear of feeling the lack of conversation: I find the youth so entertaining. You will
give my book to Lucceius. I am sending you one by
Demetrius of Magnesia, so that there may be a messenger handy to bring back your answer at once.

XII

CICERO TO ATTICUS, GREETING.

Egnatius is at Rome: but I pleaded Halimetus' *May, B.C. 55*
cause strongly with him at Antium. He assured me
he would speak seriously to Aquilius. You can look
him up, if you like. I hardly think I can keep the
appointment with Macro: for I see that the auction
at Larinum is on the 15th and the two following
days. Pray forgive me, since you think so highly of
Macro. But as you love me, dine with me on the
2nd, and bring Pilia with you. You absolutely must.
On the 1st I am thinking of dining in Crassipes'
gardens in lieu of an inn; and so I cheat the senatorial decree.[2] From there I shall proceed home

---

[1] Clodius, compared with Appuleius Saturninus.
[2] Compelling senators to attend meetings, if in Rome.

mane praesto Miloni. Ibi te igitur videbo et permanebo.[1] Domus te nostra tota salutat.

XIII

CICERO ATTICO SAL.

Scr. in Tu-
sculano m.
Nov. post
XVII K.
Dec. a. 699
Nos in Tusculanum venisse a. d. xvii Kal. Dec
video te scire. Ibi Dionysius nobis praesto fuit
Romae a. d. xiiii Kal. volumus esse. Quid dico
" volumus "? immo vero cogimur. Milonis nuptiae.
Comitiorum non nulla opinio est. Ego, ut sit rata,[2]
afuisse me in altercationibus, quas in senatu factas
audiofero non moleste. Nam aut defendissem, quod
non placeret, aut defuissem, cui non oporteret. Sed
mehercule velim res istas et praesentem statum rei
publicae, et quo animo consules ferant hunc σκυλμόν,
scribas ad me quantum pote. Valde sum ὀξύπεινος,
et, si quaeris, omnia mihi sunt suspecta. Crassum
quidem nostrum minore dignitate aiunt profectum
paludatum quam olim aequalem eius L. Paulum, item
iterum consulem. O hominem nequam! De libris
oratoriis factum est a me diligenter. Diu multumque
in manibus fuerunt. Describas licet. Illud etiam te
rogo, τὴν παροῦσαν κατάστασιν τυπωδῶς, ne istuc
hospes veniam.

[1] permanebo *Gurlitt:* promonebo *MSS.*
[2] Ego, ut sit rata *Crat. Bosius:* ergo et si irata *M.*

after dinner, so as to keep my appointment with Milo in the morning. There then I shall see you, and I will wait till you come. My whole family sends its respects.

XIII

CICERO TO ATTICUS, GREETING.

I see you know of my arrival at my Tusculan villa *Tusculum,* on the 14th of November. There I was met by *after Nov.* Dionysius. I want to be back in Rome on the 17th. *14,* B.C. *55* When I say want, I mean I have to be in town for Milo's wedding. There is some idea of an election. Even if it has come off, I am not at all sorry to have missed the disputes which I hear have taken place in the Senate. For I should either have had to give my support against my conscience or neglect my bounden duty. But I hope to goodness you will write me as full a description as possible of that affair and of the present state of politics and tell me how the consuls are taking all this pother. I am ravenous for news, and, to tell you the truth, I suspect everything. They say our friend Crassus made a less dignified start [1] in his uniform than L. Paulus of old, who rivalled him in age and in his two consulships. What a poor thing he is! I have been working hard at the books on oratory : and have had them on hand a long time and done a lot to them : you can have them copied. Again I beg you to send me a sketch of the present situation, that I may not feel an utter stranger when I get back.

[1] For Syria.

MARCUS TULLIUS CICERO

XIV

CICERO ATTICO SAL.

Scr. in Cu-
mano m. Mai.
post VI Id.
a. 700

Vestorius noster me per litteras fecit certiorem te Roma a. d. vi Idus Maias putari profectum esse tardius, quam dixeras, quod minus valuisses. Si iam melius vales, vehementer gaudeo. Velim domum ad te scribas, ut mihi tui libri pateant non secus, ac si ipse adesses, cum ceteri tum Varronis. Est enim mihi utendum quibusdam rebus ex his libris ad eos, quos in manibus habeo; quos, ut spero, tibi valde probabo. Tu velim, si quid forte novi habes, maxime a Quinto fratre, deinde a C. Caesare, et si quid forte de comitiis, de re publica (soles enim tu haec festive odorari), scribas ad me; si nihil habebis, tamen scribas aliquid. Numquam enim mihi tua epistula aut intempestiva aut loquax visa est. Maxime autem rogo, rebus tuis totoque itinere ex sententia confecto nos quam primum revisas. Dionysium iube salvere. Cura, ut valeas.

XV

CICERO ATTICO SAL.

Scr. Romae
VI K. Sext.
a. 700

De Eutychide gratum, qui vetere praenomine, novo nomine T. erit Caecilius, ut est ex me et ex te iunctus Dionysius M. Pomponius. Valde mehercule mihi gratum est Eutychidem tuam erga me benivolentiam

304

XIV

CICERO TO ATTICUS, GREETING.

Our friend Vestorius has informed me by letter *Cumae, after* that you are believed to have left Rome on the 10th *May 10,* of May, later than you said you would, because you B.C. *54* had not been quite well. I sincerely hope you are better now. Would you please write home telling them to give me the run of your books, more especially of Varro, just as though you were there? I shall have to use some passages from those books for the works I have in hand, which I hope will meet with your hearty approval. I should be glad if you would let me know if you happen to have any news from my brother Quintus particularly, or from C. Caesar, or anything about the elections and politics—you generally have a pretty scent for such things. If you have no news, write something anyhow : for no letter of yours ever seemed ill-timed or long-winded to me. But above all pray come back as soon as possible, when your business and your tour are completed to your satisfaction. Give my regards to Dionysius. Take care of yourself.

XV

CICERO TO ATTICUS, GREETING.

I am glad to hear about Eutychides. Taking your *Rome, July* old name and your new surname, he will be T. *27,* B.C. *54* Caecilius, just as Dionysius has become M. Pomponius by a combination of yours and mine. It is really a great pleasure to me that Eutychides should know that his freedom is a favour granted on my account,

305

cognosse et [1] suam illam in meo dolore συμπάθειαν neque tum mihi obscuram neque post ingratam fuisse.

Iter Asiaticum tuum puto tibi suscipiendum fuisse; numquam enim tu sine iustissima causa tam longe a tot tuis et hominibus et rebus carissimis et suavissimis abesse voluisses. Sed humanitatem tuam amoremque in tuos reditus celeritas declarabit. Sed vereor, ne lepore suo detineat diutius rhetor [2] Clodius et homo pereruditus, ut aiunt, et nunc quidem deditus Graecis litteris Pituanius. Sed, si vis homo esse, recipe te ad nos, ad quod tempus confirmasti. Cum illis tamen, cum salvi venerint, Romae vivere licebit.

Avere te scribis accipere aliquid a me litterarum. Dedi ac multis quidem de rebus ἡμερολεγδὸν perscripta omnia; sed, ut conicio, quoniam mihi non videris in Epiro diu fuisse, redditas tibi non arbitror. Genus autem mearum ad te quidem litterarum eius modi fere est, ut non libeat cuiquam dare, nisi de quo exploratum sit tibi eum redditurum.

Nunc Romanas res accipe. A. d. IIII Nonas Quintiles Sufenas et Cato absoluti, Procilius condemnatus. Ex quo intellectum est τρισαρειοπαγίτας ambitum, comitia, interregnum, maiestatem, totam denique rem publicam flocci non facere: debemus patrem familias domi suae occidere nolle, neque tamen id ipsum abunde; nam absolverunt XXII, condemnarunt XXVIII. Publius sane diserto epilogo criminans mentes iudicum commoverat. Hortalus in ea causa fuit,

[1] et *added by Bücheler.*
[2] rhetor *Bosius*: praetor M^1: p M^2.

and that his sympathy with me in my sorrow was not lost on me at the time nor forgotten afterwards.

I suppose your journey to Asia is inevitable; for you would never want to put such a distance between yourself and all your nearest and dearest friends and possessions without very good reason. But you will show your consideration and your love for your friends by the quickness with which you return. I am, however, afraid the attractions of the rhetorician Clodius and the reputed deep learning of Pituanius, who just now is devoted to Greek literature, may keep you from returning. But if you would prove yourself a good man and true, find your way back to us by the date you promised. You can live with them when they get safely to Rome.

You say you are longing for a line of some sort from me. I have written a letter full of news, with everything described as in a diary, but I suppose it was never delivered, as you don't seem to have stopped long in Epirus. Besides, my letters are generally not of a kind that I like to give to anyone, unless I can be sure he will deliver them to you.

Now I will tell you the news of the town. On the 4th of July Sufenas and Cato were acquitted, Procilius condemned. That shows us that our lights of the law care not a straw for bribery, elections, a political deadlock, treason, or the country in general. They prefer one not to murder a father of a family in his own home; but even that preference has no overwhelming majority in its favour: for 22 voted for acquittal against 28 for condemnation. Publius no doubt had awakened the sympathy of the jury by his eloquent peroration for the prosecution. Hortalus was retained and behaved as usual. I did not

cuius modi solet. Nos verbum nullum; verita est
enim pusilla, quae nunc laborat, ne animum Publi
offenderem. His rebus actis Reatini me ad sua
Τέμπη duxerunt, ut agerem causam contra Interamnates apud consulem et decem legatos, quod lacus
Velinus a M'. Curio emissus interciso monte in Nar
defluit; ex quo est illa siccata et umida tamen modice
Rosia. Vixi cum Axio; qui etiam me ad Septem
aquas duxit.

Redii Romam Fontei causa a. d. VII Idus Quinct.
Veni spectatum primum magno et aequabili plausu.
Sed hoc ne curaris. Ego ineptus, qui scripserim.
Deinde Antiphonti operam. Is erat ante manu
missus quam productus. Ne diutius pendeas, pal-
mam tulit; sed nihil tam pusillum, nihil tam sine
voce, nihil tam . . . Verum haec tu tecum habeto.
In Andromacha tamen maior fuit quam Astyanax, in
ceteris parem habuit neminem. Quaeris nunc de
Arbuscula. Valde placuit. Ludi magnifici et grati;
venatio in aliud tempus dilata.

Sequere nunc me in campum. Ardet ambitus;
σῆμα δέ τοι ἐρέω. Faenus ex triente Idibus Quincti-
libus factum erat bessibus. Dices: "Istuc quidem
non moleste fero." O virum! o civem! Memmium
Caesaris omnes opes confirmant. Cum eo Domitium
consules iunxerunt, qua pactione, epistulae committere non audeo. Pompeius fremit, queritur, Scauro

utter a word: for my little girl, who is ill, was afraid I
might offend Publius. After all this the people of
Reate took me to their " banks and braes " to plead
their cause against the Interamnates before the consul and ten commissioners, because the Veline lake,
drained by the channel cut by M'. Curius through
the mountain,[1] flowed into the Nar. By this means
the famous Rosia has been dried up, though it is still
moderately damp. I stayed with Axius, who took me
for a visit to the Seven Waters too.

For Fonteius' sake I returned to Rome on the 9th
of July. I went to the theatre and was greeted with
loud and unbroken applause—but don't bother about
that: I am a fool to mention it. Then I gave my
attention to Antiphon. He was granted his freedom
before he appeared: and, not to keep you in suspense,
he won his laurels. But there never was such a
little weakling with so little voice and so. . . . But
keep that to yourself. However, in the Andromache
he was taller than Astyanax: among the rest there
was no one of his size. You want to know next about
Arbuscula: she pleased me very much. The games
were magnificent and much liked. The wild-beast
hunt was put off till later.

Now follow me to the election field. There is an
outburst of bribery. More by token, the rate of interest has risen from 4 per cent to 8 per cent since
the 15th of July. You will say: " Well, I can put up
with that at any rate." And you call yourself a man
and a patriot! Memmius is supported by all Caesar's
influence. The consuls have coupled him with Domitius in an agreement which I dare not commit to
paper. Pompey is raging and growling and backing

[1] The passage to the waterfall of Terni, opened in 290 B.C.

studet, sed, utrum fronte an mente, dubitatur. Ἐξοχὴ
in nullo est; pecunia omnium dignitatem exaequat.
Messalla languet, non quo aut animus desit aut amici,
sed coitio consulum et Pompeius obsunt. Ea comitia
puto fore ut ducantur. Tribunicii candidati iurarunt
se arbitrio Catonis petituros. Apud eum HS quin-
gena deposuerunt, ut, qui a Catone damnatus esset,
id perderet et competitoribus tribueretur.

Haec ego pridi scribebam, quam comitia fore putabantur. Sed ad te, quinto Kal. Sextil. si facta erunt,
et tabellarius non erit profectus, tota comitia perscribam. Quae si, ut putantur, gratuita fuerint, plus
unus Cato potuerit quam omnes leges [1] omnesque
iudices. Messius defendebatur a nobis de legatione
revocatus; nam eum Caesari legarat Appius. Servilius edixit, ut adesset. Tribus habet Pomptinam,
Velinam, Maeciam. Pugnatur acriter; agitur tamen
satis. Deinde me expedio ad Drusum, inde ad
Scaurum. Parantur orationibus indices gloriosi.
Fortasse accedent etiam consules designati. In quibus si Scaurus non fuerit, in hoc iudicio valde labora-
bit.

Ex Quinti fratris litteris suspicor iam eum esse in
Britannia. Suspenso animo exspecto, quid agat.
Illud quidem sumus adepti, quod multis et magnis

---

[1] omnes leges *added by Wesenberg*.

Scaurus; but whether ostensibly or in earnest is more than one can say. None of them is romping ahead: money levels all their ranks. Messalla is not in the running, not that his heart or his friends have failed him, but the coalition of the consuls and Pompey are both against him. I think the elections will have to be postponed. The candidates for the tribunate have taken an oath to submit their conduct to Cato's approval, and have deposited £4,400 [1] with him on the condition that any one of them who is condemned by Cato shall lose it and it shall be given to his rivals.

I am writing this the day before the elections are expected to come off. But on the 28th I will give you a full account of them, if they have taken place and the messenger has not started. If they really are conducted without bribery, which people think will be the case, then Cato alone will have done more than all the laws and all the law courts can do. I am acting for Messius, who has been recalled from his office. Appius had given him a commission on Caesar's staff: but Servilius issued a warrant requiring his presence. The tribes he has to face are the Pomptine, Veline, and Maecian. It is a sharp struggle; however, it is getting on fairly well. Then I have to get ready for Drusus and after that for Scaurus. These will make grand titles for my speeches. I may even have the names of the consuls elect to add to the list; and if Scaurus is not one of them he will find himself in serious difficulties in this trial.

From my brother Quintus' letters I suspect he is now in Britain, and I am very anxious to know how he is getting on. One point I have certainly gained:

[1] 500,000 sesterces.

indiciis possumus iudicare, nos Caesari et carissimos
et iucundissimos esse. Dionysium velim salvere
iubeas et eum roges et hortere, ut quam primum
veniat, ut possit Ciceronem meum atque etiam me
ipsum erudire.

XVI

CICERO ATTICO SAL.

*Scr. Romae
ex. m. Iun
aut in. Quint.
a. 700*

Occupationum mearum vel hoc signum erit, quod
epistula librarii manu est. De epistularum frequentia te nihil accuso, sed pleraeque tantum modo mihi
nuntiabant, ubi esses : quod erant abs te, vel etiam
significabant recte esse. Quo in genere maxime delectarunt duae fere eodem tempore abs te Buthroto
datae. Scire enim volebam te commode navigasse.
Sed haec epistularum frequentia non tam ubertate
sua quam crebritate delictavit. Illa fuit gravis et
plena rerum, quam mihi M. Paccius, hospes tuus,
reddidit. Ad eam rescribam igitur et hoc quidem
primum. Paccio ratione et verbis et re ostendi, quid
tua commendatio ponderis haberet. Itaque in intimis est meis, cum antea notus non fuisset.

Nunc pergam ad cetera. Varro, de quo ad me
scribis, includetur in aliquem locum, si modo erit locus. Sed nosti genus dialogorum meorum. Ut in
oratoriis, quos tu in caelum fers, non potuit mentio
fieri cuiusquam ab iis, qui disputant, nisi eius, qui illis
notus aut auditus esset, ita hanc ego, de re publica

Caesar has given many strong proofs which assure me of his esteem and affection. Please pay my compliments to Dionysius, and beg and urge him to come as soon as possible and undertake the instruction of my son and of myself too.

XVI

CICERO TO ATTICUS, GREETING.

The bare fact that my letter is by the hand of an amanuensis will show you how busy I am. I have nothing to grumble about as regards the frequency of your letters, but most of them merely told me where you were. That they were from you showed, too, that you were well. The two of this sort which gave me the most pleasure were those dated almost simultaneously from Buthrotum: for I was anxious to know whether you had a good crossing. But it is more the regularity of this constant supply of letters which has pleased me than the richness of their contents. The one that your guest M. Paccius delivered was of importance and full of matter: so I will answer that. The first thing is that I have shown Paccius, both by word and by deed, the weight a recommendation from you carries. Accordingly, he is among my intimate friends now, though I did not know him before.

Now for the rest. You mention Varro: I will try to get him in somewhere, if I can find a place. But you know the style of my Dialogues: just as in those *On the Orator*, which you laud to the skies, I could not let the interlocutors mention anyone except persons they had known or heard of, so here, too, in the dialogue *On the Republic* which I have begun I

Rome, June or July, B.C. 54

quam institui, disputationem in Africani personam et
Phili et Laeli et Manili contuli. Adiunxi adulescentes Q. Tuberonem, P. Rutilium, duo Laeli generos, Scaevolam et Fannium. Itaque cogitabam, quoniam in singulis libris utor prohoemiis ut Aristoteles
in iis, quos ἐξωτερικοὺς vocat, aliquid efficere, ut non
sine causa istum appellarem; id quod intellego tibi
placere. Utinam modo conata efficere possim! Rem
enim, quod te non fugit, magnam complexus sum et
gravem et plurimi otii, quo ego maxime egeo.

Quod in iis libris, quos laudas, personam desideras
Scaevolae, non eam temere dimovi: sed fecit idem
in πολιτείᾳ deus ille noster Plato. Cum in Piraeum
Socrates venisset ad Cephalum, locupletem et festivum senem, quoad primus ille sermo habetur, adest
in disputando senex, deinde, cum ipse quoque commodissime locutus esset, ad rem divinam dicit se velle
discedere neque postea revertitur. Credo Platonem
vix putasse satis consonum fore, si hominem id aetatis
in tam longo sermone diutius retinuisset. Multo ego
magis hoc mihi cavendum putavi in Scaevola, qui et
aetate et valetudine erat ea, qua eum esse meministi,
et iis honoribus, ut vix satis decorum videretur eum
plures dies esse in Crassi Tusculano. Et erat primi
libri sermo non alienus a Scaevolae studiis, reliqui
libri τεχνολογίαν habent, ut scis. Huic ioculatorem
senem illum, ut noras, interesse sane nolui.

have put the discussion in the mouths of Africanus, Philus, Laelius, and Manilius, adding the youths Q. Tubero, P. Rutilius and the two sons-in-law of Laelius, Scaevola and Fannius. So I am thinking of contriving some way of mentioning him appropriately—for that, I think, is what you want—in one of the introductions. I am giving an introduction to each book, as Aristotle does in the work he called the *Exoterics*. And I only hope I may manage to get him in. For as you fully comprehend, I have set my hand to a subject of wide range and of some difficulty which requires much leisure; and that is precisely what I have not got.

While praising those books, you miss the character of Scaevola from the scene. It was not without good reason that I removed him. Our god Plato did the same in his *Republic*. When Socrates called on that wealthy and cheery old soul Cephalus in the Piraeus the old man takes part in the discussion during the introductory conversation; but after a very neat speech he pleads that he wants to go to a divine service, and does not come back again. I fancy Plato thought it would have been inartistic to keep a man of that age any longer in so lengthy a discussion. I thought there was still more reason to be careful in the case of Scaevola, who was at the age and in the state of health in which you must remember he was, and was crowned with such honours that it would hardly have been proper for him to spend several days with Crassus at his villa at Tusculum. Besides, the talk in the first book was not unconnected with Scaevola's pursuits: while the remaining books contained a technical discussion, as you know. In such I did not like the merry old man, you remember, to take a part.

De re Piliae quod scribis, erit mihi curae. Etenim
est luculenta res Aureliani, ut scribis, indiciis. Et in
eo me etiam Tulliae meae venditabo. Vestorio non
desum. Gratum enim tibi id esse intellego et, ut ille
intellegat, curo. Sed scis, qui. Cum habeat duo
faciles, nihil difficilius.

Nunc ad ea, quae quaeris de C. Catone. Lege
Iunia et Licinia scis absolutum; Fufia ego tibi nuntio
absolutum iri neque patronis suis tam libentibus quam
accusatoribus. Is tamen et mecum et cum Milone in
gratiam rediit. Drusus reus est factus a Lucretio.
Iudicibus reiciendis dies est dictus [1] a. d. v Non.
Quinct. De Procilio rumores non boni, sed iudicia
nosti. Hirrus cum Domitio in gratia est. Senatus
consultum, quod hi consules de provinciis fecerunt,
Qvicvmqve posthac —, non mihi videtur esse vali-
turum.

xvii, 2 De Messalla quod quaeris, quid scribam, nescio.
Numquam ego vidi tam pares candidatos. Messallae
copias nosti. Scaurum Triarius reum fecit. Si quaeris, nulla est magno opere commota συμπάθεια, sed
tamen habet aedilitas eius memoriam non ingratam,
et est pondus apud rusticos in patris memoria. Reliqui duo plebeii sic exaequantur, ut Domitius valeat
amicis, adiuvetur tamen non nihil [2] gratissimo munere, Memmius Caesaris commendetur militibus,
Pompei Gallia nitatur. Quibus si non valuerit, pu-

---

[1] dies est dictus, *added by Madvig.*
[2] nihil *added by Wesenberg.*

In Pilia's business I will be sure to do what you suggest: for, as you say, the point is quite clear on Aurelianus' evidence. And it will give me a chance of glorifying myself in my Tullia's eyes. I am supporting Vestorius: for I see you regard it as a favour, and I make him see it too. But you know the kind of man he is: frightfully difficult to get on with, even for two such easy-going people.

Now for your questions about C. Cato. You know he was acquitted under the Junian and Licinian law. The Fufian law will acquit him too, I assure you, and that as much to the relief of his accusers as of his supporters. However, he has made his peace with Milo and myself. Drusus is being prosecuted by Lucretius. The day for challenging the jury is fixed for the 3rd of July. About Procilius there are sinister rumours: but you know what juries are. Hirrus is on good terms with Domitius. The decree which these consuls have carried about the provinces, " whosoever henceforth," etc., I do not think will have any effect.

I don't know what to say to your question about Messalla: I have never seen candidates more evenly matched. You know Messalla's support. Scaurus has been called into court by Triarius; without any great sympathy for him being aroused, if you want to know. However, his aedileship recalls no unpleasant memories, and their remembrance of his father has some weight with the country voters. The other two plebeian candidates are about equal, as Domitius is strong in friends and his very popular gladiatorial exhibition will count for him too, while Memmius is popular with Caesar's soldiers and relies on the support of Pompey's Gaul. If that does not avail him

tant fore aliquem, qui comitia in adventum Caesaris detrudat, Catone praesertim absoluto.

Paccianae epistulae respondi. Nunc te obiurgari patere, si iure. Scribis enim in ea epistula, quam C. Decimius mihi reddidit Buthroto datam, in Asiam tibi eundum esse te arbitrari. Mihi mehercule nihil videbatur esse, in quo tantulum interesset utrum per procuratores ageres an per te ipsum, ut a tuis [1] totiens et tam longe abesses. Sed haec mallem integra re tecum egissem, profecto enim aliquid egissem. Nunc reprimam susceptam obiurgationem. Utinam valeat ad celeritatem reditus tui!

Ego ad te propterea minus saepe scribo, quod certum non habeo, ubi sis aut ubi futurus sis; huic tamen nescio cui, quod videbatur isti te visurus esse, putavi dandas esse litteras. Tu, quoniam iturum te in Asiam esse putas, ad quae tempora te exspectemus, facias me certiorem velim, et de Eutychide quid egeris.

XVII [XVIII]

CICERO ATTICO SAL.

Scr. Romae
K. Oct. a.
700 Puto te existimare me nunc oblitum consuetudinis et instituti mei rarius ad te scribere, quam solebam; sed, quoniam loca et itinera tua nihil habere certi video, neque in Epirum neque Athenas neque in Asiam cuiquam nisi ad te ipsum proficiscenti dedi litteras. Neque enim sunt epistulae nostrae eae quae si perlatae non sint, nihil ea res nos offensura sit; quae tantum habent mysteriorum, ut eas ne librariis

---

[1] ut a tuis *Boot*: mutabis *M*.

it is thought someone will block the elections till Caesar's return, especially since Cato's acquittal.

There, I have answered the letter Paccius brought. Now you must let me scold you, if you deserve it. In the letter dated from Buthrotum which was delivered by C. Decimius, you say you think you will have to go to Asia. For the life of me I cannot see any reason why it should make the least little bit of difference whether you act by proxy or in person; nor why you should so often go to such out-of-the-way places. But I wish I had tackled you about it before you had taken any steps: then I should certainly have had some influence. As it is, I will keep the rest of my scolding for another time. I only hope it may prevail on you to return quickly.

The reason why I write so seldom to you is that I do not know where you are or are going to be. But as there was someone or other who thought he might see you, I decided to give him this letter. Since you think of going to Asia, let me know when we may expect you back and what you have done about Eutychides.

XVII [XVIII]

CICERO TO ATTICUS, GREETING.

I suppose you think I have forgotten my old cus- *Rome,* tom and rule and write less frequently than I used; *Oct. 1,* but the fact is that I have not given letters to anyone B.C. *54* going to Epirus or Athens or Asia unless he was going expressly to you, because there was no certainty where you were or where you were going. For our letters are not such that it would do no harm to us if they are not delivered. They are so full of

quidem fere committamus, lepidum quid ne [1] quo excidat.

Consules flagrant infamia, quod C. Memmius candidatus pactionem in senatu recitavit, quam ipse et suus competitor Domitius cum consulibus fecisset, uti ambo HS quadragena consulibus darent, si essent ipsi consules facti, nisi tres augures dedissent, qui se adfuisse dicerent, cum lex curiata ferretur, quae lata non esset, et duo consulares, qui se dicerent in ornandis provinciis consularibus scribendo adfuisse, cum omnino ne senatus quidem fuisset. Haec pactio non verbis, sed nominibus et perscriptionibus multorum tabulis cum esse facta diceretur, prolata a Memmio est nominibus inductis auctore Pompeio. Hic Appius erat idem. Nihil sane iacturae. Corruerat alter, et plane, inquam, iacebat. Memmius autem dirempta coitione invito Calvino plane refrixerat, et eo magis nunc totus iacet,[2] quod iam intellegebamus enuntiationem illam Memmi valde Caesari displicere. Messalla noster et eius Domitius competitor liberalis in populo valde fuit. Nihil gratius. Certi erant consules. At senatus decrevit, ut tacitum iudicium ante comitia fieret ab iis consiliis, quae erant omnibus sortita, in singulos candidatos. Magnus timor candidatorum. Sed quidam iudices, in his Opimius,

xvi, 6

---

[1] quid ne *added by Tyrrell.*
[2] totus iacet *Reid*: cociace *M.*

secrets that we cannot even trust an amanuensis as a rule, for fear of some jest leaking out.

The consuls' infamy has had a lurid light thrown on it owing to C. Memmius, one of the candidates, reading out in the Senate an agreement made by himself and his fellow-candidate Domitius with them. If they were elected to the consulship they were both to give the consuls £350 each if they did not produce three augurs who would depose that they were present at the carrying of a *lex curiata*—which had never been passed; and two ex-consuls who would depose to having been present at the drafting of a decree for the fitting out of the consular provinces —though there had never been any meeting of the Senate about it at all. As this compact was alleged not to be a mere verbal compact, but one properly drawn up with the sums promised on it, drafts on the bank, and many other documents, Memmius exhibited it, with all the items entered,[1] on the suggestion of Pompey. It was all the same to Appius: he had nothing to lose by it. The other has had a sad come-down, and I may say is quite done for. Memmius, however, having dissolved the coalition against Calvinus' will, has sunk out of mind, and his ruin is all the more irretrievable because we know now that his disclosure annoyed Caesar very much. Our friend Messalla and his fellow-competitor Domitius were very liberal to the people, and could not be more popular. They are certain of election. But the Senate has decreed that a trial with closed doors should be held before the elections, and each candidate's conduct inquired into by the panels chosen by lot for all of them. The candidates are in a great fright: but some of the

[1] Or " cancelled."

Veiento, Rantius, tribunos pl. appellarunt, ne iniussu
populi iudicarent. Res cedit; comitia dilata ex senatus consulto, dum lex de tacito iudicio ferretur.
Venit legi dies. Terentius intercessit. Consules, qui
illud levi brachio egissent, rem ad senatum detulerunt. His Abdera non tacente me. Dices: "Tamen tu non quiescis?" Ignosce, vix possum. Verum
tamen quid tam ridiculum? Senatus decreverat, ne
prius comitia haberentur, quam lex lata esset; si qui
intercessisset, res integra referretur. Coepta ferri
leviter, intercessum non invitis, res ad senatum. De
ea re ita censuerunt, comitia primo quoque tempore
haberi esse e re publica.

xvi, 7 Scaurus, qui erat paucis diebus illis absolutus, cum
ego partem eius ornatissime defendissem, obnuntia-
tionibus per Scaevolam interpositis singulis diebus
usque ad pr. Kal. Octobr., quo ego haec die scripsi,
sublatis populo tributim domi suae satis fecerat. Sed
tamen, etsi uberior liberalitas huius, gratior esse
videbatur eorum, qui occuparant. Cuperem vultum
videre tuum, cum haec legeres; nam profecto spem
habes nullam haec negotia multarum nundinarum
fore. Sed senatus hodie fuerat futurus, id est Kal.
Octobribus; iam enim luciscit. Ibi loquetur praeter

jury—among them Opimus, Veiento, and Rantius—
have appealed to the tribunes to prevent their being
called upon to serve without the sanction of the
people. The affair is going on. A senatorial decree
postponed the elections until an enactment about the
trial with closed doors was carried. The day for that
enactment came, and Terentius vetoed it. The consuls, who were taking the matter very coolly, referred
the point to the Senate. Thereupon there was Bed-
lam, and I contributed my share of noise. You will
say : " Can you never hold your tongue ? " Forgive
me : I hardly can. But could anything be more ridi-
culous ? The Senate had passed a decree that the
elections should not be held before that enactment
was passed : if it was vetoed, then the matter should
be brought forward again. The law was brought forward casually ; it was vetoed to the satisfaction of the
proposers; the matter was referred to the Senate: and
they decided that it was to the interest of the State
that the elections should be held as soon as possible.

Scaurus, who was acquitted in the last few days,
after a most elaborate speech from me in his defence,
gave the requisite donations to the people tribe by
tribe at his own house, since all the days up to the
last of September, on which I am writing, had been
rendered impossible for the elections by ill omens
announced by Scaevola. But though his liberality
exceeded theirs, those who came first won the most
popularity. I should like to see your face as you read
this. For of course you have no hope that the business will be protracted over many weeks. But there
is going to be a meeting of the Senate on the first
of October, to-day, for the day is already breaking.
There no one will speak boldly except Antius and

Antium et Favonium libere nemo; nam Cato aegrotat. De me nihil timueris, sed tamen promitto nihil.

vi, 8 Quid quaeris aliud? Iudicia, credo. Drusus, Scaurus non fecisse videntur. Tres candidati fore rei putabantur, Domitius a Memmio, Messalla a Q. Pompeio Rufo, Scaurus a Triario aut a L. Caesare. " Quid poteris," inquies, " pro iis dicere?" Ne vivam, si scio; in illis quidem tribus libris, quos tu dilaudas, nihil reperio.

xvi, 13 Cognosce cetera. Ex fratris litteris incredibilia quaedam de Caesaris in me amore cognovi, eaque sunt ipsius Caesaris uberrimis litteris confirmata. Britannici belli exitus exspectatur; constat enim aditus insulae esse muratos[1] mirificis molibus. Etiam illud iam cognitum est, neque argenti scripulum esse ullum in illa insula neque ullam spem praedae nisi ex mancipiis; ex quibus nullos puto te litteris aut musicis eruditos exspectare.

xvi, 14 Paulus in medio foro basilicam iam paene refecit isdem antiquis columnis, illam autem, quam locavit, facit magnificentissimam. Quid quaeris? nihil gratius illo monumento, nihil gloriosius. Itaque Caesaris amici, me dico et Oppium, dirumparis licet, in monumentum illud, quod tu tollere laudibus solebas, ut forum laxaremus et usque ad atrium Libertatis explicaremus, contempsimus sexcenties HS; cum privatis

---

[1] muratos, *Junius, Tyrrell*: miratos *M*: munitos *E*.

Favonius: Cato is ill. You need not be afraid for me, but I won't promise anything.

What else do you want to know? Oh! the trials, I suppose. Drusus and Scaurus are thought to be innocent. Three candidates will probably be prosecuted, Domitius by Memmius, Messalla by Q. Pompeius Rufus, Scaurus by Triarius or L. Caesar. What shall I be able to find to say for them, you will ask. May I die if I know. Certainly I find no suggestions in those three books you praise so highly.

Here is the other news. From my brother's letters I hear that Caesar shows signs of extraordinary affection for me, and this is confirmed by a very cordial letter from Caesar himself. The result of the war in Britain is looked forward to with anxiety. For it is proved that the approach to the island is guarded with astonishing masses of rock and it has been ascertained, too, that there is not a scrap of silver in the island, nor any hope of booty except from slaves; but I don't fancy you will find any with literary or musical talents among them.

Paulus has almost reached the roof of his colonnade in the Forum. He has used the same old columns, but has executed most magnificently the part he put out on contract. It goes without saying that a monument like that will win for him more popularity and glory than anything. And so we friends of Caesar—myself and Oppius I mean, though you may explode with wrath at my confession—have thought nothing of spending half a million of money [1] for that public work of which you used to speak so enthusiastically, the extension of the Forum and continuation of it as far as the Hall of Liberty. We could not

---

[1] 60,000,000 sesterces.

non poterat transigi minore pecunia. Efficiemus
rem gloriosissimam ; nam in campo Martio saepta tributis comitiis marmorea sumus et tecta facturi eaque
cingemus excelsa porticu, ut mille passuum conficia-
tur.   Simul adiungetur huic operi villa etiam publica.
Dices : " Quid mihi hoc monumentum proderit ? "
At quid id laboramus ?   Habes res Romanas.   Non
enim te puto de lustro, quod iam desperatum est,
aut de iudiciis, quae lege Coctia fiant, quaerere.

XVIII

CICERO ATTICO SAL.

xvi, 9

Scr. Romae
ex. m. Oct. a.
700

. . . Nunc ut opinionem habeas rerum, ferendum
est.   Quaeris, ego me ut gesserim.   Constanter et
libere. " Quid ? ille," inquies, " ut ferebat ? "
Humaniter meaeque dignitatis, quoad mihi satis
factum esset, habendam sibi rationem putabat.   Quo
modo ergo absolutus ?   Omnino γοργεῖα γυμνά.[1]   Ac-
cusatorum incredibilis infantia, id est L. Lentuli L. f.,
quem fremunt omnes praevaricatum, deinde Pompei
mira contentio, iudicum sordes.   Ac tamen XXXII condemnarunt, XXXVIII absolverunt.   Iudicia reliqua im-

xvi, 10 pendent.   Nondum est plane expeditus.   Dices :
" Tu ergo haec quo modo fers ? "   Belle mehercule
et in eo me valde amo.   Amisimus, mi Pomponi,

[1] γοργεῖα γυμνά *Bosius :* ΠΟΡΠΑΠΥΝΝΑ *M.*

satisfy the private owners with less; but we will make it a most magnificent affair. In the Campus Martius we are going to make polling-barriers of marble for the tribal assemblies, roof them over, and surround them with a lofty colonnade a mile in circumference. And at the same time we shall join this to the Villa Publica. You will ask, "What advantage shall I derive from the work?" But we need not go into that now. That is all the public news. For I don't suppose you will want to hear about the lustration which is given up in despair, or about the trials which are taking place in accordance with the Coctian law.

XVIII

CICERO TO ATTICUS, GREETING.

. . . So now, to give you my opinion on affairs, we have got to put up with them. You want to know how I behaved. With firmness and boldness. You will ask how Pompey took things. Quite kindly, evidently thinking he must consider my dignity until satisfaction had been paid to me. How did Gabinius come to be acquitted, then? It was simply a puppet show: the behaviour of the accusers—that is to say of L. Lentulus, the younger, who is being universally accused of collusion—was incredibly infantile: Pompey exerted his influence energetically: and the jury were a rotten lot. Still 32 voted for condemnation and 38 for acquittal. Other trials are hanging over his head: he is not out of the wood yet. You will say: "How, then, do you take it?" Quite coolly, upon my word, and I congratulate myself thereon. The State, my dear Pomponius, has lost not only its sap

Rome, Oct., B.C. 54

omnem non modo sucum ac sanguinem, sed etiam colorem et speciem pristinam civitatis. Nulla est res publica, quae delectet, in qua acquiescam. " Idne igitur," inquies, " facile fers ? " Id ipsum ; recordor enim, quam bella paulisper nobis gubernantibus civitas fuerit, quae mihi gratia relata sit. Nullus dolor me angit unum omnia posse ; dirumpuntur ii, qui me aliquid posse doluerunt. Multa mihi dant solacia, nec tamen ego de meo statu demigro, quaeque vita maxime est ad naturam, ad eam me refero, ad litteras et studia nostra. Dicendi laborem delectatione oratoria consolor ; domus me et rura nostra delectant ; non recordor, unde ceciderim, sed unde surrexerim. Fratrem mecum et te si habebo, per me isti pedibus trahantur ; vobis ἐμφιλοσοφῆσαι possum. Locus ille animi nostri, stomachus ubi habitabat olim, concalluit ; privata modo et domestica nos delectant. Miram securitatem videbis ; cuius plurimae mehercule partes sunt in tuo reditu ; nemo enim in terris est mihi tam consentientibus sensibus.

xvi, 11 Sed accipe alia. Res fluit ad interregnum, et est non nullus odor dictaturae, sermo quidem multus ; qui etiam Gabinium apud timidos iudices adiuvit. Candidati consulares omnes rei ambitus. Accedit etiam Gabinius ; quem P. Sulla non dubitans, quin foris esset, postularat contra dicente et nihil obtinente

and blood, but even all its old colour and outward semblance. There is in fact no Republic to give me a feeling of joy and peace. "And is that what you find so comfortable?" you may ask. That is the very thing. For I remember its glory during the little while when I directed it, and the return that was paid me. It does not cost me a pang to see one man omnipotent: but those who were annoyed at my small power are bursting with indignation. There are many things which bring consolation to me without my stirring from my original position; and I am returning to the life which suits my nature best, to literature and my studies. For the labour of pleading I console myself by my delight in oratory. I find pleasure in my town house and my country houses. I think not of the height from which I have fallen, but of the depths from which I have risen. If I have but my brother and you with me, they may be hanged, drawn, and quartered for all I care: I can study philosophy with you. That part of my soul which used to harbour wrath has lost its power of feeling. Now only my private and personal affairs interest me. You will find me in a wonderfully peaceful state of mind, and upon my word your return is a great factor in my peace: for there is no one in the world whose spirit so harmonizes with my own.

But now I will tell you the other news. Things are drifting towards an interregnum: and a dictatorship is in the air. There is a great deal of talk about it, which helped Gabinius with timid jurors. All the candidates for the consulship are accused of bribery. Gabinius is with them too. P. Sulla applied for the prosecution of him, suspecting that he would be too out of pocket to bribe a jury. Torquatus applied too,

Torquato. Sed omnes absolventur, nec posthac quisquam damnabitur, nisi qui hominem occiderit. Hoc tamen agitur severius, itaque indicia calent. M. Fulvius Nobilior condemnatus est; multi alii urbani ne respondent quidem.

xvi, 12 Quid aliud novi? Etiam. Absoluto Gabinio stomachantes alii iudices hora post Antiochum Gabinium nescio quem e Sopolidis pictoribus libertum, accensum Gabini, lege Papia condemnarunt. Itaque dixit statim resp. lege maiestatis ΟΥΣΟΙΜΡΙΣΑΜΑΦΙΗΙ. Pomptinus vult a. d. iiii Non. Novembr. triumphare. Huic obviam Cato et Servilius praetores ad portam et Q. Mucius tribunus. Negant enim latum de imperio, et est latum hercule insulse. Sed erit cum Pomptino Appius consul. Cato tamen adfirmat se vivo illum non triumphaturum. Id ego puto ut multa eiusdem ad nihil recasurum. Appius sine lege suo sumptu in Ciliciam cogitat.

xvii, 3 A Quinto fratre et a Caesare accepi a. d. viiii Kal. Nov. litteras datas a litoribus Britanniae proximis a. d. vi Kal. Octobr. Confecta Britannia, obsidibus acceptis, nulla praeda, imperata tamen pecunia exercitum ex Britannia reportabant. Q. Pilius erat iam ad Caesarem profectus. Tu, si aut amor in te est nostri ac tuorum aut ulla veritas, aut etiam si sapis ac

but did not obtain it. But they will all be acquitted, and in future no one will be condemned except for homicide. That charge is being severely dealt with, and so informers are busy. M. Fulvius Nobilior has been condemned: and a number of others are polite enough not even to answer the charge.

Any other news? Yes. An hour after the acquittal of Gabinius another jury in indignation condemned someone called Antiochus Gabinius, out of Sopolis' studio, a freedman and attendant of Gabinius, under the Papian law. He at once said, " So the State will not acquit me of treason as it did you." [1]

Pomptinus wants to celebrate his triumph on the 2nd of November. He is openly opposed by the praetors Cato and Servilius and the tribune Q. Mucius, who declare that no authority was ever given for a triumph: and it certainly was given in the most absurd manner. However, Pomptinus will have the consul Appius on his side. Cato declares he shall never triumph as long as he lives. I fancy it will all come to nothing like most similar affairs. Appius is thinking of going to Cilicia without authority and at his own expense.

On the 24th of October I received a letter from my brother Quintus and from Caesar, dated from the nearest point on the coast of Britain on the 25th of September. Britain is settled, hostages taken, no booty, but a tribute imposed; and they are bringing back the army from the place. Q. Pilius was just on his way to Caesar. If you have any affection for me and your family, if any trust can be put in your word, nay, if you have any sense and want to enjoy your

---

[1] The Greek words here are corrupt. The translation follows Schuckburgh's emendation οὐ σοί κεν ἄρ᾿ ἰσά μ᾿ ἀφείη.

frui tuis commodis cogitas, adventare et prope adesse
iam debes.   Non mehercule aequo animo te careo ; te
autem quid mirum, qui Dionysium tanto opere desi-
derem ?   Quem quidem abs te, cum dies venerit, et
ego et Cicero meus flagitabit.   Abs te proximas litteras habebam Epheso a. d. v Idus Sextil. datas.

XIX [XVII]

CICERO ATTICO SAL.

Scr. Romae
ex. m. Nov.
a. 700

O exspectatas mihi tuas litteras ! o gratum adventum ! o constantiam promissi et fidem miram ! o navi-
gationem amandam ! quam mehercule ego valde
timebam recordans superioris tuae transmissionis
δέρρεις. Sed, nisi fallor, citius te, quam scribis,
videbo. Credo enim te putasse tuas mulieres in
Apulia esse. Quod cum secus erit, quid te Apulia
moretur ? Num Vestorio dandi sunt dies et ille Lati-
nus ἀττικισμὸς ex intervallo regustandus ? Quin tu
huc advolas et invisis illius nostrae rei publicae germa-
nae imaginem.[1] Disputavi de nummis ante comitia

xviii, 3

tributim uno loco divisis palam, inde absolutum Gabinium : remp. in [2] dictaturam ruere [3] iustitio et omnium rerum licentia. Perspice aequitatem animi mei
et lauda meam [4] contemptionem Seleucianae provinciae et mehercule cum Caesare suavissimam coniunc-
tionem (haec enim me una ex hoc naufragio tabula

---

[1] imaginem *added by Wesenberg.* disputavi *Madvig*: putavi *MSS.*
[2] remp. in *added by Madvig.*   [3] ruere *Madvig*: fruere *M.*
[4] lauda meam *Boot*: ludum et *M.*

blessings, you ought to be on your way home and very close at hand too. Upon my word, I cannot endure your absence. And what wonder that I want you, when I miss Dionysius so much? Him both I and little Marcus shall demand from you at the proper time. The last letter I had from you was posted from Ephesus on the 9th of August.

XIX [XVII]

CICERO TO ATTICUS, GREETING.

How I have longed for this letter! And how glad *Rome, Nov.* I am to hear of your arrival! You have kept your B.C. *54* promise with marvellous exactitude and fidelity. What a charming voyage! Of that I was really very much afraid, remembering the fur-coats of your former crossing. But, unless I am mistaken, I shall see you earlier than you say. I fancy you think your ladies are still in Apulia. That is not the case, so there will be nothing to keep you there. You surely won't throw days away on Vestorius and have another taste of his Latin Greek after all this interval. Fly hither rather, and visit the remains of what was once our genuine Republic. I have discussed the open bribery of the people tribe by tribe before the elections, and the consequent acquittal of Gabinius. Things are tending to a dictatorship, what with the deadlock and the general licence. Observe my placidity and praise my contempt for the Seleucinian province,[1] and my really delightful association with Caesar. That is the one plank left in this shipwreck to delight my eyes. Heavens! how he does load

---

[1] The whole of this passage is very doubtful, and the reference in *Seleucianae provinciae* is unknown.

delectat); qui quidem Quintum meum tuumque, di boni! quem ad modum tractat honore, dignitate, gratia! non secus ac si ego essem imperator. Hiberna legionis eligendi optio delata commodum, ut ad me Quintus scribit. Hunc tu non ames? quem igitur istorum?

Sed heus tu! scripseramne tibi me esse legatum Pompeio et extra urbem quidem fore ex Idibus Ianuariis? Visum est hoc mihi ad multa quadrare. Sed quid plura? Coram, opinor, reliqua, ut tu tamen aliquid exspectes. Dionysio plurimam salutem; cui quidem ego non modo servavi, sed etiam aedificavi locum. Quid quaeris? ad summam laetitiam meam, quam ex tuo reditu capio, magnus illius adventus cumulus accedit. Quo die ad me venies, fac ut, si me amas, apud me cum tuis maneas.

your and my Quintus with honours and dignities and favours! Just as though I were a commander-in-chief. The choice of any of the army winter-quarters has just been given him, as Quintus writes me. If one does not fall in love with such a man, which of the others could one fall in love with?

By the bye, had I told you I am on Pompey's staff, and from the 13th of January shall not be in Rome? It seemed to me to square with a good many things. I need not say more. I think I will leave the rest till we meet to give you something to look forward to. My best respects to Dionysius. I have not merely kept a place for him; I have built one. In fact, his coming will add a finishing stroke to the great joy I shall find in your return. The day you arrive, I must insist on you and your company staying with me.

M. TULLI CICERONIS
EPISTULARUM AD ATTICUM
LIBER QUINTUS

I

CICERO ATTICO SAL.

Scr. Mentur-
nis III aut
prid. Non.
Mai. a. 703

Ego vero et tuum in discessu vidi animum et meo
sum ipse testis. Quo magis erit tibi videndum, ne
quid novi decernatur, ut hoc nostrum desiderium ne
plus sit annuum. De Annio Saturnino curasti probe.
De satis dando vero te rogo, quoad eris Romae, tu
ut satis des. Et sunt aliquot satisdationes secundum
mancipium veluti Mennianorum praediorum vel
Atilianorum. De Oppio factum est, ut volui, et
maxime quod $\overline{\text{DCCC}}$ aperuisti. Quae quidem ego
utique vel versura facta solvi volo, ne extrema exactis
nostrorum nominum exspectetur.

Nunc venio ad transversum illum extremae epistulae tuae versiculum, in quo me admones de sorore.
Quae res se sic habet. Ut veni in Arpinas, cum ad
me frater venisset, in primis nobis sermo isque multus
de te fuit. Ex quo ego veni ad ea, quae fueramus
ego et tu inter nos de sorore in Tusculano locuti.
Nihil tam vidi mite, nihil tam placatum, quam tum
meus frater erat in sororem tuam, ut, etiam si qua

336

CICERO'S LETTERS
TO ATTICUS
BOOK V

I

CICERO TO ATTICUS, GREETING.

Yes, I did see your feelings when we parted, and *Menturnae*, to my own I can testify. That is an additional *May 5 or 6,* reason why you should take care that no new decrees B.C. *51* are passed to prevent this painful separation from lasting more than one year. You have taken the right steps with Annius Saturninus. As to the guarantee, please give it yourself, while you are in town. There are some proofs of ownership, for instance those for Mennius' or rather Atilius' estate. You have done exactly what I wanted in Oppius' case, especially in putting the £7,000 [1] to his credit. I must have that paid off without waiting till I've got in all my arrears, even if I have to get into the hands of the Jews [2] over it.

Now I come to the line you wrote crosswise at the end of your letter, in which you give me a word of advice about your sister. The facts of the case are that when I reached Arpinum and my brother had come the first thing we did was to have a long talk about you. After that I brought the talk round to the discussion you and I had about your sister at Tusculum. My brother's behaviour then to your sister was gentleness and kindness itself. If there

---

[1] 800,000 sesterces.
[2] *Versuram facere* = to borrow money to pay off a previous loan.

fuerat ex ratione sumptus offensio, non appareret.
Ille sic dies. Postridie ex Arpinati profecti sumus.
Ut in Arcano Quintus maneret, dies fecit, ego Aquini,
sed prandimus in Arcano. Nosti hunc fundum. Quo
ut venimus, humanissime Quintus " Pomponia " inquit, " tu invita mulieres, ego arcivero viros." Nihil
potuit, mihi quidem ut visum est, dulcius idque cum
verbis tum etiam animo ac vultu. At illa audientibus
nobis " Ego ipsa sum " inquit " hic hospita," id autem
ex eo, ut opinor, quod antecesserat Statius, ut pran-
dium nobis videret. Tum Quintus " En " inquit mihi
" haec ego patior cotidie." Dices : " Quid, quaeso,
istuc erat ? " Magnum ; itaque me ipsum commoverat ; sic absurde et aspere verbis vultuque respon-
derat. Dissimulavi dolens. Discubuimus omnes praeter illam, cui tamen Quintus de mensa misit. Illa
reiecit. Quid multa ? nihil meo fratre lenius, nihil
asperius tua sorore mihi visum est ; et multa prae-
tereo, quae tum mihi maiori stomacho quam ipsi
Quinto fuerunt. Ego inde Aquinum. Quintus in
Arcano remansit et Aquinum ad me postridie mane
venit mihique narravit nec secum illam dormire
voluisse et, cum discessura esset, fuisse eius modi, qualem ego vidissem. Quid quaeris ? vel ipsi hoc dicas
licet, humanitatem ei meo iudicio illo die defuisse.

Haec ad te scripsi fortasse pluribus, quam necesse
fuit, ut videres tuas quoque esse partes instituendi et
monendi. Reliquum est, ut, antequam proficiscare,
mandata nostra, exhaurias, scribas ad me omnia, Pom-

ever was any quarrel about expense, there were no signs of it. So passed that day. On the next day we started from Arpinum. A festival caused Quintus to stop at Arcanum, and me at Aquinum: but we lunched together at Arcanum. You know his place there. Well, when we reached it Quintus said most politely, " Pomponia, you invite the ladies, I will ask the men." Nothing, so far as I could see, could have been more gentle than his words or his intention or his expression. But before us all she answered, " I'm only a stranger here "; just because Statius had been sent on in front to get dinner ready for us, I suppose. Says Quintus to me: " There you are. That's what I have to put up with every day." You may say there surely was not much in that. But there was a good deal: indeed, she upset me myself; she answered with such uncalled-for acrimony in word and look. I concealed my annoyance. We all took our places except her: but Quintus sent her something from the table, which she refused. In a word, it seemed to me that my brother was as good-tempered and your sister as cross as could be, and I have omitted a lot of things that aroused my wrath more than Quintus'. Then I went on to Aquinum. Quintus stayed at Arcanum, and came to me the next morning, and told me that she would not sleep with him, and when she was leaving she was as cross as when I saw her. In fact, I don't care if you tell her herself, that to my mind she behaved with a lack of courtesy that day.

I have said perhaps more than necessary about it to show you that it is your turn to do a little instructing and advising too. It only remains for you to fulfil all my commissions before you start, and send me an account of all of them, to rout Pomptinus out, and

339

ptinum extrudas, cum profectus eris, cures, ut sciam,
sic habeas, nihil mehercule te mihi nec carius esse nec
suavius. A. Torquatum amantissime dimisi Men-
turnis, optimum virum; cui me ad te scripsisse aliquid
in sermone significes velim.

II

CICERO ATTICO SAL.

Scr. in Pom-
peiano VI
Id. Mai. a.
703

A. d. vi Idus Maias, cum has dabam litteras, ex
Pompeiano proficiscebar, ut eo die manerem in Trebulano apud Pontium. Deinde cogitabam sine ulla
mora iusta itinera facere. In Cumano cum essem,
venit ad me, quod mihi pergratum fuit, noster Hortensius; cui deposcenti mea mandata cetera universe
mandavi, illud proprie, ne pateretur, quantum esset
in ipso, prorogari nobis provincias. In quo eum tu
velim confirmes gratumque mihi fecisse dicas, quod
et venerit ad me et hoc mihi, praetereaque si quid
opus esset, promiserit. Confirmavi ad eam causam
etiam Furnium nostrum, quem ad annum tribunum
pl. videbam fore. Habuimus in Cumano quasi pusil-
lam Romam. Tanta erat in his locis multitudo; cum
interim Rufio noster, quod se a Vestorio observari
videbat, strategemate hominem percussit; nam ad
me non accessit. Itane? cum Hortensius veniret et
infirmus et tam longe et Hortensius, cum maxima
praeterea multitudo, ille non venit? Non, inquam.
" Non vidisti igitur hominem? " inquies. Qui potui
non videre, cum per emporium Puteolanorum iter

when you have left to let me know, believing that
there is nothing I hold dearer than yourself, nothing
that gives me more delight. I bade that good fellow,
A. Torquatus, a most affectionate farewell at Menturnae. I should like you to tell him I mentioned him
in a letter.

II

CICERO TO ATTICUS, GREETING.

On the 10th of May, the date of this letter, I set
out from my villa at Pompeii to spend the day with
Pontius in his villa at Trebula. Thereafter I mean to
do my day's journey regularly without delay. While
I was in my villa at Cumae our friend Hortensius
paid me a very welcome visit. He asked if I had
any commissions, and I gave him commissions in
general, and in particular to prevent to the best of
his ability extension of my term of office in my province. Please keep him up to it, and tell him that
I was much gratified at his visit, and at his promises
on that particular point and of any other assistance
I might need. I have bound our friend Furnius, who,
I see, will be tribune next year, to help me in the
same matter. My villa at Cumae was a miniature
Rome; there were such a lot of people in the neighbourhood. In the middle of it all our friend Rufio,
seeing that Vestorius was on his tracks, baffled the
man by a ruse; for he did not come to me. You may
be surprised that he did not come, seeing that Hortensius came, who is ill, lives afar off, and is a great
man, and crowds of other people came as well. I
repeat he did not come. You may infer I did not
see him. How could I fail to see him when I travelled

*Pompeii,
May 10,
B.C. 51*

facerem? In quo illum agentem aliquid, credo, salu-
tavi, post etiam iussi valere, cum me exiens e sua
villa, numquid vellem, rogasset. Hunc hominem
parum gratum quisquam putet aut non in eo ipso
laudandum, quod audiri non laborarit? Sed redeo
ad illud.

Noli putare mihi aliam consolationem esse huius
ingentis molestiae, nisi quod spero non longiorem
annua fore. Hoc me ita velle multi non credunt ex
consuetudine aliorum; tu, qui scis, omnem diligentiam adhibebis tum scilicet, cum id agi debebit, cum
ex Epiro redieris. De re publica scribas ad me velim,
si quid erit, quod odorere. Nondum enim satis huc
erat allatum, quo modo Caesar ferret de auctoritate
perscripta, eratque rumor de Transpadanis eos iussos
IIII viros creare. Quod si ita est, magnos motus
timeo. Sed aliquid ex Pompeio sciam.

III

CICERO ATTICO SAL.

Scr. in Tre-
bulano V
Id. Mai. a.
703

A. d. VI Idus Maias veni in Trebulanum ad Pontium. Ibi mihi tuae litterae binae redditae sunt
tertio abs te die. Eodem autem exiens e Pompeiano

through the market of Puteoli? He was busy about something there, I fancy, when I greeted him. On a subsequent occasion, I bade him a brief good-bye when he came out of his villa and asked if I had any commands. Is one to reckon such a man ungrateful, or does he not rather deserve praise for not striving to get audience? But I return to my former point.

Pray don't imagine that I have any consolation for this tremendous nuisance beyond a hope that my office will not outlast a year. A number of people do not believe in this wish of mine, judging me by others. You, who know my mind, will please use every effort, I mean when the time comes for action, on your return from Epirus. Please write me on state politics, and tell me any secrets you may scent out. For at present we have no sufficient news as to how Caesar takes the recorded opinion of the Senate on his case, and there was a report too that the Transpadani were ordered to create a board of four municipal officers.[1] If that is the case I fear great disturbance: but I shall learn some news from Pompey.

III

CICERO TO ATTICUS, GREETING.

On the 10th of May I came to Pontius' villa at Tre- *Trebula,* bula. There two letters from you were delivered to *May 11,* me on the third day after leaving your hands. On B.C. *51* that same day, as I was quitting my place at Pompeii,

---

[1] Caesar wished to give Transpadane Gaul the full *civitas*; in which case they would become a *municipium* and elect a yearly board of *quattuorviri*, instead of *duoviri*.

Philotimo dederam ad te litteras; nec vero nunc erat
sane, quod scriberem. Qui de re publica rumores,
scribe, quaeso; in oppidis enim summum video timorem, sed multa inania. Quid de his cogites et
quando, scire velim. Ad quas litteras tibi rescribi
velis, nescio. Nullas enim adhuc acceperam, praeter
quae mihi binae simul in Trebulano redditae sunt;
quarum alterae edictum P. Lentuli habebant (erant
autem Nonis Maiis datae), alterae rescriptae ad
meas Menturnenses. Quam vereor, ne quid fuerit
σπουδαιότερον in iis, quas non accepi, quibus rescribi
vis! Apud Lentulum ponam te in gratia.

Dionysius nobis cordi est. Nicanor tuus operam
mihi dat egregiam. Iam deest, quod scribam, et
lucet. Beneventi cogitabam hodie. Nostra continentia et diligentia esse satis [1] faciemus satis.

A Pontio ex Trebulano a. d. v Idus Maias.

IV

CICERO ATTICO SAL.

Scr. Bene-
venti IV Id.
Mai. a. 703 Beneventum veni a. d. v Idus Maias. Ibi accepi
eas litteras, quas tu superioribus litteris significaveras
te dedisse, ad quas ego eo ipso die dederam ex Trebulano a Pontio. Ac binas quidem tuas Beneventi accepi, quarum alteras Funisulanus multo mane mihi
dedit, alteras scriba Tullius. Gratissima est mihi tua
cura de illo meo primo et maximo mandato; sed tua
profectio spem meam debilitat. Ac de illo illuc

[1] *The text here is corrupt.*

I gave Philotimus a letter to you: nor have I at present any news. I beg you write me what reports there are on the political situation. In the country towns I notice there is much panic: but a great deal is nonsense. Please let me know your opinion about this and the date of the impending crisis. I do not know to which of your letters you ask for a reply. I have received no letter so far, except the two which were handed me together at my villa in Trebula. One of these contained the edict of P. Lentulus, and was dated the 7th of May: the other was a reply to my letter from Menturnae. I fear there may have been some matter more important in a letter I did not receive, to which you ask for a reply. I will put you in Lentulus' good graces.

Dionysius is my bosom friend. Your Nicanor does me excellent service. I have no more to say, and day is breaking. I think of going to Beneventum to-day. My continence and diligence shall satisfy . . .

From the house of Pontius at Trebula, May 11th.

IV

CICERO TO ATTICUS, GREETING.

I reached Beneventum on the 11th of May. There *Beneventum,* I received the note which you said in your last letter *May 12,* had been despatched. I answered that letter on B.C. *51* the day I received it from Pontius' villa at Trebula. And indeed two letters of yours reached me at Beneventum, one of them handed to me by Funisulanus in the early morning, and the other by my secretary Tullius. I am very grateful to you for your trouble about my first and most important commission. But your departure from Rome lessens my

quidem labor,[1] non quo —, sed inopia cogimur eo
contenti esse. De illo altero, quem scribis tibi visum
esse non alienum, vereor, adduci ut nostra possit, et
tu ais δυσδιάγνωστον esse. Equidem sum facilis, sed
tu aberis, et me absente res habebit mei rationem?[2]
Nam posset aliquid, si utervis nostrum adesset, agente
Servilia Servio fieri probabile. Nunc, si iam res pla-
ceat, agendi tamen viam non video.

Nunc venio ad eam epistulam, quam accepi a
Tullio. De Marcello fecisti diligenter. Igitur, senatus consultum si erit factum, scribes ad me; si
minus, rem tamen conficies; mihi enim attribui opor-
tebit, item Bibulo. Sed non dubito, quin senatus
consultum expeditum sit, in quo praesertim sit com-
pendium populi. De Torquato probe. De Masone
et Ligure, cum venerint. De illo, quod Chaerippus
(quoniam hic quoque πρόσνευσιν sustulisti), o provincia! etiamne hic mihi curandus est? curandus
autem hactenus, ne quid ad senatum " consule ! "
aut " numera ! " Nam de ceteris — sed tamen commode, quod cum Scrofa. De Pomptino recte scribis.
Est enim ita, ut, si ante Kal. Iunias Brundisi futurus
sit, minus urguendi fuerint M. Anneius et L. Tullius.
Quae de Sicinio audisti, ea mihi probantur, modo ne
illa exceptio in aliquem incurrat bene de nobis meri-
tum. Sed considerabimus, rem enim probo. De

[1] de illo, illuc quidem labor *Kayser*: me ille illud quod
labat *Z*b*N*: me ille illud *M with a marginal variant* me illud
quidem labat.

[2] res habebis mirationem *M*. *The text is Tyrrell's emen-*
dation. Many others have been made, e.g. *Palmer's* res
haerebit. Habebis mei rationem.

hope. As regards the man you mention, I am slipping into your view, not that—— but for want of a better we are compelled to be satisfied with him. As for the other man who, you say, appears a not unlikely candidate, I fear my daughter could not be persuaded, and, as you add, there is not a pin to choose between them. For myself I am reasonable; but you will be away, and will any account be taken of me in my absence? For if either of us were on the spot a good face might be put on the matter with Servius through the agency of Servilia. Now, even if it were a thing I favoured, I see no way of bringing it to pass.

Now I come to that letter which I received from Tullius. You have been very energetic about Marcellus: so if a decree should be passed, please inform me: but if not, try to carry the matter through: a grant ought to be made to me and to Bibulus. But I am confident that the decree will be passed, especially as it saves the people's pocket. That is fine about Torquatus. As for Maso and Ligur, we can wait till they come. As to Chaerippus' request, since you have given me no tip on the matter—— hang the province! Must I trouble about him too? Well, I must take enough trouble to prevent any debate on the matter or count out in the House. As for others—— however, you do well to have spoken with Scrofa. As to Pomptinus you are right. It comes to this, if Pomptinus will be at Brundisium before June M. Anneius and L. Tullius need not hurry out of Rome. As to your news from Sicinius, I am satisfied, provided this restriction does not apply to anyone who has obliged me. But I will think it over, as the plan pleases me. I will let you know

nostro itinere quod statuero, de quinque praefectis quid Pompeius facturus sit, cum ex ipso cognoro, faciam, ut scias. De Oppio bene curasti, quod ei de $\overline{\text{DCCC}}$ exposuisti, idque, quoniam Philotimum habes, perfice et cognosce rationem et, ut agam amplius, si me amas, priusquam proficiscaris, effice. Magna me cura levaris.

Habes ad omnia. Etsi paene praeterii chartam tibi deesse. Mea captio est, si quidem eius inopia minus multa ad me scribis. Tu vero aufer ducentos; etsi meam in eo parsimoniam huius paginae contractio significat. Dumtaxat rumores, vel etiam si qua certa habes de Caesare, exspecto. Litteras et aliis et Pomptino de omnibus rebus diligenter dabis.

V

CICERO ATTICO SAL.

Scr. Venu-
siae Id. Mai.
a. 703

Plane deest, quod scribam; nam, nec quod mandem, habeo (nihil enim praetermissum est), nec quod narrem (novi enim nihil), nec iocandi locus est; ita me multa sollicitant. Tantum tamen scito, Idibus Maiis nos Venusia mane proficiscentes has dedisse. Eo autem die credo aliquid actum in senatu. Sequantur igitur nos tuae litterae, quibus non modo res

348

what course I have determined to adopt as regards my route, and also as to Pompey's policy about the five prefects,[1] when I have heard from him. As for Oppius, you have done well to explain to him the matter of the £7,000.[2] Please arrange the business since Philotimus is with you. Examine the account and, to go further in my request, if you love me settle the debt before you leave town. You will relieve me of great anxiety.

I have replied to all your points. But your want of paper I had almost forgotten. It is my loss if for lack of it your letter is shorter. Take a couple of hundred sheets,[3] though the shortness of this page betokens my stinginess in paper. In return I look for information and gossip and any certain news of Caesar. You will write a letter to Pomptinus, as well as others, about everything.

V

CICERO TO ATTICUS, GREETING.

I have absolutely nothing to write about. Having forgotten nothing, I have no commission for you. Having no news, I have nothing to relate. And this is no place for jests considering the number of my cares. Still you must know that I despatched this letter setting out from Venusia on the morning of the 15th of May. I believe something has been done in the Senate to-day. So send a letter after

Venusia, May 15, B.C. 51

---

[1] Five new prefects were to be appointed in each of the Spains.
[2] 800,000 sesterces.
[3] Understanding *chartas*, which is used by the older Latin authors as a masculine noun, cf. Nonius 196, 17. Others, however, understand *sestertios*.

omnes, sed etiam rumores cognoscamus. Eas accipiemus Brundisi; ibi enim Pomptinum ad eam diem,
quam tu scripsisti, exspectare consilium est. Nos
Tarenti quos cum Pompeio διαλόγους de re publica
habuerimus, ad te perscribemus. Etsi id ipsum scire
cupio, quod ad tempus recte ad te scribere possim,
id est quam diu Romae futurus sis, ut aut, quo dem
posthac litteras, sciam, aut ne dem frustra. Sed,
antequam proficiscare, utique explicatum sit illud
HS. $\overline{xx}$ et $\overline{\text{DCCC}}$. Hoc velim in maximis rebus et
maxime necessariis habeas, ut, quod auctore te velle
coepi, adiutore adsequar.

VI

CICERO ATTICO SAL.

Scr. Tarenti
XIV K.
Iun. a. 703

Tarentum veni a. d. xv Kal. Iunias. Quod Pomptinum statueram exspectare, commodissimum duxi
dies eos, quoad ille veniret, cum Pompeio consumere
eoque magis, quod ei gratum esse id videbam, qui
etiam a me petierit, ut secum et apud se essem cotidie. Quod concessi libenter. Multos enim eius
praeclaros de re publica sermones accipiam, instruar
etiam consiliis idoneis ad hoc nostrum negotium.

Sed ad te brevior iam in scribendo incipio fieri
dubitans, Romaene sis an iam profectus. Quod tamen quoad ignorabo, scribam aliquid potius quam
committam, ut, tibi cum possint reddi a me litterae,
non reddantur. Nec tamen iam habeo, quod aut
mandem tibi aut narrem. Mandavi omnia; quae

350

me, giving not only all the facts but the gossip too. I shall get it at Brundisium. For it is there that I intend to await Pomptinus up to the date that you have mentioned. I will write you of the *causeries* I had with Pompey at Tarentum about politics. Although there is one thing I want to know, up to what time I can safely write to you at Rome, that is how long you will be in town, so that I may have your address after your removal and may not send letters in vain. Before you go, settle the business of the £180 and the £7,000.[1] Please count it most important and most necessary, that with your help I may achieve what I began to wish for at your instance.

VI

CICERO TO ATTICUS, GREETING.

I came to Tarentum on the 18th of May. As I had decided to await Pomptinus, I thought it most convenient to spend the days before his arrival with Pompey, the more so because I saw it pleased him. Indeed, he begged me to see him and to be at his house every day; and I am glad to give him my company. I shall have some grand conversations with him about the political situation, and shall get useful advice on this business of mine.

Tarentum, May 19, B.C. 51

I am beginning to send you shorter letters, as I do not know whether you are in Rome or have now started on your journey. However, so long as I am ignorant of your whereabouts I will write you a line rather than run the risk of not sending you a letter, when a letter from me can reach you. I have no commission for you and nothing to say. I have given

[1] 20,000 and 800,000 sesterces.

quidem tu, ut polliceris, exhauries. Narrabo, cum aliquid habebo novi. Illud tamen non desinam, dum adesse te putabo, de Caesaris nomine rogare ut confectum relinquas. Avide exspecto tuas litteras et maxime, ut norim tempus profectionis tuae.

VII

CICERO ATTICO SAL.

Scr. Tarenti XIII K. Iun. a. 703

Cotidie vel potius in dies singulos breviores litteras ad te mitto; cotidie enim magis suspicor te in Epirum iam profectum. Sed tamen, ut mandatum scias me curasse, quo de ante, ait se Pompeius quinos praefectos delaturum novos vacationis iudiciariae causa. Ego cum triduum cum Pompeio et apud Pompeium fuissem, proficiscebar Brundisium a. d. XIII Kal. Iunias. Civem illum egregium relinquebam et ad haec, quae timentur, propulsanda paratissimum. Tuas litteras exspectabo, cum ut, quid agas, tum ut, ubi sis, sciam.

VIII

CICERO ATTICO SAL.

Scr. Brundisi IV ant III Non. Iun. a. 703

Me et incommoda valetudo, e qua iam emerseram, utpote cum sine febri laborassem, et Pomptini exspectatio, de quo adhuc ne rumor quidem venerat, tenebat duodecimum iam diem Brundisi; sed cursum exspectabamus. Tu, si modo es Romae (vix enim puto), sin es, hoc vehementer animadvertas velim.

352

you all my commissions, and please execute them as
you promise. I will send you any fresh news, when
I have it. One matter I shall not cease to request
so long as I think you are in town,—that you will
leave my debt to Caesar settled. I await eagerly a
letter from you, especially that I may know the date
of your leaving Rome.

VII

CICERO TO ATTICUS, GREETING.

Daily, or rather more and more every day, I send *Tarentum,*
you shorter letters: for daily I suspect more than *May 20,*
ever that you have started for Epirus. However, to B.C. *51*
inform you that I have taken in hand your previous
commission: Pompey says that he will appoint five
new prefects, exempting them from serving on juries.
For myself, after spending three days with Pompey at
his house, I am setting out for Brundisium on the 20th
of May. I am leaving behind me a noble citizen, well
prepared to ward off the dangers we fear. I shall
await your letters to inform me of your actions and
whereabouts.

VIII

CICERO TO ATTICUS, GREETING.

Tiresome indisposition, from which I have re- *Brundisium,*
covered, as there was no fever with my ailment, and *June 2 or 3,*
also my awaiting Pomptinus, of whom so far no news B.C. *51*
has reached me, have detained me now twelve days
at Brundisium: but I am looking for an opportunity
to sail. I scarcely imagine that you are in town;
but if you are, please give your closest attention to

Roma acceperam litteras Milonem meum queri per
litteras iniuriam meam, quod Philotimus socius esset
in bonis suis. Id ego ita fieri volui de C. Duroni
sententia, quem et amicissimum Miloni perspexeram
et talem virum, qualem tu iudicas, cognoram. Eius
autem consilium meumque hoc fuerat, primum ut in
potestate nostra esset res, ne illum malus emptor
alienus manicipiis, quae permulta secum habet, spo-
liaret, deinde ut Faustae, cui cautum ille esse voluis-
set, ratum esset. Erat etiam illud, ut ipsi nos, si
quid servari posset, quam facillime servaremus. Nunc
rem totam perspicias velim; nobis enim scribuntur
saepe maiora. Si ille queritur, si scribit ad amicos,
si idem Fausta vult, Philotimus, ut ego ei coram
dixeram, mihique ille receperat, ne sit invito Milone
in bonis. Nihil nobis fuerat tanti. Sin haec leviora
sunt, tu iudicabis. Loquere cum Duronio. Scripsi
etiam ad Camillum, ad Lamiam eoque magis, quod
non confidebam Romae te esse. Summa erit haec.
Statues, ut ex fide, fama reque mea videbitur.

IX

CICERO ATTICO SAL.

Scr. Acti
XVII K.
Quint. a. 703 Actium venimus a. d. xvii Kal. Quinctiles, cum
quidem et Corcyrae et Sybotis muneribus tuis, quae
et Araus et meus amicus Eutychides opipare et φιλο-
προσηνέστατα nobis congesserant, epulati essemus

the following. I have received a letter from Rome, saying that my friend Milo writes complaining of ill-treatment from me, for allowing Philotimus to have a hand in the purchase of his property. I acted on the advice of C. Duronius, a man whom I saw to be most friendly to Milo, and just such a person as you suppose him to be. His plan and mine was this, firstly, to keep a hold over Milo's property for fear some hard bargainer, a stranger to us, should rob him of his slaves, of whom a great number were with him; and secondly, that the settlement he intended to make on Fausta should be respected. There was the further intention that we ourselves should have the readiest means of saving anything that could be saved. Now please review the whole matter, for letters to me often exaggerate. If Milo complains and writes to his friends, and if Fausta wishes, as I told Philotimus and as he agreed, I would not have him purchase the property against Milo's wish. Nothing would compensate for offending Milo. You will judge if the matter has been exaggerated. Please consult Duronius. I have written also to Camillus and to Lamia, among other reasons because I do not feel sure you are in town. To sum up, in deciding be careful of my honour, reputation, and interests.

IX

CICERO TO ATTICUS, GREETING.

I reached Actium on the 14th of June, after feast-ing like an alderman both at Corcyra and the Sybota islands, thanks to your gifts which Araus and my good friend Eutychides heaped on me with lavish

Actium, June 14, B.C. 51

Saliarem in modum. Actio maluimus iter facere pedibus, qui incommodissime navigassemus, et Leucatam flectere molestum videbatur, actuariis autem minutis Patras accedere sine impedimentis non satis visum est decorum. Ego, ut saepe tu me currentem hortatus es, cotidie meditor, praecipio meis, faciam denique, ut summa modestia et summa abstinentia munus hoc extraordinarium traducamus. Parthus velim quiescat, et fortuna nos iuvet, nostra praestabimus.

Tu, quaeso, quid agas, ubi quoque tempore futurus sis, quales res nostras Romae reliqueris, maxime de $\overline{XX}$ et $\overline{DCCC}$ cura ut sciamus. Id unis diligenter litteris datis, quae ad me utique perferantur, consequere. Illud tamen, quoniam nunc abes, cum id non agitur, aderis autem ad tempus, ut mihi rescripsti, memento curare per te et per omnes nostros, in primis per Hortensium, ut annus noster maneat suo statu, ne quid novi decernatur. Hoc tibi ita mando, ut dubitem, an etiam te rogem, ut pugnes, ne intercaletur. Sed non audeo tibi omnia onera imponere; annum quidem utique teneto.

Cicero meus, modestissimus et suavissimus puer, tibi salutem dicit. Dionysium semper equidem, ut scis, dilexi, sed cotidie pluris facio, et mehercule in primis quod te amat nec tui mentionem intermitti sinit.

kindness. From Actium I preferred to travel by land, in view of the wretched passage we had and the danger of rounding Leucatas. It did not seem to me quite dignified to go ashore at Patrae in small boats without my baggage. I will really take care to fulfil this unusual office of mine with all propriety and honesty, as you have often urged me, who was ready to run at your bidding; and daily I bethink me of your advice and impress it on my staff. Please God, the Parthians keep quiet and fortune favour me, I will answer for myself.

I beg that you will let me know what you are doing, your movements from time to time, how you left my business at Rome, particularly in the matter of the £180 and the £7,000. Please do this in a letter carefully addressed to reach me anyhow. You are away at this present moment of inaction, but you have promised me to be in town for the occasion, and remember to use your best endeavours and to employ all my friends, especially Hortensius, that my year of office may conclude without any extension. This commission should perhaps be accompanied by a request for you to fight that no extra days may be added to the calendar: but I hardly like to give you all this trouble. Anyhow, insist on the year.

My son, a boy of charming manners, sends greetings to you. I have always liked Dionysius, as you know, but I make more of him every day, especially because he is your admirer and lets slip no chance of mentioning you.

MARCUS TULLIUS CICERO

X

CICERO ATTICO SAL.

Scr. Athenis Ut Athenas a. d. vi Kal. Quinctiles veneram, ex-
prid. K. aut spectabam ibi iam quartum diem Pomptinum neque
K. Quint. a. de eius adventu certi quicquam habebam. Eram
703 autem totus, crede mihi, tecum et, quamquam sine iis
per me ipse, tamen acrius vestigiis tuis monitus de te
cogitabam. Quid quaeris? non mehercule alius ullus
sermo nisi de te. Sed tu de me ipso aliquid scire
fortasse mavis. Haec sunt. Adhuc sumptus nec in
me aut publice aut privatim nec in quemquam comi-
tum. Nihil accipitur lege Iulia, nihil ab hospite.
Persuasum est omnibus meis serviendum esse famae
meae. Belle adhuc. Hoc animadversum Graecorum
laude et multo sermone celebratur. Quod superest,
elaboratur in hoc a me, sicut tibi sensi placere. Sed
haec tum laudemus, cum erunt perorata. Reliqua
sunt eius modi, ut meum consilium saepe reprehen-
dam, quod non aliqua ratione ex hoc negotio emer-
serim. O rem minime aptam meis moribus! o illud
verum ἔρδοι τις! Dices: "Quid adhuc? nondum
enim in negotio versaris." Sane scio et puto mole-
stiora restare. Etsi haec ipsa fero equidem fronte, ut
puto, et voltu bellissime, sed angor intimis sensibus;
ita multa vel iracunde vel insolenter vel in omni
genere stultitiae insulse adrogantur et dicuntur et
tacentur cotidie; quae non, quo te calem, non per-

358

X

CICERO TO ATTICUS, GREETING.

I came to Athens on the 25th of June, and I have *Athens, June* waited three days for Pomptinus, but have heard *29 or July 1,* nothing certain of his coming. Believe me, you are B.C. *51* with me all the time, and, though it did not need associations to turn my thoughts towards you, still I was reminded of you more than ever by treading in your footsteps. Indeed, we talk of nothing else but you; but perhaps you prefer to have news about myself. So far no public body or private person has spent money on me or on my staff. I have not even taken the barest necessities allowed by the law of Julius, nor have I billeted myself on anyone. My staff have made up their minds that they must uphold my good name. So far everything has gone well : the Greeks have noted it and are full of outspoken praise. For the rest I am endeavouring to act as I know you would like. But let us reserve our praise for the end of the story. In other respects I often blame my mistake in not having found some method of escape from this flood of affairs. The business is little suited to my tastes. It is a true saying, " Cobbler, stick to your last." [1] You will say : " What, already ? You have not yet begun your work." Too true, and I fear worse is to come. I put up with things with cheerful brow and smiling face ; but I suffer in my heart of hearts. There is so much ill temper and insolence, such stupid folly of every kind, such arrogant talk and such sullen silence to be put up with every day. I pass over this, not because I wish to conceal

---

[1] ἔρδοι τις ἣν ἕκαστος εἰδείη τέχνην (Aristophanes, *Vespae* 1431).

scribo, sed quia δυσεκλάλητα sunt. Itaque admira-
bere meam βαθύτητα, cum salvi redierimus; tanta
mihi μελέτη huius virtutis datur.

Ergo haec quoque hactenus; etsi mihi nihil erat
propositum ad scribendum, quia, quid ageres, ubi
terrarum esses, ne suspicabar quidem. Nec hercule
umquam tam diu ignarus rerum mearum fui, quid de
Caesaris, quid de Milonis nominibus actum sit; ac
non modo nemo domo, ne Roma quidem quisquam, ut
sciremus, in re publica quid ageretur. Quare, si quid
erit, quod scias de iis rebus, quas putabis scire me
velle, per mihi gratum erit, si id curaris ad me
perferendum.

Quid est praeterea? Nihil sane nisi illud. Valde
me Athenae delectarunt urbe dumtaxat et urbis orna-
mento et hominum amore in te et in nos quadam
benevolentia; sed multa in [1] ea philosophia sursum
deorsum, si quidem est in Aristo, apud quem eram.
Nam Xenonem tuum vel nostrum potius Quinto con-
cesseram, et tamen propter vicinitatem totos dies
simul eramus. Tu velim, cum primum poteris, tua
consilia ad me scribas, ut sciam, quid agas, ubi quoque
tempore, maxime quando Romae futurus sis.

XI

CICERO ATTICO SAL.

*Scr. Athenis
pr. Non.
Quint. a.
703*

Hui, totiesne me litteras dedisse Romam, cum ad
te nullas darem? At vero posthac frustra potius
dabo quam, si recte dari potuerint, committam, ut
non dem. Ne provincia nobis prorogetur, per fortunas! dum ades, quicquid provideri poterit, provide.

---

[1] multum *M*: multa in *Reid*.

it, but because to explain is difficult. You shall
marvel at my self-restraint when I return home safe.
I have so much practice in the virtue.

Enough of this topic too. Though indeed I have
nothing to make me write to you at all, because I
have no idea of what you are doing or where you
are, and I have never been so long ignorant about
my own concerns—as to what has been done about
the debt to Caesar and Milo's money matters : and
there has come no messenger from Rome much less
from my house to inform me of political affairs. So,
if you have information you may think I should like
to know I shall be delighted if you will take care to
send it to me.

I have only one thing to add. Athens pleases me
greatly, that is the material city, its embellishments,
your popularity, and the kind feeling shown to me :
but its philosophy is topsy-turvy, that is, if it is repre-
sented by Aristus with whom I am staying : for I
gave up Xeno your friend and mine to Quintus. Still
we are close neighbours and meet every day. Please
write me as soon as possible of your plans, and tell
me what you are doing, where you are from time to
time, and especially when you will be in town.

XI

CICERO TO ATTICUS, GREETING.

What, write so often to Rome, and never a line to *Athens,*
you! Well, in future, rather than do such a thing *July 6,*
as not to write a letter than can reach you safely, I B.C. *51*
will despatch a letter that may go astray. In the
name of heaven, while you are in town, take every
possible precaution against the term of my office

Non dici potest, quam flagrem desiderio urbis, quam vix harum rerum insulsitatem feram.

Marcellus foede in Comensi. Etsi ille magistratum non gesserat, erat tamen Transpadanus. Ita mihi videtur non minus stomachi nostro quam Caesari fecisse. Sed hoc ipse viderit. Pompeius mihi quoque videbatur, quod scribis Varronem dicere, in Hispaniam certe iturus. Id ego minime probabam; qui quidem Theophani facile persuasi nihil esse melius quam illum nusquam discedere. Ergo Graecus incumbet. Valet autem auctoritas eius apud illum plurimum.

Ego has pr. Nonas Quinctiles proficiscens Athenis dedi, cum ibi decem ipsos fuissem dies. Venerat Pomptinus, una Cn. Volusius; aderat quaestor; tuus unus Tullius aberat. Aphracta Rhodiorum et dicrota Mytilenaeorum habebam et aliquid ἐπικώπων. De Parthis erat silentium. Quod superest, di iuvent!

Nos adhuc iter per Graeciam summa cum admiratione fecimus, nec mehercule habeo, quod adhuc quem accusem meorum. Videntur mihi nosse nostram causam et condicionem profectionis suae; plane serviunt existimationi meae. Quod superest, si verum illud est οἷάπερ ἡ δέσποινα, certe permanebunt.

being extended. I cannot describe how ardently I long for town, how hard I find it to bear the stupidity of life here.

Marcellus acted disgracefully over the man from Comum : [1] even if he had not been a magistrate, still he was a Transpadane. So Marcellus' action seems to me as likely to anger Pompey as Caesar ; but that is his own look-out. I agree with Varro's statement, which you quote in your letter, that Pompey will surely go to Spain. I by no means approve of the policy, and indeed I convinced Theophanes easily that Pompey's presence in Rome was the very best course. So the Greek will put pressure on Pompey ; and his opinion weighs with him a great deal.

I despatch this letter on the 6th of July, being about to leave Athens, where I have stayed just ten days. Pomptinus has come along with Cn. Volusius. My quaestor is here. Your friend Tullius is the one absentee. I have some open boats of Rhodes and two-deckers from Mitylene and a few despatch boats. There is no news of the Parthians. For the rest, God help us.

So far our journey through Greece has provoked great admiration, and I have no fault at all to find with my staff at present. They seem to understand what my case is, and the terms on which they stand. They do everything to maintain my good name. For the rest, if the saying be true, " Like master, like man," [2] assuredly they will stick to their good be-

[1] He had ordered him to be flogged, disregarding the fact that Caesar had sent 5,000 colonists to Transpadane Gaul. Magistrates of a *colonia* had the full *civitas*.

[2] The proverb ends τοία χή κύων (" the dog is like its mistress ") according to the Scholiast on Plato *De Repub.*, viii, 563.

Nihil enim a me fieri ita videbunt, ut sibi sit delinquendi locus. Sin id parum profuerit, fiet aliquid a nobis severius. Nam adhuc lenitate dulces sumus et, ut spero, proficimus aliquantum. Sed ego hanc, ut Siculi dicunt, ἀνεξίαν in unum annum meditatus sum. Proinde pugna, ne, si quid prorogatum sit, turpis inveniar.

Nunc redeo, ad quae mihi mandas. In praefectis excusatio: iis, quos voles, deferto. Non ero tam μετέωρος, quam in Appuleio fui. Xenonem tam diligo quam tu, quod ipsum sentire certo scio. Apud Patronem et reliquos barones te in maxima gratia posui et hercule merito tuo feci. Nam mihi Ister dixit te scripsisse ad se mihi ex illius litteris rem illam curae fuisse, quod ei pergratum erat. Sed, cum Patro mecum egisset, ut peterem a vestro Ariopago, ὑπομνηματισμὸν tollerent, quem Polycharmo praetore fecerant, commodius visum est et Xenoni et post ipsi Patroni me ad Memmium scribere, qui pridie, quam ego Athenas veni, Mitilenas profectus erat, ut is ad suos scriberet posse id sua voluntate fieri. Non enim dubitabat Xeno, quin ab Ariopagitis invito Memmio impetrari non posset. Memmius autem aedificandi consilium abiecerat; sed erat Patroni iratus. Itaque scripsi ad eum accurate; cuius epistulae misi ad te exemplum.

Tu velim Piliam meis verbis consolere. Indicabo enim tibi, tu illi nihil dixeris. Accepi fasciculum, in quo erat epistula Piliae. Abstuli, aperui, legi. Valde scripta est συμπαθῶς. Brundisio quae tibi epistulae

haviour, for they will see no excuse for misconduct in any act of mine. If example be futile I must try severer means. So far I have been mild and kind, and I hope I am making headway. But I have looked forward to playing patience, as the Sicilians say, for one year only. So fight for me, for fear extension of office might spoil my conduct.

To return to the commissions you have given me. Prefects have exemption from serving on a jury. Give the office to whom you will. I shall not be so *difficile* as I was in the case of Appuleius. I am as fond of Xeno as you are, and I am sure he knows it. I have put you in well-deserved favour with Patro and the other blockheads. Ister has told me you have written to him that you learned from Patro's letter I was taking an interest in the point, much to his delight. But when Patro urged me to ask your Areopagus to cancel the minute they had made when Polycharmus was praetor, it seemed better to Xeno and afterwards to Patro himself that I should send a letter to Memmius, who had set out to Mitylenae the day before I arrived at Athens, asking him to inform his agents that the minute could be cancelled with his free consent. For Xeno was sure the Areopagus would refuse to act against his will. Memmius had abandoned his plan of building a house; but he was angry with Patro. I enclose a copy of the careful letter I wrote him.

Please convey my condolences to Pilia. I will tell you a secret you are not to repeat to her: I received the parcel containing her letter, took it out, opened and read it. It was written in terms of sympathy for Quintus. Please consider the letters you got from Brundisium without one from me as having

redditae sunt sine mea, tum videlicet datas, cum ego me non belle haberem. Nam illam νομαίαν ἀργίας[1] excusationem ne acceperis. Cura, ut omnia sciam, sed maxime ut valeas.

XII

CICERO ATTICO SAL.

Scr. in medio mari med. m. Quint. a. 703

Negotium magnum est navigare atque id mense Quinctili. Sexto die Delum Athenis venimus. Pr. Nonas Quinctiles a Piraeo ad Zostera vento molesto; qui nos ibidem Nonis tenuit. Ante VIII Idus ad Ceo iucunde; inde Gyarum saevo vento, non adverso; hinc Syrum, inde Delum, utroque citius, quam vellemus, cursum confecimus. Nam nosti aphracta Rhodiorum; nihil, quod minus fluctum ferre possit. Itaque erat in animo nihil festinare nec me Delo movere, nisi omnia ἀκρωτήρια Γυρέων vidissem.

De Messalla ad te, statim ut audivi, de Gyaro dedi litteras et—id ipsum consilium nostrum—etiam ad Hortensium, cui quidem valde συνηγωνίων. Sed tuas de eius iudicii sermonibus et mehercule omni de rei publicae statu litteras exspecto πολιτικώτερον quidem scriptas, quoniam meos cum Thallumeto nostro pervolutas libros, eius modi, inquam, litteras, ex quibus ego, non quid fiat (nam id vel Helonius, vir gravissimus, potest efficere, cliens tuus), sed quid futurum sit, sciam.

Cum haec leges, habebimus consules. Omnia per-

---

[1] νομαίαν ἀργίας *Tyrrell*: νομαναρια me *MSS.*

been despatched when I was indisposed. I won't
ask you to accept the lazy man's stock excuse, my
business. Take great care to keep me well posted
up in news, and still greater care to preserve your
health.

XII

CICERO TO ATTICUS, GREETING.

A sea voyage is a big business, especially in the *At sea,*
month of July. Six days after leaving Athens I *July,*
came to Delos. On the 6th of July I got from the B.C. *51*
Piraeus to Zoster with a contrary wind which kept
us there on the 7th. On the 8th we reached Ceos in
fine weather. From there we came to Gyaros, with a
wind strong, but not contrary : thence to Syros, and
from Syros to Delos ; in both cases sailing quicker
than we could have wished. You know by this time
what the open boats of Rhodes are like, poor things
in a rough sea. So I have made up my mind not
to hurry and not to stir from Delos until I see " all
the peaks of Gyrae " clear.

I sent you a letter about Messalla at once from
Gyaros as soon as I heard, and another on my own
initiative to Hortensius, for I felt much sympathy
with him. I await a letter from you to give me the
gossip about the verdict and about the political
situation, dealing, if I may say so, more with public
topics, since now, with the aid of Thallumetus, you
are running through my books. I don't want a letter
to tell me what is actually happening, for that tiresome fellow your client Helonius can do that : but I
want to know what is likely to happen.

By the time you read this, consuls will have been

spicere poteris de Caesare, de Pompeio, de ipsis
iudiciis. Nostra autem negotia, quoniam Romae
commoraris, amabo te, explica. Cui rei fugerat me
rescribere, de strue laterum, plane rogo, de aqua, si
quid poterit fieri, eo sis animo, quo soles esse; quam
ego cum mea sponte tum tuis sermonibus aestimo
plurimi. Ergo tu id conficies. Praeterea, si quid
Philippus rogabit, quod in tua re faceres, id velim
facias. Plura scribam ad te, cum constitero. Nunc
eram plane in medio mari.

XIII

CICERO ATTICO SAL.

*Scr. Ephesi
VII K. Sext.
a. 703*
Ephesum venimus a. d. XI Kal. Sextiles sexagesimo
et quingentesimo post pugnam Bovillanam. Naviga-
vimus sine timore et sine nausea, sed tardius propter
aphractorum Rhodiorum imbecillitatem. De concursu legationum, privatorum, et de incredibili multitudine, quae mihi iam Sami, sed mirabilem in modum
Ephesi praesto fuit, aut audisse te puto aut " Quid ad
me attinet ? " Verum tamen decumani, quasi venissem cum imperio, Graeci quasi Ephesio praetori se
alacres obtulerunt. Ex quo te intellegere certo scio
multorum annorum ostentationes meas nunc in dis-
crimen esse adductas. Sed, ut spero, utemur ea
palaestra, quam a te didicimus, omnibusque satis
faciemus et eo facilius, quod in nostra provincia con-

elected. You will be able to have clear views about Caesar and Pompey and the trials themselves. And please arrange my affairs, since you are staying in town. Oh, I forgot to answer one question about the brickwork: as to the aqueduct, without entering into particulars, please be as kind as you always are, if anything can be done. To the last item, my own views as well as your letters lead me to attach very great importance: so please get it done. Furthermore, if the contractor puts you any questions, please act as you would in your own case. I will write a longer letter when I am on dry land. At present I am far out at sea.

XIII

CICERO TO ATTICUS, GREETING.

I reached Ephesus on the 22nd of July, the five *Ephesus,* hundred and sixtieth day after the battle of Bovillae.[1] *July 26,* B.C. The voyage caused me no alarm and no sickness, but *51* was slow owing to the crankiness of the open boats. I imagine you have heard about the crowd of legations and of private suitors and about the astonishing number of people who met me even at Samos, and even more noticeably at Ephesus; or you may say it does not interest you. Still the tax-collectors thrust themselves on my notice as though I had come with an army behind me, and the Greeks as if I were governor of Asia. You will see that the professions of my life are now being put to the test. I hope I shall employ the training I have learned from you and satisfy everybody, the more easily because in my province the contracts have been settled. But

[1] The murder of Clodius, January 18, B.C. 52.

fectae sunt pactiones. Sed hactenus, praesertim cum cenanti mihi nuntiarit Cestius se de nocte proficisci.

Tua negotiola Ephesi curae mihi fuerunt, Thermoque tametsi ante adventum meum liberalissime erat pollicitus tuis omnibus, tamen Philogenem et Seium tradidi, Apollonidensem Xenonem commendavi. Omnino omnia se facturum recepit. Ego praeterea rationem Philogeni permutationis eius, quam tecum feci, edidi. Ergo haec quoque hactenus.

Redeo ad urbana. Per fortunas! quoniam Romae manes, primum illud praefulci atque praemuni, quaeso, ut simus annui, ne intercaletur quidem. Deinde exhauri mea mandata maximeque, si quid potest de illo domestico scrupulo, quem non ignoras, dein de Caesare, cuius in cupiditatem te auctore incubui, nec me piget. Et, si intellegis, quam meum sit scire et curare, quid in re publica fiat—fiat autem? immo vero etiam quid futurum sit, perscribe ad me omnia, sed diligentissime imprimisque, ecquid iudiciorum status aut factorum aut futurorum etiam laboret. De aqua, si curae est, si quid Philippus aget, animadvertes.

XIV

CICERO ATTICO SAL.

Scr. Tralli-bus VI K. Sext. a. 703 Antequam aliquo loco consedero, neque longas a me neque semper mea manu litteras exspectabis; cum autem erit spatium, utrumque praestabo. Nunc iter conficiebamus aestuosa et pulverulenta via. De-

enough of this, especially as Cestius has interrupted my dinner with news that he is starting to-night.

I attended to your little jobs at Ephesus, and although before my arrival Thermus had given the most lavish promises to all your people, still I introduced Philogenes and Seius to him, and recommended Xeno of Apollonis. He undertook to do everything. In addition I submitted to Philogenes an account of the sum I got from you by negotiating a bill of exchange. So enough of this too.

I return to town affairs. Since you are staying in Rome, in heaven's name, do support and establish my plea to be let off with one year of office without additions to the calendar. Execute all my commissions; particularly get over that hitch in my private affairs of which you are aware, and over the business with Caesar. It was you who led me to try to pay my debt, and I am glad. If you understand my *penchant* to know and trouble about what is happening in public life, or rather what is going to happen, write to me in full and with accuracy, especially whether there is any break-down at all in the trials that have been held or are going to be held. If you are interested about the aqueduct, and if the contractor is at work, please give it your attention.

XIV

CICERO TO ATTICUS, GREETING.

You must not expect long letters from me nor always letters in my own handwriting, till I have settled down somewhere. When I have time I will guarantee both. I am now engaged on a hot and dusty journey. I wrote yesterday from Ephesus; to-day

Tralles, July 27, B.C. 51

371

deram Epheso pridie; has dedi Trallibus. In provincia mea fore me putabam Kal. Sextilibus. Ex ea die, si me amas, παράπηγμα ἐνιαύσιον commoveto. Interea tamen haec mihi, quae vellem, adferebantur, primum otium Parthicum, dein confectae pactiones publicanorum, postremo seditio militum sedata ab Appio stipendiumque eis usque ad Idus Quinctiles persolutum.

Nos Asia accepit admirabiliter. Adventus noster nemini ne minimo quidem fuit sumptui. Spero meos omnes servire laudi meae. Tamen magno timore sum, sed bene speramus. Omnes iam nostri praeter Tullium tuum venerunt. Erat mihi in animo recta proficisci ad exercitum, aestivos menses reliquos rei militari dare, hibernos iuris dictioni.

Tu velim, si me nihilo minus nosti curiosum in re publica quam te, scribas ad me omnia, quae sint, quae futura sint. Nihil mihi gratius facere potes; nisi tamen id erit mihi gratissimum, si, quae tibi mandavi, confeceris imprimisque illud ἐνδόμυχον, quo mihi scis nihil esse carius. Habes epistulam plenam festinationis et pulveris; reliquae subtiliores erunt.

XV

CICERO ATTICO SAL.

Scr.
Laodiceae
III Non.
Sext. a.
703
Laodiceam veni pridie Lal. Sextiles. Ex hoc die clavum anni movebis. Nihil exoptatius adventu meo,

I write from Tralles. I expect to be in my province on the 1st of August. Let that day, if you love me, be notched [1] as the first of my year of office. Meantime the following welcome news has reached me, that the Parthians are at peace; secondly, that the contracts with the tax-farmers have been settled, and lastly that Appius has quelled a mutiny of his soldiers and paid them up to the 15th of July.

Asia has given me an astonishing welcome. My coming has cost no one a penny. I trust that my staff are cherishing my good name. I am very nervous: but I hope for the best. All of them have joined me except your friend Tullius. I intend to go straight to my army, to devote the remaining summer months to military matters, and the winter to judicial business.

As you know that I am as interested as you in political business, please write to me everything that is happening and is likely to happen. You can do me no greater service, except the greatest service of all, which is to carry out my commissions, particularly that household matter with which you know I am greatly concerned. This letter is full of dust and hurry: others shall be more in detail.

XV

CICERO TO ATTICUS, GREETING.

I reached Laodicea on the 31st of July. So notch that day as the beginning of my year of office. My arrival has been looked forward to with desire and *Laodicea, Aug. 3, B.C. 51*

---

[1] παράπηγμα ἐνιαύσιον corresponds to *clavus anni* of the next letter. The expression arose from the custom of driving a nail into the right wall of the Temple of Jupiter on the Ides of September every year to keep count of the years.

nihil carius. Sed est incredibile, quam me negotii taedeat, non habeat satis magnum campum ille tibi non ignotus cursus animi et industriae meae, prae-clara opera cesset. Quippe, ius Laodiceae me dicere, cum Romae A. Plotius dicat, et, cum exercitum noster amicus habeat tantum, me nomen habere duarum legionum exilium? Denique haec non desidero, lucem, forum, urbem, domum, vos desidero. Sed feram, ut potero, sit modo annuum. Si pro-rogatur, actum est. Verum perfacile resisti potest, tu modo Romae sis.

Quaeris, quid hic agam. Ita vivam, ut maximos sumptus facio. Mirifice delector hoc instituto. Ad-mirabilis abstinentia ex praeceptis tuis, ut verear, ne illud, quod tecum permutavi, versura mihi solvendum sit. Appi vulnera non refrico, sed apparent nec occuli possunt. Iter Laodicea faciebam a. d. iii Non. Sextiles, cum has litteras dabam, in castra in Lycaoniam. Inde ad Taurum cogitabam, ut cum Moeragene signis collatis, si possem, de servo tuo deciderem.

> " Clitellae bovi sunt impositae ; plane non est
> nostrum onus."

Sed feremus, modo, si me amas, sim annuus. Adsis tu ad tempus, ut senatum totum excites. Mirifice sollicitus sum, quod iam diu mihi ignota sunt ista omnia. Quare, ut ad te ante scripsi, cum cetera tum res publica cura ut mihi nota sit. Plura scribam. Tarde tibi redditu iri,[1] sed dabam familiari homini ac domestico, C. Andronico Puteolano. Tu autem

---

[1] *The text here is uncertain.*

longing. You would never believe how sick I am of the business, and I cannot find sufficient scope for the wide interests and energy you know I possess, and do nothing noticeable. To think that I hold court in Laodicea, while A. Plotius does so at Rome, and that I have the nominal command of two skeleton legions, while Caesar has a huge army! However, it is not these advantages I miss: it is the world, the Forum, the city, my home, and you. I will bear as best I can a year of office: an extension would kill me. Still we may combat that very easily if only you are at Rome.

You ask what I am doing. Upon my life I am spending a fortune. I am marvellously pleased with the rule of conduct I have formed: and you have taught me to be so admirably self-restrained that I fear I may have to borrow to pay off the money I took from you. I avoid opening the wounds which Appius has inflicted on the province: but they are patent and cannot be hidden. I travel from Laodicea on the 3rd of August, the date of this letter, to the camp in Lycaonia. Thence I intend to go to Taurus, so that I may settle the matter of your slave, if possible, by pitched battle with Moeragenes.

" 'Tis the ox that bears the load, not I."

I can endure; but, for heaven's sake, let it be only for a year. You must be in town at the proper time to stir up every member of the House. I am marvellously anxious, because it is so long since I have had news: so, as I wrote before, give me news of political matters as well as other things. I will write more fully. [This letter I know] will be a long time in reaching you: but I am giving it to a trusty and intimate friend, C. Andronicus of Puteoli.

saepe dare tabellariis publicanorum poteris per
magistros scripturae et portus nostrarum dioecesium.

XVI

CICERO ATTICO SAL.

Scr. in
itinere a
Synnada ad
Philomelium
inter a. d.
V et III. Id.
Sext. a. 703

   Etsi in ipso itinere et via discedebant publicanorum tabellarii, et eramus in cursu, tamen surripien-
dum aliquid putavi spatii, ne me immemorem mandati tui putares. Itaque subsedi in ipsa via, dum
haec, quae longiorem desiderant orationem, sum-
matim tibi perscriberem. Maxima exspectatione in
perditam et plane eversam in perpetuum provinciam
nos venisse scito pridie Kal. Sextiles, moratos triduum
Laodiceae, triduum Apameae, totidem dies Synnade.
Audivimus nihil aliud nisi imperata ἐπικεφάλια
solvere non posse, ὠνὰς omnium venditas, civitatum
gemitus, ploratus, monstra quedam non hominis,
sed ferae nescio cuius immanis. Quid quaeris?
taedet omnino eos vitae. Levantur tamen miserae
civitates, quod nullus fit sumptus in nos neque in
legatos neque in quaestorem neque in quemquam.
Scito non modo nos foenum, aut quod e lege Iulia
dari solet, non accipere, sed ne ligna quidem, nec
praeter quattuor lectos et tectum quemquam accipere
quicquam, multis locis ne tectum quidem, et in taber-
naculo manere plerumque. Itaque incredibilem in

You, however, will be able to get the contractors for the pasture-dues and harbour-duties of my districts to send yours by the tax-gatherers' messengers.

XVI

CICERO TO ATTICUS, GREETING.

Though the tax-farmers' messengers are actually on their road and I am travelling, still I think I must snatch a moment for fear you may imagine I have forgotten your commission. So I sit down on the high road to scribble you a summary of what really calls for a long epistle. You must know that my arrival in this province, which is in a state of lasting ruin and desolation, was expected eagerly. I got here on the 31st of July. I stayed three days at Laodicea, three at Apamea, and as many at Synnas.[1] Everywhere I heard the same tale. People could not pay the poll-tax: they were forced to sell out their investments: groans and lamentations in the towns, and awful conduct of one who is some kind of savage beast rather than a man. All the people are, as you may suppose, tired of life. However, the poor towns are relieved that they have had to spend nothing on me, my legates, or a quaestor, or anyone. For you must know that I not only refused to accept pay, or what is a proper perquisite under the Julian law, but that none of us will take firewood or anything beyond four beds and a roof; and in many places we do not accept even a roof, but remain mostly under canvas. So extraordinary

On the road from Synnada to Philomelium, between Aug. 9 and 11, B.C. 51

---

[1] This name is found in three forms in classical authors— Synnada (neut. pl.), Synnada (fem. sing.), as in the superscription to this letter, and Synnas, as here.

modum concursus fiunt ex agris, ex vicis, ex domibus
omnibus. Mehercule etiam adventu nostro re-
viviscunt. Iustitia, abstinentia, clementia tui Ciceronis itaque opiniones omnium superavit. Appius,
ut audivit nos venire, in ultimam provinciam se con-
iecit Tarsum usque. Ibi forum agit. De Partho
silentium est, sed tamen concisos equites nostros a
barbaris nuntiabant ii, qui veniebant. Bibulus ne
cogitabat quidem etiam nunc in provinciam suam
accedere; id autem facere ob eam causam dicebant,
quod tardius vellet decedere. Nos in castra properabamus, quae aberant bidui.

XVII

CICERO ATTICO SAL.

Scr. in iti-
nere ad
castra inter
IV Id. et
prid. Id.
Sext. a. 703

Accepi Roma sine epistula tua fasciculum litterarum; in quo, si modo valuisti et Romae fuisti, Philotimi duco esse culpam, non tuam. Hanc epistulam
dictavi sedens in raeda, cum in castra proficiscerer, a
quibus aberam bidui. Paucis diebus habebam certos
homines, quibus darem litteras. Itaque eo me servavi. Nos tamen, etsi hoc te ex aliis audire malo, sic
in provincia nos gerimus, quod ad abstinentiam attinet, ut nullus terruncius insumatur in quemquam.
Id fit etiam et legatorum et tribunorum et praefecto-
rum diligentia; nam omnes mirifice συμφιλοδο-
ξοῦσιν gloriae meae. Lepta noster mirificus est. Sed
nunc propero. Perscribam ad te paucis diebus omnia.
Cicerones nostros Deiotarus filius, qui rex ab senatu

throngs of people have come to meet me from farms and villages and every homestead. Upon my word my very coming seems to revive them. Your friend Cicero has won all hearts by his justice and self-restraint and kind bearing. When Appius heard of my arrival he betook himself to the extreme border of the province, right up by Tarsus. There he holds court. There is no news of the Parthians, but chance arrivals report that they have cut up our cavalry. Even now, Bibulus is not thinking of coming to his province: people say because he desires to be late in departing from it. I am hurrying into camp, which is two days' journey away.

XVII

CICERO TO ATTICUS, GREETING.

I got a bundle of letters from Rome without one from you. Supposing you are well and in town, I imagine the fault was Philotimus' and not yours. This letter is dictated as I sit in my carriage on my road to the camp, from which I am distant two days' journey. In a few days' time I have trusty messengers: so I reserve myself for that time. I should like you to hear the news from others; but I can't help saying that I am conducting myself in the province with such restraint that not a halfpenny is spent on any of us. For that I have to thank the conduct of the legates, tribunes, and praetors. For all of them take a surprising pride in maintaining my good name. Our friend Lepta is wonderful. I am in a hurry now, and will write everything in a few days' time. The younger Deiotarus, who was styled king by the Senate, has taken the two boys to his court.

On the same journey, between Aug. 10 and 12, B.C. 51

appellatus est secum in regnum. Dum in aestivis nos essemus, illum pueris locum esse bellissimum duximus.

Sestius ad me scripsit, quae tecum esset de mea domestica et maxima cura locutus, et quid tibi esset visum. Amabo te, incumbe in eam rem et ad me scribe, quid et possit, et tu censeas. Idem scripsit Hortensium de proroganda nostra provincia dixisse nescio quid. Mihi in Cumano diligentissime se, ut annui essemus, defensurum receperat. Si quicquam me amas, hunc locum muni. Dici non potest, quam invitus a vobis adsim; et simul hanc gloriam iustitiae et abstinentiae fore inlustriorem spero, si cito decesserimus, id quod Scaevolae contigit, qui solos novem menses Asiae praefuit.

Appius noster, cum me adventare videret, profectus est Tarsum usque Laodicea. Ibi forum agit, cum ego sim in provincia. Quam eius iniuriam non insector. Satis enim habeo negotii in sanandis vulneribus, quae sunt imposita provinciae; quod do operam ut faciam quam minima cum illius contumelia. Sed hoc Bruto nostro velim dicas, illum fecisse non belle, qui adventu meo, quam longissime potuerit, discesserit.

XVIII

CICERO ATTICO SAL.

Scr. in castris ad Cybistra Cappadociae XI K. Oct. a. 703

Quam vellem Romae esses, si forte non es. Nihil enim certi habebamus nisi accepisse nos tuas litteras a. d. xiiii Kal. Sextil. datas, in quibus scriptum esset te in Epirum iturum circiter Kal. Sextil. Sed, sive Romae es sive in Epiro, Parthi Euphraten transi-

So long as I am in my summer camp, I fancied that would be the best place for them.

Sestius wrote me an account of his conversation with you about my pressing domestic affairs, and of your opinion. Please devote yourself to the business and write to me what can be done and what you think. Sestius told me that Hortensius has said something or other about extending my term of office. He undertook at Cumae to take good care that it should not outlast a year. If you have any regard for me, get that point fixed up squarely. I cannot describe my dislike to being away from you. Moreover, I hope that my justice and restraint may become more famous if I leave soon: for it was so in the case of Scaevola, who governed Asia only nine months.

On seeing that I was about to arrive, our friend Appius left Laodicea and went up to Tarsus. I am not offended at the slight he has done me by holding court while I am in the province, for I have enough business to heal the wounds that he has inflicted on it: and I try to do this with as little reflection on him as possible. But please tell our friend Brutus that his father-in-law has not acted well in going away as far as he could on my arrival.

XVIII

CICERO TO ATTICUS, GREETING.

If you don't happen to be in town I wish to good-ness you were. I have no positive news beyond your letter dated the 19th of July, in which you said you were going to Epirus about the 1st of August. But whether you are at Rome or in Epirus, the Parthians have crossed the Euphrates under the leadership of

In camp at Cybistra in Cappadocia, Sept. 20, B.C. 51

erunt duce Pacoro, Orodis regis Parthorum filio,
cunctis fere copiis. Bibulus nondum audiebatur esse
in Syria; Cassius in oppido Antiochia est cum omni
exercitu, nos in Cappadocia ad Taurum cum exercitu,
ad Cybistra; hostis in Cyrrhestica, quae Syriae pars
proxima est provinciae meae. His de rebus scripsi
ad senatum, quas litteras, si Romae es, videbis pu-
tesne reddendas, et multa, immo omnia, quorum
κεφάλαιον, ne quid inter caesa et porrecta, ut aiunt,
oneris mihi addatur aut temporis. Nobis enim hac
infirmitate exercitus, inopia sociorum, praesertim
fidelium, certissimum subsidium est hiems. Ea si
venerit, nec illi ante in meam provinciam transierint,
unum vereor, ne senatus propter urbanarum rerum
metum Pompeium nolit dimittere. Quodsi alium ad
ver mittit, non laboro, nobis modo temporis ne quid
prorogetur. Haec igitur, si es Romae; sin abes, aut
etiam si ades, haec negotia sic se habent. Stamus
animis et, quia consiliis, ut videmur, bonis utimur,
speramus etiam manu. Tuto consedimus copioso a
frumento, Ciliciam prope conspiciente, expedito ad
mutandum loco parvo exercitu, sed, ut spero, ad benevolentiam erga nos consentiente. Quem nos Deio-
tari adventu cum suis omnibus copiis duplicaturi
eramus. Sociis multo fidelioribus utimur, quam
quisquam usus est; quibus incredibilis videtur nostra
et mansuetudo et abstinentia. Dilectus habetur

Pacorus, a son of the Parthian king Orodes, with nearly all their forces. There is no news of the presence of Bibulus in Syria: Cassius is in the town of Antioch with his whole army. I am in Cappadocia near the Taurus with my army close to Cybistra. The enemy is in Cyrrhestica, a district of Syria adjoining my province. I have sent a despatch to the Senate on the situation. If you are in Rome, please look at the despatch and say whether you think it ought to be delivered: and so for my other affairs, chief of which is lest there be, as the saying goes, any slip between the cup and the lip,[1] I mean that I may not be burdened with an extension of office. Considering the weakness of my army, my want of allies, especially faithful allies, my most sure support is the winter weather. If winter comes and the enemy have not first crossed into my province, I am afraid the Senate may refuse to let Pompey leave Rome owing to fear of disturbance at home. But if it sends someone else by spring I don't care, provided that there be no extension of my term of office. Those are my commissions, if you are in town. If you are out of town, or even if you are not, the situation is this. I am in excellent spirits; and I hope, as my plans are well laid, that I am not too sanguine about my preparations. I have pitched camp in a safe spot, well supplied on the score of corn, almost within sight of Cilicia, convenient for change of quarters, with an army small but, I hope, very loyal to me, which will be doubled by the arrival of Deiotarus with all his forces. I have found our allies far more loyal than any of my predecessors have found them. They cannot understand my mildness and self-abnegation. A

---

[1] Lit. " Between the slaying and the offering of the victim."

civium Romanorum; frumentum ex agris in loca tuta comportatur. Si fuerit occasio, manu, si minus, locis nos defendemus. Quare bono animo es. Video enim te et, quasi coram adsis, ita cerno συμπάθειαν amoris tui. Sed te rogo, si ullo pacto fieri poterit, si integra in senatu nostra causa ad Kal. Ianuarias manserit, ut Romae sis mense Ianuario. Profecto nihil accipiam iniuriae, si tu aderis. Amicos consules habemus, nostrum tribunum pl. Furnium. Verum tua est opus adsiduitate, prudentia, gratia. Tempus est necessarium. Sed turpe est me pluribus verbis agere tecum.

Cicerones nostri sunt apud Deiotarum, sed, si opus erit, deducentur Rhodum. Tu, si es Romae, ut soles, diligentissime, si in Epiro, mitte tamen ad nos de tuis aliquem tabellarium, ut et tu, quid nos agamus, et nos, quid tu agas quidque acturus sis, scire possimus. Ego tui Bruti rem sic ago, ut suam ipse non ageret. Sed iam exhibeo pupillum neque defendo; sunt enim negotia et lenta et inania. Faciam tamen satis tibi quidem, cui difficilius est quam ipsi; sed certe satis faciam utrique.

levy is being held of Roman citizens: corn is being brought from the country into safe strongholds. Should occasion arise, I should defend myself by force, but otherwise I shall depend on my position. So be of good cheer. You are always in my mind's eye, and I understand your affectionate sympathy as if you were standing here. But I beseech you, if it can be arranged and supposing that my case is not debated in the House up to the first of January, to be in Rome during that month. I shall be treated fairly if you are there. The consuls are my friends; Furnius the tribune of the people is devoted to me: but I want you with your ingratiating and skilful persistence. It is a critical time. But it would be a shame for me to press you further.

My son and nephew are staying with Deiotarus. If necessary, they shall be sent to Rhodes. If you are in Rome send me a message with your usual regularity. And even if you are in Epirus send me one of your messengers, that you may know my proceedings, and I may know your present and future plans. I am managing your friend Brutus' business better than he could himself. But I now hand my ward [1] over to the creditors and refuse to set up any plea for him. They are an impracticable and impecunious lot. However, I shall satisfy you, which is more difficult even than satisfying Brutus. Indeed, I will satisfy you both.

[1] Ariobarzanes, King of Cappadocia, who owed money to Brutus.

MARCUS TULLIUS CICERO

XIX

CICERO ATTICO SAL.

Scr. in castris ad Cybistra XI K. Oct. a. 703

Obsignaram iam epistulam eam, quam puto te modo perlegisse scriptam mea manu, in qua omnia continentur, cum subito Apellae tabellarius a. d. XI Kal. Octobres septimo quadragesimo die Roma celeriter (hui tam longe!) mihi tuas litteras reddidit. Ex quibus non dubito, quin tu Pompeium exspectaris, dum Arimino rediret, et iam in Epirum profectus sis, magisque vereor, ut scribis, ne in Epiro sollicitus sis non minus, quam nos hic sumus.

De Atiliano nomine scripsi ad Philotimum, ne appellaret Messallam. Itineris nostri famam ad te pervenisse laetor magisque laetabor, si reliqua cognoris. Filiolam tuam tibi caram ac [1] iucundam esse gaudeo, eamque quam numquam vidi, tamen et amo et amabilem esse certo scio. Etiam atque etiam vale.

De Patrone et tuis condiscipulis quae de parietinis in Melita laboravi, ea tibi grata esse gaudeo. Quod scribis libente te repulsum tulisse eum, qui cum sororis tuae filii patruo certarit, magni amoris signum. Itaque me etiam admonuisti, ut gauderem; nam mihi in mentem non venerat. " Non credo," inquis. Ut

---

[1] caram ac *Müller*: iam Romae *MSS.*: tam moratum *Tyrrell*.

XIX

CICERO TO ATTICUS, GREETING.

I had already sealed the letter, which I fancy you *In the camp* must have just read, written in my own handwriting *at Cybistra,* and containing a full account of events, when sud- *Sept. 20,* B.C. denly your letter was delivered to me on September *51* the 20th by a letter carrier of Apelles, who had done a journey express from Rome in forty-seven days. Ah, what a long way it is! It makes me sure that you awaited Pompey's return from Ariminum, and have now set out for Epirus, and I fear from your tone that you may be in as great straits in Epirus as I am here.

I have written to my wife's steward not to dun Messalla for the money due from Atilius. I am delighted you have heard reports of my official progress, and I shall be still more delighted if you hear of my other good deeds. I am glad that you are pleased with your little daughter. I have never seen her, but I love her and I am sure she is lovable. Goodbye, again good-bye.

Talking of Patro and your friends of his school, I am glad you liked my efforts about the ruins in Melita. It is a sign of great affection on your part, to rejoice in the defeat of a man [1] who opposed the uncle of your sister's son. You have put it into my head to rejoice too. It had not occurred to me. You need not believe me, if you like: but really I

---

[1] Probably C. Hirrus, who had just failed to obtain the curule aedileship. He had previously stood for the augurate, when Cicero had been successful. Others, however, suggest M. Calidius, who had criticized Cicero's oratorical style and prosecuted Q. Gallius in 64 B.C., when Cicero defended him.

libet; sed plane gaudeo, quoniam τὸ νεμεσᾶν interest
τοῦ φθονεῖν.

XX

CICERO ATTICO SAL.

*Scr. in
Cilicia a.
703 inter a.
d. XII et
IV K. Ian.*

Saturnalibus mane se mihi Pindenissitae dedide-
runt septimo et quinquagesimo die, postquam oppu-
gnare eos coepimus. " Qui, malum! isti Pindenissitae qui sunt? " inquies; " nomen audivi numquam."
Quid ego faciam? num potui Ciliciam Aetoliam aut
Macedoniam reddere? Hoc iam sic habeto, nec hoc
exercitu nec hic tanta negotia geri potuisse. Quae
cognosce ἐν ἐπιτομῇ; sic enim concedis mihi proxumis
litteris. Ephesum ut venerim, nosti, qui etiam mihi
gratulatus es illius diei celebritatem, qua nihil me
umquam delectavit magis. Inde in oppidis iis, qua
iter erat, mirabiliter accepti Laodiceam pridie Kal.
Sextiles venimus. Ibi morati biduum perillustres
fuimus honorificisque verbis omnes iniurias revellimus
superiores, quod idem Colossis, dein Apameae quinque dies morati et Synnadis triduum, Philomeli
quinque dies, Iconi decem fecimus. Nihil ea iuris
dictione aequabilius, nihil lenius, nihil gravius. Inde
in castra veni a. d. vii Kalendas Septembres. A. d.
iii exercitum lustravi apud Iconium. Ex his castris,
sum graves de Parthis nuntii venirent, perrexi in
Ciliciam per Cappadociae partem eam, quae Ciliciam
attingit, eo consilio, ut Armenius Artavasdes et ipsi

am glad, because righteous indignation is different from malice.

XX

CICERO TO ATTICUS, GREETING.

On the morning of the 17th of December the Pindenissitae surrendered to me, on the fifty-seventh day from the commencement of my siege. "The Pindenissitae!" you will exclaim, "Who the deuce are they? I never heard the name." That is not my fault. Could I turn Cilicia into Aetolia or Macedonia? Take this for granted that with my army and in my position such a big business was impossible. Here is a synopsis of the affair. You agreed to that in your last letter. You are aware of my arrival at Ephesus, for you have congratulated me on the reception I got on the day of arrival, which delighted me beyond words. Thence, after a marvellous welcome in the towns on my way, I reached Laodicea on the 31st of July. I stayed there two days in great state and with flattering speeches took the sting out of all past injuries. I did the same at Colossae and during a stay of five days at Apamea, three at Synnada, five at Philomelus, and ten at Iconium. Nothing could be more fair, lenient, or dignified than my legal decisions. From there I came to camp on the 24th of August. On the 28th I reviewed the army at Iconium. On receipt of grave news about the Parthians I left camp for Cilicia travelling through that part of Cappadocia which borders on Cilicia, intending that the Armenian Artavasdes and the Parthians themselves should realize they were cut off from entering Cappadocia. After camp-

In Cilicia, between Dec. 19 and 27, B.C. 51

389

Parthi Cappadocia se excludi putarent. Cum dies
quinque ad Cybistra Cappadociae castra habuissem,
certior sum factus Parthos ab illo aditu Cappadociae
longe abesse, Ciliciae magis imminere. Itaque con-
festim iter in Ciliciam feci per Tauri pylas. Tarsum
veni a. d. iii Nonas Octobres. Inde ad Amanum contendi, qui Syriam a Cilicia in aquarum divertio
dividit; qui mons erat hostium plenus sempiterno-
rum. Hic a. d. iii Idus Octobr. magnum numerum
hostium occidimus. Castella munitissima nocturno
Pomptini adventu, nostro matutino cepimus, incendi-
mus. Imperatores appellati sumus. Castra paucos
dies habuimus ea ipsa, quae contra Darium habuerat
apud Issum Alexander, imperator haud paulo melior
quam aut tu aut ego. Ibi dies quinque morati
direpto et vastato Amano inde discessimus. Interim
(scis enim dici quaedam πανικά, dici item τὰ κενὰ
τοῦ πολέμου) rumore adventus nostri et Cassio, qui
Antiochia tenebatur, animus accessit, et Parthis
timor iniectus est. Itaque eos cedentes ab oppido
Cassius insecutus rem bene gessit. Qua in fuga
magna auctoritate Osaces dux Parthorum vulnus
accepit eoque interiit paucis post diebus. Erat in
Syria nostrum nomen in gratia. Venit interim Bibulus; credo, voluit appellatione hac inani nobis esse
par. In eodem Amano coepit loreolam in mustaceo
quaerere. At ille cohortem primam totam perdidit
centurionemque primi pili, nobilem sui generis, Asi-

ing five days at Cybistra in Cappadocia I got information that the Parthians were far distant from that
entrance into Cappadocia, and rather were threatening Cilicia. So I made a forced march into Cilicia by
the gates of Taurus. I reached Tarsus on the 5th of
October. Thence I hurried to Amanus, which divides
Syria from Cilicia by its watershed, a mountain that
has always been full of our enemies. Here on the
13th of October we cut up a large body of the enemy.
I captured some strongly fortified posts by a night
assault of Pomptinus and a day assault of my own;
and we burned them. I was hailed as " General."
For a few days I pitched camp at the very spot near
Issus where Alexander had camped against Darius.
He was rather a better general than you or I. We
plundered and devastated Amanus, and after a stay
of five days took our departure. Meantime (for you
know there are such words as " panic " and the " un-
certainties of war ") report of my arrival gave heart
to Cassius, who was shut up in Antioch, and it inspired fear in the Parthians. So, as the Parthians
retreated from the town, Cassius pursued them and
scored a success. In their retreat one of their leaders,
Osaces, a man of high rank, was wounded and died
a few days afterwards. I was in high favour in Syria.
Meantime Bibulus came. I fancy he wanted to be
my peer in the matter of that empty title. On
this same mountain Amanus he begins his task of
looking for a needle in a bottle of hay.[1] But the
whole of his first squadron was lost as well as Asinius
Dento, a centurion of the first line and of noble

[1] Lit. " a bay leaf in a wedding cake." They were baked
on bay leaves.

nium Dentonem, et reliquos cohortis eiusdem et Sex.
Lucilium, T. Gavi Caepionis locupletis et splendidi
hominis filium, tribunum militum. Sane plagam
odiosam acceperat cum re tum tempore. Nos ad Pin-
denissum, quod oppidum munitissimum Eleuthero-
cilicum omnium memoria in armis fuit. Feri homines
et acres et omnibus rebus ad defendendum parati.
Cinximus vallo et fossa, aggere maximo, vineis, turre
altissima, magna tormentorum copia, multis sagit-
tariis, magno labore, apparatu, multis sauciis nostris,
incolumi exercitu negotium confecimus. Hilara sane
Saturnalia militibus quoque, quibus equis exceptis
reliquam praedam concessimus. Mancipia venibant
Saturnalibus tertiis. Cum haec scribebam in tribu-
nali res erat ad HS |c̄x̄x̄|. Hinc exercitum in hiberna
agri male pacati deducendum Quinto fratri dabam;
ipse me Laodiceam recipiebam.

Haec adhuc. Sed ad praeterita revertamur. Quod
me maxime hortaris et, quod pluris est quam omnia,
in quo laboras, ut etiam Ligurino μώμῳ satis facia-
mus, moriar, si quicquam fieri potest elegantius. Nec
iam ego hanc continentiam appello, quae virtus volup-

blood,[1] and other centurions of the same squadron, and a military tribune, Sex. Lucilius son of T. Gavius Caepio, who has wealth and position. It was really a mortifying reverse and inopportune. I was at Pindenissus, the most strongly fortified town in Eleutherocilicia and engaged in war so long as men can remember. The inhabitants were keen warriors, thoroughly prepared to withstand a siege. We compassed it with a stockade and ditch, with big entrenchments, penthouses, a tall tower, a large supply of artillery, and a number of archers. With much toil and preparation I settled the business without loss of life, though many were wounded. I am keeping a festive holiday, as also are my soldiers, to whom I gave all the spoils except the horses. The captives were sold on the third day of the festival of Saturn.[2] At the time of writing, the sum realized at the auction has reached about £100,000.[3] I am giving my army to my brother Quintus to take into winter quarters in the more disturbed part of the province, while I am returning myself to Laodicea.

So much for that. To recur to old topics. As for the point of your exhortation, which is more important than anything else about which you are concerned—that I may satisfy even my carping Ligurian critic [4]—may I die if conduct could be more fastidious than mine. I am not going to talk of

---

[1] Or "noble in his own class" (i.e. a good soldier), or "a noble of his own kidney," with a play on Asinius and *asinus*.

[2] December 19.

[3] 12,000,000 sesterces.

[4] Probably P. Aelius Ligur, who sided against Cicero at the time of his banishment.

tati resistere videtur. Ego in vita mea nulla umquam voluptate tanta sum adfectus, quanta adficior
hac integritate, nec me tam fama, quae summa est,
quam res ipsa delectat. Quid quaeris? fuit tanti.
Me ipse non noram nec satis sciebam, quid in hoc
genere facere possem. Recte πεφύσημαι. Nihil est
praeclarius. Interim haec λαμπρά. Ariobarzanes
opera mea vivit, regnat; ἐν παρόδῳ consilio et auctoritate et, quod insidiatoribus eius ἀπρόσιτον me,
non modo ἀδωροδόκητον praebui, regem regnumque
servavi. Interea e Cappadocia ne pilum quidem.
Brutum abiectum, quantum potui, excitavi; quem
non minus amo quam tu, paene dixi, quam te.
Atque etiam spero toto anno imperii nostri terruncium sumptus in provincia nullum fore.

Habes omnia. Nunc publice litteras Romam mittere parabam. Uberiores erunt, quam si ex Amano
misissem. At te Romae non fore! Sed est totum
in eo, quid Kalendis Martiis futurum sit. Vereor
enim, ne, cum de provincia agetur, si Caesar resistet,
nos retineamur. His tu si adesses, nihil timerem.

Redeo ad urbana, quae ego diu ignorans ex tuis
iucundissimis litteris a. d. v Kal. Ianuarias denique
cognovi. Eas diligentissime Philogenes, libertus tuus,
curavit perlonga et non satis tuta via perferendas.

continence, a quality connoting resistance of pleasure: for nothing in my life has given me more pleasure than this rectitude. And it is not so much the enhancement of my reputation, though that is important, as the exercise of the virtue that delights me. I can tell you my exile has been worth while, for I did not understand myself nor realize of what I was capable in this line. I may well be puffed up. It is splendid. Meantime I have made a *coup* in this: it is thanks to me that Ariobarzanes lives and reigns a king. In my progress through the province I have saved a king and a kingdom by the weight of my advice and official position and by refusing to entertain even the visits much less the bribes of conspirators against him. Meantime from Cappadocia not the value of a hair. I stirred up Brutus out of his dejection as much as I could. I love him as well as you do. I had almost said as well as I do you. And I hope that during the whole of my year of office there will not be a penny's expense in my province.

That is the whole story. I am now preparing to send an official despatch to Rome. It will be richer in detail than if I had sent it from Amanus. But fancy your not being in town! Everything hangs on what happens on the 1st of March, for I fear, when the question of the provinces is under debate, that I may be kept here if Caesar refuses to give up his province. Were you there to take part in the matter, I should have no fears.

To revert to city news, with which I was put in touch only on the 26th of December from your delightful letter. It was the letter which your freedman Philogenes brought to me with scrupulous care after a long and risky journey; for I have not received

Nam, quas Laeni pueris scribis datas, non acceperam. Iucunda de Caesare, et quae senatus decrevit, et quae tu speras. Quibus ille si cedit, salvi sumus. Incendio Plaetoriano quod Seius ambustus est, minus moleste fero. Lucceius de Q. Cassio cur tam vehemens fuerit, et quid actum sit, aveo scire.

Ego, cum Laodiceam venero, Quinto, sororis tuae filio, togam puram iubeor dare. Cui moderabor diligentius. Deiotarus, cuius auxiliis magnis usus sum, ad me, ut scripsit, cum Ciceronibus Laodiceam venturus erat. Tuas etiam Epiroticas exspecto litteras, ut habeam rationem non modo negotii, verum etiam otii tui. Nicanor in officio est et a me liberaliter tractatur. Quem, ut puto, Romam cum litteris publicis mittam, ut et diligentius perferantur, et idem ad me certa de te et a te referat. Alexis quod mihi totiens salutem adscribit, est gratum; sed cur non suis litteris idem facit, quod meus ad te Alexis facit? Phemio quaeritur κέρας. Sed haec hactenus. Cura, ut valeas, et ut sciam, quando cogites Romam. Etiam atque etiam vale.

Tua tuosque Thermo et praesens Ephesi diligentissime commendaram et nunc per litteras ipsumque intellexi esse perstudiosum tui. Tu velim, quod antea

the letter which you say was entrusted to the slaves of Laenius. It was glad tidings that you wrote me about Caesar and the decree of the House and your own hopes. If Caesar falls in with this I shall be safe from any extension of office. I am not much concerned that Seius was singed in Plaetorius' fire.[1] I want to know why Lucceius was so keen about Q. Cassius and what has happened.

I am commissioned to celebrate the coming of age of Quintus, your sister's son, on arrival at Laodicea. I shall keep a careful hold upon him. Deiotarus, who has been of great help to me, has written that he will come to me at Laodicea with the two boys. I am awaiting another letter from you from Epirus, that I may have an account not only of your work-a-day life, but also of your holiday life. Nicanor is doing his duty by me, and is being well treated. I think I shall send him to Rome with my official despatch, that it may be promptly delivered and at the same time that he may bring me certain news about you and from you. I am pleased that Alexis so often sends greetings to me; but why cannot he put them in a letter of his own, as Tiro, who is my Alexis, does for you. I am searching for a horn for Phemius.[2] But enough now. Keep your health and let me know when you intend to go to town. Good-bye, again good-bye.

I have been at pains to recommend your interests and your people to Thermus, both personally at Ephesus and now by letter, and I have gathered that he is very solicitous on your behalf. Please execute

---

[1] M. Plaetorius Cestianus was condemned for extortion, and M. Seius as an accessory after the fact.

[2] A musical slave belonging to Atticus.

ad te scripsi, de domo Pammeni des operam, ut, quod tuo meoque beneficio puer habet, cures, ne qua ratione convellatur. Utrique nostrum honestum existimo; tum mihi erit pergratum.

XXI

CICERO ATTICO SAL.

Scr. Laodiceae Id. Febr. a. 704

Te in Epirum salvum venisse et, ut scribis, ex sententia navigasse vehementer gaudeo, non esse Romae meo tempore pernecessario submoleste fero. Hoc me tamen consolor uno, spero te istic iucunde hiemare et libenter requiescere. C. Cassius, frater Q. Cassi, familiaris tui, pudentiores illas litteras miserat, de quibus tu ex me requiris, quid sibi voluerint, quam eas, quas postea misit, quibus per se scribit confectum esse Parthicum bellum. Recesserant illi quidem ab Antiochia ante Bibuli adventum, sed nullo nostro εὐημερήματι; hodie vero hiemant in Cyrrhestica, maximumque bellum impendet. Nam et Orodi, regis Parthorum, filius in provincia nostra est, nec dubitat Deiotarus, cuius filio pacta est Artavasdis filia, ex quo sciri potest, quin cum omnibus copiis ipse prima aestate Euphraten transiturus sit. Quo autem die Cassi litterae victrices in senatu recitatae sunt, datae Nonis Octobribus, eodem meae tumultum nuntiantes. Axius noster ait nostras auctoritatis plenas fuisse, illis negat creditum. Bibuli nondum erant allatae; quas certo scio plenas timoris fore.

my former commissions to look after Pammenes' house, so that the boy may not be robbed of what he owes to your kindness and mine. This, I think, will redound to our honour and will please me much.

XXI

CICERO TO ATTICUS, GREETING.

I am very glad that you have reached Epirus safely, and that you report a voyage to your liking. But I am rather upset that you are absent from Rome at a moment so critical for me. However, I have one consolation : I hope you will have a pleasant winter where you are and a nice rest. You ask me the purport of a letter that C. Cassius, the brother of Q. Cassius, your friend, sent me. The letter he wrote is more modest than a subsequent epistle in which he claimed to have ended the Parthian war. The Parthians to be sure had retired from Antioch before the arrival of Bibulus : but it was not thanks to any *coup de main* of our troops. To-day the enemy is wintering in Cyrrhestica and a serious war is imminent : for the son of Orodes the king of the Parthians is in a Roman province, and Deiotarus, to whose son the daughter of Artavasdes is betrothed, a very competent authority, is positive that the king himself will cross the Euphrates with all his forces in the early summer. On the very day on which Cassius' despatch, dated the 7th of October, announcing victory was read in the Senate, came mine announcing trouble. My friend Axius says that Cassius' despatch gained no belief and mine was considered worthy of attention. Bibulus' despatch had not yet arrived : but I know for a fact that it will express alarm.

Laodicea,
Feb. 13,
B.C. *50*

Ex his rebus hoc vereor, ne, cum Pompeius propter metum rerum novarum nusquam dimittatur, Caesari nullus honos a senatu habeatur, dum hic nodus expediatur, non putet senatus nos, antequam successum sit, oportere decedere nec in tanto motu rerum tantis provinciis singulos legatos praeesse. Hic, ne quid mihi prorogetur, quod ne intercessor quidem sustinere possit, horreo, atque eo magis, quod tu abes, qui consilio, gratia, studio multis rebus occurreres. Sed dices me ipsum mihi sollicitudinem struere. Cogor, ut velim ita sit; sed omnia metuo. Etsi bellum ἀκροτελεύτιον habet illa tua epistula, quam dedisti nauseans Buthroto: "Tibi, ut video et spero, nulla ad decedendum erit mora." Mallem "ut video," nihil opus fuit "ut spero." Acceperam autem satis celeriter Iconi per publicanorum tabellarios a Lentuli triumpho datas. In his γλυκύπικρον illud confirmas, moram mihi nullam fore, deinde addis, si quid secus, te ad me esse venturum. Angunt me dubitationes tuae; simul et vides, quas acceperim litteras. Nam, quas Hermonis centurionis caculae ipse scribis te dedisse, non accepi. Laeni pueris te dedisse saepe ad me scripseras. Eas Laodiceae denique, cum eo venissem, III Idus Februar. Laenius mihi reddidit datas a. d. x Kal. Octobres. Laenio tuas commendationes et statim verbis et reliquo tempore re probabo. Eae litterae cetera vetera habe-

This makes me fear that the Senate may pay no respect to Caesar's demands, refusing to let Pompey quit Rome, when revolution is imminent. Until this trouble is unravelled, it may decline to allow me to leave the province before my successor comes, and not be willing to entrust such important provinces in troublous times to legates. So I shudder to think that the term of my office may be extended without even any tribune being able to veto it; and the more so on account of your absence, when you might interfere in many cases with your advice, influence, and efforts. You will say I am raising imaginary alarms. I am forced to hope that my alarms may be idle, but everything frightens me. Though your letter written at Buthrotum in sickness had a charming *finale*, "As I see and hope, there will be nothing to hinder your departure," still I should prefer the phrase "as I see" and there was no need for the words "and hope." I have received a letter dated just after the triumph of Lentulus, which was brought post haste to Iconium by the tax-farmers' messengers. In it you repeat that bitter-sweet saying, that there will be no delay, with a postscript, that if anything goes wrong you yourself will come to me. I am tortured by the doubts you express: and you may see which of your letters I have received, for I have not got the letter which you say was handed to Hermo the centurion's orderly. You have repeatedly told me you entrusted a letter to the slaves of Laenius. That letter, which was dated the 21st of September, was handed to me at last by Laenius on my arrival at Laodicea on the 11th of February. I will show Laenius at once in word and in the future in deed that your recommendation carries weight. Besides old topics the letter had

bant, unum hoc novum de Cibyratis pantheris.
Multum te amo, quod respondisti M. Octavio te non
putare. Sed posthac omnia, quae recta non erunt,
pro certo negato. Nos enim et nostra sponte bene
firmi et mehercule auctoritate tua inflammati vicimus
omnes (hoc tu ita reperies) cum abstinentia tum iustitia, facilitate, clementia. Cave putes quicquam
homines magis umquam esse miratos quam nullum
terruncium me obtinente provinciam sumptus factum
esse nec in rem publicam nec in quemquam meorum
praeterquam in L. Tullium legatum. Is ceteroqui
abstinens, sed Iulia lege transitans,[1] semel tamen in
diem, non, ut alii solebant, omnibus vicis (praeter eum
semel nemo accepit) facit, ut mihi excipiendus sit,
cum terruncium nego sumptus factum. Praeter eum
accepit nemo. Has a nostro Q. Titinio sordes ac-
cepimus.

Ego aestivis confectis Quintum fratrem hibernis et
Ciliciae praefeci. Q. Volusium, tui Tiberi generum,
certum hominem et mirifice abstinentem, misi in
Cyprum, ut ibi pauculos dies esset, ne cives Romani,
pauci qui illic negotiantur, ius sibi dictum negarent;
nam evocari ex insula Cyprios non licet. Ipse in
Asiam profectus sum Tarso Nonis Ianuariis, non mehercule dici potest qua admiratione Ciliciae civitatum
maximeque Tarsensium. Postea vero quam Taurum
transgressus sum, mirifica exspectatio Asiae nostrarum dioecesium, quae sex mensibus imperii mei
nullas meas acceperat litteras, numquam hospitem

---

[1] transitans *Manutius*: transitam *M*: pransitans *Peerlkamp*: in transitu *Tyrrell*.

one fresh one, the panthers from Cibyra. I am in-
debted to you for telling M. Octavius that you
thought it would be impracticable. But in future
give a direct " no " to any undesirable requests.
Firm fixed in my own determination and fired by the
weight of your opinion, I have overcome everybody
as you will find by my justice, self-abnegation, and
easy courtesy. People were never more astonished
than to learn that not a farthing has been spent during my tenure of office, either on public objects or
on any of my staff, except on my legate L. Tullius.
He has behaved well on the whole, but under the
Julian law on one occasion *en passage* and for the
day's needs, and not as others would at every ham-
let, he did take something. He is the sole offender;
and forces me to add a rider to my remark that not
a farthing has been spent upon us. Besides him no
one has taken a penny. That blot I owe to my friend
Q. Titinius.

When the camp was struck at the end of the summer I put my brother Quintus in charge of the
winter camp and of Cilicia. Q. Volusius, son-in-law
of your friend Tiberius, a safe man and wonderfully
unselfish, I have sent to Cyprus, ordering him to stay
a few days, that the few Roman citizens in business
there may not say they have no facilities for legal
process: the inhabitants cannot be summoned to a
court outside the island. I myself set out for Asia
from Tarsus on the fifth of January. I cannot describe how the cities in Cilicia and especially the
people of Tarsus looked up to me. After crossing
the Taurus I found Asia, that is so far as my district
extends, very keen to welcome me. For during the
six months of my administration there had been no

403

viderat. Illud autem tempus quotannis ante me
fuerat in hoc quaestu. Civitates locupletes, ne in
hiberna milites reciperent, magnas pecunias dabant,
Cyprii talenta Attica cc; qua ex insula (non
ὑπερβολικῶς, sed verissime loquor) nummus nullus
me obtinente erogabitur. Ob haec beneficia, quibus
illi obstupescunt, nullos honores mihi nisi verborum
decerni sino, statuas, fana, τέθριππα prohibeo, nec
sum in ulla re alia molestus civitatibus—sed fortasse
tibi, qui haec praedicem de me. Perfer, si me amas;
tu enim me haec facere voluisti. Iter igitur ita per
Asiam feci, ut etiam fames, qua nihil miserius est,
quae tum erat in haec mea Asia (messis enim nulla
fuerat), mihi optanda fuerit. Quacumque iter feci,
nulla vi, nullo iudicio, nulla contumelia, auctoritate
et cohortatione perfeci, ut et Graeci et cives Romani,
qui frumentum compresserant, magnum numerum
populis pollicerentur. Idibus Februariis, quo die
has litteras dedi, forum institueram agere Laodiceae Cibyraticum et Apamense, ex Idibus Martiis
ibidem Synnadense, Pamphylium (tum Phemio dis-
piciam κέρας), Lycaonium, Isauricum; ex Idibus
Maiis in Ciliciam, ut ibi Iunius consumatur, velim
tranquille a Parthis. Quinctilis, si erit, ut volumus,
in itinere est per provinciam redeuntibus consu-
mendus. Venimus enim in provinciam Laodiceam
Sulpicio et Marcello consulibus pridie Kalendas Sex-

requisitions and not a single case of billeting. Before
my time this season had been devoted every year to
the pursuit of gain. The richer states used to pay
large sums to escape from having soldiers billeted on
them for the winter. The people of Cyprus used to
pay nearly £50,000,[1] while under my administration,
in literal truth, not a penny will be demanded. I
will take no honours except speechifying in return for
these kindnesses which have so amazed people. I
allow neither statues, nor shrines, nor sculptured
chariots: and I don't annoy the states in any other
respects—but perhaps I may annoy you by my
egotism. Bear with it from your regard for me. It
was you who wished me to act as I have. My tour
through Asia was such that even the crowning misery
of famine, which existed in my province owing to the
failure of the crops, gave me a welcome opportunity.
Wherever I went, without force, without legal process, without hard words, by my personal influence
and exhortations, I induced Greeks and Roman
citizens, who had stored corn, to promise a large
quantity to the communities. On the 13th of February, the date on which I despatch this letter, I
have arranged to try cases from Cibyra and Apamea
at Laodicea; from the 15th of March, from Synnada,
Pamphylia (when I will look out for a horn for Phemius), Lycaonia, and Isaurum at the same place.
After the 15th of May I set out to spend June
in Cilicia: I hope without being troubled by the
Parthians. July, if things turn out as I hope, is to
be spent on my journey back through the province.
I entered the province at Laodicea during the consulship of Sulpicius and Marcellus on the 31st of July.

[1] 200 Attic talents, which were of the value of £243 15s.

tiles. Inde nos oportet decedere a. d. III Kalendas
Sextiles. Primum contendam a Quinto fratre, ut se
praefici patiatur, quod et illo et me invitissimo fiet.
Sed aliter honeste fieri non potest, praesertim cum
virum optimum, Pomptinum, ne nunc quidem retinere possim. Rapit enim hominem Postumius
Romam, fortasse etiam Postumia.

Habes consilia nostra; nunc cognosce de Bruto.
Familiares habet Brutus tuus quosdam creditores Sa-
laminiorum ex Cypro, M. Scaptium et P. Matinium;
quos mihi maiorem in modum commendavit. Matinium non novi. Scaptius ad me in castra venit.
Pollicitus sum curaturum me Bruti causa, ut ei Salaminii pecuniam solverent. Egit gratias. Praefecturam petivit. Negavi me cuiquam negotianti dare
(quod idem tibi ostenderam. Cn. Pompeio petenti
probaram institutum meum, quid dicam Torquato de
M. Laenio tuo, multis aliis?); sin praefectus vellet
esse syngraphae causa, me curaturum, ut exigeret.
Gratias egit, discessit. Appius noster turmas aliquot
equitum dederat huic Scaptio, per quas Salaminios
coerceret, et eundem habuerat praefectum; vexabat
Salaminios. Ego equites ex Cypro decedere iussi.
Moleste tulit Scaptius. Quid multa? ut ei fidem
meam praestarem, cum ad me Salaminii Tarsum
venissent et in iis Scaptius, imperavi, ut pecuniam
solverent. Multa de syngrapha, de Scapti iniuriis.
Negavi me audire; hortatus sum, petivi etiam pro

I ought to quit it on the 30th of July. First, however, I must ask my brother Quintus to be good enough to take charge, which will be against the grain with us both. But it will be the only fair course, especially since even now I cannot keep that excellent fellow Pomptinus; for Postumius is dragging him back to town, and perhaps Mrs. Postumius too.

Those are my plans. Now let me tell you about Brutus. Among his intimates your friend Brutus has some creditors of the people of Salamis in Cyprus, M. Scaptius and P. Matinius, whom he recommended to me warmly. Matinius I have not met: Scaptius came to see me in camp. For the sake of Brutus I promised that the people of Salamis should settle their debts to him. The fellow thanked me, and asked for the post of prefect. I informed him I always refused business men, as I have told you. This rule Cn. Pompeius accepted when he made a similar request. So did Torquatus, M. Laenius, and many others. However, I told Scaptius that if he wanted the post on account of his bond, I would see that he got paid. He thanked me and took his leave. Our friend Appius had given him some squadrons to put pressure on the people of Salamis, and had also given him the office of prefect. He was causing trouble to the people of Salamis. I gave orders that his cavalry should leave the island. That annoyed him. In short, to keep faith with him, I ordered the people, when they came along with Scaptius to see me at Tarsus, to pay the money. They had a good deal to say about the bond, and about the harm that Scaptius had done them. I refused to listen. I prayed and besought them to

meis in civitatem beneficiis, ut negotium conficerent,
denique dixi me coacturum. Homines non modo
non recusare, sed etiam hoc dicere, se a me solvere.
Quod enim praetori dare consuessent, quoniam ego
non acceperam, se a me quodam modo dare, atque
etiam minus esse aliquanto in Scapti nomine quam in
vectigali praetorio. Collaudavi homines. " Recte,"
inquit Scaptius, " sed subducamus summam." Interim, cum ego in edicto translaticio centesimas me
observaturum haberem cum anatocismo anniversario,
ille ex syngrapha postulabat quaternas. " Quid
ais ? " inquam, " possumne contra meum edictum ? "
At ille profert senatus consultum Lentulo Philippoque
consulibus, Vt, qvi Ciliciam obtineret, ivs ex illa
syngrapha diceret. Cohorrui primo; etenim erat
interitus civitatis. Reperio duo senatus consulta isdem consulibus de eadem syngrapha. Salaminii cum
Romae versuram facere vellent, non poterant, quod
lex Gabinia vetebat. Tum iis Bruti familiares freti
gratia Bruti dare volebant quaternis, si sibi senatus
consulto caveretur. Fit gratia Bruti senatus consultum, Vt neve Salaminiis, neve qvi eis dedisset,
fravdi esset. Pecuniam numerarunt. At postea

settle the business in consideration of the good that
I had done their state.   Finally, I threatened to com-
pel them.   So far from refusing to settle, the people
said that really they would be paying out of my
pocket, in the sense that I had refused to take the
present usually given to the governor, which they
admitted would be more than the amount they owed
to Scaptius.   I praised their attitude.   " Very well,"
said Scaptius, " but let us reckon up the total."   Now
in my traditionary edict [1] I had fixed the rate of
interest at 12 per cent compound interest, reckoned
by the year.   But Scaptius demanded 48 per cent
in accordance with the terms of the bond.   I declared
that I could not break the rule laid down in my edict.
But he produced a decree of the Senate, made in the
consulship of Lentulus and Philippus,[2] ordering that
the governor of Cilicia should give judgement according to the bond.   At first I was horror stricken,
for it spelled ruin to the community.   I find there
are two decrees of the Senate in the same year about
this identical bond.   When the people of Salamis
wanted to raise a loan in town to pay off another
they were obstructed by a law of Gabinius which forbade lending to provincials.   Then these intimates of
Brutus, depending on his support, professed willing-
ness to lend at 48 per cent if they were protected by
a decree of the Senate.   Brutus induced the Senate to
make a decree that the transaction between the
people of Salamis and the money-lenders should be
exempted from the provisions of the law.   They paid
down the money.   Afterwards it came into the heads

[1] The edict is called *translaticium,* because it was handed
down with alterations from governor to governor.
[2] 56 B.C.

venit in mentem faeneratoribus nihil se iuvare illud
senatus consultum, quod ex syngrapha ius dici lex
Gabinia vetaret. Tum fit senatus consultum, VT EX
EA SYNGRAPHA IVS DICERETVR, non ut alio iure ea syngrapha [1] esset quam ceterae, sed ut eodem. Cum
haec disseruissem, seducit me Scaptius; ait se nihil
contra dicere, sed illos putare talenta cc se debere.
Ea se velle accipere. Debere autem illos paulo minus. Rogat, ut eos ad ducenta perducam. "Optime," inquam. Voco illos ad me remoto Scaptio.
"Quid? vos quantum," inquam, "debetis?" Respondent cvi. Refero ad Scaptium. Homo clamare.
"Quid? opus est," inquam, "rationes conferatis?"
Adsidunt, subducunt; ad nummum convenit. Illi se
numerare velle, urguere, ut acciperet. Scaptius me
rursus seducit, rogat, ut rem sic relinquam. Dedi
veniam homini impudenter petenti; Graecis queren-
tibus, ut in fano deponerent, postulantibus non concessi. Clamare omnes, qui aderant, nihil impudentius Scaptio, qui centesimis cum anatocismo contentus
non esset; alii nihil stultius. Mihi autem impudens
magis quam stultus videbatur; nam aut bono nomine
centesimis contentus non [2] erat aut non bono quaternas centesimas sperabat.

Habes meam causam. Quae si Bruto non probatur, nescio, cur illum amemus. Sed avunculo eius
certe probabitur, praesertim cum senatus consultum
modo factum sit, puto, postquam tu es profectus, in

---

[1] IVS—syngrapha *is added by Boot.*
[2] non *is added by Ernesti.*

of the money-lenders that the decree would be futile, because Gabinius' law forbade any legal process on the bond. Then the Senate passed a decree that the bond should be good at law, giving this bond the same validity as other bonds and nothing more. When I pointed this out, Scaptius took me aside. He said that he had no objection to my ruling; but that the people of Salamis imagined they owed him nearly £50,000. That he wanted to get that sum, but that they owed rather less. He begged me to induce them to fix it at that amount. "Very well," said I. I sent Scaptius away, and summoned the people and asked them the amount of the debt. They replied something over £25,000. I consulted Scaptius again. He was loud in his protests. I said that the only plan was for them to check their accounts. They sat down and made out the account. It agreed to a penny with their statement. They wanted to pay, and begged him to receive the money. Again Scaptius led me aside, and asked me to let the matter stand over. The request was impertinent, but I consented. I would not listen to the complaints of the Greeks and their demand to deposit the sum in the temple treasury. The bystanders all declared that the conduct of Scaptius was outrageous in refusing 12 per cent with compound interest. Others said he was a fool. He seemed to me to be more of a knave than a fool: for either he was not content with 12 per cent on good security or he hoped for 48 per cent on very doubtful security.

There is my case. If Brutus does not approve, there is no reason why I should be friendly with him. Certainly his uncle will approve, especially since a decree of the Senate has been passed (after you left

creditorum causa ut centesimae perpetuo faenore
ducerentur. Hoc quid intersit, si tuos digitos novi,
certe habes subductum. In quo quidem, ὁδοῦ πάρερ-
γον, L. Lucceius M. f. queritur apud me per litteras
summum esse periculum, ne culpa senatus his decretis res ad tabulas novas perveniat; commemorat, quid
olim mali C. Iulius fecerit, cum dieculam duxerit;
numquam rei publicae plus. Sed ad rem redeo.
Meditare adversus Brutum causam meam, si haec
causa est, contra quam nihil honeste dici potest,
praesertim cum integram rem et causam reliquerim.

Reliqua sunt domestica. De ἐνδομύχῳ probo idem
quod tu Postumiae filio, quoniam Pontidia nugatur.
Sed vellem adesses. A Quinto fratre his mensibus
nihil exspectaris; nam Taurus propter nives ante
mensem Iunium transiri non potest. Thermum, ut
rogas, creberrimis litteris fulcio. P. Valerium negat
habere quicquam Deiotarus rex eumque ait a se sus-
tentari. Cum scies, Romae intercalatum sit necne,
velim ad me scribas certum, quo die mysteria futura
sint. Litteras tuas minus paulo exspecto, quam si
Romae esses, sed tamen exspecto.

Rome, I think) in the matter of money-lenders, that 12 per cent simple interest shall be the rate. The difference between the two totals you will already have arrived at, if I do not belie your skill as a ready-reckoner. *Apropos* of this, by the way, L. Lucceius, son of Marcus, writes me a petulant letter that there is great danger of a general repudiation of debts resulting from these decrees. He recalls the harm that C. Julius did once when he allowed a little postponement of the day of payment: public credit never received a worse blow. But to return to my point. Think over my case against Brutus, if it is a case, when there are no fair arguments on the other side, especially as I have left the matter as it stood.

To wind up with family matters. As to my *boudoir* business, I agree with you in preferring Postumia's son,[1] since Pontidia is playing the fool. But I wish you were there. You must expect no letters from Quintus at this season. The snows prevent passage of the Taurus until June. I am supporting Thermus, as you request, by frequent letters. As for P. Valerius, Deiotarus says that he has nothing and is his pensioner. When you know whether there are to be additions to the calendar at Rome or not, please write me positive news as to the date of the Mysteries. I look forward to your letters rather less eagerly than if you were in town; still I do look forward to them.

---

[1] Servius Sulpicius, as a husband for Tullia.

M. TULLI CICERONIS
EPISTULARUM AD ATTICUM
LIBER SEXTUS

I

CICERO ATTICO SAL.

Scr.
Laodiceae
VI K. Mart
a. 704
Iliad, vi, 235

Accepi tuas litteras a. d. quintum Terminalia Laodiceae; quas legi libentissime plenissimas amoris, humanitatis, officii, diligentiae. Iis igitur respondebo non χρύσεα χαλκείων (sic enim postulas) nec οἰκονομίαν meam instituam, sed ordinem conservabo tuum. Recentissimas a Cybistris te meas litteras habere ais a. d. x Kalendas Octobres datas et scire vis, tuas ego quas acceperim. Omnes fere, quas commemoras, praeter eas, quas scribis Lentuli pueris et Equotutico et Brundisio datas. Quare non οἴχεται tua industria, quod vereris, sed praeclare ponitur, si quidem id egisti, ut ego delectarer. Nam nulla re sum delectatus magis.

Quod meam βαθύτητα in Appio tibi, liberalitatem etiam in Bruto probo, vehementer gaudeo; ac putaram paulo secus. Appius enim ad me ex itinere bis terve ὑπομεμψιμοίρους litteras miserat, quod quaedam a se constituta rescinderem. Ut si medicus, cum aegrotus alii medico traditus sit, irasci velit ei medico, qui sibi successerit, si, quae ipse in curando constituerit, mutet ille, sic Appius, cum ἐξ ἀφαιρέσεως provinciam curarit, sanguinem miserit, quicquid potuit, detraxerit, mihi tradiderit enectam,

414

CICERO'S LETTERS
TO ATTICUS
BOOK VI

I

CICERO TO ATTICUS, GREETING.

I got your letter on the 5th day before the Termi- *Laodicea*
nalia [1] at Laodicea. I was delighted at its tone of *Feb. 24,*
affection, kindness, and obliging zeal. I will not B.C. *50*
pay " gold for brass " (for that is what you ask for),
nor will I start an arrangement of my own, but will
keep to your order. You say that the last letter
you got from me was from Cybistra dated the 21st
of September, and you want to know which of yours
I have received. Almost all you mention except
those which you say were entrusted to Lentulus'
servants at Equotuticus and Brundisium. So your
energy is not a dead loss as you fear, but has been
well spent, if you aimed at giving me pleasure. For
nothing has ever given me more pleasure.

I am exceedingly glad that you approve of my
reserve in the case of Appius and my generosity
even in the matter of your friend Brutus. I had
feared you might not quite like it. For Appius on
his journey sent me two or three letters showing
pique, because I revoked some of his enactments.
It is as if a doctor, when a patient has been placed
under the care of another, should be angry with his
successor for changing his prescription. So Appius,
having starved the province, let blood, and tried
every lowering treatment, hands it to me drained of

---

[1] I.e. the 19th of February, the Terminalia being on the 23rd.

προσανατρεφομένην eam a me non libenter videt, sed
modo suscenset, modo gratias agit. Nihil enim a
me fit cum ulla illius contumelia; tantum modo
dissimilitudo meae rationis offendit hominem. Quid
enim potest esse tam dissimile quam illo imperante
exhaustam esse sumptibus et iacturis provinciam,
nobis eam obtinentibus nummum nullum esse eroga-
tum nec privatim nec publice? Quid dicam de
illius praefectis, comitibus, legatis etiam? de rapinis,
de libidinibus, de contumeliis? Nunc autem domus
mehercule nulla tanto consilio aut tanta disciplina
gubernatur aut tam modesta est quam nostra tota
provincia. Haec non nulli amici Appi ridicule
interpretantur, qui me idcirco putent bene audire
velle, ut ille male audiat, et recte facere non meae
laudis, sed illius contumeliae causa. Sin Appius, ut
Bruti litterae, quas ad te misit, significabant, gratias
nobis agit, non moleste fero, sed tamen eo ipso die,
quo haec ante lucem scribebam, cogitabam eius
multa inique constituta et acta tollere.

Nunc venio ad Brutum, quem ego omni studio
te auctore sum complexus, quem etiam amare
coeperam; sed ilico me revocavi, ne te offenderem.
Noli enim putare me quicquam maluisse, quam ut
mandatis satis facerem, nec ulla de re plus laborasse.
Mandatorum autem mihi libellum dedit, isdemque
de rebus tu mecum egeras. Omnia sum diligentissime persecutus. Primum ab Ariobarzane sic
contendi, ut talenta, quae mihi pollicebatur, illi daret.
Quoad mecum rex fuit, perbono loco res erat; post
a Pompei procuratoribus sescentis premi coeptus est.

416

life and cannot bear to see it being fed up by me. Sometimes he is angry, sometimes he thanks me; for no act of mine has reflected on his policy. It is only the difference of my *regime* that annoys him. There is a very wide difference between a province worn out by expense and losses under his rule and not having to pay a penny out of private or public purse under my administration. I need not mention his prefects, his staff and his legates, the acts of robbery, of rape, and insult. But now, upon my word, no private house is managed with such judgement or such economy, or is so well ordered as my whole province. Some friends of Appius put an absurd construction on my policy and declare that I am seeking popularity to damage him, and am acting honourably, not for the sake of my own reputation, but to cause him shame. However, if Appius, as the letter from Brutus which you forward to me shows, expresses his thanks I am content: but the very day on which I write this letter before dawn I am thinking of annulling many of his wrong enactments and decisions.

I come now to the matter of Brutus. On your advice I zealously cultivated his friendship, I had even begun to feel a real liking for him: but there I pull myself up for fear I should vex you. For do not imagine that there is anything I should prefer better than to execute his commission, or anything on which I have taken more pains. He gave me a volume of commissions, and you spoke to me about his affairs. I have done my best with all of them; first of all I induced Ariobarzanes to pay him the money he promised me. So long as his highness was with me the business was on a good footing: but later the king was dunned by scores of agents from

Pompeius autem cum ob ceteras causas plus potest
unus quam ceteri omnes, tum quod putatur ad
bellum Parthicum esse venturus. Ei tamen sic nunc
solvitur, tricensimo quoque die talenta Attica xxxiii
et hoc ex tributis. Nec inde satis efficitur in usuram
menstruam. Sed Gnaeus noster clementer id fert;
sorte caret, usura nec ea solida contentus est. Alii
neque solvit cuiquam nec potest solvere; nullum
enim aerarium, nullum vectigal habet. Appi instituto tributa imperat. Ea vix in faenus Pompei
quod satis sit efficiunt. Amici regis duo tresve
perdivites sunt, sed ii suum tam diligenter tenent
quam ego aut tu. Equidem non desino tamen per
litteras rogare, suadere, accusare regem. Deiotarus
etiam mihi narravit se ad eum legatos misisse de re
Bruti; eos sibi responsum rettulisse illum non
habere. Et mehercule ego ita iudico, nihil illo regno
spoliatius, nihil rege egentius. Itaque aut tutela
cogito me abdicare aut ut pro Glabrione Scaevola
faenus et impendium recusare. Ego tamen, quas
per te Bruto promiseram praefecturas, M. Scaptio
L. Gavio, qui in regno rem Bruti procurabant, detuli;
nec enim in provincia mea negotiabantur. Tu
autem meministi nos sic agere, ut, quot vellet praefecturas, sumeret, dum ne negotiatori. Itaque duas

Pompey. Pompey has more influence than anyone for many reasons and because it is rumoured that he will come to conduct the war against the Parthians. Even to him, however, payment is made on the following terms. On every thirtieth day some £8,000 is paid and that by tribute imposed on the king's subjects. Even such a sum will not cover the amount of monthly interest. However, our friend Gnaeus is an easy-going creditor. He is willing to forgo his capital and is content with interest, and that not in full. The king pays no one else and has no means to pay. He has no treasury and no regular tribute: he levies taxes on the method of Appius. They are scarcely sufficient to pay the interest on Pompey's money. His highness has two or three very wealthy friends, but they look after their own pockets as well as you or I. Still I do not cease to write dunning, coaxing, and scolding his highness. Deiotarus, too, has told me that he has sent messengers to him about his debt to Brutus: and they came back with the reply that he has no assets. I can quite believe it, for I have never seen a kingdom more plundered or a king more needy. So I am thinking of resigning my guardianship or, as Scaevola did for Glabrio, of repudiating both capital and interest. However, I have conferred the office of prefect, which I promised Brutus through you, on M. Scaptius and L. Gavius, who are his agents in the kingdom; for they were not conducting their business in my province. You will remember that my principle was that he might have as many offices of prefect at his disposal as he liked, provided he did not give them to business men: so I offered him two others besides. But

ei praeterea dederam. Sed ii, quibus petierat, de provincia decesserant.

Nunc cognosce de Salaminiis, quod video tibi etiam novum accidisse tamquam mihi. Numquam enim ex illo audivi illam pecuniam esse suam; quin etiam libellum ipsius habeo, in quo est: " Salaminii pecuniam debent M. Scaptio et P. Matinio, familiaribus meis." Eos mihi commendat; adscribit etiam et quasi calcar admovet intercessisse se pro iis magnam pecuniam. Confeceram, ut solverent centesimis sexennii ductis cum renovatione singulorum annorum. At Scaptius quaternas postulabat. Metui, si impetrasset, ne tu ipse me amare desineres; nam ab edicto meo recessissem et civitatem in Catonis et in ipsius Bruti fide locatam meisque beneficiis ornatam funditus perdidissem. Atque hoc tempore ipso impingit mihi epistulam Scaptius Bruti rem illam suo periculo esse, quod nec mihi umquam Brutus dixerat nec tibi, etiam ut praefecturam Scaptio deferrem. Id vero per te exceperamus, ne negotiatori; quodsi cuiquam, huic tamen non. Fuerat enim praefectus Appio et quidem habuerat turmas equitum, quibus inclusum in curia senatum Salamine obsederat, ut fame senatores quinque morerentur. Itaque ego, quo die tetigi provinciam, cum mihi Cyprii legati Ephesum obviam venissent, litteras misi, ut equites ex insula statim decederent. His de causis credo Scaptium iniquius de me aliquid ad Brutum scripsisse. Sed tamen hoc

the gentlemen for whom he asked them had left my province.

Now to talk about the people of Salamis, a matter which I see came as a surprise to you as it did to me. Brutus never told me that that money was his. Indeed, I have his own memorandum stating " The people of Salamis owe money to M. Scaptius and P. Matinius, my friends." He recommends these gentlemen to me, and to spur me adds a postscript that he has gone security to them for a large sum. I had arranged that they should pay in compound interest for six years at 12 per cent. But Scaptius demanded 48 per cent. I was afraid if he got his request that you too would cease to be my friend, for I should have departed from the terms of my own edict, and have ruined utterly a state enjoying the protection of Cato and Brutus himself and distinguished by my attentions. At this very point Scaptius thrusts a letter of Brutus into my hand, stating what Brutus had never told me or you, that Brutus himself was the party concerned, and asking me to give the office of prefect to his agent. But that was the very proviso I had authorized you to make, that no office could be given to a business man, above all to such a fellow as Scaptius. For he had been a prefect of Appius, and indeed had had some squadrons of cavalry, which he had used to beset the Senate at Salamis in their own chamber, so that five Members of the House died of starvation. Accordingly, on the day I reached the province, since an embassy from Cyprus had already met me at Ephesus, I sent orders that his cavalry should leave the island at once. This, I fancy, had led Scaptius to write somewhat bitterly about me to Brutus. However, my attitude

sum animo. Si Brutus putabit me quaternas centesimas oportuisse decernere, cum tota provincia singulas
observarem itaque edixissem, idque etiam acerbissi-
mis faeneratoribus probaretur, si praefecturam negotiatori denegatam queretur, quod ego Torquato nostro in tuo Laenio, Pompeio ipsi in Sex. Statio negavi
et iis probavi, si equites deductos moleste feret, accipiam equidem dolorem mihi illum irasci, sed multo
maiorem non esse eum talem, qualem putassem.
Illud quidem fatebitur Scaptius, me ius dicente sibi
omnem pecuniam ex edicto meo auferendi potestatem fuisse. Addo etiam illud, quod vereor tibi ipsi
ut probem. Consistere usura debuit, quae erat in
edicto meo. Deponere volebant: impetravi a Salaminiis, ut silerent. Veniam illi quidem mihi dederunt, sed quid iis fiet, si huc Paulus venerit? Sed
totum hoc Bruto dedi; qui de me ad te humanissimas
litteras scripsit, ad me autem, etiam cum rogat aliquid, contumaciter, adroganter, ἀκοινονοήτως solet
scribere. Tu autem velim ad eum scribas de his
rebus, ut sciam, quo modo haec accipiat; facies enim
me certiorem.

Atque haec superioribus litteris diligenter ad te
perscripseram, sed plane te intellegere volui mihi non
excidisse illud, quod tu ad me quibusdam litteris scripsisses, si nihil aliud de hac provincia nisi illius benevolentiam deportassem, mihi id satis esse. Sit sane,
quoniam ita tu vis, sed tamen cum eo, credo, quod

is this. If Brutus thinks that I ought to have allowed
48 per cent, when throughout my province I have
recognized only 12 per cent, and have fixed this rate
in my edict, with the approval of the most grasping
usurers; if he complains of my refusal to give office
to a business man, which I made also to our friend
Torquatus in the case of your acquaintance Laenius,
and to Pompey himself in the case of Sex. Statius,
without annoying either of them; if he is angry at
the disbanding of his cavalry, well, I shall be sorry
that he is angry with me, but I shall be far sorrier
at discovering he is not the man I imagined he was.
Scaptius will admit that he had the opportunity of
getting by my decision all the money allowed by
my edict. I will add a point which I fear you may
not like, the interest allowed by my edict ought to
have ceased to run.[1] The people of Salamis wished
to deposit the sum in a temple; but I begged them
not to raise the point. They gave way to me:
but what will happen to them if Brutus' brother-in-
law, Paulus, comes here? I allowed Brutus all this
privilege: and he has written very kind letters
about me to you; but to me, even when he asks a
favour, he writes in an arrogant, bold tone and
uncivilly. Please write to Brutus about the matter,
that I may know how he takes it. You can inform
me.

To be sure, I had given you the full story in a
former letter: but I wanted you to understand clearly
that I had not forgotten a remark in one of your
letters, that if I took nothing else away from this
province except Brutus' goodwill, that would be
enough. Be it as you wish, provided it can be so

[1] If the money was deposited in a temple.

sine peccato meo fiat. Igitur meo decreto soluta res
Scaptio stat. Quam id rectum sit, tu iudieabis; ne
ad Catonem quidem provocabo. Sed noli me putare
ἐγκελεύσματα illa tua abiecisse, quae mihi in visceri-
bus haerent. Flens mihi meam famam commendasti;
quae epistula tua est, in qua non eius mentionem
facias? Itaque irascatur, qui volet; patiar. Τὸ γὰρ
εὖ μετ᾽ ἐμοῦ, praesertim cum sex libris tamquam prae-
dibus me ipse obstrinxerim, quos tibi tam valde probari gaudeo. E quibus unum ἱστορικὸν requiris de Cn.
Flavio, Anni filio. Ille vero ante decemviros non fuit,
quippe qui aedilis curulis fuerit, qui magistratus
multis annis post decemviros institutus est. Quid
ergo profecit, quod protulit fastos? Occultatam putant quodam tempore istam tabulam, ut dies agendi
peterentur a paucis. Nec vero pauci sunt auctores
Cn. Flavium scribam fastos protulisse actionesque
composuisse, ne me hoc vel potius Africanum (is
enim loquitur) commentum putes. Οὐκ ἔλαθέ σε
illud de gestu histrionis. Tu sceleste suspicaris, ego
ἀφελῶς scripsi. De me imperatore scribis te ex
Philotimi litteris cognosse; sed credo te, iam in
Epiro cum esses, binas meas de omnibus rebus accepisse, unas a Pindenisso capto, alteras Laodicea,

Aristophanes,
Acharnians, 659

without loss of honour to me. So I have given judgement that the payment of the people of Salamis to Scaptius is good at law. The equity of this course I will leave to your consideration. I will not even appeal to Cato : but don't think I have let slip your exhortations. They are fixed in my heart. With tears in your eyes, you told me to think of my reputation. Is there any letter of yours which does not touch on the topic? So let who will be angry. I can put up with it. " The right is on my side," especially since I have bound myself to good conduct, with six volumes [1] for bail. I am glad you like the books so much, though there is one point of history which you question, that about Cn. Flavius, the son of Annius. He did not flourish before the days of the decemviri, since he held a curule aedileship which was instituted long after their time. What good, then, did he do by publishing the official calendar? It is thought that at one time the calendar was not exposed in public, so that a privileged few might be the sole source of information as to days propitious for business. Moreover, several authorities maintain that this Cn. Flavius was the first man to publish the calendar and to draw up a digest of the forms of legal procedure. So don't think that I, or rather my spokesman Africanus, invented a fiction. You took my remark about the actor's mannerism, and suspected a satirical meaning : [2] but I wrote in all *naïveté*. You tell me that Philotimus wrote to you about my being hailed imperator ; but I fancy that, now you are in Epirus, you have got my two letters about the business, one from Pindenissus after its capture, another from Laodicea,

---

[1] The *De Republica*.
[2] That it was a hit at Hortensius.

utrasque tuis pueris datas. Quibus de rebus propter casum navigandi per binos tabellarios misi Romam publice litteras.

De Tullia mea tibi adsentior scripsique ad eam et ac Terentiam mihi placere. Tu enim ad me iam ante scripseras: "Ac vellem te in tuum veterem gregem rettulisses." Correcta vero epistula Memmiana nihil negotii fuit; multo enim malo hunc a Pontidia quam illum a Servilia. Quare adiunges Saufeium nostrum, hominem semper amantem mei, nunc, credo, eo magis, quod debet etiam fratris Appi amorem erga me cum reliqua hereditate crevisse; qui declaravit, quanti me faceret, cum saepe tum in Bursa. Ne tu me sollicitudine magna liberaris.

Furni exceptio mihi non placet; nec enim ego ullum aliud tempus timeo, nisi quod ille solum excipit. Sed scriberem ad te de hoc plura, si Romae esses. In Pompeio te spem omnem otii ponere non miror. Ita res est, removendumque censeo illud " dissimulantem." Sed enim οἰκονομία si perturbatior est, tibi assignato. Te enim sequor σχεδιάζοντα.

Cicerones pueri amant inter se, discunt, exercentur, sed alter, uti dixit Isocrates in Ephoro et Theopompo, frenis eget, alter calcaribus. Quinto togam puram

both delivered to your slaves. For fear of accidents at sea, I sent the public despatch on my campaign to Rome in duplicate by different carriers.

As to my daughter Tullia I agree with you, and I have written to her and her mother giving my consent. For a former letter of yours to me said, " I could wish you had returned to your old associates." There was no occasion to alter the letter that came from Memmius: for I much prefer to accept this candidate from Pontidia than the other from Servilia. So get our friend Saufeius to help you in this business. He always liked me, and now I trust he will like me all the more, since he is bound to have inherited his brother Appius' liking for me along with the rest of his inheritance, and Appius often expressed great affection for me, especially in the trial of Bursa. Indeed, you will relieve me of a source of great anxiety.

I do not like Furnius' proviso; there is nothing else I fear, except the point which he makes his sole proviso.[1] I would write to you more fully on the point if you were in Rome. I am not surprised that you depend entirely on Pompey for keeping the peace. That is quite right, and I think you must delete your phrase " insincere." If the order of my paragraphs is muddled you have yourself to blame, as I am following your own harum-scarum way.

My son and nephew are fond of one another, learn their lessons and take their exercise together: but to quote Isocrates' remark about Ephorus and Theopompus, one wants the rein and the other the spur.

[1] Apparently a proposal by a tribune that the governors of Syria and Cilicia could quit their provinces at the end of the year, provided the Parthians were not aggressive.

Liberalibus cogitabam dare; mandavit enim pater
Ea sic observabo, quasi intercalatum non sit. Dionysius mihi quidem in amoribus est; pueri autem aiunt
eum furenter irasci; sed homo nec doctior nec
sanctior fieri potest nec tui meique amantior. Thermum, Silium vere audis laudari. Valde honeste se
gerunt. Adde M. Nonium, Bibulum, me, si voles.
Iam Scrofa vellem haberet, ubi posset; est enim
lautum negotium. Ceteri infirmant πολίτευμα Catonis. Hortensio quod causam meam commendas,
valde gratum. De Amiano spei nihil putat esse Dionysius. Terenti nullum vestigium adgnovi. Moeragenes certe periit. Feci iter per eius possessionem,
in qua animal reliquum nullum est. Haec non noram
tum, cum Democrito tuo cum locutus sum. Rhosica
vasa mandavi. Sed heus tu! quid cogitas? in felicatis
lancibus et splendidissimis canistris holusculis nos
soles pascere; quid te in vasis fictilibus appositurum
putem? Κέρας Phemio mandatum est; reperietur,
modo aliquid illo dignum canat.

Parthicum bellum impendet. Cassius ineptas litteras misit, necdum Bibuli erant allatae. Quibus
recitatis puto fore ut aliquando commoveatur senatus.
Equidem sum in magna animi perturbatione. Si, ut
opto, non prorogatur nostrum negotium, habeo

I intend to celebrate Quintus' coming of age [1] on the feast of Bacchus.[2] His father asked me to do this, and I shall act on the assumption that there will be no addition to the calendar. Dionysius is in my good graces; but the boys say he is liable to mad fits of temper. However, one could not get a master of more learning and better character and more liking for you and me. The praise you hear of Thermus and Silius is deserved: they conduct themselves in very honourable fashion. You may praise M. Nonius, Bibulus, and myself too if you like. I only wish Scrofa had scope for his tact. He is a fine fellow. The rest do little credit to Cato's caucus. I am much obliged to you for recommending my case to Hortensius. As to Amianus, Dionysius says there is no help. I have met with no trace of Terentius. Moeragenes has certainly been killed. I made a tour through his district and found not a living thing. I did not know this when I spoke to your agent Democritus. I have ordered the Rhosian ware for you. But what the deuce will you serve up in porcelain, when you are accustomed to give us vegetarian fare on fern-pattern plates and in magnificent baskets? I have ordered a horn for Phemius, and one will be got. I only hope that his tune will be worthy of the instrument.

A war with the Parthians is imminent. Cassius' despatch was futile, Bibulus' has not yet come. I think the reading of it will stir the House to action at last. I am very anxious myself. If, as I hope, my tenure of office is not extended I have June and July

---

[1] On coming of age, which took place at about fifteen or sixteen, the Roman boy left off the purple-bordered *toga praetexta* and assumed the pure white *toga virilis*.

[2] March 17.

Iunium et Quinctilem in metu. Esto; duos quidem
menses sustinebit Bibulus. Quid illo fiet, quem reli-
quero, praesertim si fratrem? quid me autem, si non
tam cito decedo? Magna turba est. Mihi tamen
cum Deiotaro convenit, ut ille in meis castris esset
cum suis copiis omnibus. Habet autem cohortes
quadringenarias nostra armatura xxx, equitum ↀ
ↀ. Erit ad sustentandum, quoad Pompeius veniat;
qui litteris, quas ad me mittit, significat suum negotium illud fore. Hiemant in nostra provincia Parthi;
exspectatur ipse Orodes. Quid quaeris? aliquantum
est negotii.

De Bibuli edicto nihil novi praeter illam excep-
tionem, de qua tu ad me scripseras, " nimis gravi
praeiudicio in ordinem nostrum." Ego tamen habeo
ἰσοδυναμοῦσαν, sed tectiorem, ex Q. Muci P. f. edicto
Asiatico, Extra qvam si ita negotivm gestvm est, vt
eo stari non oporteat ex fide bona, multaque sum
secutus Scaevolae, in iis illud, in quo sibi libertatem
censent Graeci datam, ut Graeci inter se disceptent
suis legibus. Breve autem edictum est propter hanc
meam διαίρεσιν, quod duobus generibus edicendum
putavi. Quorum unum est provinciale, in quo est de
rationibus civitatum, de aere alieno, de usura, de syn-
graphis, in eodem omnia de publicanis, alterum, quod
sine edicto satis commode transigi non potest, de

to fear. Very good. Bibulus can check them for two months, but what will happen to the man whom I leave behind, especially if he be my brother? Or what will be my own fate if I do not depart so speedily? It is a great bother. However, Deiotarus has decided to join my camp in full force. He has thirty squadrons of four hundred men each armed in our fashion, and two thousand cavalry. He can hold out till Pompey comes. A letter he writes to me presumes that he will conduct the campaign. The Parthians spend the winter in a Roman province. Orodes is expected in person. You may take my word it is a big business.

As to Bibulus' edict there is no new feature, except that proviso of which you wrote "it is a very grave reflection on our order." [1] However, I have a similar proviso, in more circumspect language, borrowed from the Asiatic edict of Q. Mucius, son of Publius, "Provided that the agreement is not such as contravenes equity." I have followed Scaevola in many details, among them in the stipulation which the Greeks hold as the salvation of their freedom, that Greek cases are to be settled according to Greek law. The edict is short on account of the division I have made, as I considered it fell better under two heads. The one concerns provincial matters and deals with town accounts, debt, the rate of interest, contracts, and includes all matters referring to the tax-collectors. The second head, embracing matters which cannot properly be settled without an edict,

---

[1] Bibulus had excepted from debts recoverable in his court cases in which *vis* or *dolus malus* had been used. The clause was directed against *publicani* and *negotiatores* who belonged to the *equites*.

hereditatum possessionibus, de bonis possidendis, vendendis, magistris faciendis, quae ex edicto et postulari et fieri solent. Tertium de reliquo iure dicundo ἄγραφον reliqui. Dixi me de eo genere mea decreta ad edicta urbana accommodaturum. Itaque curo et satis facio adhuc omnibus. Graeci vero exsultant, quod peregrinis iudicibus utuntur. " Nugatoribus quidem," inquies. Quid refert? tamen se αὐτονομίαν adeptos putant. Vestri enim, credo, graves habent Turpionem sutorium et Vettium mancipem.

De publicanis quid agam, videris quaerere. Habeo in deliciis, obsequor, verbis laudo, orno; efficio, ne cui molesti sint. Τὸ παραδοξότατον, usuras eorum, quas pactionibus adscripserant, servavit etiam Servilius. Ego sic. Diem statuo satis laxam, quam ante si solverint, dico me centesimas ducturum; si non solverint, ex pactione. Itaque et Graeci solvunt tolerabili faenore, et publicanis res est gratissima, si illa iam habent pleno modio, verborum honorem, invitationem crebram. Quid plura? sunt omnes ita mihi familiares, ut se quisque maxime putet. Sed tamen μηδὲν αὐτοῖς—scis reliqua.

De statua Africani (ὢ πραγμάτων ἀσυγκλώστων! sed me id ipsum delectavit in tuis litteris) ain tu? Scipio hic Metellus proavum suum nescit censorem non

deals with inheritance, ownership and sale, the appointment of official receivers, matters where suits are wont to be brought and settled in accordance with the terms of an edict. A third head dealing with the rest of judicial procedure I left unwritten. I stated that in such matters my decrees would be based on those of Rome. I observe this rule, and so far satisfy everybody. The Greeks are jubilant at having foreign jurors. You may say that the jurors are wasters: however, the Greeks flatter themselves that they have got home rule, and your own jurors are men of the lofty standing of Turpio the shoemaker and Vettius the broker.

You ask how I am dealing with the tax-gatherers. I pet them, indulge them, praise and honour them: and take care they trouble no one. It is very odd that the rates of interest specified in their bonds were upheld even by Servilius. My procedure is this. I name a day fairly remote, before which, if the debtors pay up, I lay down that I shall allow only 12 per cent. But if they have not paid, judgement will be according to the bond. Accordingly, the Greeks pay their debts at a fair rate of interest, and the farmers are gratified, provided they get their fill of compliments and invitations. In short, they are all so intimate with me that each man thinks himself my special favourite. But still you know the old saw.[1]

As to the statue of Africanus (what a medley of topics! but that was the delightful feature of your letter, to my mind), do you really mean that Metellus Scipio does not know his great-grandfather was

[1] The quotation is incomplete, and the ending of it unknown. Probably it contained advice either against trusting or humouring people too much.

fuisse? Atqui nihil habuit aliud inscriptum nisi cos. ea statua, quae ad Opis nuper [1] posita in excelso est. In illa autem, quae est ad Πολυκλέους Herculem, inscriptum est CENS; [2] quam esse eiusdem status, amictus, anulus, imago ipsa declarat. At mehercule ego, cum in turma inauratarum equestrium, quas hic Metellus in Capitolio posuit, animadvertissem in Serapionis subscriptione Africani imaginem, erratum fabrile putavi, nunc video Metelli. Ὁ ἀνιστορησίαν turpem! Nam illud de Flavio et fastis, si secus est, commune erratum est, et tu belle ἠπόρησας, et nos publicam prope opinionem secuti sumus, ut multa apud Graecos. Quis enim non dixit Εὔπολιν, τὸν τῆς ἀρχαίας, ab Alcibiade navigante in Siciliam deiectum esse in mare? Redarguit Eratosthenes; adfert enim, quas ille post id tempus fabulas docuerit. Num idcirco Duris Samius, homo in historia diligens, quod cum multis erravit, inridetur? Quis Zaleucum leges Locris scripsisse non dixit? Num igitur iacet Theophrastus, si id a Timaeo, tuo familiari, reprensum est? Sed nescire proavum suum censorem non fuisse turpe est, praesertim cum post eum consulem nemo Cornelius illo vivo censor fuerit.

Quod de Philotimo et de solutione HS |xxDC| scribis, Philotimum circiter Kal. Ianuarias in Chersonesum audio venisse. At mi ab eo nihil adhuc. Reliqua mea Camillus scribit se accepisse. Ea quae

---

[1] nuper *Boot*; per te *MSS*.
[2] *I have adopted Tyrrell's transposition of* COS. (=CONSUL) *and* CENS. (=CENSOR), *though with doubts of its correctness.*

never censor? Certainly the statue which has lately been placed on high near the temple of Ops has only the inscription cos. But the statue near the Hercules of Polycles bears the inscription CENS. : and the pose, the dress, the ring, and the likeness prove that it is a statue of the same person. As a matter of fact, when among the crowd of gilded knights placed by Metellus on the Capitol, I noticed a likeness of Africanus with the name Serapio on the pedestal, I thought it was a workman's error, but now I see it is Metellus' mistake. What gross ignorance of history! For that misconception about Flavius and the calendar, if it is such, is widely held : and you were quite right in having doubts about it. I have followed the view which is almost universal, as Greek authors often do. Everyone says that Eupolis, the poet of the old Comedy, was thrown into the sea by Alcibiades on his voyage to Sicily. Eratosthenes confutes this, producing plays exhibited by him after that date. But that is no reason for laughing at Duris of Samos, who is an accurate historian, because he follows a vulgar error. All historians agree that Zaleucus drew up laws for the Locrians. It is not therefore fatal to Theophrastus if he is called to account for that by your friend Timaeus. But not to know that one's great-grandfather was not censor is shocking, especially as after his consulship no Cornelius was censor during his lifetime.

As for your remarks about Philotimus and the payment of £182,000,[1] I hear that Philotimus came to the Chersonese about the beginning of January, but so far I have heard nothing from him. Camillus writes that he has received my balance. I don't know

[1] 20,600,000 sesterces.

sint, nescio et aveo scire. Verum haec posterius et coram fortasse commodius.

Illud me, mi Attice, in extrema fere parte epistulae commovit; scribis enim sic; Τί λοιπόν; deinde me obsecras amantissime, ne obliviscar vigilare et ut animadvertam, quae fiant. Num quid de quo inaudisti? Etsi nihil eius modi est; πολλοῦ γε καὶ δεῖ. Nec enim me fefellisset nec fallet. Sed ista admonitio tua tam accurata nescio quid mihi significare visa est.

De M. Octavio iterum iam tibi rescribo te illi probe respondisse; paulo vellem fidentius. Nam Caelius libertum ad me misit et litteras accurate scriptas et de pantheris et civitatibus. Rescripsi alterum me moleste ferre, si ego in tenebris laterem, nec audiretur Romae nullum in mea provincia nummum nisi in aes alienum erogari, docuique nec mihi conciliare pecuniam licere nec illi capere monuique eum, quem plane diligo, ut, cum alios accusasset, cautius viveret; illud autem alterum alienum esse existumatione mea, Cibyratas imperio meo publice venari.

Lepta tua epistula gaudio exsultat; etenim scripta belle est meque apud eum magna in gratia posuit. Filiola tua gratum mihi fecit, quod tibi diligenter mandavit, ut mihi salutem adscriberes, gratum etiam Pilia, sed illa officiosius, quod mihi, quem iam pridem numquam vidit. Igitur tu quoque salutem

436

how much it is, and I should like to know. However, we can discuss this later and more conveniently when we meet.

That remark at the end of your letter, my dear Atticus, upset me. You used the phrase, " What more is there to say," and follow it by a most affectionate warning not to forget to be on the watch and to keep an eye on events. Have you heard anything about any of my staff ? I am sure there has been no wrongdoing, *pas du tout*. It could not have escaped my notice, and it will not. But your earnest entreaty seemed to hint something.

As for M. Octavius, I repeat that your reply was excellent. I could wish it had been in more positive terms. For Caelius has sent me a freedman of his and a carefully worded letter about panthers and an offer from the townships to furnish contributions. I replied that the second item is annoying, if my conduct is still a secret and the news has not reached town that in my province no money is exacted except in satisfaction of debts : and I have told him that it would be improper for me to allow payment and for him to take it. I have a sincere regard for him and have warned him that after his prosecution of other people he should conduct himself on more careful lines. As to the second point, I have told him it would be a blot on my escutcheon that the people of Cibyra should have a public hunt during my governorship.

Lepta leaps with joy over your letter ; for it was nicely written and puts me in his good graces. Your tiny daughter has done me a favour in ordering you earnestly to send me her greetings. It was kind of Pilia and very dutiful of your daughter to send greetings to one whom as yet she has never met. So please

utrique adscribito. Litterarum datarum dies pr. Kal.
Ianuar. suavem habuit recordationem clarissimi iuris
iurandi, quod ego non eram oblitus. Magnus enim
praetextatus illo die fui. Habes ad omnia. Non ut
postulasti, χρύσεα χαλκείων, sed paria paribus re-
spondimus.

Ecce autem alia pusilla epistula, quam non relinquam ἀναντιφώνητον. Bene mehercule potuit Lucceius Tusculanum, nisi forte (solet enim) cum suo
tibicine. Et velim scire, qui sit eius status. Lentulum quidem nostrum omnia praeter Tusculanum pro-
scripsisse audio. Cupio hos expeditos videre, cupio
etiam Sestium, adde sis Caelium; in quibus omnibus
est

Iliad vii, 93   Αἴδεσθεν μὲν ἀνήνασθαι, δεῖσαν δ᾽ ὑποδέχθαι.

De Memmio restituendo ut Curio cogitet, te audisse
puto. De Egnati Sidicini nomine nec nulla nec
magna spe sumus. Pinarium, quem mihi commendas, diligentissime Deiotarus curat graviter aegrum.
Respondi etiam minori.

Tu velim, dum ero Laodiceae, id est ad Idus Maias,
quam saepissime mecum per litteras colloquare, et
cum Athenas veneris (iam enim sciemus de rebus
urbanis, de provinciis, quae omnia in mensem Mar-
tium sunt conlata), utique ad me tabellarios mittas.
Et heus tu! iamne vos a Caesare per Herodem talenta
Attica ʟ extorsistis? in quo, ut audio, magnum odium
Pompei suscepistis. Putat enim suos nummos vos

438

give my greetings to both of them in return. The date of your letter, the last day of December, reminded me pleasantly of the famous and unforgotten oath I took.[1] I was a Pompey in state robes that day. There you have my answer to all your points: not as you asked " gold for copper," but like for like.

There was another short letter which I will not leave unanswered. Lucceius to be sure was able to do something for the villa at Tusculum, unless perhaps there was the old obstacle of the flute player[2]; and I should like to know its condition. Our friend Lentulus, I hear, has advertised all his property except that at Tusculum. I should like to see these gentlemen free from debt as well as Sestius, and you may add Caelius too. To all of them one may apply the quotation, " ashamed to refuse, but yet afraid to take." I suppose you have heard of Curio's idea to recall Memmius. As for the debt due from Egnatius of Sidicinum, I have some hope, but not much. Deiotarus is taking very great care of Pinarius, whom you recommended to me, in a serious illness. So there is my answer to your little letter.

While I am at Laodicea, which will be up to the 15th of May, please correspond with me as often as possible, and on your arrival at Athens at any rate send me letter carriers, since by that time we shall know what has been done in town and about the provinces, of which the affairs are settled in March. By the by, have you yet got Herodes to wring from Caesar that £12,000? I hear you have excited the animosity of Pompey in the matter. He thinks that

[1] Cicero refers to the day on which he laid down the consulship. Cf. *Ad. Fam.* v, 2.
[2] Or " prop." But the whole passage is uncertain.

comedisse, Caesarem in Nemore aedificando diligen-
tiorem fore. Haec ego ex P. Vedio, magno nebulone,
sed Pompei tamen familiari, audivi. Hic Vedius
mihi obviam venit cum duobus essedis et raeda equis
iuncta et lectica et familia magna, pro qua, si Curio
legem pertulerit, HS centenos pendat necesse est.
Erat praeterea cynocephalus in essedo, nec deerant
onagri. Numquam vidi hominem nequiorem. Sed
extremum audi. Deversatus est Laodiceae apud
Pompeium Vindullum. Ibi sua deposuit, cum ad me
profectus est. Moritur interim Vindullus ; quae res
ad Magnum Pompeium pertinere putabatur. C.
Vennonius domum Vindulli venit. Cum omnia obsi-
gnaret, in Vedianas res incidit. In his inventae sunt
quinque imagunculae matronarum, in quibus una
sororis amici tui hominis " bruti," qui hoc utatur, et
illius " lepidi," qui haec tam neglegenter ferat. Haec
te volui παριστορῆσαι. Sumus enim ambo belle
curiosi.

Unum etiam velim cogites. Audio Appium πρό-
πυλον Eleusine facere. Num inepti fuerimus, si nos
quoque Academiae fecerimus ? " Puto," inquies.
Ergo id ipsum scribes ad me. Equidem valde ipsas
Athenas amo. Volo esse aliquod monumentum ; odi
falsas inscriptiones statuarum alienarum. Sed, ut
tibi placebit, faciesque me, in quem diem Romana in-

you have snapped up money which was his, and that it will not lessen Caesar's energy in building a palace near the sacred grove of Diana. This bit of news came to me from P. Vedius, a shady character, but an intimate of Pompey. The fellow met me on the road with two chariots, a carriage and horses and a litter and a large following. If Curio carries his law [1] he will have to pay £1 apiece. Besides other things, there was a dog-faced baboon in a chariot, and some wild asses. I never met such a rascal. But listen to the end of the story. At Laodicea Vedius put up with Pompeius Vindullus, and left his belongings with him, while he came to meet me. Meantime Vindullus died, and his property is supposed to go to Pompeius Magnus. C. Vennonius went to the house and, while sealing all the goods, found Vedius' baggage. Among this baggage there were five little busts of Roman married ladies, among them one of the sister of your friend Brutus—a brute indeed to be acquainted with the fellow—and one of the wife of Lepidus, whose easy conduct agrees with the meaning of his name. I wanted to tell you this little tale *en passant*, for we are both nice gossips.

There is one thing I wish you to consider. I hear that Appius is putting up a porch at Eleusis. Shall I look a fool if I do so in the Academy? I dare say you may think so: say so plainly if you do. I am very fond of the city of Athens. I should like it to have some memorial of myself. I dislike lying titles on the statues of other folk. But as you think best. And please let me know the date of the

[1] In *Ad Fam.* viii, 6, a *lex viaria* and a *lex alimentaria* are mentioned. Possibly travellers with a large retinue were taxed under the first of these.

cidant mysteria, certiorem, et quo modo hiemaris.
Cura, ut valeas. Post Leuctricam pugnam die septin-
gentesimo sexagesimo quinto.

II

CICERO ATTICO SAL.

Scr. Laodi-
ceae in. m.
Mai. a. 704

Cum Philogenes, libertus tuus, Laodiceam ad me
salutandi causa venisset et se statim ad te navigatu-
rum esse diceret, has ei litteras dedi, quibus ad eas
rescripsi, quas acceperam a Bruti tabellario. Et respondebo primum postremae tuae paginae, quae mihi
magnae molestiae fuit, quod ad te scriptum est a Cincio de Stati sermone; in quo hoc molestissimum est,
Statium dicere a me quoque id consilium probari.
Probari autem? De isto hactenus dixerim, me vel
plurima vincla tecum summae coniunctionis optare,
etsi sunt amoris artissima; tantum abest, ut ego ex
eo, quo astricti sumus, laxari aliquid velim. Illum
autem multa de istis rebus asperius solere loqui saepe
sum expertus, saepe etiam lenivi iratum. Id scire te
arbitror. In hac autem peregrinatione militiave nostra saepe incensum ira vidi, saepe placatum. Quid ad
Statium scripserit, nescio. Quicquid acturus de tali
re fuit, scribendum tamen ad libertum non fuit. Mihi
autem erit maxumae curae, ne quid fiat secus, quam
volumus, quamque oportet. Nec satis est in eius modi
re se quemque praestare, ac maxumae partes istius

442

mysteries at Rome, and how you are passing the winter. Keep well. I write this on the seven hundred and sixty-fifth day after the battle of Leuctra.[1]

II

Your freedman Philogenes has come to visit me at Laodicea and tells me that he is on the point of sailing to join you : so I give him this letter in reply to your letter which I got from Brutus' letter-carrier. First I will answer your last page which caused me much concern : that is about Cincius' communication on the talk he had with Statius. I was particularly concerned at Statius' remark that the plan had my approval. Approval indeed ! I need only say thus much. I wish the ties of friendship to be as many and close as possible between us, though none can be so close as those of our common liking. I am far from wanting the tie between us to be relaxed. Quintus, however, to my knowledge will often use bitter language on his private affairs, and often I have pacified his anger, as I think you know. On my late tour or military campaign I have seen him often fly in a temper and often calm again. I don't know what he wrote to Statius ; whatever he meant to do, he ought not to have informed a freedman. However, I will do my best to prevent any course contrary to our wishes and to propriety. In a case like this it is not enough for a man to make himself responsible for his own conduct only : and

Laodicea, May, B.C. 50

---

[1] Cicero refers thus to the killing of Clodius on January 18, 52 B.C., comparing it with the defeat of the Spartans by Epaminondas at Leuctra in 371 B.C.

officii sunt pueri Ciceronis sive iam adulescentis;
quod quidem illum soleo hortari. Ac mihi videtur
matrem valde, ut debet, amare teque mirifice. Sed est
magnum illud quidem, verum tamen multiplex pueri
ingenium; in quo ego regendo habeo negotii satis.

Quoniam respondi postremae tuae paginae prima
mea, nunc ad primam revertar tuam. Peloponnesias
civitates omnes maritimas esse hominis non nequam,
sed etiam tuo iudicio probati, Dicaearchi, tabulis credidi. Is multis nominibus in Trophoniana Chaeronis
narratione Graecos in eo reprendit, quod mare tantum
secuti sint, nec ullum in Peloponneso locum excipit.
Cum mihi auctor placeret (etenim erat ἱστορικώτατος
et vixerat in Peloponneso), admirabar tamen et vix
adcredens communicavi cum Dionysio. Atque is
primo est commotus, deinde, quod de isto Dicaearcho non minus bene existumabat quam tu de C.
Vestorio, ego de M. Cluvio, non dubitabat, quin ei
crederemus. Arcadiae censebat esse Lepreon quoddam maritumum; Tenea autem et Aliphera et Tritia
νεόκτιστα ei videbantur, idque τῷ τῶν νεῶν καταλόγῳ
confirmabat, ubi mentio non fit istorum. Itaque istum
ego locum totidem verbis a Dicaearcho transtuli.
" Phliasios " autem dici sciebam, et ita fac ut habeas;
nos quidem sic habemus. Sed primo me ἀναλογία
deceperat, Φλιοῦς, Ὀποῦς, Σιποῦς, quod Ὀπούντιοι,
Σιπούντιοι. Sed hoc continuo correximus.

Laetari te nostra moderatione et continentia video.

indeed the principal share of responsibility attaches to the boy, or young man as he is now, Quintus. This I am always telling him. To me he seems to love his mother greatly, as he should, and to be extremely fond of you. He is a lad of high but complex character, and I have enough to do to guide his conduct.

Having devoted my first page to answering your last, I will now return to your first. I relied on the maps of Dicaearchus, a writer of no mean standing and an authority you accept, for the information that all the states of the Peloponnese bordered on the sea. In the account of the cave of Trophonius, which he puts into the mouth of Chaeron, he blames the Greeks on many scores for sticking to the sea coast; and he does not except a single district in the Peloponnese. He was a very accurate historian and lived in the Peloponnese, so that his evidence seemed trustworthy. Still I was surprised and communicated my doubts to Dionysius. Dionysius was startled at first, but finally accepted his authority, since he had as good an opinion of Dicaearchus as you have of C. Vestorius or I of M. Cluvius. Arcadia he agreed had a seaport Lepreon: but Tenea, Aliphera, and Tritia were, he considered, more modern, a view he supported by the omission of these places from Homer's catalogue of the ships. Accordingly, I borrowed the passage from Dicaearchus in so many words. I know that Phliasii is the proper form. Please make it so in your copy. I read it in mine. But first of all thinking of Phlious I was misled by a vicious analogy of Opuntii from Opous and Sipuntii from Sipous. But I altered it at once.

I see that you are pleased at my unselfish modera-

Tum id magis faceres, si adesses. Atque hoc foro, quod egi ex Idibus Februariis Laodiceae ad Kal. Maias omnium dioecensium praeter Ciliciae, mirabilia quaedam effecimus. Ita multae civitates omni aere alieno liberatae, multae valde levatae sunt, omnes suis legibus et iudiciis usae αὐτονομίαν adeptae revixerunt. His ego duobus generibus facultatem ad se aere alieno liberandas aut levandas dedi, uno, quod omnino nullus in imperio meo sumptus factus est (nullum cum dico, non loquor ὑπερβολικῶς), nullus, inquam, ne terruncius quidem. Hac autem re incredibile est quantum civitates emerserint. Accessit altera. Mira erant in civitatibus ipsorum furta Graecorum, quae magistratus sui fecerant. Quaesivi ipse de iis, qui annis decem proximis magistratum gesserant. Aperte fatebantur. Itaque sine ulla ignominia suis umeris pecunias populis rettulerunt. Populi autem nullo gemitu publicanis, quibus hoc ipso lustro nihil solverant, etiam superioris lustri reddiderunt. Itaque publicanis in oculis sumus. " Gratis," inquis, " viris." Sensimus. Iam cetera iuris dictio nec imperita et clemens cum admirabili facilitate ; aditus autem ad me minime provinciales ; nihil per cubicularium ; ante lucem inambulabam domi ut olim candidatus. Grata haec et magna mihique nondum laboriosa ex illa vetere militia.

Nonis Maiis in Ciliciam cogitabam. Ibi cum

tion. You would be more pleased if you were here. In this very assize which I have been holding at Laodicea from the 13th of February to the 1st of May for all the districts except Cilicia, I have done wonders. See how many states have been freed from debt and how many have had their burden lightened. All have revived on acquiring home rule, and using their own enactments in law. I have given them in two ways the chance of freeing themselves or relieving themselves from debt. First by causing them no expense during my administration (and in saying no expense I mean literally not one farthing), which has helped them astonishingly out of their trouble. Secondly, the states had suffered from surprising corruption in their own countrymen, that is to say their magistrates. I questioned the men who had held the office of magistrate during the last ten years. They concealed nothing. So without exposure they took on their own backs the repayment of the money : and the communities which had paid the tax-farmers nothing for the present five years have now without any complaints paid up arrears for the last five years too. So I am the apple of their eye to the tax-farmers. " Grateful fellows," you exclaim. Yes I have experienced their gratitude. The rest of my judicial conduct has been enlightened, but mild and marvellously courteous. There has been none of the difficulty of access so characteristic of provincial governors ; and no backstairs jobbery. Before daybreak I walk up and down in my house, as I did of yore when a candidate for office. This is popular and a great boon, and I have not felt it a burden owing to my old training.

On the 7th of May I intend to go to Cilicia.

Iunium mensem consumpsissem (atque utinam in pace! magnum enim bellum inpendet a Parthis), Quinctilem in reditu ponere. Annuae enim mihi operae a. d. III Kal. Sextil. emerentur. Magna autem in spe sum mihi nihil temporis prorogatum iri. Habebam acta urbana usque ad Nonas Martias; e quibus intellegebam Curionis nostri constantia omnia potius actum iri quam de provinciis. Ergo, ut spero, prope diem te videbo.

Venio ad Brutum tuum, immo nostrum; sic enim mavis. Equidem omnia feci, quae potui aut in mea provincia perficere aut in regno experiri. Omni igitur modo egi cum rege et ago cotidie per litteras scilicet. Ipsum enim triduum quadriduumve mecum habui turbulentis in rebus, quibus eum liberavi. Sed et tum praesens et postea creberrimis litteris non destiti rogare et petere mea causa, suadere et hortari sua. Multum profeci, sed quantum, non plane, quia longe absum, scio. Salaminios autem (hos enim poteram coërcere), adduxi, ut totum nomen Scaptio vellent solvere, sed centesimis ductis a proxuma quidem syngrapha nec perpetuis, sed renovatis quotannis. Numerabantur nummi: noluit Scaptius. Tu qui ais Brutum cupere aliquid perdere? Quaternas habebat in syngrapha. Fieri non poterat, nec, si posset, ego pati possem. Audio omnino Scaptium

After spending the month of June there (and I pray it may be in peace, for a serious war with the Parthians is certainly coming), July I shall spend on my journey home. I shall have served my year on July the 30th. I have great hopes that my tenure of office may not be extended. I have the city gazette up to the 7th of March. I gather that, thanks to the persistence of my friend Curio, appointments to the province will be the last business to be considered. So, as I hope, I shall see you soon.

I come now to Brutus, your friend or rather mine, since you prefer it. I have done everything that I could accomplish in my own province or attempt in the kingdom of Cappadocia. I have taken every measure with the king and still do so daily—by letter. The king himself was in my company only for three or four days and at a crisis in his affairs from which I released him. But both then in person and subsequently in repeated letters I have continually begged and besought him in my own name and advised and persuaded him in his own interest. My efforts have borne fruit: but how much at this distance I cannot tell for certain. The people of Salamis, however, whom I could influence, I have induced to consent to settle all their debt with Scaptius, but with interest at 12 per cent calculated from the date of the last contract, and not at simple but compound interest. The money was counted down: but Scaptius refused to take it. What kind of a figure do you cut, who say that Brutus will make a sacrifice? Forty-eight per cent was written in the bond. It was an impossible sum. It could not be paid, nor could I have permitted it. I hear after all

paenitere. Nam, quod senatus consultum esse dicebat, ut ius ex syngrapha diceretur, eo consilio factum
est, quod pecuniam Salaminii contra legem Gabiniam
sumpserant. Vetabat autem Auli lex ius dici de ita
sumpta pecunia. Decrevit igitur senatus, ut ius
diceretur ex ista syngrapha. Nunc ista habet iuris
idem quod ceterae, nihil praecipui. Haec a me
ordine facta puto me Bruto probaturum; tibi nescio;
Catoni certe probabo.

Sed iam ad te ipsum revertor. Ain tandem, Attice,
laudator integritatis et elegantiae nostrae,

> " ausus es hoc ex ore tuo——,"

inquit Ennius, ut equites Scaptio ad pecuniam cogen-
dam darem, me rogare? An tu, si mecum esses, qui
scribis morderi te interdum, quod non simul sis, pate-
rere me id facere, si vellem? " Non amplius," inquis,
" quinquaginta." Cum Spartaco minus multi primo
fuerunt. Quid tandem isti mali in tam tenera insula
non fecissent? Non fecissent autem? immo quid
ante adventum meum non fecerunt? Inclusum in
curia senatum habuerunt Salaminium ita multos dies,
ut interierint non nulli fame. Erat enim praefectus
Appi Scaptius et habebat turmas ab Appio. Id me
igitur tu, cuius mehercule os mihi ante oculos solet
versari, cum de aliquo officio ac laude cogito, tu me,
inquam, rogas, praefectus ut Scaptius sit? Alias hoc
statueramus, ut negotiatorem neminem, idque Bruto
probaramus. Habeat is turmas? Cur potius quam

450

that Scaptius is sorry. As to his argument from a decree of the Senate ordering judgement to be given according to the bond, the reason for that was that in borrowing the money the people of Salamis contravened the law of Gabinius. Aulus' law forbade that judgement should be given for money so borrowed. So the Senate decreed that judgement might be given on that particular bond. Now the bond in question has the same validity as other bonds, and no special privilege. I fancy Brutus will admit that my behaviour has been proper. I do not know if you will take that view, but certainly Cato will.

Now I come back to yourself. My dear friend, you have praised the nice honour of my conduct " and can you dare with your own mouth," as Ennius says, ask me to give Scaptius cavalry to collect his debts? Or would you, if you were here,—you who say that you chafe sometimes at not being with me,—would you suffer me to do such a thing, if I wanted? " Not more than fifty men," you say. Spartacus had fewer men than that at first. The blackguards would have done indescribable damage in such a weak island. Do you say they would have refrained? Look at the damage they did before I came here. They kept the members of the local Senate prisoners in their Chamber for so long that some died of hunger. For Scaptius was a prefect of Appius, and was allowed some cavalry. Your face is always before my eyes when I think of duty and honour, and can you, you, I repeat, ask me to give the fellow the office of prefect? I had settled in other cases never to give the office to a man of business, a course which had won the approval of Brutus: and is a fellow like Scaptius to have cavalry? Why should he not be content with a

cohortes? Sumptu iam nepos evadit Scaptius. " Volunt," inquit, " principes." Scio; nam ad me Ephesum usque venerunt flentesque equitum scelera et
miserias suas detulerunt. Itaque statim dedi litteras,
ut ex Cypro equites ante certam diem decederent, ob
eamque causam, tum ob ceteras Salaminii nos in caelum decretis suis sustulerunt. Sed iam quid opus equi-
tatu? solvunt enim Salaminii; nisi forte id volumus
armis efficere, ut faenus quaternis centesimis ducant.
Et ego audebo legere umquam aut attingere eos
libros, quos tu dilaudas, si tale quid fecero? Nimis,
inquam, in isto Brutum amasti, dulcissime Attice,
nos vereor ne parum. Atque haec scripsi ego ad
Brutum scripsisse te ad me. Cognosce nunc cetera.

Pro Appio nos hic omnia facimus, honeste tamen,
sed plane libenter. Nec enim ipsum odimus et
Brutum amamus, et Pompeius mirifice a me conten-
dit, quem mehercule plus plusque in dies diligo. C.
Caelium quaestorem huc venire audisti. Nescio,
quid sit: sed Pammenia illa mihi non placent. Ego
me spero Athenis fore mense Septembri. Tuorum
itinerum tempora scire sane velim. Εὐήθειαν Sem-
proni Rufi cognovi ex epistula tua Corcyraea. Quid
quaeris? invideo potentiae Vestori.

Cupiebam etiam nunc plura garrire, sed lucet;
urget turba, festinat Philogenes. Valebis igitur et
valere Piliam et Caeciliam nostram iubebis litteris et
salvebis a meo Cicerone.

company of foot? He is beginning to live in spend-
thrift style. The leading people of Salamis insist,
he declares. Of course; that is why they came to me
and with tears told me of his men's atrocities and
their own miseries. Accordingly, I sent a letter at
once ordering the cavalry to quit Cyprus by a certain
day, and that, as well as other acts of mine, has
caused the people of Salamis to praise me to the
skies in their decrees. There is no need of cavalry
now, for the people are ready to pay,—unless perhaps
I want to use force to make them pay 48 per cent
interest. Were I to do such a thing, I could never
venture to read or touch those volumes which you
praise. You, my dear fellow, have had far too much
regard for Brutus in the matter. I perhaps not
enough. I have informed Brutus of the drift of
your letter. Now for the remaining topics.

I am pleased to do all I can for Appius here con-
sistently with my honour. I do not dislike him and I
like Brutus: and Pompey, for whom I have a higher
regard every day, is surprisingly importunate. You
have heard that C. Caelius comes here as quaestor.
I don't know why, but I don't like that affair of Pammenes. I hope to be at Athens in the month of
September. Please let me know the dates of your
travels. I understood the *naïveté* of Sempronius
Rufus from your letter written in Corcyra. I am
really quite jealous of the influence of Vestorius.

I should like to keep on chatting, but day dawns,
the crowd is pressing in, and Philogenes is in a hurry.
Good-bye, give my greetings to Pilia, when you
write, and to your daughter: and accept greetings
from my son.

MARCUS TULLIUS CICERO

III

Etsi nil sane habebam novi, quod post accidisset, quam dedissem ad te Philogeni, liberto tuo, litteras, tamen, cum Philotimum Romam remitterem, scribendum aliquid ad te fuit. Ac primum illud, quod me maxume angebat—non quo me aliquid iuvare posses. Quippe, res enim est in manibus, tu autem abes longe gentium;

πολλὰ δ᾽ ἐν μεταιχμίῳ
νότος κυλίνδει κύματ᾽ εὐρείης ἁλός.

Obrepit dies, ut vides (mihi enim a. d. III Kal. Sextil. de provincia decedendum est), nec succeditur. Quem relinquam, qui provinciae praesit? Ratio quidem et opinio hominum postulat fratrem, primum quod videtur esse honos, nemo igitur potior; deinde quod solum habeo praetorium. Pomptinus enim ex pacto et convento (nam ea lege exierat) iam a me discesserat; quaestorem nemo dignum putat; etenim est " levis, libidinosus, tagax." De fratre autem primum illud est. Persuaderi ei non posse arbitror; odit enim provinciam, et hercule nihil odiosius, nihil molestius. Deinde, ut mihi nolit negare, quidnam mei sit officii? cum bellum esse in Syria magnum putetur, id videatur in hanc provinciam erupturum, hic praesidii nihil sit, sumptus annuus decretus sit, videaturne aut pietatis esse meae fratrem relinquere aut diligentiae nugarum aliquid relinquere? Magna igitur, ut vides, sollicitudine adficior, magna inopia consilii. Quid quaeris?

III

CICERO TO ATTICUS, GREETING.

Though I have no fresh news, since I handed a *Cilicia,* letter for you to your freedman Philogenes, still I *before June* must write you a line, since I am sending Philotimus *26,* B.C. *50* back to Rome. First a thing which gives me much anxiety—not that you can help me at all—for the business is in hand, and you are far away in a foreign land

> " and by south wind tossed
>   Between us rolls the wide estranging sea."

The days steal on, as you see (for I am due to leave my province on the 30th of July), and no successor is appointed. Whom can I leave in charge? Policy and public opinion point to my brother: first because it is right that he should have the honour by preference to anyone else, and secondly because he is the only officer of praetorian rank that I have: for Pomptinus, who came out on that condition, has left me already according to his agreement. My quaestor is notoriously unsuitable; he is " unsteady, wanton, and light-fingered." There is one objection to my brother's appointment,—he will probably refuse, as he hates provincial life. Certes, it is a hateful bore. Then, supposing he does not like to refuse, what is my proper course? Seeing that a great war is likely in Syria, which will apparently break forth into this district, where there is no protection and only the ordinary supplies have been voted for the year, it would certainly seem unnatural to leave my brother, and careless to leave some nincompoop. As you see, I am troubled greatly and badly want advice. In

toto negotio nobis opus non fuit. Quanto tua provincia melior! Decedes, cum voles, nisi forte iam decessisti; quem videbitur, praeficies Thesprotiae et Chaoniae. Necdum tamen ego Quintum conveneram, ut iam, si id placeret, scirem, possetne ab eo impetrari; nec tamen, si posset, quid vellem, habebam. Hoc est igitur eius modi.

Reliqua plena adhuc et laudis et gratiae, digna iis libris, quos dilaudas, conservatae civitates, cumulate publicanis satis factum, offensus contumelia nemo, decreto iusto et severo perpauci, nec tamen quisquam, ut queri audeat, res gestae dignae triumpho; de quo ipso nihil cupide agemus, sine tuo quidem consilio certe nihil. Clausula est difficilis in tradenda provincia. Sed haec deus aliquis gubernabit.

De urbanis rebus scilicet plura tu scis; saepius et certiora audis; equidem doleo non me tuis litteris certiorem fieri. Huc enim odiosa adferebantur de Curione, de Paulo; non quo ullum periculum videam stante Pompeio vel etiam sedente, valeat modo; sed mehercule Curionis et Pauli, meorum familiarium, vicem doleo. Formam igitur mihi totius rei publicae, si iam es Romae aut cum eris, velim mittas, quae mihi obviam veniat, ex qua me fingere possim et praemeditari, quo animo accedam ad urbem. Est enim quiddam advenientem non esse peregrinum atque hospitem. Et, quod paene praeterii, Bruti tui

short, I made a mistake over the whole matter. Your sphere is far preferable. You can depart at pleasure; and perhaps you have left already. You can put Thesprotia and Chaonia [1] in charge of anyone you like. I have not yet met my brother to know whether he would consent if I want him to take it over; nor, should he consent, am I settled in my plans. So much for that.

The rest so far is full of honour and glory and worthy of the volumes which you praise. Communities have found salvation, the whole body of tax-collectors has been satisfied, no one has been annoyed by ill-considered conduct, very few by the severity of upright justice—none so that he could dare complain —and a campaign has been conducted in a way that deserves a triumph, though I shall not seek it greedily, nor seek it at all without your advice. The conclusion is difficult in the matter of handing over the province. But some god will direct my course.

About doings in town of course you know more, as your information comes more frequently and more surely. I am sorry that you do not pass on your news in a letter, for tiresome tidings have reached me about Curio and Paulus, not that there would seem anything to fear if Pompey keeps his influence or even his inactivity. Only let him recover his health. But I am annoyed for Curio and Paulus, my friends. So if you are now in town, or when you are there, please send me a sketch of the political situation to meet me on my way, that I may mould my conduct upon it and bethink me of the proper spirit in which to approach Rome. It is something not to arrive as a foreigner and a stranger. There was one point I nearly omitted. As I have said often,

[1] The country round Atticus' house in Epirus.

causa, ut saepe ad te scripsi, feci omnia. Cyprii numerabant; sed Scaptius centesimis renovato in singulos annos faenore contentus non fuit. Ariobarzanes non in Pompeium prolixior per ipsum quam per me in Brutum. Quem tamen ego praestare non poteram; erat enim rex perpauper, aberamque ab eo ita longe, ut nihil possem nisi litteris; quibus pugnare non destiti. Summa haec est. Pro ratione pecuniae liberalius est Brutus tractatus quam Pompeius. Bruto curata hoc anno talenta circiter c, Pompeio in sex mensibus promissa cc. Iam in Appi negotio quantum tribuerim Bruto, dici vix potest. Quid est igitur, quod laborem? Amicos habet meras nugas, Matinium, Scaptium. Qui quia non habuit a me turmas equitum, quibus Cyprum vexaret, ut ante me fecerat, fortasse suscenset, aut quia praefectus non est, quod ego nemini tribui negotiatori, non C. Vennonio, meo familiari, non tuo, M. Laenio, et quod tibi Romae ostenderam me servaturum; in quo perseveravi. Sed quid poterit queri is, qui, auferre pecuniam cum posset, noluit? Scaptio, qui in Cappadocia fuit, puto esse satis factum. Is a me tribunatum cum accepisset, quem ego ex Bruti litteris ei detulissem, postea scripsit ad me se uti nolle eo tribunatu.

Gavius est quidam, cui cum praefecturam detulissem Bruti rogatu, multa et dixit et fecit cum quadam mea contumelia, P. Clodi canis. Is me nec proficiscentem Apameam prosecutus est, nec, cum postea in castra venisset atque inde discederet, num

I have done everything for your friend Brutus. The people of Cyprus were paying down the money. Scaptius was not content with 12 per cent compound interest. Ariobarzanes is not more accommodating to Pompey for his own sake than to Brutus for mine. Still I could not go bail for him, for he is a very needy monarch and I was such a long way off that I could only press him on paper, as I did continually. The conclusion is this. In proportion to the sum lent, Brutus has been treated more liberally than Pompey: for Brutus there has been got this year about £24,400. To Pompey has been promised £48,800 within six months. In the business of Appius, my concessions to Brutus are almost incalculable. I have no reason to distress myself. Brutus' friends are men of straw, Matinius, and Scaptius, who is perhaps angry because he could not get troops to harry Cyprus has he had done before my time, or because he was not made a prefect, an office I have not granted to any man of business, not to C. Vennonius, my friend, nor to your friend M. Laenius. I have persevered in the course that I told you at Rome I should keep : but a man who refused to take his money, when he could, cannot grumble. The other Scaptius who was in Cappadocia, I think, is satisfied. First of all he accepted a military tribuneship from me, which a letter from Brutus had persuaded me to offer him ; but he wrote me afterwards that he did not want to take it up.

There is a person Gavius, who, after I had offered him a post as prefect at Brutus' request, said and did a good deal to disparage me. He is Clodius' puppy-dog. He did not condescend to be one of my escort when I left Apamea, nor, when he came into camp later and was leaving it, did he ask if I had any com-

quid vellem, rogavit, et fuit aperte mihi nescio quare
non amicus. Hunc ego si in praefectis habuissem,
quem tu me hominem putares? Qui, ut scis, poten-
tissimorum hominum contumaciam numquam tule-
rim, ferrem huius adseculae? etsi hoc plus est quam
ferre, tribuere etiam aliquid beneficii et honoris. Is
igitur Gavius, cum Apameae me nuper vidisset Romam proficiscens, me ita appellavit, ut Culleolum vix
auderem: " Unde," inquit, " me iubes petere cibaria
praefecti? " Respondi lenius, quam putabant oportuisse, qui aderant, me non instituisse iis dare cibaria,
quorum opera non essem usus. Abiit iratus. Huius
nebulonis oratione si Brutus moveri potest, licebit
eum solus ames, me aemulum non habebis. Sed illum
eum futurum esse puto, qui esse debet. Tibi tamen
causam notam esse volui et ad ipsum haec perscripsi
diligentissime. Omnino (soli enim sumus) nullas
umquam ad me litteras misit Brutus, ne proxime
quidem de Appio, in quibus non inesset adrogans,
ἀκοινονόητον aliquid. Tibi autem valde solet in ore
esse :

" Granius autem

Lucilius.   Non contemnere se et reges odisse superbos."

In quo tamen ille mihi risum magis quam stomachum
movere solet. Sed plane parum cogitat, quid scribat
aut ad quem.

Q. Cicero puer legit, ut opinor, et certe, epistulam
inscriptam patri suo. Solet enim aperire idque de
meo consilio, si quid forte sit, quod opus sit sciri.
In ea autem epistula erat idem illud de sorore quod
ad me. Mirifice conturbatum vidi puerum. Lacri-

missions. For some unknown reason he was an open enemy of mine. If I had counted such a fellow among my prefects, you might doubt what kind of creature I am. You know I will not brook discourtesy from men of power, and should I put up with it from this hanger-on? Though, to be sure, gracious bestowal of honour is something more than putting up with a man. So Gavius, when on his road to Rome he saw me lately at Apamea, addressed me as I should scarcely address Culleolus. " Where," said he, " am I to look for my pickings?" I answered less sternly than those present thought proper, that I was not accustomed to give pickings to men whose services I had not used. He went off in a temper. If Brutus listens to the talk of such a shady customer you may have him to yourself. I shall not be your rival. But I think he will behave all right. However, I wanted you to know the circumstances, and I have recounted the matter very fully to Brutus. Between ourselves, Brutus has never sent me a letter, not even lately about Appius, without a touch of arrogance and intolerance. You often quote the lines,

> " But Granius too
> Has self-conceit and hates the pride of kings."

However, in this business he excites my laughter rather than my rage, and evidently he does not consider sufficiently what he writes and to whom.

The young Quintus, I fancy, yes I am sure, read your letter addressed to his father, for he usually opens his father's letters—and that by my advice—in case there is anything he ought to know. The letter contained that same passage about your sister that you wrote to me. The boy was awfully upset. He

mans mecum est questus. Quid quaeris? miram in
eo pietatem, suavitatem humanitatemque perspexi.
Quo maiorem spem habeo nihil fore aliter, ac deceat.
Id te igitur scire volui.

Ne illud quidem praetermittam. Hortensius filius
fuit Laodiceae gladiatoribus flagitiose et turpiter.
Hunc ego patris causa vocavi ad cenam, quo die venit,
et eiusdem patris causa nihil amplius. Is mihi dixit
se Athenis me exspectaturum, ut mecum decederet.
" Recte," inquam; quid enim dicerem? Omnino
puto nihil esse, quod dixit; nolo quidem, ne offendam
patrem, quem mehercule multum diligo. Sin fuerit
meus comes, moderabor ita, ne quid eum offendam,
quem minime volo.

Haec sunt; etiam illud. Orationem Q. Celeris
mihi velim mittas contra M. Servilium. Litteras
mitte quam primum; si nihil, nihil fieri vel per tuum
tabellarium. Piliae et filiae salutem. Cura, ut
valeas.

IV

CICERO ATTICO SAL.

Scr. in itinere
paulo post
Non. Iun.
a. 704

Tarsum venimus Nonis Iuniis. Ibi me multa mo-
verunt, magnum in Syria bellum, magna in Cilicia
latrocinia, mihi difficilis ratio administrandi, quod
paucos dies habebam reliquos annui muneris, illud
autem difficillimum, relinquendus erat ex senatus con-

came to me complaining in tears. I saw much good feeling in him, and a kind and courteous disposition, which increases my hope for a satisfactory issue to the matter: so I want you to know it.

There is one thing I must not pass over. The young Hortensius, during the gladiatorial exhibition at Laodicea, behaved in a shameful and scandalous way. For his father's sake I invited him to my table on the day of his arrival, and for the same father's sake treated him handsomely.[1] He said that he would await my departure in Athens, that we might go home together. I could only say, "Very well." But I don't fancy at all that he meant what he said. I hope not, lest I offend his father, who is my very good friend. But if he comes in my suite I will arrange so as to avoid offence to a man I don't want to offend.

So much for that, there is one thing more. Please send me Q. Celer's speech against M. Servilius. Write to me at your first opportunity. If there is no news, write to say so, or even send a verbal message. Give my love to your wife and daughter. Keep well.

IV

CICERO TO ATTICUS, GREETING.

I came to Tarsus on the 5th of June. There I was *On the road,* upset by many troubles: a big war in Syria, big cases *shortly after* of robbery in Cilicia, my difficulty in arranging things, *June 5,* considering there are only a few days left of my year B.C. *50* of office: but the hardest problem of all is that, according to a decree of the Senate, someone must

---

[1] Or "did nothing more for him."

sulto, qui praeesset. Nihil minus probari poterat
quam quaestor Mescinius. Nam de Caelio nihil
audiebamus. Rectissimum videbatur fratrem cum
imperio relinquere; in quo multa molesta, discessus
noster, belli periculum, militum improbitas, sescenta
praeterea. O rem totam odiosam! Sed haec fortuna
viderit, quoniam consilio non multum uti licet.

Tu, quando Romam salvus, ut spero, venisti, videbis, ut soles, omnia, quae intelleges nostra interesse,
imprimis de Tullia mea, cuius de condicione quid
mihi placeret, scripsi ad Terentiam, cum tu in Grae-
cia esses; deinde de honore nostro. Quod enim tu
afuisti, vereor, ut satis diligenter actum in senatu sit
de litteris meis.

Illud praeterea μυστικώτερον ad te scribam, tu
sagacius odorabere. Τῆς δάμαρτός μου ὁ ἀπελεύθερος
(οἶσθα, ὃν λέγω) ἔδοξέ μοι πρώην, ἐξ ὧν ἀλογευό-
μενος παρεφθέγγετο, πεφυρακέναι τὰς ψήφους ἐκ
τῆς ὠνῆς τῶν ὑπαρχόντων τοῦ Κροτωνιάτου τυραν-
νοκτόνου. Δέδοικα δή, μή τι νοήσῃς. Εἰς δήπου
τοῦτο δὴ περισκεψάμενος τὰ λοιπὰ ἐξασφάλισαι.
Non queo tantum, quantum vereor, scribere; tu
autem fac, ut mihi tuae litterae volent obviae.
Haec festinans scripsi in itinere atque agmine.
Piliae et puellae Caeciliae bellissimae salutem dices.

be left in charge. The quaestor Mescinius is by no means a suitable person. Of Caelius I hear nothing. The proper thing seems to be to leave my brother with military power, but that involves many difficulties—our separation, risk of war, mutiny in the troops, a thousand other hazards. A hateful business altogether. But fortune must look to it, since reason serves our purpose little.

You, having come safe to Rome, as I hope, will as usual look to everything that concerns me, especially the matter of my daughter, about whose marriage settlement I have written to Terentia expressing my intentions, since you were in Greece. Then please look after my triumph. For as you were absent from town, I fear the Senate hardly paid sufficient attention to my despatch.

The following point I will write to you in dark phrases: your cleverness will scent my meaning. My wife's freedman (you know whom I mean) seemed to me lately from casual words of his to have cooked his accounts on the sale of the goods of the Crotonian tyrannicide.[1] I fear you have noticed something. Look into this matter yourself alone, and secure what is left. I cannot write all my fears. Take care that your letter flies to meet me. I write in haste on the march and with my army. Give my love to your wife and to your very charming little daughter.

[1] T. Annius Milo, who assumed the name Milo in honour of the well-known athlete of Croton of that name. The freedman referred to is Philotimus. From v, 8 it appears that he bought for Cicero at the sale of Milo's property.

MARCUS TULLIUS CICERO

V

CICERO ATTICO SAL.

Scr. in castris
V K. Quint.
a. 704

Nunc quidem profecto Romae es. Quo te, si ita est, salvum venisse gaudeo; unde quidem quam diu afuisti, magis a me abesse videbare, quam si domi esses; minus enim mihi meae notae res erant, minus etiam publicae. Quare velim, etsi, ut spero, te haec legente aliquantum iam viae processero, tamen obvias mihi litteras quam argutissimas de omnibus rebus crebro mittas, imprimis de quo scripsi ad te antea. Τῆς ξυναόρου τῆς ἐμῆς οὐξελεύθερος ἔδοξέ μοι θαμὰ βατταρίζων καὶ ἀλύων ἐν τοῖς ξυλλόγοις καὶ ταῖς λέσχαις ὑπό τι πεφυρακέναι τὰς ψήφους ἐν τοῖς ὑπάρχουσιν τοῖς τοῦ Κροτωνιάτου. Hoc tu indagu, ut soles, ast hoc magis. Ἐξ ἄστεως ἐπταλόφου στείχων παρέδωκεν μνῶν κδ', μή ὀφείλημα τῷ Καμίλλῳ, ἑαυτόν τε ὀφείλοντα μνᾶς κδ' ἐκ τῶν Κροτωνιατικῶν καὶ ἐκ τῶν Χερρονησιτικῶν μή καὶ μνᾶς κληρονομῆσαι χμ', χμ'. Τούτων δὲ μηδὲ ὀβολὸν διευθετῆσθαι πάντων ὀφειληθέντων τοῦ δευτέρου μηνὸς τῇ νουμηνίᾳ. Τὸν δὲ ἀπελεύθερον αὐτοῦ ὄντα ὁμώνυμον τῷ Κόνωνος πατρὶ μηδὲν ὁλοσχερῶς πεφροντικέναι. Ταῦτα οὖν πρῶτον μέν, ἵνα πάντα σώζηται, δεύτερον δέ, ἵνα μηδὲ τῶν τόκων ὀλιγωρήσῃς τῶν ἀπὸ τῆς προεκκειμένης ἡμέρας. Ὅσας αὐτὸν ἠνέγκαμεν, σφόδρα δέδοικα· καὶ γὰρ παρῆν πρὸς ἡμᾶς κατασκεψόμενος καί

466

V

CICERO TO ATTICUS, GREETING.

You must certainly be at Rome now. If you are, *In camp,* I am glad of your safe arrival. So long as you were *June 26,* away from town, you seemed to me to be farther off B.C. *50* than if you were in Rome, for I heard less of my own business and less of the business of the state. So please send plenty of chatty letters on every kind of subject to meet me, though I hope, when you read this, I shall be well on my journey home. Above all, write me on the subject I raised in my former letter. From the stuttering hesitation of my wife's freedman in our meetings and talks I infer that he has been cooking his accounts a little in the matter of the sale of the Crotonian's [1] goods. Investigate the matter with your usual care, but pay still more attention to this. When leaving the city of the seven hills he tendered an account of debts of some £100 and £200 [2] to Camillus, and put himself down as owing £100 from Milo's goods and £200 from the property in the Chersonese, and as having inherited two sums of £2,600,[3] of which not a penny had been paid, though all were due on the 1st of the second month. Milo's freedman, Timotheus, the namesake of Conon's father, he said, had never given a thought to the matter. Now first try to secure the whole amount, and secondly don't overlook the interest from the afore-mentioned day. All the time I had to endure him I was much upset. He came to me to spy out

---

[1] I.e. T. Annius Milo.
[2] 24 and 48 minae, worth a little over £4 each.
[3] 640 minae.

MARCUS TULLIUS CICERO

τι σχεδὸν ἐλπίσας· ἀπογνοὺς δ' ἀλόγως ἀπέστη
ἐπειπών " εἴκω· αἰσχρόν τοι δηρόν τε μένειν "—

meque obiurgavit vetere proverbio τὰ μὲν διδόμενα—.
Reliqua vide et, quantum fieri potest, perspiciamus.

Etsi annuum tempus prope iam emeritum habebamus (dies enim xxxiii erant reliqui), sollicitudine
provinciae tamen vel maxime urgebamur. Cum enim
arderet Syria bello, et Bibulus in tanto maerore suo
maximam curam belli sustineret, ad meque legati
eius et quaestor et amici eius litteras mitterent, ut
subsidio venirem, etsi exercitum infirmum habebam,
auxilia sane bona, sed ea Galatarum, Pisidarum, Ly-
ciorum (haec enim sunt nostra robora), tamen esse
officiummeum putavi exercitum habere quam pro-
xume hostem, quoad mihi praeesse provinciae per
senatus consultum liceret. Sed, quo ego maxime
delectabar, Bibulus molestus mihi non erat, de omnibus rebus scribebat ad me potius. Et mihi decessio-
nis dies λεληθότως obrepebat. Qui cum advenerit,
ἄλλο πρόβλημα, quem praeficiam, nisi Caldus quaestor
venerit; de quo adhuc nihil certi habebamus.

Cupiebam mehercule longiorem epistulam facere,
sed nec erat res, de qua scriberem, nec iocari prae
cura poteram. Valebis igitur et puellae salutem
Atticulae dices nostraeque Piliae.

468

the land, and had some hopes. When he lost them he left without an explanation, saying: " I give in, 'Twere shame to tarry long," and casting in my teeth the old proverb " take the goods the gods provide you." [1] Look after the rest, and let us investigate the matter as thoroughly as possible.

Though I have nearly served my year (for only thirty-three days remain), still I am greatly concerned about my province. Syria is ablaze with war, and Bibulus is burdened with its cares in the midst of his own great sorrow,[2] and his legates, quaestor, and friends write to me to go to his aid: so, although the army I have is weak—the auxiliaries certainly are good, Galatians, Pisidians, Lycians, the main strength of my force—I have thought it my duty to keep an army facing the foe so long as I am authorized by the Senate's decree to be in charge of my province. But what pleases me greatly is that Bibulus gives no trouble. He writes to me about any other topic by preference, and the day of my departure creeps on unnoticed. When it arrives there is the further problem of my substitute, unless my quaestor Caldus comes, of whom so far I have no news.

I should like to write a longer letter, but I have no news, and care keeps me from jesting; so goodbye, and love to your little daughter and to your wife.

---

[1] This proverb is referred to in Plato's *Gorgias* 499c, and given in full by Olympiodorus in the form τὰ ἐκ τῆς τύχης διδόμενα κόσμει " make the best of what fortune gives."

[2] The murder of his sons in Egypt.

VI

Scr. Rhodi
circ. IV Id.
Sext. a. 704

Ego, dum in provincia omnibus rebus Appium orno, subito sum factus accusatoris eius socer. " Id quidem," inquis, " di adprobent! " Ita velim teque ita cupere certo scio. Sed, crede mihi, nihil minus putaram ego, qui de Ti. Nerone, qui mecum egerat, certos homines ad mulieres miseram; qui Romam venerunt factis sponsalibus. Sed hoc spero melius; mulieres quidem valde intellego delectari obsequio et comitate adulescentis. Cetera noli ἐξακανθίζειν.

Sed heus tu! πυροὺς εἰς δῆμον Athenis? placet hoc tibi? Etsi non impediebant mei certe libri. Non enim ista largitio fuit in cives, sed in hospites liberalitas. Me tamen de Academiae προπύλῳ iubes cogitare, cum iam Appius de Eleusine non cogitet? De Hortensio te certo scio dolere; equidem excrucior; decreram enim cum eo valde familiariter vivere.

Nos provinciae praefecimus Caelium. " Puerum," inquies, " et fortasse fatuum et non gravem et non continentem! " Adsentior; fieri non potuit aliter. Nam, quas multo ante tuas acceperam litteras, in quibus ἐπέχειν te scripseras, quid esset mihi faciendum de relinquendo, eae me pungebant; videbam enim, quae tibi essent ἐποχῆς causae, et erant eaedem

VI

CICERO TO ATTICUS, GREETING.

While in my province I show Appius every honour, *Rhodes,* suddenly I find myself father-in-law of Dolabella his *circa Aug.* accuser. You invoke heaven's benison. So say I, *10,* B.C. *50* and you I know are sincere. Believe me, it was the last thing I had expected. Indeed, I had even sent trusty agents to Terentia and Tullia about the suit of Ti. Nero, who had made proposals to me : but they arrived in town only when the betrothal was over. However, I hope the better course has been taken. I understand that my women folk are highly pleased with the young man's obliging and courteous temper. As for the rest, don't pick holes in him.

Good gracious! Do you approve of corn doles to Athens? My own books to be sure do not forbid such a dole, for it was not a largesse to fellow-citizens, but a graceful present in return for hospitality. Still do you encourage me in the matter of the porch for the Academy, when Appius has abandoned his design of a porch at Eleusis? I am sure you are sorry about the news of Hortensius. Personally I am distracted : for it had been my intention to live on intimate terms with him.

I have put Caelius in charge of my province. "A mere boy" you will object, "and perhaps silly, and lacking in dignity and self-control." I agree; but there was no alternative. The letter I got from you some time ago, in which you said you suspended judgement as to what I ought to do about my substitute, caused me a pang; for I understood the

mihi. Puero tradere? fratri autem? Illud non utile nobis. Nam praeter fratrem nemo erat, quem sine contumelia quaestori, nobili praesertim, anteferrem. Tamen, dum impendere Parthi videbantur, statueram fratrem relinquere aut etiam rei publicae causa contra senatus consultum ipse remanere. Qui posteaquam incredibili felicitate discesserunt, sublata dubitatio est. Videbam sermones: " Hui, fratrem reliquit! Num est hoc non plus annum obtinere provinciam? Quid, quod senatus eos voluit praeesse provinciis, qui non praefuissent? At hic triennium!" Ergo haec ad populum. Quid, quae tecum? Numquam essem sine cura, si quid iracundius aut contumeliosius aut neglegentius, quae fert vita hominum. Quid, si quid filius puer et puer bene sibi fidens? qui esset dolor? quem pater non dimittebat teque id censere moleste ferebat. At nunc Caelius non dico equidem " quod egerit—," sed tamen multo minus laboro. Adde illud. Pompeius, eo robore vir, iis radicibus, Q. Cassium sine sorte delegit, Caesar Antonium; ego sorte datum offenderem, ut etiam inquireret in eum, quem reliquissem? Hoc melius, et huius rei plura exempla, senectuti quidem nostrae profecto aptius.

grounds of your hesitation and felt them myself.
Could I hand it over to a boy? But ought I to hand
it over to my brother? The latter is prejudicial to
my own interests. My brother was the only man it
would not be an insult to prefer to the quaestor,
especially as that officer was of noble birth. Still,
while the Parthians seemed threatening, I determined to leave my brother in charge, or even to run
counter to the decree of the Senate and for the sake
of the Republic remain here myself. Their marvellously opportune retirement removed my doubts. I
foresaw the world's comment. " So he has left his
brother in charge! Is this holding a province for one
year only? And what about the decree of the Senate
that ex-governors should not be eligible? Why, his
brother was governor for three years." These are
the arguments for the public; but for you I have
private reasons. I should have been in constant
anxiety as to some exhibition of temper or over-
bearingness or negligence; for such things will
happen. Perhaps his son, a mere headstrong lad,
would have given me cause for distress: his
father would not send him away, and was annoyed
with you for saying that he ought. As for Caelius,
I cannot say that I am unconcerned about his
past behaviour: but still I am far less concerned.
Then there is another point. Pompey (and think
of his power and position) chose Q. Cassius without regard to the lot, and Caesar, too, chose Antony.
I could not affront Caelius who had been given
to me by lot, and so make him a spy on the
actions of my successor. No; my present course
is better, accords well with precedent, and is well
suited to my time of life. But, heavens, how I have

At te apud eum, di boni, quanta in gratia posui!
Eique legi litteras non tuas, sed librarii tui.

Amicorum litterae me ad triumphum vocant, rem
a nobis, ut ego arbitror, propter hanc παλιγγενεσίαν
nostram non neglegendam. Quare tu quoque, mi
Attice, incipe id cupere, quo nos minus inepti videamur.

VII

CICERO ATTICO SAL.

Scr. Tarsi
ante III K.
Sext. a. 704 Quintus filius pie sane me quidem certe multum
hortante, sed currentem, animum patris sui sorori
tuae reconciliavit. Eum valde tuae litterae excita-
runt. Quid quaeris? confido rem, ut volumus, esse.

Bis ad te antea scripsi de re mea familiari, si modo
tibi redditae litterae sunt, Graece ἐν αἰνιγμοῖς. Scilicet nihil est movendum; sed tamen ἀφελῶς per-
contando de nominibus Milonis et, ut expediat, ut
mihi receperit, hortando, aliquid tu proficies.

Ego Laodiceae quaestorem Mescinium exspectare
iussi, ut confectas rationes lege Iulia apud duas civitates possem relinquere. Rhodum volo puerorum
causa, inde quam primum Athenas, etsi etesiae valde
reflant; sed plane volo his magistratibus, quorum voluntatem in supplicatione sum expertus. Tu tamen
mitte mihi, quaeso, obviam litteras, numquid putes
rei publicae nomine tardandum esse nobis. Tiro ad

474

put you in his good books. I read him a letter, not in your own hand, but in that of your secretary.[1]

Friends write me to come home to my triumph, a matter, I think, in view of my political renaissance, hardly to be neglected. So I hope, my dear Atticus, that you will look forward to it too, to make me appear less foolish.

VII

CICERO TO ATTICUS, GREETING.

The boy Quintus has contrived to reconcile his father to your sister. He showed the proper feeling of a son, and I gave him much encouragement, which he received nothing loath. He was greatly moved by your letter. I trust that matters are as we wish. *Tarsus, before July 30, B.C. 50*

I have written to you twice about a domestic matter of mine in Greek and in riddles, if only my letters have reached you. Don't take decided steps : but still you may do some good by questioning the man simply about Milo's accounts, and urging him to settle the business as he promised.

I have ordered my quaestor Mescinius to wait at Laodicea, so that in accordance with the Julian law I may leave copies of my accounts in two cities. I want to go to Rhodes for the sake of the boys, thence as soon as possible to Athens, though the Etesian winds are very contrary. But I wish to reach Rome during the magistracy of men whose goodwill I experienced over that thanksgiving in my honour. However, please send a letter to meet me, saying if you think there can be any political reason for delay.

[1] Presumably dictated to him by Cicero himself.

te dedisset litteras, nisi eum graviter aegrum Issi
reliquissem. Sed nuntiant melius esse. Ego tamen
angor; nihil enim illo adulescente castius, nihil diligentius.

VIII

CICERO ATTICO SAL.

*Scr. Ephesi
K. Oct.
a. 704*
Cum instituissem ad te scribere calamumque sumpsissem, Batonius e navi recta ad me venit domum
Ephesi et epistulam tuam reddidit pridie Kal. Octobres. Laetatus sum felicitate navigationis tuae, op-
portunitate Piliae, etiam hercule sermone eiusdem
de coniugio Tulliae meae. Batonius autem miros
terrores ad me attulit Caesarianos, cum Lepta etiam
plura locutus est, spero falsa, sed certe horribilia,
exercitum nullo modo dimissurum, cum illo praetores
designatos, Cassium tribunum pl., Lentulum consulem facere, Pompeio in animo esse urbem relinquere.

Sed heus tu! numquid moleste fers de illo, qui
se solet anteferre patruo sororis tuae filii? at a quibus victus! Sed ad rem.

Nos etesiae vehementissime tardarunt; detraxit xx
ipsos dies etiam aphractus Rhodiorum. Kal. Octobr.
Epheso conscendentes hanc epistulam dedimus L.
Tarquitio simul e portu egredienti, sed expeditius
naviganti. Nos Rhodiorum aphractis ceterisque lon-
gis navibus tranquillitates aucupaturi eramus; ita
tamen properabamus, ut non posset magis.

Tiro would have written you a letter, but I left him at Issus seriously ill. However, a message has reached me that he is better. Still I am upset: for he is a model youth and very attentive.

VIII

CICERO TO ATTICUS, GREETING.

Just as I had determined to write to you and had *Ephesus,* taken up my pen, Batonius came straight from his *Oct. 1,* B.C. ship to my house at Ephesus and gave me your *50* letter on the 29th of September. I am delighted about your good voyage, and your opportune meeting with your wife and also at her remarks about the marriage of my daughter. But Batonius brought news that was simply awful about Caesar, and was even more frank in conversation with Lepta. I hope his news is false: it was certainly terrifying. He says that Caesar will refuse to disband his army, that the officials elect, praetors, Cassius the tribune, and Lentulus the consul take his part, and that Pompey thinks of leaving Rome.

But by the by, are you so sorry for the fellow that thinks himself superior to the uncle of your sister's son? What fine opponents to beat him! But to business.

The Etesian winds have hindered me much: the open Rhodian boats, too, caused me a delay of exactly twenty days. On the 1st of October, as I am embarking from Ephesus, I give this letter to L. Tarquitius, who is leaving the harbour at the same time, but sailing by a faster boat. I have had to wait for fair weather owing to the undecked boats and other war vessels of the Rhodians. However, I am hurrying as fast as possible.

De raudusculo Puteolano gratum. Nunc velim
dispicias res Romanas, videas, quid nobis de triumpho
cogitandum putes, ad quem amici me vocant. Ego,
nisi Bibulus, qui, dum unus hostis in Syria fuit, pe-
dem porta non plus extulit quam domi [1] domo sua,
adniteretur de triumpho, aequo animo essem. Nunc
vero αἰσχρὸν σιωπᾶν. Sed explora rem totam, ut,
quo die congressi erimus, consilium capere possimus.

Sat multa, qui et properarem et ei litteras darem,
qui aut mecum aut paulo ante venturus esset. Cicero
tibi plurimam salutem dicit. Tu dices utriusque nostrum verbis et Piliae tuae et filiae.

IX

CICERO ATTICO SAL.

*Scr. Athenis
Id. Oct. a.
704*
In Piraeea cum exissem pridie Idus Octobr., accepi
ab Acasto, servo meo, statim tuas litteras. Quas
quidem cum exspectassem iam diu, admiratus sum,
ut vidi obsignatam epistulam, brevitatem eius, ut
aperui, rursus σύγχυσιν litterularum, quia solent tuae
compositissimae et clarissimae esse, ac, ne multa,
cognovi ex eo, quod ita scripseras, te Romam venisse
a. d. xii Kal. Oct. cum febri. Percussus vehementer
nec magis, quam debui, statim quaero ex Acasto.
Ille et tibi et sibi visum et ita se domi ex tuis audisse,

---

[1] domi *is added by Tyrrell and Purser.*

Many thanks for paying the man of Puteoli [1] his pence. Now please consider politics, and see what you think I should do about the triumph, to which my friends invite me. I should have been quite happy, had not Bibulus been trying for a triumph, though the man never set his foot outside his house so long as there was one enemy in Syria any more than he set foot out of his house in town when he was consul. But as it is " 'twere base to hold one's peace." [2] But consider the whole matter, that we may be able to decide something on the day we meet.

That's enough, considering I am in a hurry and am giving this letter to a man who will arrive at the same time as myself or just before me. My son pays you his best respects. Please give the compliments of both of us to your wife and daughter.

IX

CICERO TO ATTICUS, GREETING.

As soon as I landed in port on the 14th of October I received your letter from my slave Acastus. I have been looking forward to it so long that I was surprised at its brevity, as I looked at the letter before breaking the seal. Again, when I opened it, I was startled at the illegibility of the scribble, for your hand is generally very fine and legible. In short I gathered from the style of writing that you had arrived in town, as you stated, on the 19th of September, suffering from an attack of fever. Much disturbed, as I was bound to be, I questioned my slave. He said that both he

Athens, Oct. 15, B.C. 50

---

[1] Vestorius.

[2] Euripides; Frag. αἰσχρὸν σιωπᾶν βαρβάρους δ' ἐᾶν λέγειν.

ut nihil esset incommode. Id videbatur approbare, quod erat in extremo, febriculam tum te habentem scripsisse. Sed te amavi tamen admiratusque sum, quod nihilo minus ad me tua manu scripsisses. Quare de hoc satis. Spero enim, quae tua prudentia et temperantia est, et hercule, ut me iubet Acastus, confido te iam, ut volumus, valere.

A Turranio te accepisse meas litteras gaudeo. Παραφύλαξον, si me amas, τὴν τοῦ φυρατοῦ φιλοτιμίαν αὐτότατα. Hanc, quae mehercule mihi magno dolori est (dilexi enim hominem), procura, quantulacumque est, Precianam hereditatem prorsus ille ne attingat. Dices nummos mihi opus esse ad apparatum triumphi. In quo, ut praecipis, nec me κενὸν in expetendo cognosces nec ἄτυφον in abiciendo.

Intellexi ex tuis litteris te ex Turranio audisse a me provinciam fratri traditam. Adeon ego non perspexeram prudentiam litterarum tuarum? Ἐπέχειν te scribebas. Quid erat dubitatione dignum, si esset quicquam, cur placeret, fratrem et talem fratrem relinqui? Ἀθέτησις ista mihi tua, non ἐποχὴ videbatur. Monebas de Q. Cicerone puero, ut eum quidem neutiquam relinquerem. Τοὐμὸν ὄνειρον ἐμοί. Eadem omnia, quasi conlocuti essemus, vidimus. Non fuit faciendum aliter, meque ἐπιχρονία ἐποχὴ tua dubitatione liberavit. Sed puto te accepisse de hac re epistulam scriptam accuratius.

and you thought that it was nothing serious and that he had gathered as much from your people. This view seemed to be supported by a remark at the end of your letter that at the time of writing you had a touch of fever. However, I was greatly surprised and pleased at your writing to me in your own hand in the circumstances. So I will say no more. For I hope considering your careful and temperate life— and to be sure Acastus bids me be confident—that you are now as well as I could wish.

I am glad you got my letter from Turranius. Keep a very strict eye, as you love me, on the untimely designs of that cooker of accounts Philotimus. As to this legacy from Precius, which is a great sorrow to me—for I loved him indeed—don't let the fellow lay a finger on it, small as it is. You will say that I want money for the outfit of my triumph. You shall see that following your advice I will not show foolish vanity in seeking a triumph, nor be phlegmatic enough to refuse it.

I gather from your letter that you heard from Turranius I had given over my province to my brother. Do you imagine that I overlooked the cautious tone of your letter? You wrote that you were doubtful. There could have been no reason for doubts, if there had been grounds for leaving a brother and such a brother in charge. I took your doubts for dogmatic rejection. You warn me on no account to leave the young Quintus. Your words repeat my dream. The same vision came to us both, as though we had talked it over. There was nothing else to be done, and your long doubt has relieved me of hesitation. But I fancy you must have already got a letter on this topic written in more detail.

MARCUS TULLIUS CICERO

Ego tabellarios postero die ad vos eram missurus; quos puto ante venturos quam nostrum Saufeium. Sed eum sine meis litteris ad te venire vix rectum erat. Tu mihi, ut polliceris, de Tulliola mea, id est de Dolabella, perscribes, de re publica, quam praevideo in summis periculis, de censoribus, maximeque de signis, tabulis quid fiat, referaturne. Idibus Octobribus has dedi litteras, quo die, ut scribis, Caesar Placentiam legiones IIII. Quaeso, quid nobis futurum est? In arce Athenis statio mea nunc placet.

END OF VOL. I

I mean to send letter-carriers to you to-morrow, who I fancy will arrive before our friend Saufeius: but it was hardly proper that he should come to you without a letter from me. Please write me fully, as you promise, about my little daughter, that is about her husband Dolabella, about the political situation in which I foresee much trouble, about the censors, and above all about the business of statues and pictures, and whether the matter will come up before the Senate.[1] The 15th of October is the date of this letter, a day on which you say Caesar is going to bring four legions to Placentia. I wonder what will be our fate. My present quarters on the Acropolis at Athens seem to me the best place.

[1] The censors had fixed a limit on private expenditure on works of art; but their edict required the confirmation of the Senate before it became law.

CHRONOLOGICAL ORDER OF THE LETTERS.[1]

[1] In many cases the dates and order are only approximate and authorities differ about them. I have generally accepted the dates given in the Teubner edition.

[2] Some date this letter early in 67, and the next towards the end of January, 67.

CHRONOLOGICAL ORDER OF THE LETTERS

INDEX OF NAMES.

[*The references are to the pages of Latin text.*]

487

INDEX OF NAMES

INDEX OF NAMES

INDEX OF NAMES

INDEX OF NAMES

491

INDEX OF NAMES

INDEX OF NAMES

INDEX OF NAMES

494

INDEX OF NAMES

495

INDEX OF NAMES

Printed in Great Britain by
Richard Clay (The Chaucer Press), Ltd.,
Bungay, Suffolk

THE LOEB CLASSICAL LIBRARY

VOLUMES ALREADY PUBLISHED

Latin Authors

AMMIANUS MARCELLINUS. Translated by J. C. Rolfe. 3 Vols.

APULEIUS: THE GOLDEN ASS (METAMORPHOSES). W. Adlington (1566). Revised by S. Gaselee.

ST. AUGUSTINE: CITY OF GOD. 7 Vols. Vol. I. G. E. McCracken Vol. II. W. M. Green. Vol. III. D. Wiesen. Vol. IV. P. Levine. Vol. V. E. M. Sanford and W. M. Green. Vol. VI. W. C. Greene.

ST. AUGUSTINE, CONFESSIONS OF. W. Watts (1631). 2 Vols.

ST. AUGUSTINE, SELECT LETTERS. J. H. Baxter.

AUSONIUS. H. G. Evelyn White. 2 Vols.

BEDE. J. E. King. 2 Vols.

BOETHIUS: TRACTS and DE CONSOLATIONE PHILOSOPHIAE. Rev. H. F. Stewart and E. K. Rand.

CAESAR: ALEXANDRIAN, AFRICAN and SPANISH WARS. A. G. Way.

CAESAR: CIVIL WARS. A. G. Peskett.

CAESAR: GALLIC WAR. H. J. Edwards.

CATO: DE RE RUSTICA; VARRO: DE RE RUSTICA. H. B. Ash and W. D. Hooper.

CATULLUS. F. W. Cornish; TIBULLUS. J. B. Postgate; PERVIGILIUM VENERIS. J. W. Mackail.

CELSUS: DE MEDICINA. W. G. Spencer. 3 Vols.

CICERO: BRUTUS, and ORATOR. G. L. Hendrickson and H. M. Hubbell.

[CICERO]: AD HERENNIUM. H. Caplan.

CICERO: DE ORATORE, etc. 2 Vols. Vol. I. DE ORATORE, Books I. and II. E. W. Sutton and H. Rackham. Vol. II. DE ORATORE, Book III. De Fato; Paradoxa Stoicorum; De Partitione Oratoria. H. Rackham.

CICERO: DE FINIBUS. H. Rackham.

CICERO: DE INVENTIONE, etc. H. M. Hubbell.

CICERO: DE NATURA DEORUM and ACADEMICA. H. Rackham.

CICERO: DE OFFICIIS. Walter Miller.

CICERO: DE REPUBLICA and DE LEGIBUS; SOMNIUM SCIPIONIS. Clinton W. Keyes.

Cicero: De Senectute, De Amicitia, De Divinatione. W. A. Falconer.

Cicero: In Catilinam, Pro Flacco, Pro Murena, Pro Sulla. Louis E. Lord.

Cicero: Letters to Atticus. E. O. Winstedt. 3 Vols.

Cicero: Letters to His Friends. W. Glynn Williams. 3 Vols.

Cicero: Philippics. W. C. A. Ker.

Cicero: Pro Archia Post Reditum, De Domo, De Haruspicum Responsis, Pro Plancio. N. H. Watts.

Cicero: Pro Caecina, Pro Lege Manilia, Pro Cluentio, Pro Rabirio. H. Grose Hodge.

Cicero: Pro Caelio, De Provinciis Consularibus, Pro Balbo. R. Gardner.

Cicero: Pro Milone, In Pisonem, Pro Scauro, Pro Fonteio, Pro Rabirio Postumo, Pro Marcello, Pro Ligario, Pro Rege Deiotaro. N. H. Watts.

Cicero: Pro Quinctio, Pro Roscio Amerino, Pro Roscio Comoedo, Contra Rullum. J. H. Freese.

Cicero: Pro Sestio, In Vatinium. R. Gardner.

Cicero: Tusculan Disputations. J. E. King.

Cicero: Verrine Orations. L. H. G. Greenwood. 2 Vols.

Claudian. M. Platnauer. 2 Vols.

Columella: De Re Rustica. De Arboribus. H. B. Ash, E. S. Forster and E. Heffner. 3 Vols.

Curtius, Q.: History of Alexander. J. C. Rolfe. 2 Vols.

Florus. E. S. Forster; and Cornelius Nepos. J. C. Rolfe.

Frontinus: Stratagems and Aqueducts. C. E. Bennett and M. B. McElwain.

Fronto: Correspondence. C. R. Haines. 2 Vols.

Gellius, J. C. Rolfe. 3 Vols.

Horace: Odes and Epodes. C. E. Bennett.

Horace: Satires, Epistles, Ars Poetica. H. R. Fairclough.

Jerome: Selected Letters. F. A. Wright.

Juvenal and Persius. G. G. Ramsay.

Livy. B. O. Foster, F. G. Moore, Evan T. Sage, and A. C. Schlesinger and K. M. Geer (General Index). 14 Vols.

Lucan. J. D. Duff.

Lucretius. W. H. D. Rouse.

Martial. W. C. A. Ker. 2 Vols.

Minor Latin Poets: from Publilius Syrus to Rutilius Namatianus, including Grattius, Calpurnius Siculus, Nemesianus, Avianus, and others with " Aetna " and the " Phoenix." J. Wight Duff and Arnold M. Duff.

Ovid: The Art of Love and Other Poems. J. H. Mozley.

2

Ovid: Fasti. Sir James G. Frazer.

Ovid: Heroides and Amores. Grant Showerman.

Ovid: Metamorphoses. F. J. Miller. 2 Vols.

Ovid: Tristia and Ex Ponto. A. L. Wheeler.

Persius. Cf. Juvenal.

Petronius. M. Heseltine; Seneca; Apocolocyntosis. W. H. D. Rouse.

Phaedrus and Babrius (Greek). B. E. Perry.

Plautus. Paul Nixon. 5 Vols.

Pliny: Letters, Panegyricus. Betty Radice. 2 Vols.

Pliny: Natural History.
10 Vols. Vols. I.–V. and IX. H. Rackham. Vols. VI.–VIII. W. H. S. Jones. Vol. X. D. E. Eichholz.

Propertius. H. E. Butler.

Prudentius. H. J. Thomson. 2 Vols.

Quintilian. H. E. Butler. 4 Vols.

Remains of Old Latin. E. H. Warmington. 4 Vols. Vol. I. (Ennius and Caecilius.) Vol. II. (Livius, Naevius, Pacuvius, Accius.) Vol. III. (Lucilius and Laws of XII Tables.) Vol. IV. (Archaic Inscriptions.)

Sallust. J. C. Rolfe.

Scriptores Historiae Augustae. D. Magie. 3 Vols.

Seneca: Apocolocyntosis. Cf. Petronius.

Seneca: Epistulae Morales. R. M. Gummere. 3 Vols.

Seneca: Moral Essays. J. W. Basore. 3 Vols.

Seneca: Tragedies. F. J. Miller. 2 Vols.

Sidonius: Poems and Letters. W. B. Anderson. 2 Vols.

Silius Italicus. J. D. Duff. 2 Vols.

Statius. J. H. Mozley. 2 Vols.

Suetonius. J. C. Rolfe. 2 Vols.

Tacitus: Dialogus. Sir Wm. Peterson. Agricola and Germania. Maurice Hutton.

Tacitus: Histories and Annals. C. H. Moore and J. Jackson. 4 Vols.

Terence. John Sargeaunt. 2 Vols.

Tertullian: Apologia and De Spectaculis. T. R. Glover. Minucius Felix. G. H. Rendall.

Valerius Flaccus. J. H. Mozley.

Varro: De Lingua Latina. R. G. Kent. 2 Vols.

Velleius Paterculus and Res Gestae Divi Augusti. F. W. Shipley.

Virgil. H. R. Fairclough. 2 Vols.

Vitruvius: De Architectura. F. Granger. 2 Vols.

3

Greek Authors

ACHILLES TATIUS. S. Gaselee.

AELIAN: ON THE NATURE OF ANIMALS. A. F. Scholfield. 3 Vols.

AENEAS TACTICUS, ASCLEPIODOTUS and ONASANDER. The Illinois Greek Club.

AESCHINES. C. D. Adams.

AESCHYLUS. H. Weir Smyth. 2 Vols.

ALCIPHRON, AELIAN, PHILOSTRATUS: LETTERS. A. R. Benner and F. H. Fobes.

ANDOCIDES, ANTIPHON, Cf. MINOR ATTIC ORATORS.

APOLLODORUS. Sir James G. Frazer. 2 Vols.

APOLLONIUS RHODIUS. R. C. Seaton.

THE APOSTOLIC FATHERS. Kirsopp Lake. 2 Vols.

APPIAN: ROMAN HISTORY. Horace White. 4 Vols.

ARATUS. Cf. CALLIMACHUS.

ARISTOPHANES. Benjamin Bickley Rogers. 3 Vols. Verse trans.

ARISTOTLE: ART OF RHETORIC. J. H. Freese.

ARISTOTLE: ATHENIAN CONSTITUTION, EUDEMIAN ETHICS, VICES AND VIRTUES. H. Rackham.

ARISTOTLE: GENERATION OF ANIMALS. A. L. Peck.

ARISTOTLE: HISTORIA ANIMALIUM. A. L. Peck. Vols. I.–II.

ARISTOTLE: METAPHYSICS. H. Tredennick. 2 Vols.

ARISTOTLE: METEOROLOGICA. H. D. P. Lee.

ARISTOTLE: MINOR WORKS. W. S. Hett. On Colours, On Things Heard, On Physiognomies, On Plants, On Marvellous Things Heard, Mechanical Problems, On Indivisible Lines, On Situations and Names of Winds, On Melissus, Xenophanes, and Gorgias.

ARISTOTLE: NICOMACHEAN ETHICS. H. Rackham.

ARISTOTLE: OECONOMICA and MAGNA MORALIA. G. C. Armstrong; (with Metaphysics, Vol. II.).

ARISTOTLE: ON THE HEAVENS. W. K. C. Guthrie.

ARISTOTLE: ON THE SOUL. PARVA NATURALIA. ON BREATH. W. S. Hett.

ARISTOTLE: CATEGORIES, ON INTERPRETATION, PRIOR ANALYTICS. H. P. Cooke and H. Tredennick.

ARISTOTLE: POSTERIOR ANALYTICS, TOPICS. H. Tredennick and E. S. Forster.

ARISTOTLE: ON SOPHISTICAL REFUTATIONS. On Coming to be and Passing Away, On the Cosmos. E. S. Forster and D. J. Furley.

ARISTOTLE: PARTS OF ANIMALS. A. L. Peck; MOTION AND PROGRESSION OF ANIMALS. E. S. Forster.

ARISTOTLE: PHYSICS. Rev. P. Wicksteed and F. M. Cornford. 2 Vols.

ARISTOTLE: POETICS and LONGINUS. W. Hamilton Fyfe; DEMETRIUS ON STYLE. W. Rhys Roberts.

ARISTOTLE: POLITICS. H. Rackham.

ARISTOTLE: PROBLEMS. W. S. Hett. 2 Vols.

ARISTOTLE: RHETORICA AD ALEXANDRUM (with PROBLEMS. Vol. II). H. Rackham.

ARRIAN: HISTORY OF ALEXANDER and INDICA. Rev. E. Iliffe Robson. 2 Vols.

ATHENAEUS: DEIPNOSOPHISTAE. C. B. GULICK. 7 Vols.

BABRIUS AND PHAEDRUS (Latin). B. E. Perry.

ST. BASIL: LETTERS. R. J. Deferrari. 4 Vols.

CALLIMACHUS: FRAGMENTS. C. A. Trypanis.

CALLIMACHUS, Hymns and Epigrams, and LYCOPHRON. A. W. Mair; ARATUS. G. R. MAIR.

CLEMENT of ALEXANDRIA. Rev. G. W. Butterworth.

COLLUTHUS. Cf. OPPIAN.

DAPHNIS AND CHLOE. Thornley's Translation revised by J. M. Edmonds; and PARTHENIUS. S. Gaselee.

DEMOSTHENES I.: OLYNTHIACS, PHILIPPICS and MINOR ORATIONS. I.–XVII. AND XX. J. H. Vince.

DEMOSTHENES II.: DE CORONA and DE FALSA LEGATIONE. C. A. Vince and J. H. Vince.

DEMOSTHENES III.: MEIDIAS, ANDROTION, ARISTOCRATES, TIMOCRATES and ARISTOGEITON, I. AND II. J. H. Vince.

DEMOSTHENES IV.–VI.: PRIVATE ORATIONS and IN NEAERAM. A. T. Murray.

DEMOSTHENES VII.: FUNERAL SPEECH, EROTIC ESSAY, EXORDIA and LETTERS. N. W. and N. J. DeWitt.

DIO CASSIUS: ROMAN HISTORY. E. Cary. 9 Vols.

DIO CHRYSOSTOM. J. W. Cohoon and H. Lamar Crosby. 5 Vols.

DIODORUS SICULUS. 12 Vols. Vols. I.–VI. C. H. Oldfather. Vol. VII. C. L. Sherman. Vol. VIII. C. B. Welles. Vols. IX. and X. R. M. Geer. Vol. XI. F. Walton. Vol. XII. F. Walton. General Index. R. M. Geer.

DIOGENES LAERTIUS. R. D. Hicks. 2 Vols.

DIONYSIUS OF HALICARNASSUS: ROMAN ANTIQUITIES. Spelman's translation revised by E. Cary. 7 Vols.

EPICTETUS. W. A. Oldfather. 2 Vols.

EURIPIDES. A. S. Way. 4 Vols. Verse trans.

EUSEBIUS: ECCLESIASTICAL HISTORY. Kirsopp Lake and J. E. L. Oulton. 2 Vols.

GALEN: ON THE NATURAL FACULTIES. A. J. Brock.

THE GREEK ANTHOLOGY. W. R. Paton. 5 Vols.

GREEK ELEGY AND IAMBUS with the ANACREONTEA. J. M. Edmonds. 2 Vols.

THE GREEK BUCOLIC POETS (THEOCRITUS, BION, MOSCHUS). J. M. Edmonds.

GREEK MATHEMATICAL WORKS. Ivor Thomas. 2 Vols.

HERODES. Cf. THEOPHRASTUS: CHARACTERS.

HERODIAN. C. R. Whittaker. 2 Vols.

HERODOTUS. A. D. Godley. 4 Vols.

HESIOD AND THE HOMERIC HYMNS. H. G. Evelyn White.

HIPPOCRATES and the FRAGMENTS OF HERACLEITUS. W. H. S. Jones and E. T. Withington. 4 Vols.

HOMER: ILIAD. A. T. Murray. 2 Vols.

HOMER: ODYSSEY. A. T. Murray. 2 Vols.

ISAEUS. E. W. Forster.

ISOCRATES. George Norlin and LaRue Van Hook. 3 Vols.

[ST. JOHN DAMASCENE]: BARLAAM AND IOASAPH. Rev. G. R. Woodward, Harold Mattingly and D. M. Lang.

JOSEPHUS. 9 Vols. Vols. I.–IV.; H. Thackeray. Vol. V.; H. Thackeray and R. Marcus. Vols. VI.–VII.; R. Marcus. Vol. VIII.; R. Marcus and Allen Wikgren. Vol. IX. L. H. Feldman.

JULIAN. Wilmer Cave Wright. 3 Vols.

LIBANIUS. A. F. Norman. Vol. I.

LUCIAN. 8 Vols. Vols. I.–V. A. M. Harmon. Vol. VI. K. Kilburn. Vols. VII.–VIII. M. D. Macleod.

LYCOPHRON. Cf. CALLIMACHUS.

LYRA GRAECA. J. M. Edmonds. 3 Vols.

LYSIAS. W. R. M. Lamb.

MANETHO. W. G. Waddell: PTOLEMY: TETRABIBLOS. F. E. Robbins.

MARCUS AURELIUS. C. R. Haines.

MENANDER. F. G. Allinson.

MINOR ATTIC ORATORS (ANTIPHON, ANDOCIDES, LYCURGUS, DEMADES, DINARCHUS, HYPERIDES). K. J. Maidment and J. O. Burtt. 2 Vols.

NONNOS: DIONYSIACA. W. H. D. Rouse. 3 Vols.

OPPIAN, COLLUTHUS, TRYPHIODORUS. A. W. Mair.

PAPYRI. NON-LITERARY SELECTIONS. A. S. Hunt and C. C. Edgar. 2 Vols. LITERARY SELECTIONS (Poetry). D. L. Page.

PARTHENIUS. Cf. DAPHNIS and CHLOE.

PAUSANIAS: DESCRIPTION OF GREECE. W. H. S. Jones. 4 Vols. and Companion Vol. arranged by R. E. Wycherley.

PHILO. 10 Vols. Vols. I.–V.; F. H. Colson and Rev. G. H. Whitaker. Vols. VI.–IX.; F. H. Colson. Vol. X. F. H. Colson and the Rev. J. W. Earp.

6

PHILO: two supplementary Vols. (*Translation only.*) Ralph Marcus.

PHILOSTRATUS: THE LIFE OF APOLLONIUS OF TYANA. F. C. Conybeare. 2 Vols.

PHILOSTRATUS: IMAGINES; CALLISTRATUS: DESCRIPTIONS. A. Fairbanks.

PHILOSTRATUS and EUNAPIUS: LIVES OF THE SOPHISTS. Wilmer Cave Wright.

PINDAR. Sir J. E. Sandys.

PLATO: CHARMIDES, ALCIBIADES, HIPPARCHUS, THE LOVERS, THEAGES, MINOS and EPINOMIS. W. R. M. Lamb.

PLATO: CRATYLUS, PARMENIDES, GREATER HIPPIAS, LESSER HIPPIAS. H. N. Fowler.

PLATO: EUTHYPHRO, APOLOGY, CRITO, PHAEDO, PHAEDRUS. H. N. Fowler.

PLATO: LACHES, PROTAGORAS, MENO, EUTHYDEMUS. W. R. M. Lamb.

PLATO: LAWS. Rev. R. G. Bury. 2 Vols.

PLATO: LYSIS, SYMPOSIUM, GORGIAS. W. R. M. Lamb.

PLATO: REPUBLIC. Paul Shorey. 2 Vols.

PLATO: STATESMAN, PHILEBUS. H. N. Fowler; ION. W. R. M. Lamb.

PLATO: THEAETETUS and SOPHIST. H. N. Fowler.

PLATO: TIMAEUS, CRITIAS, CLITOPHO, MENEXENUS, EPISTULAE. Rev. R. G. Bury.

PLOTINUS: A. H. Armstrong. Vols. I.–III.

PLUTARCH: MORALIA. 16 Vols. Vols. I.–V. F. C. Babbitt. Vol. VI. W. C. Helmbold. Vols. VII. and XIV. P. H. De Lacy and B. Einarson. Vol. VIII. P. A. Clement and H. B. Hoffleit. Vol. IX. E. L. Minar, Jr., F. H. Sandbach, W. C. Helmbold. Vol. X. H. N. Fowler. Vol. XI. L. Pearson and F. H. Sandbach. Vol. XII. H. Cherniss and W. C. Helmbold. Vol. XV. F. H. Sandbach.

PLUTARCH: THE PARALLEL LIVES. B. Perrin. 11 Vols.

POLYBIUS. W. R. Paton. 6 Vols.

PROCOPIUS: HISTORY OF THE WARS. H. B. Dewing. 7 Vols.

PTOLEMY: TETRABIBLOS. Cf. MANETHO.

QUINTUS SMYRNAEUS. A. S. Way. Verse trans.

SEXTUS EMPIRICUS. Rev. R. G. Bury. 4 Vols.

SOPHOCLES. F. Storr. 2 Vols. Verse trans.

STRABO: GEOGRAPHY. Horace L. Jones. 8 Vols.

THEOPHRASTUS: CHARACTERS. J. M. Edmonds. HERODES, etc. A. D. Knox.

THEOPHRASTUS: ENQUIRY INTO PLANTS. Sir Arthur Hort, Bart. 2 Vols.

THUCYDIDES. C. F. Smith. 4 Vols.

TRYPHIODORUS. Cf. OPPIAN.
XENOPHON: CYROPAEDIA. Walter Miller. 2 Vols.
XENOPHON: HELLENICA. C. L. Brownson. 2 Vols.
XENOPHON: ANABASIS. C. L. Brownson.
XENOPHON: MEMORABILIA AND OECONOMICUS. E. C. Marchant.
SYMPOSIUM AND APOLOGY. O. J. Todd.
XENOPHON: SCRIPTA MINORA. E. C. Marchant and G. W.
Bowersock.

IN PREPARATION

Greek Authors

ARISTIDES: ORATIONS. C. A. Behr.
MUSAEUS: HERO AND LEANDER. T. Gelzer and C. H.
WHITMAN.
THEOPHRASTUS: DE CAUSIS PLANTARUM. G. K. K. Link and
B. Einarson.

Latin Authors

ASCONIUS: COMMENTARIES ON CICERO'S ORATIONS.
G. W. Bowersock.
BENEDICT: THE RULE. P. Meyvaert.
JUSTIN-TROGUS. R. Moss.
MANILIUS. G. P. Goold.

DESCRIPTIVE PROSPECTUS ON APPLICATION

London   WILLIAM HEINEMANN LTD
Cambridge, Mass.   HARVARD UNIVERSITY PRESS

Date Due